'The autobiography of a nation'

STUDIES IN DESIGN

general editor:
CHRISTOPHER BREWARD

founding editor:
PAUL GREENHALGH

'The autobiography of a nation'

THE 1951 FESTIVAL OF BRITAIN

Becky E. Conekin

Manchester University Press

Manchester and New York

distributed exclusively in the USA by Palgrave

Published by Manchester University Press
Oxford Road, Manchester M13 9NR, UK
and Room 400, 175 Fifth Avenue, New York, NY 10010, USA
www.manchesteruniversitypress.co.uk

Distributed exclusively in the USA by
Palgrave, 175 Fifth Avenue, New York NY 10010, USA

Distributed exclusively in Canada by
UBC Press, University of British Columbia, 2029 West Mall,
Vancouver, BC, Canada V6T 1Z2

British Library Cataloguing-in-Publication Data
A catalogue record for this book is available from the British Library

Library of Congress Cataloging-in-Publication Data
A catalog record for this book is available from the Library of Congress

ISBN 13: 978 0 7190 6060 1

First published by Manchester University Press 2003

First digital paperback edition published 2008

Printed by Lightning Source

For Adam

In 1951, to celebrate the opening of a happier decade, the government decreed a Festival. Monstrous constructions appeared on the south bank of the Thames, the foundation stone was solemnly laid for a National Theatre, but there was little popular exuberance among the straitened people and the dollar-bearing tourists curtailed their visits and sped to the countries of the Continent where, however precarious their condition, they ordered things better. (Evelyn Waugh, 'Epilogue: The Festival of Britain', in *Unconditional Surrender*, 1961.)

even the grumblers intend to turn out to see what's to be seen and maybe cheer themselves up for the trials ahead by having a civilized good time. (The *New Yorker*, May 1951.)

There's been no hidebound, blue-nosed, ultra conservative dead hand on this Festival planning. Youth has been given its head ... and the results they will achieve will make Festival visitors gasp ... Despite those who clamour to have the whole affair scrapped; despite those who resent the Festival because its happening while the Labour Government is in power; despite those people who believe the world is too unsettled for such an event; there seems little doubt that the Festival ... should be a roaring financial and prestige building success. (The *Sydney Daily Telegraph*, May 1951.)

The great Exhibition of 1951 surpasses by far the one which took place a hundred years ago ... It will be the greatest that ever happened in England or indeed, in the world. It will demonstrate the economic vitality of the nation and their trust in the future. (*Lisbon O Secuto Illustrado*, May 1951.)

(These three quotations and many more
from a range of international newspapers
were published in the *Picture Post*, 5 May 1951)

Contents

List of illustrations

Acknowledgements

As is true with any academic project spanning a number of years, I have incurred many debts and been offered much assistance in the course of researching and writing this book. First, I thank my parents who in their separately inimitable ways set me the challenge of completing a PhD at a very young age. That challenge has led to this book. Next, I would like to thank the various institutions that funded this project: the American Council of Learned Societies and the Social Science Research Council's (SSRC) Program in Western Europe; the History Department of the University of Michigan, Ann Arbor; the Rackham Graduate School of the University of Michigan, including its Hewlett International Dissertation Research Fellowship; the Program in British Studies and the International Institute of the University of Michigan, as well as my current institution, the London College of Fashion (LCF), the London Institute. LCF offered me a part-time Senior Research Fellowship at exactly the right time. The (UK) Arts and Humanities Research Board provided me with a small grant in aid of publication. Specifically, Kent Worcester, then Program Director of the Western Europe Program of the SSRC, Geoff Eley and David Cohen, both of the University of Michigan, and most recently Elizabeth Rouse, Christopher Breward and Adam Briggs of LCF, have all in very different ways encouraged this project. Janice Miller of LCF helped me with last-minute, good-humoured copy-editing. I also owe Christopher Breward a debt of gratitude for suggesting this book appear in this series, which he edits. Thank you.

I would like to acknowledge the assistance offered by the staff and librarians of a number of archives I have consulted, including Marian Pringle, Senior Librarian and Royal Shakespeare Theatre Librarian, The Shakespeare Birthplace Trust; Carol Edwards, Assistant Librarian, The National Library of Wales; Roger Strong, of the Public Record Office of Northern Ireland; A. Franklin, Assistant Librarian, The Manx Museum, Douglas, Isle of Man; Richard Temple, the Assistant Archivist of the Modern Records Centre at the University of Warwick; and the librarians and staff of the British Library, the Public Record Office at Kew, the National Sound Archive, the National Labour Party Archives, the Thomas Cook Travel Archive, and the Victoria and Albert Archive of Art and Design. Additionally, I would like to thank a few individuals whom I came to know in British institutions in the course of the research for this project: Kevin Rogers, who helped me at the National Art Library; Javier Pes, then Assistant Curator, Department of Later London History, Museum of London; Toby Haggith of the Film Department of the Imperial War Museum, who invited me to a private screening of Ministry of Information films; and Armand De Filipo who assisted me and cheered me up at the BBC Written Archives, Caversham.

B. Frank generously allowed me to live in her home in Primrose Hill for far below the going rate while I conducted research and began writing in London. Richard Weight, one of the few people it seems other than myself who has ever trudged through the

Festival material at the PRO, I thank for sharing some bad canteen coffee there, as well as his resulting PhD thesis chapter with me. Hannah Tooze graciously shared her expertise and gave me helpful citations regarding planning in twentieth-century Britain.

I would also like to express my gratitude to the organisers and participants of various seminars and conferences to which I have had the pleasure and challenge of presenting papers on the Festival: especially Carolyn Steedman, of the then Centre for the Study of Social History seminar at the University of Warwick; Kelly Boyd of the *History Workshop Journal* seminar; James Ryan of the Institute of Historical Research (London), Postgraduate Seminar in Theory and Method; Abigail Beach and Richard Weight, convenors of 'The Right to Belong' colloquium, University College London; Chris Waters, Program Director of the North American Conference on British Studies; Frank Mort, convenor of the one-day symposium on 'Cultural and Political Histories: Britain and Germany in the 20th Century' at the University of Portsmouth; Margaret Gallick of the Courtauld Institute of Art; Christopher Breward, organiser of the historical and cultural studies research seminar at the London College of Fashion; Simon Gunn, organiser of the cultural studies research seminar at Leeds Metropolitan University; Kelly Boyd, co-organiser of Middlesex University's 'Aspects of London Life in the Twentieth-Century' conference; Jakob Vogel and Ralph Jessen, co-convenors of the 'Wissenschaft und Nation' (Science and Nation) Conference of the Centre for Comparative History of Europe, Free University, Berlin; and Miles Taylor, co-organiser of the 'The Victorians Since 1901' strand of the 'Locating the Victorians' Conference, held at the Science Museum. Thanks also goes to Gareth Stedman Jones and Emma Rothschild at the Centre for History and Economics, King's College, Cambridge, for suggesting and supporting a one-day colloquium funded by the Rockefeller Foundation, for which I had the pleasure of bringing together some of Britain's most impressive scholars to discuss 'Exhibiting Britain: 1851, 1951 and 2000'.

Picture research can be perilous, but I received generous assistance with this book. Andrew Mead of the Architectural Press kindly granted permission to publish a number of photographs from the *Architectural Review*. With Lynne Jackson's permission, Tamsyn Hill took the photograph of the page of the *Architectural Review* featuring the crystal structure patterns. Anne Woodward of the National Monuments Record, English Heritage also granted me kind permission to use three photos from their collections. Alan Powers of the Twentieth Century Society offered me copies of photographs and invaluable help with obtaining permissions. I am grateful to you all. Thank you to Jackie Barry and Alan and Irene Cook for allowing me permission to publish their photos. Thanks also to Martin Packer and Brenda Cobon for finding the Cooks and their photographs of Trowell in 1951.

In the past few months I have had the great good fortune of meeting via electronic mail Martin Packer of the Festival of Britain Society, the creator of a website, and Charles Plouviez, who was the assistant to the Director of Exhibitions for the 1951 Festival of Britain. Martin Packer compiled and analysed the information that appears as Appendix 2 at the end of this book. Both of these men have shared with me their knowledge and love of the Festival and I am greatly indebted to them. Their feedback and encouragement often kept me going when my own enthusiasm was flagging.

Many other mentors, colleagues and friends have offered invaluable advice and support along the way. The University of Michigan, Ann Arbor proved a near-perfect place to be a graduate student while I was there. There was a lively interdisciplinary research culture, with more seminars and conferences every week than most people could manage to attend, where graduate students were treated as equals. One of the key instigators of that culture, to my mind, is Geoff Eley. In 1990 we chose each other to work with and he has been an extremely important mentor ever since. Thank you. For helping me to formulate and write my initial proposal for this project, I would like to thank him, along with: Marjorie Bryer, Laura Lee Downs, Alice Echols, Kali Israel, Susan Johnson, Pat Simons, Jackie Stevens and Martha Vicinus. For providing me with very good early feedback on the project at my dissertation prospectus defence, I am grateful to them, as well as Michael MacDonald and Carolyn Steedman. For co-chairing this project as a PhD dissertation over the long haul and for persevering with me and my ideas, I thank Sonya Rose, who is ever the thoughtful and practical critic. For always believing in me and this project, even when sometimes I didn't, I thank all of the above and Deborah Cohen, Janene Furness, Craig Koslofsky, Peter Mandler, Frank Mort, Kathy Pence, Dana Rabin, James Vernon, Chris Waters, Kent Worcester, and Peggy and Arthur Wynn. A special thank you goes to Don LaCoss, not only for his continual encouragement and good humour, but also for the many acts of friendship, often verging on the truly heroic, he has performed for me over the ten or so years we have known each other. Such demonstrations of his loyalty and love have always had a positive impact on my sometimes-shaky work life. You all, spread as you are over at least two continents and too many miles, are my community and I thank you for being that for me. It means more than you can ever know. Unfortunately for me, any errors, omissions or other acts of stupidity are, of course, my responsibility alone.

The external reader for Manchester University Press provided me with thorough constructive criticism of the entire manuscript and the book has improved because of it. Thank you. For the sort of help and support only she could offer, I wish to thank Fiona Sinclair. She understands better than most what the publication of this book represents. For giving me a new and very different reason to complete this book, I thank my daughter, Edith Elizabeth. Edie, once you came into our lives, I had to finish this book for two conflicting reasons: to have more time with you and to show you that women do serious work. Finally, I must thank Adam Tooze. For years now he has helped me make a home, offering me financial security, a critical, careful reader, fabulous cups of coffee, and someone with whom to engage intellectually at almost any time of day. For the past year, since the arrival of Edie, he has also generously provided extra childcare in all its many guises. At one time, he would have been called a comrade; I am extraordinarily lucky to be able to call him my husband. My debt to him cannot really be expressed in words. The best I can do is to offer him the dedication.

I

INTRODUCING THE FESTIVAL

1 ✧ The background: history and historiography

The background: history and historiography

I N 1976, to mark the twenty-fifth anniversary of the Festival of Britain, the then Director of the Victoria and Albert Museum, Roy Strong, commissioned an exhibition, primarily to celebrate the Festival as 'the last really great stylistic statement this country made'.[1] He opened the accompanying catalogue, however, with his own reminiscences of that 1951 summer, at which time he was fifteen years old: 'all of us who grew up then remember it and its concomitant fete, the Coronation, as culminations of a great reawakening of the arts after years of privation, particularly sharp for those whose formative years were the ones of austerity'[2] (Figure 1). Ignoring for the time being the issue of whether or not the Coronation celebrations and the 1951 festivities should be considered 'concomitant', as well as the generational differences that underlie the experiences of people in the immediate post-war period, Strong's memories are not dissimilar from most British people's.[3] The Festival was planned as a 'pat on the back' for winning the war, as well as 'a tonic to the nation' in the age of austerity.[4] Mary Banham in the 1976 catalogue asserted that:

> The significance of the Festival for us today is not so much that it made a particularly important stylistic statement in design but that it was a genuinely national popular public event of amazing proportions, unexpectedly successful and still remembered more than any other event of this kind ... the Festival provided colour (after the drabness of war), light (after the darkness of the blackout) and fun in the traditional fairground sense. But the Festival organising team would not have been seen to have done their job unless visiting families went away feeling instructed and, in some undefined way, improved.[5]

Yet, surely, not every twenty-fifth anniversary warrants an exhibition in a national museum. So, what was it about the year 1976 that made

1 The South Bank Concourse facing the People of Britain and Transport Pavilions

these London museum administrators, architects and planners wish to celebrate the 1951 Festival of Britain and its visions of Britain and Britishness? Was it the state of the Labour government, with the resignation of Wilson in that year? Or was it the state of the British economy, which 'from the end of 1973 ... had nose-dived into recession for two full years: the first time that output had shown a significant year-on-year decline since the early 1930s'?[6] Or the consistently high level of unemployment under Labour, with the unemployed numbering one million, now a 'commonplace'?[7] Or was it what many contemporary commentators foresaw as the end of one of the central planks of the structure of the post-war welfare settlement, the abandonment of the commitment to full employment as stated by Prime Minister Callaghan at the Labour Party Conference, when he proclaimed: 'You cannot now, if you ever could, spend your way out of a recession'?[8]

Charles Plouviez, the Festival's Assistant to the Director of Exhibitions, wrote in 2001 that 1976 was 'a bad time ... the country was racked by industrial disputes and financial crises ... Culturally, the swinging sixties had left nothing much behind, and the reaction against modernism in architecture had reached its peak. The Festival survivors were defensive, their juniors bemused or simply scornful'.[9] In the conflicted and disappointed times of 1976, the surviving planners and contributors to the Festival surely wished to stress the goals and visions of that earlier optimistic moment.

Adrian Forty clearly stated the 1951 Festival's aspirations in the 1976 volume. There he wrote that: 'As reconstruction and reform were not distinguished in the Labour party programme, the Festival could not fail to be a celebration of both, and that was how it was understood by the majority of visitors.'[10] The Festival of Britain set the broad parameters of a social democratic agenda for a new and modern Britain. The expertise of architects, industrial designers, scientists and town planners was enlisted in this government project to construct representations of the nation's past and future. As well as acting as 'a tonic to the nation', the Festival's stated intention was to project 'the belief that Britain will have contributions to make in the future'.[11] These projections stressed progress and modernity, with science and planning evoked as the answers to the question of *how* to build a better Britain. Everything from living conditions to 'culture' and from industrial design to farm management was henceforward to be different, especially for those whose limited incomes had restricted their life experiences. The goals of diffusing knowledge and constructing a modern, cultured citizenry were ones that the Festival planners shared with many within the post-war Labour Party. As such, the Festival can be read simultaneously as a public celebration and a government-sponsored educational event.

The 1951 Festival was conceived in the immediate post-war period, a period characterised by housing shortages and the continuation, and even extension, of wartime restrictions and rationing, as well as the initial stages of the dissolution of the British Empire. It was to be both a celebration of Britain's victory in the Second World War and a proclamation of its national recovery. There were nine official, government-funded exhibitions in England, Scotland, Northern Ireland and Wales, twenty-three designated arts festivals, as well as a pleasure garden in Battersea.[12] Eight and a half million people visited the London South Bank exhibition and the BBC aired 2,700 Festival-related broadcasts. On the local level, close to two thousand cities, towns and villages across the United Kingdom organised and funded a Festival event of some kind.

Even so, there is no historical monograph on the Festival of Britain.[13] Most studied by students of design and architectural history in the context of the 'Festival style' or 'brutalism', surprisingly, the 1951 Festival has never received a full-length treatment before now.[14] Neither a design history nor an architectural history *per se*, this book examines the reconstruction of post-war British national identity in the context of the social democratic project which was the Festival of Britain. As a consciously constructed cultural and educational event – or, rather, series of events – the Festival provides an opportunity to see a society and a government struggling to recast national identity after the experience of the Second World War: a war fought on the home front as well as the battlefield, with devastating, yet unifying, effects.[15]

In the autumn of 2001, Wolfgang Behringer wrote in the journal *Social History* that 'cultural history ... seems to need intellectual, economic and social history'.[16] Such a synthetic work is, of course, most historians' ideal. This book attempts to take into account various intellectual, economic and social factors that influenced the representations on show in the summer of 1951. But, primarily, what follows is a study of how Britain and Britishness were portrayed in the 1951 Festival's exhibitions and events. After the two introductory chapters, the book is divided into two main thematic sections: time and place. In the time section representations of the future (Chapter 3) and the present and the past (Chapter 4) are explored. Under the heading of 'place', representations of the metropole and the regions are the subject of Chapter 5 and those of the local, Chapter 6. Two different sorts of places are the topics of the two chapters that follow: Chapter 7 examines the place that was barely represented, the empire, and the possible reasons for this, and Chapter 8 looks at the Festival's Battersea Pleasure Gardens as 'the place of fun and fantasy, escape and edification'. There is then a conclusion, which briefly compares the 1951 Festival to the 1953 Coronation of Queen Elizabeth II and the Millennium Dome – a very different kind of Labour extravaganza.

The historiography of post-war Britain

Most historical assessments of British post-war reconstruction focus on the successes and failures of the Labour Government's economic and social reform policies, such as the creation of the welfare state, decolonisation and nationalisation.[17] Although over the past decade it has become acceptable for historians to work on the post-war period (as opposed to Michael Sissons and Philip French's finding in 1963 that the decade after the Second World War had received little examination 'beyond the inevitably partisan memoirs of the political protagonists'), there are still some problems with much of the resulting scholarship.[18] There has been a tendency amongst historians of the British post-war period to construct narratives within a narrow conception of what constitutes the legitimate fields of historical inquiry, as well as legitimate methodologies.[19] This has resulted in the historiography being dominated by 'high' political narratives and characters.[20] Unlike eighteenth- and nineteenth-century British history, or histories of twentieth-century France, the studies that have attempted to address the realms of what they call 'culture' and 'society' generally do so as a separate, discrete realm or historical sub-field, divorced from the world of 'politics' and 'the economy'.[21] Oddly, it is as if the very demarcations between the 'soft' arts topics and the 'harder' more practical and important topics of the social sciences, so debated in the inter-war period amongst teachers in adult- and workers' education institutes, have lived on, only to become reified in university history departments in Britain.[22]

But, there are some works, produced primarily by a generation of younger historians, that attempt to bridge these gaps, even though they are officially working within the field of British post-war political history. Such work has begun to focus on the political culture of the 1940s and 1950s, rather than political elites and the machinery of government, for example. These studies include work on the Labour Party by Martin Francis, Nick Tiratsoo, Jon Lawrence and Miles Taylor.[23] Meanwhile, a new approach to the political culture of the Conservatives in wartime and post-war Britain has been pioneered by Ina Zweiniger-Bargielowska.[24]

Yet, the strange compartmentalisation of the study of post-war British history has meant that most who consider themselves its scholars do not refer to the work of Robert Hewison, much less the more methodologically challenging studies covering the post-war period, which have their origins in cultural studies, women's studies, literary theory, historical geography, or even in English, departments.[25] Alan Sinfield's very important *Literature, Politics and Culture in Postwar Britain* is generally not acknowledged by British political and social historians of the period. The work of interdisciplinary scholars seems not to have made a great impact on mainstream historical education and writing in British institutions.[26] The new interpretative frameworks offered and new methodologies utilised by such scholars have often been dismissed by established British historians for their rejection of traditional modes of enquiry.[27]

On the other hand, it is also true that much of cultural studies has actually remained ahistorical. In 1982 Bernard Waites, Tony Bennett and Graham Martin observed in relation to the field that 'the post-war period has not yet been a subject of serious historical interest. Contemporary cultural studies have been emphatically "contemporary".[28] Ten years later, the publication of one of the field's most influential readers, *Cultural Studies*, revealed that this was still generally true.[29] In that reader, Carolyn Steedman charged British cultural studies with the task of deciding 'what it will *do* with history, and what kind of historical thinking it will ask its students to perform.'[30] Answering Steedman's challenge, this study is situated within and attempting to contribute to both fields. Using the traditional archival sources of the historian, *The autobiography of a nation* engages with issues of representation generally more familiar to students and scholars in cultural studies.[31]

The Festival: 'culture' and 'politics' and national identity

The Festival of Britain provides us with a rare moment of conscious celebration across the United Kingdom. It was by its nature involved in ideas, politics, arts, 'culture', leisure, science, visions of the future and imaginings of the past. As an event four years in the making, at a cost of eleven million pounds of badly needed public funds, the Festival was deeply enmeshed in the economics and politics of the day.[32] It is not possible to write an adequate history of the Festival that sits easily and firmly either in the 'hard' (masculine) camp of politics and economics or in the 'soft' (feminised) land of arts and 'culture'. As Geoff Eley and Ron Suny have convincingly argued, if politics was 'the ground upon which the category of the nation was first proposed, culture was the terrain where it was elaborated'.[33] This more general statement of how nations are 'constituted discursively, through processes of imaginative ideological labour' is directly applicable to the Festival as a concerted effort of national imagining at a time of great change for the British nation.[34]

The 1951 Festival of Britain was necessarily a heterogeneous event. To adequately encompass its complexity it is necessary to elaborate a notion of the functioning of the state/governmental apparatus which is indebted to Michel Foucault, as well as a historically specific analysis of the post-war period and its Labour Party. In other words, given its huge scale and its decentralised organisation, the Festival was a governmental project. Located primarily in London, a loose coalition of actors – national politicians, ex-military officers, writers, artists and musicians, members of the Design and Arts Councils, the British Film Institute, former members of the Ministry of Information and panels of 'experts' in fields such as architecture, design, science, and landscape gardening (with many of these hats being worn on the same heads) – both within and beyond the boundaries of the state apparatus was responsible for shaping the agendas of the festivities. This hodgepodge of individuals, led by a newspaper editor, is not constitutive of what historians have traditionally been trained to view as 'the state'. But, after Foucault, some historians have become aware that often governing does not only occur in the places we traditionally believed 'the state' to reside.[35] For example, Nikolas Rose and Peter Miller have argued that:

> Government is the historically constituted matrix within which are articulated all those dreams, schemes, strategies and manoeuvres of authorities

that seek to shape beliefs and conduct of others in desired directions by
acting upon their will, their circumstances or their environment ... Central
to the possibility of modern forms of government ... are the associations
formed between entities constituted as 'political' and the projects, plans,
practices of those authorities – economic, legal, spiritual, medical, technical
– who endeavour to administer the lives of others in the light of conceptions
of what is good, healthy, normal, virtuous, efficient or profitable.[36]

Based on such a conceptualisation of 'governmentality',[37] this study reads
the Festival of Britain as a tool of government used to act on an object
of government, namely, national identity.

However, as will become apparent, this is not the end of the Festival
story. The Festival took the specific shape that it did thanks to the contours
of the particular post-war moment and the influences the war, amongst
other things, had had on its planners. It was the event it was – with its
odd conjunction of imaginings of the past and visions of the future,
emphasis on the metropole, yet acknowledgement of the importance of
regional and local industries, ideas and traditions – because of the operative
discourses in mid-twentieth-century Britain. These discourses included
stories about time, place, class and gender, as various groups of actors
attempted to create new meanings for the terms 'Britain' and 'Britishness'.[38]

Moreover, it seems at this point that few scholars would disagree with
the assertion first made by Benedict Anderson that a nation is an 'imagined
political community'.[39] But, how that imagined political community elicits
identification with, and even loyalty from, its members is a further question.
Stuart Hall has provided us with many useful insights relating to this
problem. For example, he has written that national cultures create meanings
with which we identify because they:

> are composed not only of cultural institutions, but of symbols and repre-
> sentations ... [and] a national culture is a *discourse* ... which influences
> and organises both our actions and our conceptions of ourselves. National
> cultures construct identities by producing meanings about "the nation" with
> which we can identify; these are contained in the stories which are told
> about it, memories which connect its present with its past, and images
> which are constructed of it.[40]

The Festival of Britain's meanings about 'the nation' are the subject of
this book. Building on Hall, I would argue that one of the reasons why
these constructed identities possess such powers is that they are multifarious.
As the Festival of Britain illustrates, the pasts and futures and 'invented
traditions' that are evoked in national commemorations can be so diverse
as to allow for numerous points of identification, while still claiming to
be relating the coherent meaning of 'Britishness'.[41]

A dimension of variety that has at times been marginalised in many formulations of British national identities is the regional or local.[42] The Festival of Britain had an agenda both to the display of the British 'regions' and to encourage every town, city and village across the country to participate in whatever way it could in the 1951 celebrations. Chapter 5 discusses the regional exhibitions, which were planned from London, and Chapter 6 explores a cross section of local events planned by the communities themselves. An examination of the official brochures, guidebooks, posters, blueprints, and planning minutes – as well as BBC features and news coverage, and newspaper treatments of numerous festivities – at times exposes tensions among the representations of 'Britain' and 'Britishness' promulgated by these various celebrations.

The Festival's agendas within the wartime and post-war cultural landscape

The Festival planners imagined 'New Britain' as a consensual, unified society in need of edifying entertainment. The Festival of Britain was simultaneously a public celebration, an educational undertaking, and a constructed vision of a new, democratic national community. It was part of what Peter Hennessy has called 'a kind of full enjoyment policy to go with full employment'.[43] Its organisers agreed that after the destruction and deprivation of the war years and the further hardships of reconstruction, 'the people' deserved a fete. This study also demonstrates that the post-war Labour government set an agenda for the roles of culture and education in the remaking of British society. Labour was the party which 'continually reiterated throughout the 1940s' that it was 'the "People's Party"'.[44] G. D. H. Cole had popularised the use of the term 'the people' and the idea of 'people's culture and history', particularly through his 1938 book written with Postgate, *The Common People, 1746–1938*, as well as his earlier work *The People's Front* (1937) published by the Left Book Club.[45] Clearly, there is a much longer genealogy here, the tracing of which is beyond the limits of the present study. However, it is noteworthy that, according to Gareth Stedman Jones, the Chartists used the language of 'the people' beginning in 1832 in place of 'the working classes'.[46]

The Festival embodied the post-war British ideal of universal, popular access to and understanding of 'culture'. After the Second World War – the 'People's War' – 'there were attempts by those in authority to regulate leisure in socially beneficial directions especially where it spilled over into culture'.[47] Martin Francis has argued that Labour's policies during the period point up the ways in which the party's policy-makers were committed, however modestly, to a version of socialism 'concerned with … an improvement of the "quality of life" in its widest sense, and not merely with questions of economic power and material improvement'.[48] These ideals, which at times had cross-party appeal, were perhaps personified by the Liberal patrician figure of Lord Keynes, who in the summer of 1945 had announced the formation of the state-funded Arts Council, stating: 'We look forward to a time when the theatre and concert hall and art gallery will be a living element in everybody's upbringing, and regular attendance at the theatre and at concerts a part of organised education.'[49] The Festival of Britain sought to contribute to this project of cultivating the nation's taste through education in 'culture' and, more generally, through the diffusion of various forms of knowledge. The diffusion of knowledge emerges, alongside the familiar programmes of economic intervention and social welfare, as a key element of the Labour Party's post-war agenda. The Festival symbolised the Labour Party's commitment to the democratic potential of a shared national culture. It was part of a much longer and larger conversation about culture among politicians, intellectuals, writers, artists, and social theorists, ranging from the British Broadcasting Corporation (BBC) to the Workers' Educational Association (WEA).

It has been said (in not entirely complimentary terms) of Ellen Wilkinson, the Minister of Education between 1945 and 1947, that she wanted Britain to become a '"Third Programme" Nation'.[50] The BBC – especially thanks to its Director-General from 1922 to 1938, John Reith – has gained a reputation for being paternalistic and dismissive of popular or 'people's' culture.[51] This was indeed often the case, especially before the Second World War. Yet, as Raphael Samuel has reminded us, the BBC also 'could be said to have gone about nationalising the arts'.[52] Its goal was '"not levelling but cultural upgrading" or, as Reith put in it *Broadcasting Over Britain* (1924), "to bring the best of things into the greatest number of homes"'.[53] In a country as riven by issues of class as Britain was at this time, a publicly funded institution with such a motto is not simply to be criticised.

The BBC was the home of the hugely popular Brains Trust programme, in which five 'Brains' answered eight or ten questions, generally of a scientific or philosophical nature. Usually one more light-hearted question featured, as well. Memorable ones included 'How does a fly land on the ceiling?' and 'Why can't you tickle yourself?'. During the war there was 'a real increase of public interest in serious drama and there was a growing avidity for general knowledge of all kinds which gobbled down the Brains Trust week after week'.[54] One worker in a chemical factory, for example, recorded in his diary in the autumn of 1941: 'Favourite topic on Mondays seems to be the previous day's Brains Trust session, hardly anyone ever confesses that he didn't hear it, or if they do, take care to give adequate reason for so doing.'[55] Its creator, Howard Thomas, had 'borrowed' the name 'Brains Trust' from Roosevelt's name for his chosen advisors and its goal was to give listeners not what *you* wanted them to hear but what *they* wanted to hear without always realizing they did'.[56] Only J. B. Priestley's 'Postscripts' and the news bulletins were as popular as the Brains Trust.[57]

There were other signs that during the Second World War British people from all walks of life were in search of new knowledge. In the late 1930s, more people were reading, according to surveys, than ever before. The publishing house, Victor Gollancz, launched its Left Book Club in 1936 and by 1939 it was dispatching a book a month, costing half-a-crown (12½p) to 58,000 members. These books were subsequently discussed in 1,200 Left Book Club groups. And by 1941, when George Orwell published *The Lion and the Unicorn: Socialism and the English Genius*, he could state that although public education had not been properly funded in recent years, 'it has nevertheless improved, largely owing to the devoted efforts of teachers, and the habit of reading has become enormously more widespread. To an increasing extent, the rich and poor read the same books.'[58] Alongside more readers and a new interest in informative radio programmes, there was a great increase after the Second World War in the number of people involved in adult education. Adult education had spread during the war through informal groups in the armed forces and the Army Bureau of Current Affairs (ABCA), as well as among civilians attempting to understand the war and what the future might hold once it was over.[59] Evening institutes changed, becoming less orientated towards training young people in vocations and more committed to adult non-vocational education.[60] The number of such institutes more than doubled between 1947 and 1950, from just over 5,000 to almost 11,000, with the number of students increasing from approximately 825,000 to 1,250,000 in the same period.[61] The Labour Party was one great force in this change. For instance, a 1947 Ministry of Education pamphlet proclaimed:

> given understanding, the human spirit can rise to the challenge of events ... therefore the aim of any programme of adult education must be to provide men and women with opportunities for developing a maturity of outlook and judgment, for increasing their sense of responsibility and awareness, for helping them to evolve a philosophy of life, and to develop interests which will enrich their leisure.[62]

Although on one level this commitment to adult education is admirable, on another, the language resonates with that of regulating 'leisure in socially beneficial directions'. Clearly, there was a desire to constitute a new type of better-educated citizenry. Yet, what these citizens were to be educated in seems to have been primarily against popular culture; they were to develop interests that would 'enrich their leisure' – something it was becoming apparent they would have more of than ever before.

Like the BBC and similar institutions, the Festival was at times denounced as being patronising or as presenting an overwhelming display of information organised by Hampstead intellectuals, the leadership of the Labour Party, and the 'radical middle-class do-gooders' who were the Festival's planners and script-writers.[63] Some critics claimed that its organisers were seriously out of touch with 'the people' of Britain. Yet the popularity of the 'Brains Trust' programme, the increase in the number of 'ordinary people' who read regularly, and the extension of and growing participation in adult education in many British communities suggest that these critics missed the mark.

In addition, the Festival's Director-General was a journalist – Gerald Barry, the managing editor of the *News Chronicle* – who, according to Huw Wheldon of the Arts Council, 'preferred fireworks to ballet'.[64] Barry himself stressed in his call for local involvement in the Festival that the celebrations should be 'gay and entertaining – not "precious" or "highbrow"', explaining that 'There is no reason either now, or still less, in 1951, to be afraid of being amused'.[65] And in the event, there were fireworks on the South Bank and at the Battersea Pleasure Gardens, while the closing ceremonies featured Geraldo and his Orchestra, Gracie Fields, and the humour of Kenneth Horne and Richard Murdoch (the stars of *Much-Binding-in the Marsh*, a post-war Light Programme series referred to by Compton Mackenzie on the Third as an 'earnestly comic topographical serial').[66] Gracie Fields was, of course, the 'so-English' Lancastrian singer and dancer, as well as the extremely popular star of a number of inter-war Ealing comedies, whose rendition of 'There'll Always Be An England' became the Second World War equivalent of the First World War's 'Tipperary'.[67] There were enough improving agendas in evidence in the Festival to make the BBC types happy, but there was also some acknowledgement that if the politician in charge of the Festival, who came to be called 'Lord Festival', Herbert Morrison, wanted '"everyone in Britain ... to take part in it, to enjoy it", if he wanted to "hear the people sing"', as he said he did, then the Festival would need to give them music they knew and liked, rather than the Reithian ideal of what they *needed*, yet did not yet *know* they wanted.[68]

Labour was committed to class co-operation, rather than conflict, and this 'was why the likes of Morrison took so much heart from the social solidarity allegedly promoted by the Second World War', according to Fielding, Thompson and Tiratsoo.[69] Although among historians 'class' is now a heavily scrutinised category of analysis and a hotly debated topic, it is an appropriate concept to explore in relation to the post-war period because it was relevant to people and politicians at the time.[70] Often discussed in terms of 'the people', the creation of a classless society was one of post-war Labour's proclaimed goals. But, at times, even Labour's conception of class was an impressively complicated one. For example, it aimed to 'promote alliances between the "useful people", a category which embraced all manual workers, bank clerks, factory managers and even owners of industrial capital'.[71]

Since the inter-war period, 'culture' had been seen as having a particular role to play in healing the wounds of class society. The 1921 Board of Education's report, *The Teaching of English in England*, which came to be known as the 'Newbolt' Report after its Chairman, declared: 'Culture unites classes'. It argued that a liberal arts education based on the teaching of English 'would form a new element of national unity, linking together the mental life of all classes'.[72] This agenda for English was not one which would 'supplant the study of classics, which was still implicitly assumed to be the appropriate education for the ruling elite, but it was seen as part of a much wider mission of cultural renewal, with the task of co-opting the lower classes into the national settlement'.[73]

And by the period following the Second World War, the 'national settlement' rested on 'the lower classes', particularly the 'organized working class'. Ross McKibbin contends in his *Classes and Cultures: England 1918– 1951* that the experiences and discourses of the Second World War transformed the 1930s' definition of democracy. In the inter-war period, Britain's democracy was defined as 'individualistic', with its advocates mainly 'a modernized middle class'. But, by the 1940s, according to McKibbin, 'the ruling definition was social-democratic and its proponents chiefly the organized working class'.[74] He explains that this 'social-demo-cratic definition of democracy ... was incomplete' and that 'a powerful rhetorical device of both the war and the Attlee government emphasized social harmony and "fair shares"'.[75] With the help of 'culture', 'the people' of Britain could have a fairer, more egalitarian society under Labour.

In its own way, the Festival contributed to the once-taken-for-granted notion of the post-war consensus. Popular memory has it that the Festival of Britain was the British people's well-deserved pat on the back for their Second World War victory and continued endurance of the sacrifices and stringencies of austerity. However, this study reveals that even over this 'tonic to the nation' – the Festival of Britain – there was no consensus.

In the 1994 edition of his *The Road to 1945*, first published in 1975, Paul Addison wrote an epilogue explaining why in 1975 he believed that Britain was a consensus society in the post-war period and why by 1994 he no longer did so. By 1994, post-Thatcherite Britain had made it clear that post-war Britain 'was another country', he explained. He had written the original book in a spirit of optimism 'in which the past and the present were interconnected', with pride in Britain's role in the Second World War. Addison points out that he did not believe that class or political differences had been eradicated, but he did see 'in the home front the paradox that social stability worked in favour of the Left ... The collective experience of war ended the Conservative hegemony which had prevailed since 1918. Labour and the trade unions advanced, Beveridge unveiled his Report, and the spirit of wartime collectivism was distilled by the Attlee governments into the managed economy and welfare state.' This he viewed as 'one of those irreversible turning-points in history, like the extension of the franchise in 1918'. Of course, Addison admits that by 1974 it was obvious that there were problems and that the '"post-war consensus" was under pressure'. But, he believed that the answer was to shift 'the post-war settlement further to the Left'. Of course, Addison acknowledged that the Conservatives would not be pleased with this, but that 'in the end they would reconcile themselves to the facts, as they had so often in the past'. For Addison, whatever Margaret Thatcher intended when she became Prime Minister, 'did not imagine that any government had the power to repeal the post-war settlement. I was wrong, of course: society had changed'. If he had been writing *The Road to 1945* in the mid-1990s, he says that his 'account would [have been] ... overshadowed by the knowledge that the brave new world of Attlee, Beveridge and Keynes was never the enduring structure it appeared to be. It was more like a Ministry of Works prefab, intended for some deserving young couple at the end of the war ... But finally it was bulldozed away in spite of many pleas to preserve it as a memorial to a more civilized era'. Addison argues that with that bulldozing of the structure of the welfare state 'there departed the essential wartime vision of a society in which the state maintained a framework of social justice and citizenship for all'.[76]

The myth of the post-war consensus, as Addison's eloquent account illustrates, was the result of a generation of historians, like Addison, who both celebrated the post-war political achievements and sought to ground them historically. Samuel Beer, for example, wrote in *British Politics in the Collectivist Age* (1966) of the 'modernization of British politics' and announced how it was a harbinger of the present, stating: 'Happy is the country in which consensus and conflict are ordered in a dialectic that makes of the political arena at once a market of interests and a forum for debate of fundamental concerns'.[77] Beer and other historians and social scientists attempted to find in the past the antecedents of the achievements of the post-war consensus.[78] Such optimistic accounts of the consensual nature of post-war British society and politics were widely circulated in the 1960s and 1970s, but there were sceptics even then. For example, as early as the late 1950s, Titmuss in his *Essays on the 'Welfare State'* was calling the notion of consensus into question.[79] So were Smith and Townsend, who, along with Titmuss, were 'rediscovering' poverty.[80] But, as Addison has indicated, it was the erosion of the post-war settlement in the 1970s and 1980s, which seriously began to undermine the myth of consensus.[81] By the 1990s, Corelli Barnett, in the most sustained arguments, criticised the aspirations and policies of the post-war governments, arguing that the creation of the welfare state was a costly avoidance of the truth of economic decline.[82]

The Festival of Britain itself was deeply contested by particular Conservatives and the Beaverbrook press.[83] Beaverbrook's *Evening Standard* began in August of 1949 calling the Festival: 'Mr. Morrison's multi-million-pound baby', and from then to its opening the *Standard* and the *Express* boasted Festival critiques, employing turns of phrases such as: 'Mr. Morrison's Monument', 'Morrison's Folly' and 'This gigantic waxworks *cum* circus *cum* carnival', with daily headline complaints including: 'Resort-Guide Paper Taken for Festival', 'Up Up Up Go Hotel Prices', 'Up Go the Costs of the Festival'. In addition, Conservative MP Cyril Osborne declared he was against the Festival on the grounds that the divorce courts were already choked with customers and the prisons were overcrowded.[84] Conversely, a Gallup Poll in the winter of 1951 showed 58 per cent in favour of the Festival, in spite of the situation in Korea. The appropriateness of the Festival in the post-war moment was clearly highly contested.

Which road to take to the future was contested, as well. There are many indications that how to be Britain and British after the Second World War, with the loss of India, was not entirely clear. Britain as a part of a wider European alliance, for example, was not considered a real alternative by many because of the state of European economies and the British Government's concerns about the political situation in Europe, especially in France and Italy, with their strong communist parties. Labour Foreign Secretary, Ernest Bevin, agreed that Britain would, under the terms established in the Brussels Treaty of 1948, co-operate on defence in relation to Europe, but he would not agree to any further British involvement in new political or economic entities such as the European Steel Community.[85]

The post-war Labour government had numerous domestic concerns as well. Bread, unrationed during the war, was rationed in 1946. The coal shortage of the horribly cold winter of 1947 proved an embarrassment and problem for the government, as was the situation in 1947 when full convertibility between sterling and dollars was re-established and sudden speculation against sterling made the pound overvalued at $4.03. This convertibility crisis continued until the autumn of 1949 when the pound was devalued to $2.80. In October of 1949, all public expenditure was cut, but the Festival survived with only a £1,000,000 reduction in its funds.[86] 'Lord Festival', Herbert Morrison, vigorously rejected calls for it to be axed. Giving up the Festival, he argued, would be like declaring national mourning: 'Is that the way to buck ourselves up when we are in difficulties?' 'I do not think it is'.[87]

Further crises followed in 1950–51. The convertibility crisis led to an increase in the price of imports. Then, due to the unforeseeable catastrophe of the Korean War, there was another rise in import prices. By late 1950 and early 1951 the United Nations was withdrawing from Korea and the British press was filled with predictions of another world war. In mid-January 1951, Rainald Wells wrote in the *Daily Telegraph* that 'More and more people, indeed, are asking whether it [the Festival] should not be postponed, or even cancelled. The overriding question is whether or not the Festival will tend to aid or hinder us in what is now our primary task – that is the strengthening of our defences.'[88] Morrison was asked on a number of occasions if it would not be more reasonable and appropriate to cancel or delay the Festival in view of war. Of course, it would not have been at all practical to stop the Festival so close to its opening, with so many resources already devoted to it, but Morrison answered the question in more lofty terms, stating 'I quite agree that there is plenty to be anxious about in the state of the world, but we do not know how long this anxiety without large scale war is going on … and … in this situation, which may continue, it is profoundly important that we should keep the self-respect and morale of the British people on a high level.'[89]

The Korean War led to post-war Labour's worst domestic crisis. Hugh Gaitskell, Chancellor of the Exchequer, had to find funds somewhere in the budget to supply the military expenditure agreed with the Americans. Gaitskell announced in April of 1951 that he had no choice but to cut all the social services, including the NHS, and that he had to introduce charges for spectacles and dentures. Aneurin Bevan, who had been responsible for the creation of the NHS (although he was no longer Minster of Health in 1951), had declared that charges would not be introduced as long as he was in the Government. Lord President of the Council, Herbert Morrison, supported Gaitskell's unpopular decision and Bevan resigned, as did Harold Wilson, the President of the Board of Trade.[90] The newspapers were full of this news, as well as the British casualties in Korea. The Festival opened two weeks later.

Speeches made at the Festival reveal uncertainty and unease about the state of Britain. The Archbishop of Canterbury, for instance, proclaimed in his sermon at the Festival's opening ceremony that:

The chief and governing purpose of the Festival is to declare our belief and trust in the British way of life, not with any boastful self-confidence nor with any aggressive self-advertisement, but with sober and humble trust that by holding fast to that which is good and rejecting from our midst that which is evil we may continue to be a nation at unity in itself and of service to the world. It is good at a time like the present so to strengthen, and in part recover, our hold on the abiding principles of all that is best in our national life.[91]

Archbishop Fisher's sermon betrays a fragility in the national feeling of 1951 – a need to boost morale 'to strengthen and in part to recover our hold on all that is best in our national life'. The hold had slipped somewhat since the trials of the war. Perhaps this was due to the slow realisation that Britain was no longer a great world power, and therefore had to console itself with either attempting to stake a claim as a 'third way' between the USA and the USSR or to align itself with the USA. Among other examples, Attlee's decision to develop the British atom bomb indicates that the idea of Britain as a 'third force' was the preferred path.[92]

The Festival's Director, Gerald Barry, declared: 'One mistake we should *not* make, we should not fall into the error of supposing we were going to produce anything conclusive. In this sceptical age, the glorious assurance of the mid-Victorians would find no echo.'[93] And, the King himself revealed the uncertainties of 1951 in a speech at its official opening. George VI explained to the nation the purpose of the Festival, stating: 'Two world wars have brought us grievous loss of life and treasure; and though the nation has made a splendid effort towards recovery new burdens have fallen upon it and dark clouds still overhang the whole world. Yet this is no time for despondency; for I see this Festival as a symbol of Britain's abiding courage and vitality.'[94]

A national celebration of 'British achievement' was what Herbert Morrison and his team of experts decided was needed to express national recovery and to enact it as well. The 1951 Festival was to be 'an act of national autobiography' and the people of every town and village with their 'local events' and 'spontaneous expression[s]' of their life and interest' were encouraged to meet the 'challenge' and 'make these traditional events better than ever before, to write the year into their memories'.[95] Along with being a co-ordinated effort at locally funded, as well as nationally funded, reconstruction projects, great and small, the Festival was also an opportunity for Labour to advertise its achievements and to attempt to actualise some of its social democratic goals. The following chapter explores this point further, as well as the question of who the Festival planners were. It also elaborates an idea of what form British national identity took in the immediate post-war period. And, finally, it illustrates how the 1951

Festival was clearly a Labour project, regardless of the repeated public pronouncements that it was apolitical.

Notes

1 Roy Strong, as quoted by B. Hillier, 'Introduction', in M. Banham and B. Hillier (eds), *A Tonic to the Nation: The Festival of Britain 1951* (London: Thames & Hudson with the co-operation of the Victoria and Albert Museum, 1976), 10–17, p. 10.

2 R. Strong, 'Prologue: Utopia Limited', in Banham and Hillier (eds), *A Tonic*: 6–9, p. 6.

3 On how I believe the Festival and Coronation were very different events, see the conclusion to this book.

4 The Festival's Director-General, Gerald Barry, is generally attributed with the well-remembered description of the Festival as 'a tonic to the nation' (see, for example, A. Forty, 'Festival Politics', in Banham and Hillier (eds), *A Tonic*: 26–38, p. 26). However, Charles Plouviez, Assistant to the Director of Exhibitions, stated in 2001 that it was 'speechwriters brainwave' (electronic mail between Charles Plouviez and Martin Packer, 10 October 2001, copied to the author).

5 M. Banham, 'A National Enterprise: Introduction', in Banham and Hillier (eds), *A Tonic*: 70–2, p. 72.

6 P. Clarke, *Hope and Glory: Britain 1900–1990* (London: Penguin Books, 1996), p. 351.

7 Clarke, *Hope and Glory*, p. 353.

8 Callaghan, September 1976, as quoted by Clarke, *Hope and Glory*, p. 351.

9 C. Plouviez, 'The Best of the Festival' [review of E. Harwood and A. Powers (eds), *Festival of Britain: Twentieth Century Architecture 5* (The Journal of The Twentieth Century Society, 2001)], *Festival Times*, newsletter of the Festival of Britain Society, 44 (March 2002).

10 Forty, 'Festival Politics', p. 34.

11 Public Record Office, London (hereafter PRO), Work 25/21 (old 3 A2/A3), I. Cox, 'The Story the Exhibition Tells: F. S. Campania, Festival of Britain 1951' (London: HMSO, 1951), p. 4.

12 Curiously, the various Festival official souvenir guide/catalogues describe anywhere from eight to twelve official exhibitions and twenty-two to twenty-four arts festivals. In an electronic mail message of 28 September 2001 Charles Plouviez, Assistant to the Director of Exhibitions, explained that he thought 'we really muddled things up so nobody would know what was "official" and what not. The confusion over the arts festivals is even worse'.

13 *A Tonic to the Nation*, mentioned above, is the only full-length treatment of the Festival of Britain 1951 and it is not a historical monograph. It is, instead, a very useful combination of primary documents, essays by architects and planners, and reminiscences. The 176-page *Festival of Britain: Twentieth Century Architecture 5* (2001) edited by Elain Harwood and Alan Powers is the most far-ranging publication on the Festival to date. Although its main focus is the Festival's architecture, other aspects are addressed. There is also the Festival of Britain Society's website at www. packer34.freeserve.co.uk, created by Martin Packer, which is very informative.

14 See, for example, R. Elwall, *Building a Better Tomorrow: Architecture in Britain in the 1950s* (Chichester: Wiley-Academy, 2000); B. Ford (ed.), *The Cambridge Guide to the Arts in Britain, Vol. 9, Since the Second World War* (Cambridge: Cambridge University Press, 1988): 259–62 and 292–7; S. Forgan, 'Festival of Science and the Two Cultures: Science, Design and Display in the Festival of Britain, 1951', *British Journal for the History of Science*, 31:2 (1988), 217–40; and A. Jackson, 'The Politics of Architecture: English Architecture 1929–1951', *Journal of the Society of Architectural Historians*, 24:1 (1965), 97–107.

15 According to Harold Perkin, 'Nearly 8 million people were in the armed forces by the last year of the war, every man between 18 and 60 was either called up or directed into the war industries, and every unmarried woman between the same ages'. H. Perkin, *The Rise of Professional Society in England Since 1880* (London and New York: Routledge, 1989), p. 407.

16 W. Behringer, Review of work by Craig Koslofsky, *Social History*, 26:3 (October 2001), 340–3, p. 343.

17 See for example: K. Middlemas, *Power, Competition and the State Vol. I: Britain in Search of Balance 1940–1961* (London: Macmillan, 1986); S. Brooke, *Labour's War: The Labour Party During the Second World War* (Oxford: Oxford University Press, 1992); P. Addison, *The Road to 1945: British Politics and the Second World War* (London: Pimlico, 1994).

18 M. Sissons and P. French (eds), *Age of Austerity, 1945–1951* (Harmondsworth: Penguin Books, 1963), p. 9.

19 For an attempt at using new methodologies and asking new questions of the post-war period, see B. Conekin, F. Mort and C. Waters (eds), *Moments of Modernity: Reconstructing Britain 1945–1964* (London: Rivers Oram Press, 1999).

20 Peter Clarke's *Hope and Glory: Britain 1900–1990* and Kenneth O. Morgan's *The People's Peace: British History 1945–1989* (Oxford: Oxford University Press, 1990) are the best general histories covering the period and both authors do to some degree take cultural issues into account when discussing politics. I do not consider here Paul Addison's *Now the War is Over: A Social History of Britain 1945–51* (London: BBC and Jonathan Cape, 1985) or Peter Hennessy's *Never Again: Britain 1945–1951* (London: Vintage Books, 1993). Both are the results of television productions and, as such, different sorts of work. They do both, however, contain much useful information.

21 Clearly, the big exception here is Alan Sinfield's widely acclaimed *Literature, Politics and Culture in Postwar Britain* (Berkeley: University of California Press, 1989). But, in a way, this exception proves the rule, as Sinfield is a Professor of English at the University of Sussex. For the more numerous histories of nineteenth-century Britain that relate these domains, see, for example: R. Colls and P. Dodd (eds), *Englishness: Politics and Culture 1880–1920* (London: Croom Helm, 1986); the work of Raphael Samuel, especially *Island Stories: Unravelling Britain, Theatres of Memory Vol. II*, ed. A. Light with S. Alexander and G. Stedman Jones (London and New York: Verso, 1998), *Theatres of Memory, Vol. I: Past and Present in Contemporary Culture* (London and New York: Verso, 1994) and his three edited volumes, *Patriotism: the Making and Unmaking of British National Identity* (London: Routledge, 1989); G. Stedman Jones, *Languages of Class* (Cambridge: Cambridge University Press, 1983); E. Hobsbawm and T. Ranger (eds), *The Invention of Tradition* (Cambridge: Cambridge University Press, 1983); J. Walkowitz, *City of Dreadful Delight: Narratives of Sexual Danger in Late-Victorian London* (London: Virago Press, 1994); and the work of

C. K. Steedman, especially *Childhood, Culture and Class in Britain: Margaret McMillan 1860–1931* (New Brunswick: Rutgers University Press, 1990). For a fine attempt for the first half of the twentieth century, see M. Daunton and B. Rieger (eds), *Meanings of Modernity: Britain from the Late Victorian Era to World War II* (Oxford and New York: Berg, 2001). On France, see: L. Hunt, *Politics, Culture and Class in the French Revolution* (Berkeley: University of California Press, 1989) and H. Lebovics, *True France: The Wars Over Cultural Identity: 1900–1945* (Ithaca: Cornell University Press, 1992).

22 On this debate in the WEA and its impact on cultural studies as a discipline, see T. Steele, *The Emergence of Cultural Studies 1945–65: Cultural Politics, Adult Education and the 'English' Question* (London: Lawrence & Wishart, 1997). Examples of post-war histories of Britain that make this demarcation between 'culture' and 'politics' are J. Obelkevich and P. Catterall (eds), *Understanding Post-War British Society* (London and New York: Routledge, 1994) and J. Fyrth (ed.), *Labour's High Noon: The Government and the Economy* (London: Lawrence & Wishart, 1993) and *Labour's Promised Land? Culture and Society in Labour Britain 1945–51* (London: Lawrence & Wishart, 1995).

23 M. Francis, *Ideas and Policies under Labour 1945–1951: Building a New Britain* (Manchester: Manchester University Press, 1997) and his 'The Labour Party: Modernisation and the Politics of Restraint', in Conekin, Mort and Waters (eds), *Moments of Modernity*, 152–70; J. Lawrence and M. Taylor (eds), *Party, State and Society: Electoral Behaviour in Britain Since 1800* (Aldershot: Scolar Press, 1997); and N. Tiratsoo, 'Popular Politics, Affluence and the Labour Party in the 1950s', in A. Gorst, L. Johnman and W. Scott Lucas (eds), *Contemporary British History 1931–1961: Politics and the Limits of Policy* (London: Pinter Press, 1991), 44–51. Francis' new work on masculinity, emotion and politics in the period promises to offer a further challenge to the field, while opening up new areas of enquiry.

24 I. Zweiniger-Bargielowska, 'Exploring the Gender Gap: The Conservative Party and Women's Vote, 1945–1964', in M. Francis and I. Zweiniger-Bargielowska (eds), *The Conservatives and British Society, 1880–1990* (Cardiff: University of Wales Press, 1996) and 'Rationing, Austerity and the Conservative Party After 1945', *Historical Journal*, 37:1 (1994), 173–97.

25 R. Hewison, *In Anger: Culture and the Cold War, 1945–60* (London: Weidenfeld & Nicolson, 1981) and *Culture and Consensus: England, Art and Politics since 1945* (London: Methuen, 1995).

26 The sort of interdisciplinary work I am referring to here includes: S. Hall and T. Jefferson (eds), *Resistance Through Rituals: Youth Subcultures in Post-War Britain* (London: Hutchinson, 1976); D. Hebdige, *Subculture: The Meaning of Style* (London: Methuen, 1979); J. Hill, *Sex, Class and Realism: British Cinema 1956–1963* (London: BFI, 1986); S. Laing, *Representations of Working-Class Life 1957–1964* (Basingtoke: Macmillan, 1986); P. Gilroy, *There Ain't No Black in the Union Jack: The Cultural Politics of Race and Nation* (London: Hutchinson, 1987); A. McRobbie, *Feminism and Youth Culture: from 'Jackie' to 'Just Seventeen'* (Basingstoke: Macmillan, 1991); F. Mort, *Cultures of Consumption: Masculinities and Social Space in Late Twentieth-Century Britain* (London: Routledge, 1996); C. Steedman, *Landscape for a Good Woman: A Story of Two Lives* (New Brunswick: Rutgers University Press, 1987) and A. Kuhn, *Family Secrets: Acts of Memory and Imagination* (London: Verso, 1995). Clearly, I am all too aware that the state of affairs in at least some American universities is different.

27 See, for example, Stefan Collini, who dismissed cultural studies as 'grievance studies'

in 'Escape from DWEMsville: is culture too important to be left to cultural studies?', *Times Literary Supplement*, 27 May 1994.

28 B. Waites, T. Bennett and G. Martin (eds), *Popular Culture: Past and Present, A Reader* (London: Croom Helm in association with the Open University, 1982), p. 18.

29 C. Nelson, L. Grossberg and P. A. Triechler (eds), *Cultural Studies* (New York: Routledge, 1992).

30 C. K. Steedman, 'Culture, Cultural Studies, and Historians', in Nelson, Grossberg and Triechler (eds), *Cultural Studies*, p. 620.

31 In this work, the term representation is understood to mean a signifying practice that can include language, discourse and image. 'Representation', as Stuart Hall has explained, 'is one of the central practices which produce[s] culture': S. Hall, 'Introduction', in S. Hall (ed.), *Representation: Cultural Representations and Signifying Practices* (London: Sage Publications in association with the Open University, 1997), p. 1.

32 Robert Hewison points out that the week of 1953 Coronation celebrations, planned by the Tories, cost one million pounds 'which for one week makes the expenditure on the whole Festival year relatively modest' (Hewison, *Culture and Consensus*, p. 65).

33 G. Eley and R. Suny, 'Introduction: From the Moment of Social History to the Work of Cultural Representation', in G. Eley and R. Suny (eds), *Becoming National: A Reader* (New York and Oxford: Oxford University Press, 1996), 3–37, p. 8.

34 *Ibid.*

35 See M. Foucault, 'Space, Knowledge and Power', in *The Foucault Reader*, ed. P. Rabinow (Harmondsworth: Penguin, 1987), p. 252.

36 N. Rose and P. Miller, 'Political Power Beyond the State: Problematics of Government', *British Journal of Sociology*, 43:2 (June 1992), 173–205, p. 175. See also P. Abrams, 'Notes on the Difficulty of Studying the State (1977)', *Journal of Historical Sociology*, 1:1 (March 1988), 58–89, p. 81. Abrams writes: 'the state is not the reality which stands behind the mask of political practice. It is itself the mask which prevents our seeing political practice as it is. It is, one could almost say, the mind of a mindless world, the purpose of purposeless conditions, the opium of the citizen. There *is* a state-system in Miliband's sense: a palpable nexus of practice and institutional structure centred in government and more or less extensive, unified and dominant in any given society. And its sources, structures and variations can be examined in fairly straight-forward empirical ways. There *is*, too, a state-idea, projected, purveyed and variously believed in different societies at different times. And its modes, effects and variations are also susceptible to research. The relationship of the state-system and the state-idea to other forms of power should and can be central concerns of political analysis'.

37 On Foucault's concept of 'governmentality', see G. Burchell, C. Gordon and P. Miller (eds), *The Foucault Effect: Studies in Governmentality with Two Lectures and an Interview with Michel Foucault* (Chicago: University of Chicago Press, 1991).

38 On Gramscian notions of 'hegemony', which is what I am grappling with here, see: *Selections from the Prison Notebooks of Antonio Gramsci*, eds and trans. Q. Hoare and G. Nowell Smith (New York: International Publishers, 1989).

39 Benedict Anderson, *Imagined Communities: Reflections on the Origin and Spread of Nationalism* (London: Verso, 1990), p. 15. Anderson, is, of course, the most influential theorist of the nationalisation of culture and national identity. But, earlier interventions moved us from 'a primordialist, essentialist notion of the nation to the

currently dominant view of the nation as constructed or invented'. These were, in particular: E. Gellner, *Thought and Change* (London: Weidenfeld & Nicolson, 1964), Chapter 7, and K. Deutsch, *Nationalism and Social Communication: An Inquiry into the Foundations of Nationality* (Cambridge MA: MIT Press, 1966 [1953]). See Eley and Suny (eds), *Becoming National*, p. 6.

40 Stuart Hall in S. Hall and D. Held (eds), *Understanding Modern Societies*, vol. 4 of *Modernity and Its Futures* (Cambridge: Polity Press, 1992), 292–3.

41 The term 'invented tradition' was first employed by Hobsbawm and Ranger in their edited volume, *The Invention of Tradition*.

42 Of course, there are exceptions. See, for example: T. Nairn, 'Scotland and Europe', in Eley and Suny (eds), *Becoming National*, 79–105; Samuel (ed.), *Patriotism, Vol. II: Minorities and Outsiders*; Hobsbawm and Ranger (eds), *The Invention of Tradition*. But, these are article-length treatments of the sub-nations. British historians have yet to produce a work similar to Celia Applegate's study, *A Nation of Provincials: The German Idea of Heimat* (Berkeley: University of California Press, 1990).

43 Hennessy, *Never Again*, p. 310.

44 S. Fielding, '"To Make Men and Women Better Than They Are": Labour and the Building of Socialism', in Fyrth (ed.), *Labour's Promised Land?*, 16–27, p. 18; H. Morrison, *The Peaceful Revolution* (London: Allen And Unwin, 1949), p. 47.

45 T. Steele, *The Emergence of Cultural Studies 1945–65*, p. 90. According to Steele, A. L. Morton's *A People's History of England* (1937) was 'pioneering' in this respect as well.

46 Stedman Jones has offered as evidence of this shift a quote from the *Northern Star* in 1838, which asserted: 'The attention of the labouring classes – the real "people" – has been successively ... aroused by the injuries they have sustained by the operation of a corrupt system of patronage.'(G. Stedman Jones, 'Rethinking Chartism', in his *Languages of Class*, p. 104) See also P. Joyce, *Visions of the People: Industrial England and the Question of Class, 1848–1914* (Cambridge: Cambridge University Press, 1991).

47 Hennessy, *Never Again*, p. 310.

48 Francis, *Ideas and Policies Under Labour*, p. 57.

49 Keynes, BBC summer of 1945, as quoted by Hennessy, *Never Again*, p. 310.

50 Lord Redcliffe-Maud, *Experiences of an Optimist* (1981), as quoted by Hennessy, *Never Again*, p. 120.

51 On Reith, his attitudes and his role at the BBC, see: D. L. LeMahieu, *A Culture for Democracy: Mass Communication and the Cultivated Mind in Britain Between the Wars* (Oxford: Clarendon Press, 1988), pp. 139–54; S. Nicholas, *The Echo of War: Home Front Propaganda and the Wartime BBC, 1939–1945* (Manchester: Manchester University Press, 1996), pp. 18–19; R. McKibbin, *Classes and Cultures: England 1918–1951* (Oxford: Oxford University Press, 1998), pp. 460–2; Samuel, *Island Stories, Theatres of Memory Vol. II*, pp. 177–88, 190.

52 Samuel, *Island Stories, Theatres of Memory Vol. II*, p. 182.

53 *Ibid.*

54 A. Calder, *The People's War: Britain 1939–1945* (London: Pimlico, 1992), pp. 364–5.

55 *Mass Observation, People in Production* (1942, p. 277), as quoted by Calder, *The People's War*, p. 364.

56 Thomas as quoted by Calder, *The People's War*, p. 364.

57 Calder, *The People's War*, p. 366.

58 G. Orwell, *The Lion and the Unicorn: Socialism and the English Genius* (London: Penguin Books, 1982 [1941]), p. 67.

59 R. Fieldhouse 'Adults Learning – for Leisure, Recreation and Democracy', in Fyrth (ed.), *Labour's Promised Land?*, 264–74, p. 264.

60 *Ibid.*

61 Fieldhouse, 'Adults Learning', p. 265.

62 'Further Education', Ministry of Education Pamphlet No. 8 (HMSO: 1947), as cited by Fieldhouse, 'Adults Learning', p. 264.

63 It was Michael Frayn who first called the Festival planners members of 'the radical middle-classes – do-gooders'. Frayn, 'Festival', in Sissons and French (eds), *Age of Austerity*, p. 331. Many people took such a characterisation as a criticism of the planners, but in a 1976 BBC interview conducted as part of the 25th anniversary celebrations, Frayn made it clear that he thought of himself as a member of such a group, rather than a critic (Frayn in 'A Tonic to the Nation', British Library, National Sound Archive, Tape T 10993, WR, Track W, copies of three BBC transmissions, BBC # T52334, played on the BBC on 28 November 1976 [recorded on 23 November]).

64 Huw Wheldon, as quoted by Hillier, 'Introduction', p. 16.

65 PRO, EL 6/23 [Arts Council], Memo by Director-General Gerald Barry to Arts Council Secretary Miss Mary Glasgow: 'When the 1851 Exhibition closed, it was finished, but 1951 ...' folder 'F. O. B. Correspondence with the Director General, April 1948 – August 1950', n.d., but other correspondence in file indicates mid-August 1949. (Ellipsis in the original.)

66 C. Mackenzie, 'What is Light Music?', 30 November 1950, a talk broadcast on the BBC Third Programme, as quoted by H. Carpenter, with research by J. Doctor, *The Envy of the World: Fifty Years of the BBC Third Programme and Radio 3, 1946–1996* (London: Weidenfield & Nicolson, 1996), p. 86. Four-page programme of the closing ceremonies included independently in I. Cox, *South Bank Exhibition, London, Festival of Britain 1951: A Guide to the Story it Tells* (London: HMSO, 1951).

67 Nicholas, *The Echo of War*, pp. 239, 230; McKibbin, *Classes and Cultures*, pp. 436–8.

68 H. Morrison, Festival of Britain opening speech, May 1951 as quoted by Forty, 'Festival Politics', p. 36. Lord Reith's motto for the BBC was: 'Give the public slightly better than it now thinks it likes'.

69 S. Fielding, P. Thompson and N. Tiratsoo, *'England Arise!': The Labour Party and Popular Politics in 1940s Britain* (Manchester: Manchester University Press, 1995), p. 217.

70 On these debates, see, for example: Stedman Jones, *Languages of Class*; Joyce, *Visions of the People*; P. Corfield (ed.), *Language, History and Class* (Oxford: Oxford University Press, 1991); D. Mayfield and S. Thorne, 'Social History and Its Discontents', *Social History*, 17 (1992), 165–87; J. Lawrence and M. Taylor, 'The Poverty of Protest', *Social History*, 18 (1993), 1–18; J. Vernon, 'Who's Afraid of the Linguistic Turn?', *Social History*, 19 (1994), 81–7; and D. Cannadine, *Class in Britain* (New Haven and London: Yale University Press, 1998).

71 Fielding, Thompson and Tiratsoo, *'England Arise!'*, p. 217.

72 Board of Education [chair: Sir Henry Newbolt], *The Teaching of English in England, Being the Report of the Departmental Committee appointed by the President of the Board of Education to Enquire into the Position of English in the Educational System of England* (London: HMSO, 1921), 248–9.

73 Steele, *The Emergence of Cultural Studies*, p. 65.

74 McKibbin, *Classes and Cultures*, p. 533.

75 *Ibid.*

76 P. Addison, 'Epilogue', in *The Road to 1945*, 280–1.

77 S. Beer, *British Politics in the Collectivist Age* (New York: Alfred A. Knopf, 1966), pp. x, 390. This section on the historiography of consensus was developed collectively by me, Frank Mort and Chris Waters for our 'Introduction' to Conekin, Mort and Waters (eds), *Moments of Modernity*.

78 D. Roberts, *Victorian Origins of the British Welfare State* (New Haven: Yale University Press, 1960) and D. Fraser, *The Evolution of the British Welfare: A History of Social Policy Since the Industrial Revolution* (London: Macmillan, 1973).

79 R. M. Titmuss, *Essays on the 'Welfare State'* (London: Allen & Unwin, 1958). For an overview on the question of a post-war consensus in Britain, see Addison, 'Epilogue'. See also work originating from the Institute of Contemporary British History which questions the post-war consensus: D. Marquand, 'The Decline of the Post-war Consensus', in A. Gorst and W. S. Lucas (eds), *Post-War Britain* (London: Pinter, 1989),1–21; D. Kavanagh and P. Morris, *Consensus from Attlee to Major* (Oxford: Blackwell, 1994) and their 'Controversy: Is the "Postwar Consensus" a Myth?' *Contemporary Record*, 2:6 (1989), 12–15.

80 B. Abel Smith and P. Townsend, *The Poor and the Poorest: A New Analysis of the Ministry of Labour's Family Expenditure Surveys of 1953 and 1960* (London: G. Bell and Sons, 1965).

81 Conversely, some scholars, witnessing the end of the post-war settlement, evoked the 1945–51 period as a time before '"casino capitalism" undermined "the hope of a society united by the service of its members to the common weal"': N. Dennis and A. H. Halsey, *English Ethical Socialism: Thomas More to R. H. Tawney* (Oxford: Oxford University Press, 1988), p. 256.

82 C. Barnett, *The Lost Victory: British Dreams, British Realities 1945–1950* (London: Macmillan, 1995) and *The Audit of War: The Illusion and Reality of Britain as a Great Nation* (London: Macmillan, 1996). Margaret Thatcher, herself, attacked the idea of the post-war consensus, attempting to replace it with a version of the period as one of hardship and petty bickering: M. Thatcher, *The Downing Street Years* (London: HarperCollins, 1993). Conversely, from the opposite side of the political spectrum, Andrew Roberts has argued that the Conservatives were responsible for the culture of decline in the 1950s that reduced Britain to its present status of 'Italy with rockets': A. Roberts, *Eminent Churchillians* (London: Weidenfeld & Nicolson, 1994), p. 3.

83 See the epigraphs of this book for Evelyn Waugh's appraisal of the Festival.

84 All the newspaper headlines and the opinion of Cyril Osborne come from Frayn, 'Festival', pp. 337–40.

85 See, for example, Forty, 'Festival Politics', pp. 26–38.

86 *Ibid.*

87 Herbert Morrison, October 1949, as quoted by Forty, 'Festival Politics', p. 32.

88 Rainald Wells, *Daily Telegraph*, 19 January 1951, as quoted by Frayn, 'Festival', pp. 345–6.

89 H. Morrison, 1951, as quoted by Forty, 'Festival Politics', p. 32.

90 Added to these crises, Attlee was in ill health and Bevin died in the spring of 1951: P. Adelman, *British Politics in the 1930s and 1940s* (Cambridge: Cambridge University Press, 1987), p. 84.

91 Archbishop of Canterbury, Speech, 17 July 1950, as printed in *The Festival of Britain* (back cover reads: *The Official Book of the Festival of Britain, 1951*) (London: HMSO, 1951), n.p., inside front cover. Hereafter referred to as *The Official Book of the Festival*.

92 Forty, 'Festival Politics', p. 35. The idea of Britain as a 'third way' is further discussed in Chapter three.

93 Gerald Barry, as quoted by Frayn, 'Festival Politics', p. 336.

94 King George VI, Speech, as quoted by Gerald Barry, 'The Festival of Britain 1951', *Journal of the Royal Society of Arts*, 100:4880 (22 August 1952).

95 *The Official Book of the Festival*, p. 68.

2 ✧ The Festival's people and purposes

TWO GENERATIONS of British people remember the Festival of Britain as London's celebration of Britain's victory and proclamation of recovery. However, the 1951 Festival had both a broader scope and a much more localised agenda than these popular memories indicate. As stated, the Festival was actually conceived across the nation and created in almost 2,000 locations from competing notions of Britain and 'British-ness'. Even the events predominantly planned from London included the Welsh Hillside Farming Scheme, the Ulster Farm and Factory Exhibition, the Glasgow Heavy Engineering Exhibition, as well as land and sea travelling exhibitions designed to transport miniature versions of London's exhibition to 'the provinces'. In addition, the Festival of Britain was a government strategy to increase foreign tourism, yet it strangely de-emphasised Britain's imperial past. And, although some Labour leaders denied it, the Festival was a Labour extravaganza, with a social democratic agenda.

The Festival of Britain was not only an event – or rather, a series of events – designed to demonstrate to the world Britain's proclaimed economic resurgence, it was also an *attempt* at national recovery – an attempt to bolster the low numbers of tourists, who could stimulate the national economy by bringing hard currency to circulate throughout Great Britain.[1] This aspect has been virtually unexplored in the previous work on the Festival of Britain. The exception is a piece by Adrian Forty, who explains that 'one of the counter-arguments that had been used to defend the Festival against those who accused it of consuming expensive imports was that it might earn foreign currency, and especially dollars, from tourists'.[2] A Board of Trade memo from the summer of 1948 supports this contention. The memo outlined a plan for direct government intervention to stimulate the tourist trade and contained special arrangements for the derequisitioning of hotels and the extra allocation of rationed goods for tourists, including that essential commodity, petrol.[3] And this memo explicitly named the Festival of Britain, 1951 as 'the outstanding tourist attraction of the next few years'.[4] The Festival's touristic agenda was clearly significant and is part of the reason why it was conceived and created in many different sites across the British Isles. An official pamphlet entitled 'Notes for Industry on the 1951 Exhibitions' stated:

> The Festival of Britain, 1951, as its name implies, is intended to be nation-wide ... Behind the Festival of Britain lies a broader and bolder plan: for the idea is that in 1951 the land of Britain itself and the people of Britain themselves will be open to view ... To fulfil this intention, the visitors to Britain will be encouraged to tour industrial and rural areas and to meet the men and women of Britain in their own surroundings.[5]

The authors of this brochure wanted industrial owners and managers to realise the Festival's potential. Everyone was to enthusiastically encourage visitors to travel to the regional centres of industry and agriculture, to meet Britons, and 'view their way of life'. Both residents and visitors were to traverse the islands of the United Kingdom in pursuit of its rich diversity – its people, land and products.

More anecdotal evidence comes from the special Festival issue of *Punch*, all of which was a parody of the Festival in one form or another. In it appeared a full-page poem entitled: 'Exhortation to All Parish and Rural District Councils', which began with the lines: 'Come local bodies, one and all unite / To make our village greens a gladsome sight'. However, the fifth and sixth lines revealed the true object of ironic criticism: 'But let it be your special aim to please / The people pouring in from overseas'. The poem went on to make fun of the idea that not only should Britain's towns act as if their economies were booming, but the town's inhabitants should be stereotypically British, in the extreme, so as to encourage and entertain foreign visitors during the Festival summer:

> All village shops might make, in playful mood,
> Facsimiles of appetizing food
> And publicans must resolutely strive
> To keep tradition splendidly alive ...
> Blacksmiths should be on duty or at ease
> In reach of real or cardboard chestnut trees ...
> Beards should be worn for cricket, every shot
> Greeted with cries of 'Jolly decent, what!' ...
> All houses should be quite devoid of heat ...
> All ladies would be well advised to wear
> Amorphous tweeds and incoherent hair.[6]

Foreign visitors, but nothing else foreign

Although the Festival had this goal of attracting foreign visitors, it did not represent anything foreign.[7] The Festival was 'a national display illustrating the British contribution to civilisation, past, present, and future, in the arts, in science and technology and in industrial design'.[8] In this respect, the 1951 Festival was a long way from the original conception. The first version of the Festival was conceived and privately suggested in 1943 by the Royal Society of Arts as an international exhibition to mark the centenary of the Great Exhibition of 1851, most remembered by its Crystal Palace. According to one official souvenir guide, the 'suggestion was based on the hope that 1951 would have seen not merely the end of the war but Britain well on the road to recovery'.[9] In 1945, John Gloag, a well-respected authority on contemporary design, wrote to *The Times* to support the idea of celebrating the centenary of 1851 with an exhibition, and shortly after Gerald Barry wrote an open letter in the *News Chronicle* to Stafford Cripps, then President of the Board of Trade, urging 'a great Trade and Cultural exhibition to be held in London' in 1951. The government set up the Ramsden Committee in 1945 to investigate the feasibility of holding an international fair or exhibition in order to boost British exports. The committee concluded in the early spring of 1946 that 'a first category international exhibition should be held in London at the first practicable date to demonstrate to the world the recovery of the United Kingdom from the effect of war in moral, cultural, spiritual and material fields'.[10] Although the government accepted the general proposal, in the end an international exhibition was deemed far too expensive and entirely out of line with post-war reconstruction pro-grammes. For example, it was calculated that at 1946 prices such a scheme would have cost the British taxpayers close to 70 million pounds, and would tie up one-third of building labour over three years just to construct the London structures.[11] This, at a time when as many as four million homes, or close to one-third of the total number of all houses, had been destroyed or damaged by bombing.[12] The decision, then, to throw a less ambitious event, costing about one-sixth the sum, was announced in March of 1947. The Festival of Britain, as a smaller, national exhibition, was placed in the charge of the Lord President of the Council, the Right Honourable Herbert Morrison, Labour MP, rather than the Board of Trade.[13] Other than real financial concerns, the decision for a national event reflects a more general mood and a move from the Empire towards the British Isles as the focus of politics and policy.

The Festival marked a drastic departure from most large-scale exhibitions sponsored by states in the nineteenth and twentieth centuries in the West. In 1951, the Festival was the result of a convergence of crises in governance, which made it an altogether different event. For instance, it was very different from the Great Exhibition of 1851. Officially named 'the Exhibition of the Works of Industry of All Nations', the 1851 exhibition sought to represent the world and its products via hundreds of courts organised according to nation. And at the Paris Exposition of 1937, the visitor was invited to experience a miniature version of France, its colonies and, to a lesser extent, the entire world. According to Elizabeth B. Mock, a journalist at the time, 'A visitor to the fair remarked insightfully that "the exposition contains in miniature all the tensions of French society"'.[14] But, the London Festival of Britain did not attempt to represent any tensions of British society or between Great Britain and the rest of the world, whatsoever. It was an isolated storybook encapsulating tales of British strengths and imagination, arranged as 'the autobiography of a nation', with chapters to be experienced in a specified order, as the guidebooks indicated to visitors. These chapters covered various aspects of 'British civilisation' ranging from the story of 'the people' to the 'lion and the unicorn',[15] symbolising 'two of the main qualities of the national character: on the one hand, realism and strength, on the other fantasy, independence and imagination'.[16]

Closer in intent to the Festival of Britain than either the Paris Expo of 1937 or the 1851 exhibition, was the British Empire Exhibition held at Wembley in 1924, also six years after a world war. It aimed to 'stimulate trade, to strengthen the bonds that bind the Mother Country to her Sister States and Daughters, to bring all into closer contact the one with the other, to enable all who owe allegiance to the British flag to meet on common ground, and to learn to know each other'.[17] Yet, the Festival of Britain's planners chose not to stress Britain's ties to anywhere else in the world. Why was this? What was the agenda for the 1951 Festival, according to the London organisers?

Gerald Barry, the driving personality behind the Festival, wrote in his unpublished memoir that:

> An exhibition on this scale devised by the methods that we are adopting implied little short of a revolution. Always before, large-scale national exhibitions had been organized in trade sections, each displaying the accomplishments of an industry ... Space was sold to firms to display their wares in their own way. This time we were going to dispense with all that. We were going to tell a consecutive story, not industry by industry, still less firm by firm, but the story of the British people and the land they live in and by. There was to be no space to let. No one would be able to have his goods on exhibit by paying to do so; they would get there by merit or not at all.[18]

The fact that Barry compared the London South Bank exhibition to a trade fair, rather than an international exhibition, a world's fair or a colonial exhibition reveals the comparatively narrow focus and intent of the Festival of Britain, as well as the serious constraints and economic crises of the immediate post-war government.

It is not difficult to comprehend why Labour decided to turn inward and focus on domestic issues after the Second World War. In addition to the severe housing shortage, there was a frighteningly low level of food imports, resulting in continued rationing. Attlee and his cabinet also faced such crises as the failure of the convertibility scheme in August of 1947, the devastating fuel shortage of the previous winter, the rapid evaporation of the American loan, and the slow growth of exports.[19] In addition to these domestic woes, by 1948 the British government had withdrawn from India, Ceylon and Burma. Although for some this was the fulfilment of Labour's promises of decolonisation, for many it indicated a loss of British power and prestige in a period of great uncertainty. The financial follies and political disturbances in most of Britain's remaining colonies including Ghana, Southern Rhodesia, Zambia, Malawi and Malaya were also destabilising.[20]

Notions of post-war national identity

Britain as a modest, peaceable nation

A turning inward did occur in the immediate post-war era, due to hardships in Britain and crises in the former colonies. Gareth Stedman Jones has written in a different context that 'the problems of defining English nationhood in the first half of the twentieth century were ... intimately tied to assumptions of imperial heritage or destiny'.[21] But by 1951 the retreat from Empire had begun, and therefore by 1949, with Labour in power, the Empire was no longer an appropriate or comfortable foundational structure around which to build British national identity.[22]

It seems that by the early 1950s, intentionally or unintentionally, Britons ranging from popular writers to politicians were busy recasting the imagined nation of Great Britain as a diverse yet united land, perhaps just as complex and fascinating as the former Empire. Sociologist Bill Williamson has argued that a 'redrawing of the emotional boundaries and images of nationhood – often around those very forms of "ordinariness" that were articulated so clearly during the war itself' took place in the post-war era due to the retreat from Empire and the gradual realisation that Great Britain was not the world power it once had been.[23]

However, historian Chris Waters has reminded us that such notions of Britishness did not spring up from nowhere. He has argued that:

> the BBC's glorification during World War II of 'ordinary people' as the heroes and heroines of the national drama did not suddenly emerge out of the blue, but instead was the result of a wholesale remapping of the symbolic representations of nationhood that had taken place earlier, a

complex process in which various individuals and institutions had contributed, from film-makers like John Grierson, to popular magazines like *Picture Post*, to novelists and social critics like George Orwell, J. B. Priestley and Walter Greenwood, to organisations like Mass Observation and the Pilgrim Trust, to social investigators like Seebohm Rowntree, and to artists like L. S. Lowry, whose visual remapping of 'the North' became central to shared perceptions of the meaning of the nation and national identity.[24]

Labour appealed to this new construction of Britishness in referring to itself throughout the 1940s as 'the People's Party'.[25]

Alison Light – whose *Forever England* focuses on literary expressions of conservatism, femininity and national identity between the two world wars – has noted the difference between the text version dating from 1938–39 and the Hollywood film version from 1942 of *Mrs Miniver*. She detects a shift from a quiet, domestic conservatism to one similar in tone, yet harnessed to the aims of fighting the Second World War.[26] Light believes the war 'provided a new heroic stage for a British people seen, not as a race of empire builders ... but, rather as an essentially unassuming nation, peaceable by temperament, who wanted nothing better than a quiet life'. She argues that the essence of this change meant the creation of 'a powerful and new sense of national history, not as the doing of the great and the good, but as that which was made by the little ordinary people at home, "muddling through"'.[27] This sense of Britishness as not 'boastful', but 'sober and humble', as not imperial, but domestic and 'ordinary'[28] was the predominant representation of national identity in the Festival of Britain's official exhibitions.[29] The British were people who lived rather quiet, cosy lives and just wanted to be left alone, but if faced with adversity they had the stamina and determination to 'muddle through'. The fact that they had succeeded in 'muddling through' meant that they deserved a fete.

Britishness as belonging rather than othering

In addition to the Festival's portrayal of Britishness as 'unassuming', yet determined, the other thing about this identity was its sense of belonging. Britons were British because they 'belonged' to Britain – there was something about their 'island' home that made them unique and different from other people. This something was related to both the soil and the sea – the land and the 'islandness' of Great Britain. In Michael Billig's phrase, this was a type of 'banal nationalism', the stuff of 'clichéd utterance, as well as heroic gesture', utilising the 'repertoire of the obvious'.[30] At the risk of over-simplifying, the immediate post-war form of Britishness was dependent on beliefs, stories and discourses constituted by 'belonging' to a place.[31] According to David Morley and Kevin Robins, 'The project of modernity is ... "to make oneself somehow at home in the maelstrom" that is daily life'.[32] Britain in the post-war period was attempting to modernise and saw itself generally as a special combination of the ancient and the modern – steeped in tradition, yet extremely forward-looking. Being 'at home' or 'belonging' to a place was key. Often this place consisted of both the British isles and a region or town with a unique sense of itself; Britons were generally self-identified as being from both Great Britain and also a town or city, a community or neighbourhood, or even a smaller country, such as Wales, Northern Ireland or Scotland. As Linda Colley has argued, 'identities are not like hats. Human beings can and do put on several at a time'.[33] Writing of a much earlier Britain (1707–1837), Colley asserts that:

> Great Britain did not emerge by way of a 'blending' of the different regional or older national cultures contained within its boundaries as is sometimes maintained, nor is its genesis to be explained primarily in terms of an English 'core' imposing its cultural and political hegemony on a helpless and defrauded Celtic periphery. As even the briefest acquaintance with Great Britain will confirm, the Welsh, the Scottish and the English remain in many ways distinct peoples in cultural terms, just as all three countries continue to be conspicuously sub-divided into different regions. The sense of a common identity here did not come into being then, because of an integration and homogenisation of disparate cultures. Instead, Britishness was superimposed over an array of internal differences.[34]

The 'array of internal differences' within Britain was emphasised in the 1951 Festival as a source of strength and even unity for the nation. By the early 1950s, however, the process through which this identity was constructed was not the same as in Colley's story, for she states that Britishness was 'superimposed' over the differences 'in response to contact with the Other, and above all in response to conflict with the Other'. One of the problems with recreating a national identity in Britain immediately following the Second World War was precisely related to this. As we shall see, at times in the official 1951 exhibitions there was the implication that to be British was to be different from particularly the Americans, Russians or Germans. The most prominent of such notions was the presentation of Britain as an independent 'third force' between the extremes of the United States and Russia in the new Cold War world.[35] But in 1951 these references were surprisingly muted and infrequent. It seems there no longer was a clear 'other'; the Germans were defeated and the Empire could not at this time serve as an uncomplicated point of reference and pride. In the New Britain struggling to emerge, with the help of Labour and left-leaning professionals, notions of 'Britishness' relied on a more positive and multi-layered process of inward identification.

However, although the Festival of Britain represented Britain and British 'contributions to civilisation' with little mention of the Empire,[36] the 1951

Festival was not merely one more example of 'Little Englandism'. From
the outset, the Festival planners in London were very committed to and
interested in presenting a modern Festival of *Britain*, not a conservative,
volkisch rendering of 'Deep England'.[37] As previously mentioned, the London-based planners devised exhibitions in Wales, Northern Ireland and
Scotland, as well as encouraging all cities, towns and villages in the United
Kingdom to plan some event or activity to celebrate 1951. And Barry saw
the Festival as an opportunity to represent 'the hopes in three dimensional
projection of a brighter and better future'.[38]

The people behind the Festival

When the government approved the final, scaled-down version of the
Festival in 1947, Herbert Morrison was deemed the appropriate head, as
the minister in charge of the domestic front and economic planning,
earning him the title of 'Lord Festival'.[39] Morrison and his under-secretary,
Max Nicholson, selected some of the key members of the Festival executive
committee, including the Festival's director, Gerald Barry [40] (Figure 2). Barry
wrote in his unpublished autobiography that 'Hateful schooling and the
war itself turned me into a rebel all right. My generation (what was left
of it) were Angry Young Men. But we also believed in Utopia'.[41] Barry was
well known to Morrison and was a friend of Nicholson's. The two of them
were founding members of the Labour think-tank, Political and Economic
Planning or PEP, and had worked together on *The Weekend Review*,
established by Barry.[42] Barry had also been a vocal advocate of the Festival
as the editor of the liberal *News Chronicle*. Nicholson deemed Barry perfect
for the job, calling him 'a great impresario'.[43]

Apart from three civil servants, Cecil Cooke of the Central Office of
Information, George Campbell from the Treasury and Bernard Sendall of
the Admiralty, the crux of the executive committee were chosen by Barry
and Nicholson in concert to serve as representatives of the constituent
councils of art, science, architecture, industrial design and the British Film
Institute (BFI). Most of those selected had particular expertise in their
fields, as well as being known to Barry. For example, Hugh Casson, who
was appointed director of the Festival's Council for Architecture, Town
Planning and Building Research, claimed that 'as an impecunious architect
I'd moonlighted, doing journalism: I used to write "What to do with the
cupboard under the stairs" ... and I wrote for Gerald Barry in the *News
Chronicle* on the future of architecture and all that sort of stuff' [44] (Figure 3).
The director of the Council of Industrial Design (COID), Gordon Russell,
represented industrial design, Huw Wheldon the Arts Council, and Denis
Forman the BFI. Ian Cox, who had worked for the Ministry of Information,

was chosen as the Festival's director of science and technology.[45] Leonard Crainford was the Secretary of the Festival Organisation, until he became the managing director of the Festival Gardens Limited, which had its own Board of Directors.[46]

Adrian Forty has described the Festival as 'in part an early experiment in technocracy', with the organisation dominated by 'professional architects, designers, engineers, etc., and not professional administrators'.[47] The Festival planners were representatives of the new post-war public sphere, dominated by experts and professionals. They had learned important lessons in their war work, including the art of teamwork and *ad hoc* decision making. Hugh Casson said more than once that the Festival organisation was indeed 'inbred', but that it had to be so. The organisers were charged with the task of putting on the exhibitions quickly; therefore, it was necessary for all members to unequivocally share the same objectives from the start.[48] According to Bevis Hillier, these 'earnest young men with double-breasted suits, brigade ties and pipes, may have made later generations smile or wince', but, he argues that their shared experiences allowed them to plan and mount the Festival exhibitions on schedule in a very short time.[49]

2 Visit of Members of the Council and the Executive Committee to the Festival of Britain South Bank site, 4 May 1950. From left: Ralph Freeman, Misha Black, Hugh Casson, Sir Wynn Wheldon, Sir Harry Lindsey, Sir Alan Herbert, Jean Mann, Sir Frederick Bain, Lady Megan Lloyd George, Sir Henry French, John Ratcliff, Sir Alan Barlow, Cecil Cooke, Gerald Barry, Leonard Crainford, Ralph Tubbs, Brigadier Greenfield and Colonel Neil

3 Hugh Casson's drawing of the view from Chichley Street of the South Bank site,
24 October 1950

The Presentation Panel was 'the creative engine for the exhibitions'.[50] This group was 'responsible for all the visual and many of the non-visual aspects of the official exhibitions, from choosing the architects and designers, to naming the restaurants', according to Hippisley Coxe.[51] Chaired by Barry, but often headed by Cecil Cooke, the Presentation Panel included: Ian Cox; George Campbell; the young designer Peter Kneebone; Antony Hippisley Coxe, as a representative of the COID; and architects James Holland, Hugh Casson, James Gardner, Ralph Tubbs and Misha Black.[52] Black had been the design co-ordinator for the MARS Group Exhibition in 1938 and Casson considered him 'one of the most experienced exhibition designers in Europe'.[53] Tubbs had written about architecture for *The Chronicle*, as well as publishing two Penguin paperbacks, *Living in Cities* (1942) and *The Englishman Builds* (1945).[54] The Design Group was a subcommittee of the Presentation Panel and it met until the Festival opened, whereas the larger group ceased earlier.[55] Hippisley Coxe was one of the theme convenors, being in charge of the Home and Gardens section and the Seaside Section. His role, in his words, was to try 'to get the designers to do more than display the best that Britain could offer. They were encouraged to make a new contribution to the post-war world by solving some of the problems that faced us'.[56]

Such was the spirit of the Festival and the agenda of its planners. They were overwhelmingly professional men of the sort Michael Frayn described as 'do-gooders; the readers of the *News Chronicle*, the *Guardian*, and the *Observer*; the signers of petitions; the backbone of the BBC'.[57] These philanthropic experts were characteristically entering early middle-age in 1951; many of them had been students in the 1930s. Architectural critic, John Summerson, wrote in October 1951 that the Festival architects, for example, were 'the troublesome students of around 1935 ... who at that date, discovered Lloyd Wright, Gropius and Le Corbusier for themselves'.[58] Some of the planners, like the landscape architect, Peter Shepheard, saw the war as an interruption to their careers, whilst others acknowledged that they had actually acquired their expertise in the war, on finding themselves working in the Ministry of Information designing camouflage or educational exhibitions.[59] Whatever their perspective, war service followed by austerity meant that most of the Festival's architects and planners saw the 1951 Festival as their first real chance to design and build modern structures in Britain.

Many other creative people were involved in making the Festival a reality and a success. For example, the writer Laurie Lee was charged with creating the texts to go along with most of the South Bank exhibitions and some of the Festival's numerous official guide-catalogues. The engineering firm Freeman Fox figured out how to make Ralph Tubbs' Dome of Discovery – at 365 feet (111 metres), the biggest span in the world at the time – actually work. Robin Day designed all the seating for the Royal Festival Hall and Lucienne Day designed its textiles.[60] Ernest Race designed his now-famous antelope chair for the South Bank, as well[61] (Figure 4). The Arts Council commissioned sixty painters and twelve sculptors to 'make their contribution' to the Festival in a wider sense. Five purchase prizes of £500 were promised. The painters were given canvases and instructed that their work should be large, with a minimum of 45 by 60 inches (114 centimetres by 152 centimetres) stipulated. The results included Lucian Freud's *Interior near Paddington*, William Gear's *Autumn Landscape*, Robert Adam's *Apocalyptic Figure*, Elinor Bellingham-Smith's *The Island*, and Robert MacBryde's *Figure and Still Life*. The reason the artists were asked to paint large works was that the sixty paintings were for the '51' exhibition, which aimed to display recent paintings to be offered to the new municipal patrons. The exhibition toured twelve provincial cities in the Festival year and the paintings were intended to be of a size suited not only to museums, but also to the important sites of the new welfare state – schools, hospitals, health centres and libraries.[62]

Separately, the Arts Council also commissioned murals for the South Bank site by John Minton, Ben Nicholson, Josef Herman and Keith Vaughan. Graham Sutherland's *Origins of the Land* and John Piper's architectural

4 Terrace of 1951 Bar with Ernest Race's 'antelope' chairs on the South Bank

panorama painted on the back of the Homes and Gardens Pavilion were other commissions. Victor Pasmore contributed a ceramic mural to the exterior of the Regatta Restaurant, as well.[63] All the commissions were approved either by the Festival's Presentation Panel or its subcommittee, the Design Group. The London County Council held the main Festival sculpture exhibition in Battersea Park, but more than thirty sculptures were displayed on the South Bank site. Most of the best-known sculptures – such as Jacob Epstein's *Youth Advances*, Barbara Hepworth's *Contrapuntal Forms* and Henry Moore's *Reclining Figure* – were Arts Council commissions. But, interestingly, the Festival of Britain Office itself spent about £10,000 on more than twenty sculptures, 'favouring "young and comparatively untried talent"'.[64] The Design Group selected the work from proposals they had solicited from 'associations representing both traditionalist and progressive artists, and encouraged the South Bank's architects to commission works from their own budgets'.[65] Hugh Casson has been quoted as saying that the sculpture selected 'was sufficiently varied to be of interest to many different people': 'We did not see why the Exhibition should be either highbrow or lowbrow ... we believed in concertina-brows'.[66] In the end work appeared by Peter Peri, Reg Butler, Lynn Chadwick, Eduardo Paolozzi, Frank Dobson, Keith Godwin, John Matthews, and émigrés including Dora Gordine, Karin Jonzen and Karel Vogel. Expressionism was represented by Georg Ehrlich and Daphne Hardy Henrion and surrealism by Mitzi Cunliffe's embracing figures in giant plant tendrils. Work by Heinz Henghes,

F. E. McWilliams, Anna Mahler and David McFall also appeared on the South Bank. The Design Group desired a 'close harmony of sculpture and building, of landscape and mural painting', in Casson's words. The exhibition 'offered an opportunity to show that sculpture could be an integral aspect of urban space without being assigned the decorative function typical of architectural sculpture', according to art historian, Robert Burstow.[67] The *Architectural Review* claimed that the exhibition was an example of the 'urban picturesque' and approved of it as 'the first modern townscape'.[68]

Conclusion

H. T. Cadbury-Brown was a commissioned architect on the South Bank given the important job of 'knitting together' the two major sections of the exhibition, the 'Upstream' and the 'Downstream', as well as many of the individual pavilions. He designed the entrance to the Land of Britain Pavilion, plinths for some of the sculptures, including Hepworth's *Contrapuntal Forms*, and all the fountains that contributed to the magical quality of the exhibition site. In August of 2000, Cadbury-Brown explained that working on the South Bank exhibition 'was joyous ..., the first big anything after years of small exhibitions, alterations, and a little housing work ... There was a real sense in which the Festival marked an upturn in people's lives ... It was an event for a new dawn, for enjoying life on modern terms, with modern technology. That was the real reason for the exhibition, and it marked a brighter socialism.'[69]

The 1951 Festival organisers, planners and architects were committed to a brighter future for Britain. Their sense of themselves as British was a complicated one, which stressed that they belonged to a nation of victorious people, who knew how to 'muddle through'. The resulting Festival was an attempt to increase tourism through a *national* display of British 'civilisation ... in the arts, in science and technology and in industrial design'.[70] It was created by professional men who had previously worked together and who were 'largely left-wing'.[71] In the Festival 'there was a real sense of celebration, that anything was possible, and that British technology was good – as shown by inventions such as radar, television and the jet engine', in Cadbury-Brown's words.[72] Such representations of the better British future are the subject of the next chapter.

Notes

1 I am indebted to Dr Peter Mandler for sharing his BBC Written Archive sources with me, as well as his thoughts on his own work on tourism and English country houses prior to the publication of *The Fall and Rise of the Stately Home* (New Haven and London: Yale University Press, 1997).

2 Forty, 'Festival Politics', p. 32. Unfortunately, due largely to American resistance to travelling abroad during the Korean war, only 14 per cent more tourists visited Britain in 1951 than in 1950.

3 PRO, BT 64/4058, 'Draft note on Tourism for inclusion in C. E. P. S. statement for O.E.E.C.', registered on 17 August 1948. See also: Parliamentary Questions, 19 May 1950, *Hansard*, p. 1615, col. 2, in which Morrison states that 'The Festival Office are very keen ... to draw the attention of overseas visitors to the Festival activities outside London. I can assure the hon. Friend that in their publicity material they will have this aspect fully in mind, so that the overseas visitors will know that there are many things outside London to see as well as the London events'.

4 *Ibid.*

5 PRO, Work 25/232, 'Notes for Industry on the 1951 Exhibitions, the Festival of Britain, 1951', p. 4.

6 D. Pettiward, 'Exhortation to All Parish and Rural District Councils', Part III – The Festival Charivari, *Punch Festival*, 30 April 1951, p. 89.

7 The Festival planners did, however, devise an incredible scheme to promote the 1951 events in Europe. 'In 1950 London Transport and the Festival of Britain organizers selected four of their latest buses to publicize the forthcoming Festival by a tour of Europe through Norway, Sweden, Denmark, Germany, Holland, Belgium, Luxembourg and France, covering 4,000 miles in three months ... The vehicles had the words "Festival of Britain 1951" as their destination and over the entrance hung a Union Jack.' In seven languages the sides of the bus displayed an explanation of the Festival. In English it read 'A nationwide demonstration, by means of exhibitions, arts festivals and other events in all parts of the United Kingdom, of Britain's continuing contributions to civilisation and of her faith in her future place in the world.' Three of the buses contained sample exhibitions, galleries and record players on which were played national anthems including 'God Save the King': D. J. Webb, assisted by R. Wilkin, 'An Advertisement on Wheels', in Banham and Hillier (eds), *A Tonic*: 170–1, p. 170.

8 PRO, EL6/1, Herbert Morrison MP, 'Proposals Regarding the 1951 Exhibition: Draft Memorandum by the Lord President of the Council', June 1947.

9 PRO, Work 25/232, *The Story of the Festival of Britain* (London: HMSO, Printed for the Festival Council, 1952).

10 PRO, Work 25/232, 'Ramsden Committee Report', pp. 2–4.

11 See, for example, Forty, 'Festival Politics', p. 31.

12 See for example, D. Childs, *Britain Since 1945: A Political History* (London: Routledge, 1992).

13 Morrison, 'Proposals Regarding the 1951 Exhibition'.

14 E. B. Mock, 'Paris Exposition', *Magazine of Art* (May 1937), 266–73, p. 273, as quoted by D. LaCoss in an unpublished paper, ' "La Leçon de L'Ile des Cygnes": Ordonnance and Social Modernity at the 1937 Paris Exposition', University of Michigan, May 1993.

15 Since 1603 the royal arms have been supported by the English lion and the Scottish unicorn. But I do not think it insignificant that George Orwell's 1941 Penguin publication on British socialism was entitled *The Lion and the Unicorn: Socialism and the English Genius*.

16 *South Bank London Exhibition, 1951, Festival of Britain* (London: HMSO, 1951) (guide consulted at the Victoria and Albert Museum, London).

17 As quoted by Roy Strong, 'Prologue', p. 7. See also: D. R. Knight, *The Lion Roars at Wembley, British Empire Exhibition 60th Anniversary 1924–25* (London: Bernard and Westwood, 1984).

18 Gerald Barry, unpublished memoir as quoted by Hillier 'Introduction', p. 15.

19 See, for example: L. J. Butler, 'The Ambiguities of British Colonial Development Policy', in A. Gorst, L. Johnman and W. S. Lucas (eds), *Contemporary British History, 1931 to 1961: Politics and the Limits of Policy* (London: Pinter Press, 1991): 119–40 for an elaboration of these problems and an exploration of how some of the Cabinet believed that the colonies, and especially Africa, could solve them.

20 For a good overview of the situation, please see Childs, *Britain Since 1945*.

21 G. Stedman Jones, 'The "cockney" and the nation, 1780–1988', in D. Feldman and G. Stedman Jones (eds), *Metropolis, London: Histories and Representations Since 1800* (London: Routledge, 1989), 272–324, p. 315.

22 Please see Chapter 7 for a fuller discussion and explanation of the virtual absence of representations of empire in the Festival.

23 B. Williamson, 'Memories, Vision and Hope: Themes in a Historical Sociology of Britain since the Second World War', *Journal of Historical Sociology*, 1 (June 1988), 161–83.

24 C. Waters, 'J. B. Priestley (1894–1984): Englishness and the Politics of Nostalgia, 1929–1951', in S. Pedersen and P. Mandler (eds), *After the Victorians: Private Conscious and Public Duty in Modern Britain, Essays in Memory of John Clive* (London and New York: Routledge, 1994), 209–28.

25 See, for example, Fielding, '"To Make Men and Women Better Than They Are"', p. 18.

26 According to Alison Light: 'in its day the collected book form of *The Times* columns was a bestseller, especially in the U. S. where it was a Book of the Month': *Forever England: Femininity, Literature and Conservatism Between the Wars* (London: Routledge, 1991), p. 111.

27 Light, *Forever England*, p. 154.

28 Archbishop of Canterbury, 17 July 1950.

29 On the gendered nature of the Festival's discourses, see especially Chapter 4.

30 M. Billig, *Banal Nationalism* (London, 1995) as quoted by G. Cubitt, 'Introduction', in G. Cubitt (ed.), *Imagining Nations* (Manchester: Manchester University Press, 1998), 1–21, p. 3.

31 I want to thank Carolyn Steedman for a conversation in the Spring of 1995 in which she helped me to think about Britishness as 'belonging', encouraging a rejection of 'othering' as the only way to think about formations of national identity. Sonya Rose also proved very enthusiastic about such a formulation.

32 D. Morley and K. Robins, 'No Place Like *Heimat*: Images of Home(land) in European Culture', *New Formations*, 12 (Winter 1990), 1–23, p. 2. They are quoting Marshall Berman on modernity: M. Berman, *All that is Solid Melts into Air: The Experience of Modernity* (London: Verso, 1983), pp. 15, 345.

33 L. Colley, *Britons: Forging the Nation, 1707–1837* (London: Pimlico, 1994), p. 6.

34 *Ibid.*

35 Such conceptions of Britain are discussed more fully in the next chapter. On the idea in the post-war moment, see for example, Forty, 'Festival Politics', pp. 27, 35.

36 There is one piece of evidence extant in which Mr Hale of the Treasury wrote to Max Nicholson, Secretary to Herbert Morrison, Lord President, that he found it 'difficult to conceive a display illustrating the British contribution to civilisation without a Commonwealth and Empire theme of some sort' (PRO, CAB 124/1332, Letter, Hale to Nicholson, 12 June 1947). However, Morrison and his staff officially stated that they believed the resources they had at hand were too limited to extend the Festival's theme beyond the boundaries of the British isles. (See for example, Ebong, Interview with Max Nicholson, 20 January 1984, as quoted by I. I. I. Ebong, 'The Origins and Significance of the Festival of Britain, 1951', PhD thesis, University of Edinburgh, 1986, p. 30.) In Chapter 7 I present a fuller analysis of why the Empire/Commonwealth was virtually absent in the 1951 Festival.

37 Here I differ with Hewison, *Culture and Consensus*, p. 59.

38 British Library of Political and Economic Science (BLPES), London, Draft Autobiography, Sir Gerald Barry Papers, Folder 57.

39 PRO, EL6/21, 'Proposals Regarding the 1951 Exhibition', June 1947, and B. Donoughue and G. W. Jones, *Herbert Morrison: Portrait of a Politician* (London: Weidenfeld & Nicolson, 1973), p. 358.

40 There was also an official Festival Council, which included the likes of Sir Kenneth Clark, T. S. Eliot, Sir Malcolm Sargent, and Lady Megan Lloyd George. However, the Council played much less of a role in creating and actualising the Festival than did the Executive Committee. The most interesting thing about the Council is that General Lord Ismay was appointed the Chair of the Festival Council. Although Ismay described himself as 'a complete ignoramus about the arts', his appointment was an extremely intelligent move. As a dear friend of Churchill's he was able to stop criticism from the Festival's most persuasive and respected critic. Quote from Lord Ismay, *The Memoirs of General Lord Ismay* (Westport: Greenwood Press, 1974), p. 448.

41 BLPES, Draft Autobiography, Sir Gerald Barry Papers, Folder 57, as quoted by S. Waters, 'In Search of Sir Gerald Barry, the Man Behind the Festival of Britain', in Harwood and Powers (eds), 37–46, p. 39.

42 Waters, 'In Search of Sir Gerald Barry', p. 41 and R. Weight, 'Pale Stood Albion: The Promotion of National Culture in Britain 1939–56', unpublished PhD thesis, University of London, 1995, p. 144.

43 M. Nicholson, quoted in Ebong, 'The Origins and Significance', p. 51.

44 Sir H. Casson, quoted by Hillier, 'Introduction', p. 15.

45 Sir P. Wright, in an interview with Ebong, in 'The Origins and Significance', p. 53.

46 *The Official Book of the Festival of Britain, 1951*, p. 71.

47 Forty, 'Festival Politics', p. 37.

48 Sir H. Casson, in an interview with Ebong, in 'The Origins and Significance', p. 55. The same assertion is made by Hillier in 'Introduction', p. 14.

49 Hillier, 'Introduction', p. 14.

50 C. Plouviez, Assistant to the Director of Exhibitions, electronic mail message to author, 26 November 2001.

51 A. Hippisley Coxe, 'I enjoyed it more than anything in my life', in Banham and Hillier (eds), *A Tonic*, 88–90, p. 88.

52 C. Plouviez, electronic mail message to author, 26 November 2001. See also Waters, 'In Search of Sir Gerald Barry', p. 43 and Banham and Hillier (eds), *A Tonic*.

53 H. Casson, 'Period Piece', in Banham and Hillier (eds), *A Tonic*, 76–81, p. 76 and electronic mail from C. Plouviez, 28 September 2001.

54 H. T. Cadbury-Brown, 'A Good Time-and-a-half was had by All', in Harwood and Powers (eds), *Festival of Britain*, 58–64, p. 59; and Hillier, 'Introduction', p. 15.

55 Plouviez, electronic mail message to author, 26 November 2001.

56 A. Hippisley Coxe, 'I enjoyed it more than anything', p. 88.

57 Frayn, 'Festival', p. 331.

58 J. Summerson, *New Statesman*, October 1951, as cited by Hewison, *In Anger*, p. 49.

59 See for example M. Girouard, 'It's Another World', *Architectural Review*, August 1974, reprinted in *Architects' Journal*, 179 (27 June 1984), p. 108.

60 'Robin and Lucienne Day: Pioneers of Modern Design', film, Maggie Norden, director/producer (A London College of Fashion Production for the Barbican, 2001).

61 R. Banham, 'The Style: "Flimsy ... Effeminate"?', in Banham and Hiller (eds), *A Tonic*, 190–8, p. 190.

62 H. Lane, 'Festival of Fifty-One', Catalogue to an Exhibition selected from the Arts Council Collection, organised by Isobel Johnstone and Hilary Lane (London: South Bank Centre, 1990).

63 W. Feaver, 'Festival Star', in Banham and Hillier (eds), *A Tonic*, p. 49.

64 R. Burstow, 'Modern Sculpture in the South Bank: Townscape', in Harwood and Powers (eds), *Festival of Britain*, 96–106, p. 97.

65 *Ibid.*

66 H. Casson, *Image* (Spring 1952), p. 58, as quoted by Burstow, 'Modern Sculpture', pp. 97–8.

67 H. Casson, 'Festival of Britain', Manuscript of RIBA lecture, 24 March 1950, p. 8, as quoted by Burstow, 'Modern Sculpture', p. 100; and Burstow, 'Modern Sculpture', p. 100.

68 *Architectural Review*, 110 (August 1951), p. 77; and Burstow, 'Modern Sculpture', p. 101.

69 Cadbury-Brown, 'A Good Time', p. 60.

70 Morrison, 'Proposals Regarding the 1951 Exhibition'.

71 Cadbury-Brown, 'A Good Time', p. 64.

72 Cadbury-Brown, 'A Good Time', p. 60.

II
TIME

Introduction

The constitutive stories of 'the autobiography of a nation', as the Festival was called, focused primarily on representations that can be divided broadly into two categories: 'time' and 'place'.[1] Emphasising a new, improved modern future, as well as an ancient past, allowed the construction of an imagined united, white British national community. Stressing the 'unity through diversity' of Britain via official regional exhibitions, as well as encouraging the participation of every British city, town and village, facilitated a multi-layered sense of Britishness. Focusing on pleasure and fun accessible to all created the (temporary) illusion of a classless, egalitarian society – a 'people's Britain'. Such are the broad parameters of the representations of Britain and Britishness projected by the Festival and explored in the next two sections of this book.

The exciting future and the ancient past: the Festival's representations of time

The present was the lens through which the past and the future were viewed. Phenomenologically, the present is defined as the moment of now, the moment occurring that is not the past or the future. It is possible, especially when considering the immediate post-war period, with its obvious example of Germany and de-Nazification, to imagine how a national event focusing on the present could have been structured. For instance, such an event might have focused on how the society was in chaos and therefore had to be understood as leaving behind its past and attempting to turn towards the future. This is distinctly *not* how the present was imagined in the 1951 Festival of Britain.

As we shall see, the future and the past were the defining moments for the post-war 'New Britain'. For something to be 'new' it must be different from the past and looking towards the future. Interestingly, however, the ugly memories of the past, such as the 'Hungry Thirties' or earlier moments in the country's history of industrialisation and its concomitant class conflict, were not emphasised in the Festival, as they were in many Labour publications.[2] There were probably numerous reasons why the Festival did not represent the past in terms of one party's political triumphs over another's. Undoubtedly, they included Herbert Morrison's commitment to the Festival as a national, rather than party, affair. And this may, indeed, have been very savvy in the face of evidence that there was 'a long-running popular unease with adversarial politics as such' and 'a deep popular yearning for a national political community worthy of respect'.[3] Instead, social harmony was portrayed as timeless in the Festival, with the topic of the industrial revolution, for example, downplayed. The Festival's primary imagining of the past was one of a trans-historical, trans-class time in which the British people came upon the shores of the British Isles. From this ancient experience sprang all the traditions of democracy, justice and fair play for which the British were supposedly so renowned. The Festival was designed to be 'the autobiography of a nation' – the story the nation told about itself – and this was their story in the immediate post-war moment. Similarly, the future, according to the Festival, would be a time where a more educated and rational citizenry would have equal access to all sorts of knowledge, from the internal structure of a molecule to the latest ideas in farming, and the nation would make a contribution to the world as the rational negotiator of post-war struggles, most evident in the Cold War. The present was the tool used to make sense of the past and the future. Between the timeless past and the exciting future, there was little space for the present in the Festival's representations of Britain and Britishness.

Notes

1 The use of the term 'place' rather than 'space' is explained in the introduction to Part III.

2 See, for example, Labour Party, *Festival*, p. 6. In a section of this publication entitled 'Ghost in the Queue' the text reads: 'in the "Hungry Thirties" we couldn't have been in the queue at all ... nowadays, they say, we have a Government which remembers and helps ordinary folk. It wasn't always like this. Both can remember when conditions were different, when for many housewives there were empty shopping baskets. There were blank places in the queue then. Those were the days when the Tories were running affairs, the lean thirties, when at one time in Glasgow one in three of the insured population was out of work.'

3 J. Hinton, '1945 and the Apathy School' (review essay), *History Workshop Journal*, 43 (spring 1997), 266–72, p. 270.

3 ✧ The Festival's representations of the future

ROBERT HEWISON has written that 'the lasting imagery' of much of the South Bank exhibition 'suggests that the Festival of Britain was more forward looking than it really was ... The modernist architecture was a lightweight framework for yet another exploration of Deep England'.[1] In contrast with Hewison's judgement, this book argues that the Festival betrayed surprisingly little nostalgia. Instead, it set the broad outlines for a social democratic agenda for modern Britain. 'Experts' from the newly constituted public sphere – in the form of architects, industrial designers, scientists and town planners – were enlisted in this government project to construct representations of the nation's future. In addition to giving 'the people' a pat on the back for winning the war and enduring austerity, the Festival's stated intention was to project 'the belief that Britain will have contributions to make in the future'.[2] Such projections stressed progress and modernity, with science and planning evoked as the answers to the question of *how* to build a better Britain. Everything from living conditions to 'culture' and from industrial design to farm management was to be different in 'New Britain', especially for those whose limited incomes had restricted their life experiences. The goals of diffusing knowledge and constructing a modern, cultured citizenry, as well as improving 'the people's' surroundings, both in the form of the built environment and everyday objects, were shared by the Festival planners with many within the post-war Labour Party.

Scandinavian social democracy and modernism and the Festival

Susan Buck-Morss has written that 'no one in Europe (or the United States) could have lived through the decade of the thirties without being aware that international expositions ... [were] back with a vengeance during the Depression years'. Buck-Morss elaborates, stating that in the 1930s, expositions were staged to enhance business, create jobs, and to offer 'state-subsidised mass entertainment that was at the same time public "education"'.[3]

As mentioned in the last chapter, the Festival's architects and planners were predominantly middle-class men, entering middle age, who as students in the mid-1930s had 'discovered Lloyd Wright, Gropius and Le Corbusier for themselves'.[4] Stockholm's modernist, social democratic exhibition of 1930 was clearly a model for the 1951 Festival. Architectural critic Reyner Banham has stated that 'the semi-official line' was that the Festival of Britain was indebted to its Scandinavian predecessor.[5] Both exhibitions marked a departure from the nineteenth-century model of international exhibitions. And in many respects, including the way in which its national intention was married to international pretensions, the 1951 Festival greatly resembled the 1930 Stockholm Exhibition.[6] The organisational structure of both exhibitions was very similar, consisting of a small executive committee, a tight-knit staff of experts, and a panel who selected the products to be exhibited.[7] Furthermore, the narrative structure of the 1951 Festival seems to have been borrowed from the Scandinavian exhibition. The Swedish project was described by Ludvig Nordstrom, one of its key planners, as laid out to be an 'amusing and interesting picture-book' with a 'pedagogic purpose'.[8] Likewise, the Festival of Britain was called 'the autobiography of a nation', and visitors were instructed how 'to go round' the South Bank displays, reading them as 'one continuous, interwoven story'.[9] The Festival brochures proudly boasted of the originality of this method of display, calling it 'something new in exhibitions'.[10]

One particular chapter or section of the Stockholm exhibition, the *Svea Rike*, 'a three-storied building topped by a cylindrical rotunda' containing exhibitions designed by an architect, the chief of the National Social Welfare Board and a well-known journalist, anticipated the 1951 exhibitions.[11] The intention of the *Svea Rike* was to 'illustrate how our country has achieved the indisputably high [international] standing that it now occupies within the economic, social and cultural spheres, and what further development possibilities the future might offer'.[12] Its planners declared *Svea Rike* would 'strengthen "*l'énergie nationale*" and "stimulate our sometimes sluggish national imagination and without self-arrogance strengthen our self-confidence as a people and a state"'.[13] Similar language was used to describe the aim of the Festival of Britain. At the Festival's opening ceremony, as quoted in Chapter 1, the Archbishop of Canterbury asserted that 'The chief and governing purpose of the Festival is to declare our belief and trust in the British way of life, ... [so] we may continue to be a nation at unity in itself and of service to the world'.[14] In 1951 the reticent British were encouraged to proclaim confidence in their nation and their way of life, just as the Scandinavians had done in 1930.

Finally, the Stockholm exhibition shared with its 1951 counterpart the goal of raising 'the taste and cultivation of our entire population'.[15] Both exhibitions sought to construct new scripts of subjectivity in those nationals who attended. Allan Pred has written that the Stockholm planners aimed, like the Social Democrats, to create a vision of a society 'peopled by rational, enlightened and socially responsible citizens'. Moreover, the organisers felt that the Swedish future should include new, functional housing for *all* its citizens.[16] Such a vision of an enlightened citizenry, enjoying better housing, was also central to the 1951 Festival of Britain.

The Labour Party and the Festival

The Festival's eclectic combination of education and leisure, didacticism and amusement, arts and pleasure was very much in keeping with the type of Labour Party agenda tabled in the late 1940s and early 1950s. At the 1949 Labour Party conference Morrison declared that 'Part of our work in politics and in industry must be to improve human nature ... we should set ourselves more than materialistic aims'.[17] The pamphlet *Labour Believes in Britain*, published in the same year, asserted 'Socialism is not bread alone. Material security and sufficiency are not the final goals. They are means to the greater end – the evolution of a people more kindly, intelligent, co-operative, enterprising and rich in culture'.[18] The document insisted that there was a need to stimulate leisure and the arts, as well as arguing for a state-funded holiday council, which would provide cheap holidays for the British people.[19] Post-war Labour's policy-makers were committed to socialism that led to 'an improvement of the "quality of life" in its widest sense'.[20]

In line with the goals of improving 'the quality of life' and constituting a more enlightened citizenry, one major aim of the Festival organisers was to distribute education, ideas and tastes, generally the preserve of elites, to 'the people' of Britain. This was not an exclusively Labour Party agenda, but in the late 1940s and early 1950s it was Labour that was promising nationalisation and common ownership. And for Labour 'the People' were those nine-tenths of the British population who worked for a living. 'In other words, Labour was the party of "the producers, the consumers, the useful people"', in Morrison's words.[21] Moreover, for many Labour leaders, such egalitarian notions extended in the direction of a commitment to the diffusion of knowledge, 'culture' and tastes.

Party politics was a sensitive issue for the Festival organisers. Perhaps sensing popular distrust in party squabbles, Morrison was adamant in asserting that 'the last thing in the world I would wish would be that this should turn into or was ever contemplated as a political venture'.[22] However, Hugh Casson, the South Bank exhibition's chief architect, stated that 'Churchill, like the rest of the Tory Party, was against the Festival which they (quite rightly) believed was the advanced guard of socialism'.[23] In addition, a number of prominent members of the Labour government considered the Festival to be an overtly Labour undertaking which would contribute to future electoral success. When Attlee wrote to Morrison to say that the autumn of 1951 was the best time to call an election, he explained that this would allow the Festival as much time as possible to amass support for the Labour Party.[24] To this end, Labour published a special Festival magazine, simply called *Festival*, in which the party was accredited with both the success of the Festival and the higher post-war standard of living. In page after page, life under Labour was proclaimed far better than it had been under the Conservatives, especially for 'ordinary British people'.[25]

The constitutive national projects of the Festival of Britain were very much in keeping with Labour Party policy statements and with the party's social democratic agenda. Diffusing knowledge through popular education, encouraging people to partake in 'culture' in their leisure time, improving their material surroundings, stimulating the arts, broadly fostering an enlightened citizenry 'rich in culture' – these were all goals shared by both the 1951 Festival and the post-war Labour Party.

Agendas for taste

A strategic site for this new politics of culture was the household. The organisers believed that expert knowledge could relay to the British public – as well as to foreign visitors – new, improved ideas about the design of everyday household goods, public buildings, neighbourhoods and homes. Scientific expertise in particular was used to validate this modern agenda for design.

Many of the London planners, especially those who were members of the Council of Industrial Design (COID) or young architects, aimed to create a large-scale change in the British public's taste. Their objective was to dispel the fussy, old-fashioned, even 'repellent extravagances of the nineteen-thirties', replacing them with simple, clean lines for interior and exterior design and household objects.[26] These middle-class arbiters of taste hoped that a newly constituted British citizenry would become educated in and eventually embrace 'good design', as defined by the COID and magazines such as *House and Garden*.[27]

The COID was established by the Board of Trade in 1944. The 'upper class socialists' at the Board of Trade – Hugh Dalton and his successor, Stafford Cripps – were motivated by their commitment to the democratisation of design, as well as their desire to rejuvenate the British manufacturing industry after the war.[28] The COID stimulated media interest in its agenda with the 1946 'Britain Can Make It' exhibition, which occupied the entire ground floor of the Victoria and Albert Museum. This exhibition, attended by well over a million people, sought to generate interest among manufacturers and the public in good design, while showing the rest of the world that British industries were producing goods of high quality which could be ordered, even after the exigencies of war.[29] Ironically, 'Britain Can Make It' was renamed 'Britain Can't Have It' by the press, due to the fact that most of the articles on display were merely prototypes or for export only.[30] The products were labelled 'now', 'soon' and 'later' – the 'later' label dominated. During the Festival of Britain itself, the COID took overall responsibility for selecting every product in the South Bank exhibition – a total of 10,000 objects in all, used in not only the official displays, but in all aspects of the exhibition, down to the toilets![31]

The COID's meticulous commitment to good design was shared by another post-war arbiter of taste – the BBC programmes such as the *Looking at Things* series, transmitted as part of the BBC schools' broadcasts, worked to a similar cultural agenda. An early instalment, aired in September of 1951, asked school listeners *Have you a Seeing Eye?* and explained that:

> Designing something means more than just drawing a picture of what it is to look like; it also means thinking about how it is to be made and making sure that it will do its job properly. Not everything you see in the shops has been carefully designed, and the most expensive things are not necessarily the best, nor are the cheapest always the worst ...
>
> A 'seeing eye' will help you to distinguish good design from bad, to choose wisely when you go shopping, and to make the best of what you have already ... you can start straight away by looking critically at the things around you – the things you use every day. Look at things in shop windows, though you may not yet be able to buy them.[32]

Such wide-ranging training in 'good design' aimed to educate young people in more aesthetically orientated consumption. The explicit intention was to encourage modernist tastes through the prioritisation of functionality and of high-quality materials.[33]

The Festival of Britain's modernist agendas in design, art and architecture aimed to encourage people of all ages to learn about and, when available, consume well-designed 'modern' artefacts. An official brochure entitled *Design in the Festival*, produced by the COID, stated that 'There is now no logical reason why well-designed things should not be available to all of us ... they affect our whole outlook, whether we admit it or not; and if we are critical we have to confess that many of them are downright ugly ... one can hardly expect to get a high standard of design unless there is a critical and appreciative public'.[34]

Not unlike the utility scheme in the Second World War or the nineteenth-century ideas of John Ruskin and William Morris, the COID's strategy rested on a type of educational popularism that appealed to the rational and cultured citizen.[35] The brochure concluded with the assertion that 'When consumer knowledge increases still further, the minority of less satisfactory appliances will be reduced to a negligible quantity'.[36] Thus, through the Festival's selective exhibition of well-designed goods, the council hoped to continue its re-education of British consumers. By increasing consumer knowledge through the display of goods of a high standard, the COID believed they were encouraging the public to demand modern, well-designed goods when they shopped.[37]

There can be little doubt that the Festival helped to shape popular definitions of good and modern design. The term 'Festival style' came to be applied to buildings utilising concrete, aluminium and plate glass, as well as to household furnishings.[38] According to William Feaver, 'the South Bank remained the popularly accepted idea of "modern" for a whole generation'. Other examples of modern design that first appeared at the Festival were canework for indoor furniture, blond wood, 'lily-of-the-valley splays' for light bulbs, 'flying staircases' and textiles sporting thorns, spikes and molecules.[39]

In the words of Raphael Samuel, the Festival 'was determinedly modernist in bias, substituting, for the moth-eaten and the traditional, vistas of progressive advance: a great looking forward after years of rationing and greyness'.[40] This agenda stretched beyond domestic artefacts to the field of public architecture. Morrison himself described the South Bank site as 'new Britain springing from the battered fabric of the old'[41] (Figure 5). In a London guide, produced in association with the *Architects' Journal* and published in May 1951, the editors asserted that the exhibition was 'the first full-scale example of modern architecture doing a popular job ... for the very first time in history it is trying to create a still greater thing than architecture, a modern *background*, a twentieth century urban environment'.[42]

Examples of the components of this modern 'urban environment' included Maxwell Fry and Jane Drew's tension-stressed concrete footbridge built between Waterloo Bridge and the Festival Hall, which was 'one of the most interesting technical experiments' in the Festival, according to Casson.[43] Edward Mills' atomic screen (which some called the 'Abacus Screen'), erected to shield the South Bank site from Waterloo Station without blocking the light, is another example. Mills has explained that he designed the screen because 'in a sense the science background to the exhibition was the atom'.[44]

Ralph Tubbs' Dome of Discovery was a key innovation structure contributing to the overall modernity of the South Bank site (Figure 6).

In the summer of 1948 the Festival Design Group had decided that the South Bank should 'have at least one building that was technologically unique, a step forward that had not been taken before', according to Tubbs. That building was his Dome of Discovery, thanks partially to the coincidence of the Group receiving 'an advertisement in the post from a firm that made aluminium domes' at about the same time.[45] Tubbs had studied at the Architectural Association, leaving in 1935 to work for Ernö Goldfinger because he 'wanted to know all about modern construction and decided that the best man for [him] was Goldfinger'.[46] He later worked for Gropius and Fry and served as Secretary of the MARS group in 1939. The Dome, with its 365-foot (111-metre) diameter, was the biggest dome in the world in 1951. The engineer, Ralph Freeman of Freeman Fox, was the man behind the Sydney Harbour Bridge and much admired by Tubbs. Freeman advised Tubbs on the Dome and provided enthusiastic support. Tubbs saw the Dome as 'a kind of mathematical poem'.[47] Due to shortages, the number of materials used had to be limited and so the Dome was primarily made of concrete and aluminium. The aluminium cladding gave the dome its 'futuristic sparkle', along with its entrance. Tubbs had devised the longest

5 'Lord Festival', Herbert Morrison MP, described the Festival's South Bank site as 'new Britain springing from the battered fabric of the old'. A view from Hungerford bridge of the progress of the South Bank site, 15 October 1949

6 The Dome of Discovery on the South Bank

unsupported escalator ever built at the time to convey the visitors into the dome so that the interior was concealed until the actual point of entry where they then encountered the beauty of its complex structure, as well as the displays dedicated to 'creative thought'[48] (Figure 7). In 1951, *The Official Book of the Festival of Britain* called 'this great dome' 'an act of exploration in the fields of architecture and engineering' whose exhibits illustrated how Britain had 'contributed to the world's enquiry about itself and about the universe and how it has applied this knowledge'.[49]

The South Bank's architects and planners were endeavouring to construct more than just an exhibition, they were attempting to build a vision of a brighter future for Britain – a future that was clean, orderly and modern after the dirt and chaos of the war. In this context, the best-remembered symbol of the Festival's modernity was the award-winning vertical feature, the Skylon. Modern engineering meant that the Skylon's steel frame of almost 300 feet (91 metres), also clad in louvred aluminium, created the illusion that it was floating 40 feet (12 metres) above the ground, especially at night when it was lit from the inside. Powell and Moya had won the competition with their design and had then consulted Moya's former Architectural Association tutor, engineer Felix Samuely, on how to make the concept a reality. The Skylon's tall, cigar-shaped body

7 Interior of the Dome of Discovery on the South Bank

was suspended almost invisibly on three cables because Samuely had 'arranged a system of hydraulic jacks underneath the three smaller pylons. Once the whole structure was assembled, he pumped up these jacks and raised the pylons. This put tension or stresses on all the cables and by doing that the whole thing became a stressed structure ... You felt that there weren't enough wires to hold it up, which made it tremendously exciting', explained Moya in 1994.[50] The joke at the time was that the Skylon was like Britain in that it had 'no visible means of support'.[51] The name 'Skylon' was chosen by a competition won by one Mrs Sheppard Fidler: 'nylon was the great new invention, and the name seemed to fit the mood of the times'.[52] Yet, not only was it modern, but it was futuristic and found itself gracing the cover of more than one science fiction magazine. Brian Aldiss, the science fiction author, wrote on the Festival's twenty-fifth anniversary that 'the South Bank Exhibition was a memorial to the future', and the Skylon was its centrepiece.[53]

The South Bank's Telekinema, designed by Wells Coates, was another 'memorial to the future'.[54] In the Festival year Dilys Powell explained in *The Times* that: 'London has had no cinema like that of the Museum of Modern Art in New York, where the public can any day see the work of directors from Griffith to Clair, and watch vanished players from the Keystone Kops to Will Rogers', but declared that this was 'to be remedied' by the building of the Telekinema, which was a specially equipped cinema designed to project new and experimental formats.[55] In the words of J. D. Ralph, the British Film Institute's representative to the Festival, 'to combine the requirements of both film and television involved rather radical alterations in accepted cinema design'.[56] The result was a building of modern architectural design, with a seating capacity of 400, considered 'to be a model of the cinema of the future, capable of exhibiting both chemical film images and electronic television images'.[57] Uniquely, upon entering the cinema the public was able to view the film projectors and sound equipment, 'probably of a complexity unparalleled'.[58] In addition to specially commissioned films, such as Humphrey Jennings's *Family Portrait* and a number of shorts, during the Festival the Telekinema showed 'brilliant experimental work in animation' and full-screen closed-circuit television, seen for the first time in the UK.[59] Accessible to all and utilising the latest technology, the Telekinema was a vision of the future (and unlike most of the South Bank's structures, it was a lasting tribute as well, since it was modified to become the National Film Theatre still on the South Bank today).

The Schools Pavilion was another testament to the future displayed on the South Bank. Much to the chagrin of many left-wing members of the party, the Schools Pavilion was the only example of a current Labour achievement on view in the Festival. The official guide-catalogue explained that the pavilion 'shows many of those devices which can contribute to the efficiency and beauty of our new schools, so that they may be places not only for study but for the spiritual refreshment of those who work there'.[60] In this pavilion references were made to recent reforms, but even here, Herbert Morrison, ever-determined that the Festival not *seem* party political, removed all mention of the controversial issue of free school

8 View of the Shot Tower on the South Bank. The Homes and Gardens Pavilion is on the right and the rear of the Royal Festival Hall is on the left

meals.[61] Yet, surely, most people would have noted that the display of recent changes in British education was meant as a further sign that Britain was on the way to a more egalitarian, 'modern' future and that Labour intended to lead them there.[62]

Similarly, although the new National Health Service was not trumpeted as a Labour achievement in the Festival, the 'most modern resources which science can place at the command of the doctor and at the service of the patient' were exhibited in 'The Land and the People' section.[63] As Gavin and Lowe have argued, 'the rapidly approaching "end of Empire" produced as a reflex a change in the nature of the pioneer', the notional explorers and discovers of 1951, were scientists, doctors and technicians – or, in other words, members of the new class of experts.[64] In the strand's 'Health' exhibition it was explained that, for doctors and surgeons, 'the human body, then, is like a land rich in prizes for its explorers'.[65] And in the Dome of Discovery visitors could 'watch the return of radar impulses which have been beamed from the top of the Shot Tower and reflected from the moon'[66] (Figure 8). Here was an oblique reference to the recent war in which British work on radar had played such an important role. The accompanying text informed the Dome's visitors that 'The cloak of Drake and Cook has now fallen on our men of science'.[67] In the post-war world, with the help of science, the body and outer space were constituted as the appropriate frontiers for discovery, rather than foreign lands.

A fusion of art and science

Science was central to the modernism of the Festival. While the South Bank structures aestheticised the scientific future, the Festival also sought to enlist science as the foundation of a new modernist aesthetic. Variations on this scientific aesthetic included Misha Black's upscale Regatta restaurant on the South Bank, decorated with molecular and crystalline motifs on furnishings and tableware and replete with a globule painting by artist John Tunnard.[68] And the Dome of Discovery, which itself contained a model atomic pile, featured atomic structures and snowflakes in the gallery and dress circle. 'Everything is made of atoms', proclaimed Basil Taylor in the Festival's *Official Book*.[69] Many of the Festival's official exhibitions, from the South Bank to Glasgow, from Belfast to London's East End, were designed to illustrate how science could influence design, architecture and planning.

The Festival's executive committee asserted that Britain was uniquely placed in the constellation of post-war powers to mark out a new course for the integration of science and the arts. They envisaged this co-ordination of the arts and science as another 'British contribution' to the contemporary world, alongside all of those already being celebrated in the 1951 London festivities. A planning document from 1948 had stated that perhaps 'the greatest single contribution which Britain could make would be to bring Science and the Humanities into step'. It had claimed that neither Russia nor the United States was capable of such co-ordination. However, Britain could and should create 'a proper co-ordination of the fine-arts, machine-work and hand-work', because this sort of 'balance' was essential 'if Western Civilisation [was] to survive'.[70] Written as it was in the immediate aftermath of the war, this rhetoric reflected a commonly held anxiety about the excesses of science exhibited in the recent global conflict – and especially about the role of the atomic bomb. Britain was in a unique position, the document argued: it was the one country capable of stabilising Cold War hostilities through the reconciliation of art and science.

Such arguments drew on an earlier pedigree. At least since the inter-war years, left-leaning scientists, as well as the Labour Party itself, had been attempting to reconcile 'the two cultures' of art and science. In a Labour Party report on reconstruction after the First World War the 'greatly increased public provision ... for scientific investigation and original re-search' was mentioned in the same breath as 'the promotion of music, literature, and fine art, which have been under Capitalism so greatly neglected'.[71] By 1951 the historian of science Dr Jacob Bronowski, who served as the caption writer for the Festival's Science Exhibition, echoed these themes and suggested that science and culture were not intrinsically opposed. Having himself written a study of William Blake, radio plays and an opera, in addition to his scientific works, he stood characteristically for the integration of the two fields:

> Science and the arts to-day are not as discordant as many people think. The difficulties which we all have as intelligent amateurs in following modern literature and music and painting are not unimportant. They are one sign of the lack of a broad and general language in our culture. The difficulties which we have in understanding the basic ideas of modern science are signs of the same lack.[72]

Bronowski believed that the British had equal problems in comprehending modern art and modern science. He insisted that both difficulties needed to be addressed by the Festival.

In addition to this rather lofty aim of reconciling 'the arts' and science for the sake of 'civilisation', more pragmatic concerns rested on the minds of the Festival's organisers. According to Angus Calder, 'in 1943, the Select Committee on National Expenditure found it necessary to warn that "The aeronautical industry in this country is suffering from an acute shortage of scientific and technical men, and there are not enough adequately qualified men available to maintain the industry at the proper level of efficiency"'.[73] Especially in the area of radar, the insufficient number of adequately trained scientists and engineers became glaringly obvious in the Second World War.[74] This had led people from both inside and outside the government to recognise a need for more Britons, especially children and young people, to be encouraged to study various aspects of science. In the first year of the new government, Labour set up a Committee on Scientific Manpower 'to consider policies governing the use and development of scientific manpower in the next ten years'.[75]

A committee, headed by Sir Alan Barlow, then Second Secretary to the Treasury, convened by Attlee to investigate a possible shortage of scientific workers, concluded:

> We do not think that it is necessary to preface our report by stating at length the case for developing our scientific resources. Never before has the importance of science been more widely recognised or so many hopes of future progress and welfare founded upon the scientist. Least of all nations can Great Britain afford to neglect whatever benefits the scientists can confer upon her ... If we are to maintain our position in the world and restore and improve our standard of living.[76]

The Barlow report proclaimed that 'scientific achievement' was central, not only to economic well-being, but to improving the British standard of living and position in the world, and even to maintaining democracy.[77]

Tom Wilkie, the author of *British Science and Politics Since 1945*, stresses that science was considered central to questions of Britain's post-war economic well-being across the political spectrum.[78] 'Throughout the 1950s, policy-makers were obsessed with what they perceived as a shortage of trained scientific manpower'.[79] As such, there were extensive efforts in the 1950s to increase science education in the grammar and public schools. The goal was to produce a new 'proconsular' elite who would be the 'new captains of industry, men of affairs and Whitehall mandarins'.[80] Gerald Barry had a similar goal for the Festival, as he stated at the inauguration of the Festival committee at the end of May 1948. He proclaimed there that:

> By the standards we set, by the wealth of talent we disclose, by the recognition which the whole idea of the Festival will give to the central importance of arts and sciences in the national life, by emphasising their indispensability in the future if we are to maintain and develop our leadership in quality ... by all these things the Festival should, as I see it, aim to produce tangible and lasting results. Among other things, it should succeed in encouraging more of the right sort of recruits into the Arts and Sciences in the future.[81]

Beyond these concerns of shortages of scientific labour, some Labour Party leaders were also eager to encourage scientists to be more integrated into 'society', and for 'society' to be more informed about science. In 1946, Morrison was Lord President of the Privy Council, and thus responsible for overseeing Britain's civilian research and development programmes. In this capacity he spoke at a conference organised by the Association of Scientific Workers.[82] There he argued that 'Great benefits have been misused because the scientists have been satisfied to be specialists and have failed to give their work a social context ... For that, society is also to blame'.[83] By broadly educating the British population in the basics of science, the Festival planners sought to remedy this disjuncture between science and society. However, they clearly also hoped to encourage specialist, as well as a generalist, interest in science which would lead to a new generation of scientists who were more integrated into other areas.

Crystallography meets industrial design: the Festival Pattern Group

The Festival Pattern Group was a unique expression of this desire for bridge-building between the arts and science. The group aimed to create a new modernist aesthetic that combined the two. Their project attempted to harness science in the pursuit of better British design. Collaborating with the COID, a group of university scientists worked to popularise science by bringing it into ordinary people's homes. The goal was to weave science into the fabric of everyday life by rendering science accessible to everyone.

Mark Hartland Thomas, a member of the COID and a distinguished architect who later founded the Modular Society, was the originator of the Pattern Group. Two years before the Festival, he had attended a weekend course organised by the Society of Industrial Artists to encourage British designers to broaden their visual archive and draw on new sources of inspiration. One of the papers read at that course was by Professor Kathleen Lonsdale on her own area of expertise, crystallography, a science in which Britain dominated at the time.[84] Lonsdale suggested that some crystal-structure diagrams could provide the bases for original textile designs.

At the same time, a junior colleague of Lonsdale's, Dr Helen Megaw, had begun preparation of an in-house publication for the design research unit. Hartland Thomas wrote immediately to Megaw and discovered that she had produced diagrams that would work well as patterns for fabric decoration. Upon seeing them, Hartland Thomas decided that the designs should not be limited to textiles. In his capacity as the head of the selection of industrial exhibits at the Festival, he convinced twenty-eight manufacturers to join the scheme and use these patterns (Figure 9). The manufacturers represented industries as divergent as plastics and pottery,

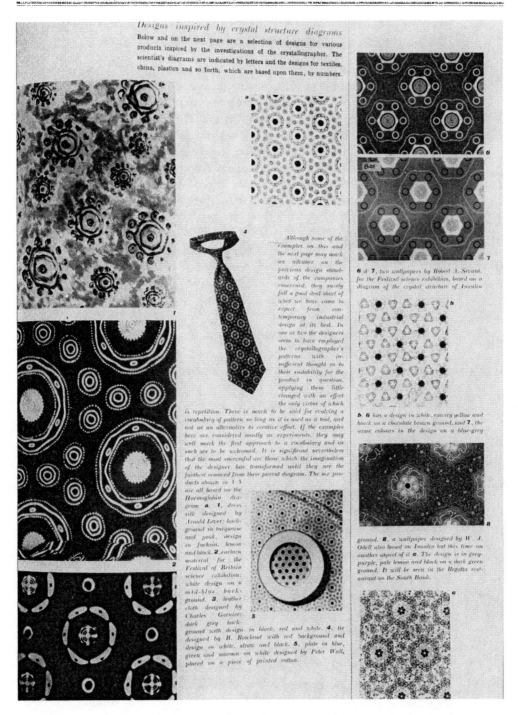

9 Examples of Crystal Structure Patterns by the Festival Pattern Group

while the patterns were derived from the molecular structures of compounds such as insulin and haemoglobin.[85] As he wrote at the time:

> I had it in mind that we were at a stage in the history of industrial design when both the public and leading designers have a feeling for more richness in style and decoration, but are somewhat at a loss for inspiration ... these crystal-structure diagrams had the discipline of exact repetitive symmetry; they were above all very pretty and were full of rich variety, yet with a remarkable family likeness; they were essentially modern because the technique that constructed them was quite recent, and yet, like all successful decorations of the past, they derived from nature – although it was nature at a submicroscopic scale not previously revealed.[86]

Hartland Thomas appealed to a classically inspired sense of natural beauty – a beauty of symmetry and repetition. Yet this was now announced as aesthetic. According to Hartland Thomas the new designs would be modern because they were based on atomic structures, only visible as a result of recent developments in science. From the point of view of the Festival organisers, crystallography was the perfect science. It was futuristic, yet had its aesthetic origins in the natural world. As such it was perceived as quintessentially British.

Moreover, the Festival's souvenir guides stressed that the idea for using crystal diagrams as the bases for decorative patterns came from the British scientists themselves: 'Crystallography, as this branch of science is called, is highly developed in Britain, and the suggestion to put the diagrams to decorative uses came originally from the crystallographers themselves'.[87] Professor Kathleen Lonsdale herself explained that 'Scientists ... derive not only useful information but great aesthetic satisfaction from their studies'.[88] This perfect science was modern and British, and the fact that the crystallographers themselves saw the beauty of their science and its potential for melding the arts and science was an added bonus.

'Growth and Form': the Independent Group's contribution to the Festival

The Independent Group's contribution to the Festival can be seen as a further attempt at a 'rebirth of understanding between scientists and artists'.[89] Featuring 'a wall-sized blow-up of an x-ray diffraction pattern of a crystal, appropriated by Richard Hamilton from Lonsdale', the 'Growth and Form' exhibition was held in the Festival summer at the Institute of Contemporary Art (ICA) in London.[90] This exhibition received no financial support from the government or the Festival Office, but that its aims were so close to many of the official exhibitions' agendas is striking. Richard Hamilton and his fellow members of the Independent Group, Reyner Banham, John McHale and Lawrence Alloway, organised 'Growth and Form' in an attempt to bridge 'the two cultures'.[91] David Mellor asserts that throughout the 1950s this group attempted 'to account for the massive post-war proliferation of scientific and technical discourses, perceived as originating mainly in the United States'.[92] The outset of this effort was this 1951 ICA exhibition.

The inspiration for the show came from the work of the late Victorian morphologist, mathematician and classicist, D'Arcy Wentworth Thompson, whom Hamilton, Henderson, Paolozzi and Turnball had discovered while at the Slade School.[93] Under the influence of D'Arcy Thompson, they had spent 'hours in the Natural History Museum examining fantastic biological forms from the fossil collection, re-accessing Surrealist biomorphism at its root'.[94] Even the title of the Independent Group's 1951 exhibition was taken from Thompson's two-volume work *On Growth and Form*, published in 1917 and expanded and republished in 1942. Hamilton found the 'beautiful theory and beautiful mathematics' in this work compelling.[95] For two years Hamilton researched 'Growth and Form', drawing on J. D. Bernal and the resources of the National Physical Laboratory.[96] For one section of the 1951 installation, Hamilton constructed a three-dimensional grid on which stood 'models of minute organisms, radiolara and sponges illustrated in Thompson's book'.[97] In Mellor's words, 'The image of a radiating stream of particles was placed by Hamilton onto a lenticular stand that acted as a housing for strobe and other optical displays: a pun on the overall eye shape of the stand that was projecting a world as being the gazed-at target'.[98] At the opening of the exhibition, Le Corbusier, 'a long-standing admirer of Thompson', said that 'this ensemble of scientific samplings was the work of a poet'.[99] Compare this to Le Corbusier's appraisal of the South Bank's Festival Hall, in which he said he preferred the inside to the outside, or Lloyd Wright's opinion of the same: 'I don't think it is a particularly wonderful building, but I think it is wonderful that your country has a new building'.[100] Clearly, in terms of modern imaginings of the future aiming to harmonise art and science, the lesser-known attempt – 'Growth and Form' – was considered by the modernist international architectural community more of a success than the Festival Hall.

Official representations of science in the London Festival: science for the British future

Yet science was not only aestheticised in the Festival. The Festival combined a somewhat fanciful vision of a modernist future with a more or less realistic appreciation of the potential of science to transform everyday life. In addition to the efforts to combine art and science, there were attempts in the official London-based exhibitions to represent science itself as fun and accessible to everyone. According to Sophie Forgan, 'Festival science was "official" science ... It looked to a "diffusion" model, to attempt [to] spread scientific knowledge as widely as possible'.[101] Forgan's notion of 'diffusion' is bolstered by the fact that numerous exhibits were intended to be donated to schools and museums at the close of the Festival, particularly the ones designed to help people 'understand "how we know" and be entranced by the beauty and excitement of science'.[102]

The draft of the catalogue-guide to the Science Exhibition of the South Kensington Science Museum explicitly stated its aims as such. For example, it maintained that 'Being well informed about scientific matters is not the same thing as understanding science and a pressing problem of the age is to bring about the latter, a task in which the former can be of great assistance – the layman needs information on the tactics and strategy of science – information of which it is largely the purpose of the Exhibition of Science to present to its viewers'[103] (Figure 10). The science fiction writer Brian Aldiss has written that he believes the Festival's message got through to him. He mused on the occasion of its twenty-fifth anniversary that: 'The science was well presented. It reinforced my feelings that technology, and the western way of thought shaping and shaped by it, was an integral part of life, not just one of its departments'.[104]

The Sea Travelling Exhibition's guide-catalogue provides a typical example of the language employed to convince all Britons of the significance of science to their lives. This exhibition, discussed further in Chapter 5,

10 Festival of Britain Science Exhibition, Science Museum, South Kensington

was housed on the decommissioned aircraft carrier, HMS Campania. Its goal was to carry the South Bank exhibitions' themes and agendas to 'the provinces'. In the catalogue, under the larger heading of 'The Physical World' and the subheading of 'Chemistry', the catalogue explained that:

> The close relationship between discovery and application is illustrated here by the display of some of the components of a typical television set. In showing what the various parts are made of and how ... they are constructed, we are demonstrating what the explorers in the field of *CHEMISTRY* have discovered ... Such knowledge enables chemists ... nowadays to make useful substances that do not occur in nature.[105]

The emphasis on 'useful substances' and the choice of the television set – although not yet in every British home, certainly a more accessible object than many which could have been chosen to illustrate concepts in chemistry – were both part of a recurring rhetoric in the science exhibitions and brochures. Repeatedly the stress was on 'ordinariness' and the 'everyday' – language which underscored that science was *already* in people's lives and once they recognised this they would realise that it was easy to learn more about it. For example, the introduction to the South Kensington Science Exhibition's guide-catalogue, written by caption writer J. Bronowski, accentuated the accessibility of science, claiming that it was simply 'common knowledge'. Bronowski wrote that:

> The Word Science means Knowledge. This is an exhibition of things we know ... People are often tempted to draw a more romantic picture of science: to see it as something remote or frightening, a magic and a mystery. Science is none of these things. Science is knowledge.
> Nor is science a strange and special kind of knowledge. Its underlying ideas are not difficult and not at all extraordinary ... This is an exhibition for everyone, in which the ideas of science are shown as common knowledge.
> Nothing in this exhibition, therefore, is meant to puzzle or astonish ... here is the modern world itself, standing straight and handsome on its base of science. The wonders of this exhibition are not larger than life; they are the fabric of modern life; and they have grown of themselves from science ... This exhibition is meant to make you feel at home with the knowledge of science, and to make you take pride in it, because it shows science as it is – fascinating, yes, but real and downright.[106]

One of the most striking aspects of this discourse is how greatly it resembles contemporary (wartime and post-war) descriptions of Britishness – of the national character as 'ordinary', unassuming, and even cosy and homey. Bronowski's discussion of science and the Festival's display of science echo these alleged British virtues. 'The exhibition is meant to make you feel at home', he says, and science is 'real and downright'. Yet, unlike inter-war discourses on Englishness (which, as Alison Light has so brilliantly shown, focused on feminised notions of the English as domestic, quiet, and unassuming), post-war Britain – modern Britain – was presented as decidedly masculine (if not phallic) in Bronowski's rendering.[107]

The Science Exhibition's official catalogue emphasised the accessibility of scientific concepts, as well. It began by stating that: 'A great obstacle in the way of popular understanding of modern science is unfamiliar words. This Exhibition consists of specially designed displays and working models so that no words need get between the visitor and the story'.[108] The text continued:

> The story, as presented, will be a new one: what we know nowadays about the way in which matter – the very substance of the world about us – is built up, and what we can do with this knowledge. It is a story that starts with the minutest of all particles and introduces the public, through their eyes, into a completely novel world. Everything is so small that the visitor must get used to the idea gradually. For this reason, he will come into the Exhibition through a series of rooms where the graphite of a lead pencil is seen to enlarge itself progressively until it is 10,000,000,000 times its natural size. Here he will see, for the first time, what an atom is really like.
>
> Having, like Alice, altered the scale of all about him, he will now be able to wander through Wonderland seeing how particular substances come to have their own peculiar properties, how new materials can be artificially made … The secret of all these things is in their minute structure, which the scientists are making plain.[109]

The *Alice in Wonderland* metaphor delivered much here. It referred not only to the size differential – that within the Exhibition 'the graphite of a lead pencil is seen to enlarge itself progressively until it is 10,000,000,000 times its natural size' – but also to a constant, found throughout all of the London-based exhibitions: that they were 'narrative exhibitions' or exhibitions which told a story and, as such, should be 'read' in a particular order, like chapters of a book. Unfortunately, the Alice metaphor may reveal something more about the London planners and brochure authors. Did they perceive many of the Festival visitors, rather like children, best capable of learning about and becoming interested in scientific educational material if it was presented as an enchanting and not-too-difficult story?[110] These narrative, London-based festivities seem to exhibit some deep ambivalence on the part of the Festival organisers – on the one hand, desires to diffuse knowledge, information and ideas to people across class, yet on the other, reservations that perhaps it was not possible. Or if it was possible, it was so only if reduced to the lowest common denominator, if the public were imagined as rather child-like, willing and able to take in new material at a rudimentary level, presented simply and told as a picture book.

Science and 'the Hall of the Future': Glasgow's Exhibition of Industrial Power

There was, however, a London-planned exhibition which stressed science and its importance to Britain's future while treating its visitors like adults capable of comprehending difficult concepts and of contemplating challenging dilemmas. It continued the story-telling metaphor, yet in a less patronising tone. The official exhibition in Scotland, the 'Exhibition of Industrial Power' in Glasgow, aimed to tell 'the story of man's conquest of "Power" and the part played by Britain in that conquest'.[111] Here, too, science was celebrated, with atomic power portrayed as the triumphant finale to this exhibition designed 'to demonstrate the harnessing of the sources of power on which all industry ultimately depends'.[112] Like most of the London displays, the Glasgow exhibition set out to show British inventiveness and its impact on the world, and in this capacity the current products of British heavy engineering dominated the Glasgow exhibition.[113]

The exhibition was planned by Alistair Borthwick, who in 1949 had recommended to the Festival's Scottish committee that such an exhibition should be held in Glasgow. As with the other official displays, the Glasgow exhibition told a story. The narrative was divided into eleven essential chapters on topics such as coal, steel, steam, electricity, civil engineering and atomic energy. Professional writers rather than subject experts were engaged to prepare scripts, since it was acknowledged that simply displaying heavy machinery and engineering equipment would not prove sufficiently interesting to most visitors. Basil Spence, the co-ordinating architect, produced a layout plan for an exhibition of 100,000 square feet (9,300 square metres), presenting the subject matter in two parallel sequences: coal and water – the nation's main sources of power. He was responsible for the design of the first hall, the Hall of Power, which illustrated this general theme and then led on to more specific displays. For example, the entrance to the Hall of Coal (designed by Hulme Chadwick) featured a symbolic sun created by a 'stroboscopic' flash contained in a perspex sphere. The entrance opened on to the huge relief sculpture of 'God the Creator' by Thomas Whalen.[114] According to the *Glasgow Herald*, this sculpture reworked the Renaissance image by presenting the 'figure of the God of Nature with right hand outstretched to the recumbent figure of man, pointing out to him the latest possibilities of coal'.[115] The grand finale of the Glasgow exhibition was the Hall of the Future, containing a spectacular presentation of the new power source – atomic energy.[116]

In the Hall of the Future, according to the guide-catalogue: 'the visitor walks in the present, looks down on the past, and looks up to the future'.[117] The end point of the display focused on atomic power, claimed as a partly British achievement, thanks to Rutherford's discoveries. The more recent work of British scientists on the atomic bomb was omitted. However, the problematic nature of the new source of power was not entirely glossed over. The catalogue pointed out that the atomic future held out both the possibility of unfathomable positive opportunities and the prospect of utter annihilation, stating:

> The use which has been made of these discoveries and the work which is being based on them today will determine whether we are entering an age of undreamed-of plenty and comfort, or whether we are working out our complete extinction. The scientists have placed a great new source of power in the hands of the engineers, the basic power of the sun. If it is used for peaceful ends, anything is possible.[118]

Such a double-edged appraisal is noteworthy when compared to more popular celebrations of atomic energy in early 1950s Britain. The tone in the Festival literature was level and considered, whereas the more prevalent, popular thinking on atomic energy was far less reasoned, presenting it simply as the solution to every kind of modern-day problem.[119]

Belfast's farmhouse of the future

The solutions to modern problems in agriculture also were to be found in science, according to the official Festival exhibition in Northern Ireland – the Ulster Farm and Factory exhibition. This Festival display was held in Belfast and organised jointly by London and Belfast committees. Visited by 156,760 people – twice as many as was originally estimated – the Belfast exhibition's farmhouse and farmyard of the future were juxtaposed with an 1851 farmstead.[120] Here was modernity with a clear and direct link to the past. The 1851 exhibit came in the shape of an authentic reconstruction.[121] Its counterpart, the farm of the future, employed new materials and a modern idiom. The buildings were functionally designed as one complete unit, to allow for tending and feeding animals easily in inclement weather. This construction also reduced capital outlay by reducing the number of necessary external walls.[122] The buildings were intended to provide maximum ventilation and light, featuring roofs covered with asbestos units and supported by light steel joists. Concrete floors with good drainage facilities were designed to ensure hygiene in the animal houses and sheds. It was all planned utilising 'building science', as it was termed in the early 1950s. The farmhouse of the future contained features that in 1951 must have seemed very modern indeed, such as a kitchen, living-room and bedroom all on the first floor and all approachable by internal and external stairways, an open, airy covered walkway connecting the house to the farm buildings, and an uninterrupted view of the farm and fields from both the living room and the balcony. The living area featured folding, sliding windows leading directly on to the balcony.[123] As Raphael Samuel has explained, 'The outside coming in was one of the architectural ideals of the period'.[124] The kitchen boasted fitted cupboards and storage cabinets, along with built-in sinks, just like the latest advertisements for fitted kitchens in the women's and home design magazines.[125] Overall, the Ulster exhibition's agricultural display combined innovations in hygienic, convenient and affordable farm management with all the latest modern designs for the home.

The Festival's Welsh 'Hillside Farming Scheme'

New and 'scientific' visions of the future in agriculture were the focus of the centrally planned Festival contribution in Wales, as well. This Festival offering was an even stranger and more ambitious endeavour which, like Glasgow's 'Hall of the Future', took its participants seriously. Also as in Glasgow, the project in Wales asserted a vision of the not-too-distant future as scientifically planned and improved. However, the scheme was of a different order than the majority of other centrally organised exhibitions. The Dolhendre 'hill farm improvement scheme', as the BBC called it in June of 1951, was planned from London as part of the Festival.[126] This scheme underscored the social democratic tendencies in the 1951 Festival, even though, as we have seen, organisers such as Morrison tended to deny any party-political affiliations.

According to William Holt, the BBC announcer who visited the Hillside Farming Scheme in North Wales as part of a series of on-site broadcasts to different Festival of Britain events, this was a rare and worthwhile undertaking. Quoting from Holt's broadcast at length preserves the tone and flavour of a contemporary description of this rather odd project. Holt announced in his Festival broadcast that the:

> activity in the heart of Wales is interesting for several reasons. It's the most important Welsh contribution to the Festival of Britain, and it's grown out of historical changes that have been taking place in Britain during this century.
>
> As you know, taxes are high in Britain, especially death duties. When a large land-owner dies, his heirs, who inherit his property, have to pay to the State a very large sum. Now, in that part of where I've been, a large part of an enormous estate has been transferred to the Government in

11 Lansbury's Live Architecture Exhibition   12 Chrisp Street Market, the Lansbury Estate,
                                                at the opening of the Clock Tower, May 1952

satisfaction of death duties – about sixty square miles, with nearly one
hundred and fifty farms on it. Although it's rough country, much of it bare
mountain, and no part of it is lower than five hundred feet above sea level
– it's the largest agricultural unit owned by the public in Britain. They're
mainly sheep farms, with small herds of Welsh black cattle that graze the
lower slopes. The Ministry of Agriculture and Fisheries had handed over
the management to the Welsh Agriculture Land Sub-Commission; and the
tenants on the estate have appointed a committee to make it easier for
ideas to be exchanged between landlord and tenant – the landlord, in this
case, being the public.[127]

Holt continued by explaining that this 'rather unusual situation in
Britain' afforded the opportunity to do 'something new in farm management'.[128] Due to rising labour and material costs since the First World
War, it had been 'difficult for landlords to find the capital to carry out
the necessary improvements and repairs'.[129] Yet, in spite of this 'these hill
farmers clung to their holdings. Some of the families have been farming
the same farm for centuries and the entire culture of the neighbourhoods
has been kept up, based on these farms. So here were people refusing to
quit, who were determined to carry on with their farming and survive.
Obviously these people were worth backing'.[130] Holt was invoking the
Dunkirk spirit; these people were 'obviously worth backing' because they

13 View of Geoffrey Jellicoe's houses on Grundy Street in the Lansbury Estate. Three-storey houses, maisonettes and ground-floor bedsits were built around two small squares

had the same spirit and resolve that it had taken to win the war. He further explained that these hardy Welsh farm families had proved 'only too willing to put in extra work themselves', and to spend 'all the money they could on improving their cultivation' once capital was provided for updating and repairing the buildings.[131]

In 1948 the Government had taken over this Welsh estate and a survey and plan for improvements commenced. The London-based Welsh Festival Committee decided that one small group of farms could be more quickly developed in the name of the Welsh Festival of Britain and that 'they could be used as an example or pattern for other hill farming districts throughout the whole of Britain'.[132] The Festival of Britain provided the opportunity to use this experiment in Wales to illustrate the future of farming for all of 'New Britain'.

East London's 'Live Architecture Exhibition'

The other centrally planned and funded exhibition most like the Dolhendre Farming Scheme was sited in Poplar in the East End of London. 'Building science' was the key to the better-known 'Live Architecture Exhibition' in which a badly bombed working-class neighbourhood was chosen as the home of a new, modern estate named after local Labour politician George Lansbury, the architect of early twentieth-century, municipal socialism [133] (Figure 11). The Lansbury estate consisted of 'scientifically' built flats and houses, as well as a school, a church and a pedestrianised shopping zone [134] (Figure 12). Science was evoked as the solution to pressing social problems. And as with the project in Wales, not only were the actual residents of the Lansbury estate to benefit from these new features, but so was all of Britain. The estate was the centrepiece of the Festival's 'Live Architecture Exhibition' and this meant that the latest British building techniques and planning schemes were 'on show' to all national and foreign visitors. The present and the future of British town planning and responsible architecture – architecture that was committed to enhancing the existing characteristics and character of an area – were displayed for all to see and scrutinise.

As in the Belfast exhibition, the view of the future was clearly linked with the past. Evocations of the frightful history of this 'slum area', as well as a version of the present, littered with 'Jerry-built and pokey dwellings' were on display. These miserable environments were counterpoised by the exhibition's well-planned, 'new urban landscape in which the buildings are growing together as a community' [135] (Figure 13). In short, the problems of the past and present were solved through modern science and planning; the future would be brighter.

One official Festival of Britain catalogue guide explained how two temporary exhibitions mounted at Poplar elucidated what building research and building science contributed to the new Lansbury estate and to British reconstruction more generally:

> A nearly full-sized model of a part of a house will show the results of bad building, why the house becomes damp, why cold water pipes burst in the winter. Then the pavilion shows how building science tackles the problem of stability, weather resistance, heating, lighting, noise and durability, and finally, how a house should be constructed. The other pavilion contains an exhibition on town planning. It explains in detail the principles upon which the new Lansbury has been designed, and tells the story of Britain's new towns.[136]

The conclusion to the brochure's section on architecture at Poplar proclaimed: 'Here at Poplar then you may catch a glimpse of that future London which is to arise from blitzed ruins and from the slums and chaotic planning of the past'.[137] 'A glimpse of the future' was what this exhibition, like so many of the others in 1951, was planned to provide.

Conclusion

These Festival projects and exhibitions reveal that their planners and architects had an agenda for bringing about a modern and scientifically assisted version of the future in Britain. The forward-looking representations on show in the summer of 1951 were projected as brighter, better planned, scientifically researched and more modern than the designs of the past or the present. However, in addition to merely portraying this new future, the planners were also attempting to alter people's experiences through popular education in the hope of creating a different world. The Festival's exhibitionary complex contained educational and cultural agendas that sought to encourage appreciation of both art and science (often melded together) as well as their incorporation into daily life. From images of the internal structure of a molecule to the latest ideas in farming, the British people were to be the recipients of new, modern knowledge.

Clearly, the exhibitions represented only one of many possible ways the post-war British nation could have been imagined. Emphasising an improving, modern future underscored the recovery and renewal of a badly shaken but victorious country – a country which could make a distinctive contribution alongside the superpowers. This collective project of imagining also created a space for an unspoken message that the post-war Labour Party was the force behind Britain's recovery and that it would continue to lead the country into a brighter, fairer 'New Britain'.

Notes

1 Hewison, *Culture and Consensus*, p. 59.

2 Cox, 'The Story the Exhibition Tells', p. 4.

3 S. Buck-Morss, *The Dialectics of Seeing: Walter Benjamin and the Arcades Project* (Cambridge MA: MIT Press, 1989), p. 323.

4 J. Summerson, *New Statesman* (October 1951), quoted in Hewison, *In Anger*, p. 49.

5 R. Banham, 'The Style: "Flimsy … Effeminate"?', in Banham and Hillier (eds), *A Tonic*, p. 193. See also H. Hopkins, *The New Look: A Social History of the Forties and Fifties in Britain* (London: Readers Union, Secker and Warburg, 1964), p. 271.

6 Alan Pred, *Recognizing European Modernities: A Montage of the Present* (London and New York: Routledge, 1995), p. 100.

7 Pred, *Recognizing European Modernities*, p. 101.

8 L. Nordstrom, 1930, quoted in Pred, *Recognizing European Modernities*, p. 134.

9 Cox, *Festival of Britain Guide, South Bank*, p. 4. See also Barry Curtis, 'One Continuous Interwoven Story', *Block*, 11 (1985–86), 48–52.

10 *Ibid.* See also Victoria and Albert Archive of Art and Design, Blythe Road, London (hereafter V&A AAD), Information Office File, AAD 5/1–1979 – 5/44–1979,

'F. O. B./Press/14/49 16th November, 1949, The 1951 Exhibition, South Bank, London'.

11 Pred, *Recognizing European Modernities*, p. 133.

12 L. Nordstrom, *Svea Rike* (1930), quoted in Pred, *Recognizing European Modernities*, pp. 133–4.

13 L. Nordstrom, 1930, and G. Paulsson, 1937, quoted in Pred, *Recognizing European Modernities*, p. 134.

14 Archbishop of Canterbury, 17 July 1950, in *The Official Book of the Festival*, inside front cover.

15 L. Nordstrom, 1930, and G. Paulsson, 1937, quoted in Pred, *Recognizing European Modernities*, p. 134.

16 Pred, *Recognizing European Modernities*, p. 106.

17 H. Morrison, quoted in M. Francis, *Ideas and Policies Under Labour, 1945–1951: Building a New Britain* (Manchester: Manchester University Press, 1997), pp. 56–7.

18 Labour Party, *Labour Believes in Britain* (London: Labour Party, 1949), p. 3. See also: Francis, *Ideas and Policies*; Fielding, Thompson and Tiratsoo, *'England Arise!'*.

19 Labour Party, *Labour Believes in Britain*, p. 3; Francis, *Ideas and Policies*, p. 57.

20 Francis, *Ideas and Policies*, p. 57.

21 Morrison, *The Peaceful Revolution*, p. 47. See also: Fielding, '"To Make Men and Women Better Than They Are"', p. 18.

22 H. Morrison, quoted in Forty, 'Festival Politics', p. 36. For example, 'a poll of March 1945 showed 55% ready to embrace an anti-Conservative popular front'. According to Hinton, this reflected 'a deep popular yearning for a national political community worthy of respect': Hinton, '1945 and the Apathy School', p. 270.

23 Sir H. Casson, quoted in Hewison, *Culture and Consensus*, p. 58.

24 Forty, 'Festival Politics', p. 37.

25 Labour Party, *Festival*, pp. 8–9.

26 J. Gloag, 'Furniture Design in Britain', in Council of Industrial Design (COID), *Design in the Festival: Illustrated Review of British Goods* (London: HMSO, 1951), p. 14.

27 For discussions of this controversial agenda see: S. MacDonald and J. Porter, 'Mid-Century Modern: The Campaign for Good Design', in *Putting on the Style: Setting up Home in the 1950s* (London: The Geffrye Museum, 1990), n.p.; A. Partington, 'Popular Fashion and Working-Class Affluence', in J. Ash and E. Wilson (eds), *Chic Thrills* (London: Pandora Press, 1992), 145–61; P. Sparke, *As Long As It's Pink: The Sexual Politics of Taste* (London: Pandora Press, 1995), 219–21.

28 MacDonald and Porter, 'Mid-Century Modern', n.p. See also P. J. Maguire and J. M. Woodham (eds), *Design and Cultural Politics in Postwar Britain: The Britain Can Make It Exhibition of 1946* (London and Washington: Leicester University Press, 1997).

29 *Ibid.*

30 *Ibid.*

31 S. MacDonald and J. Porter, 'The Festival Spirit', in *Putting on the Style*, n.p.

32 *Have You A Seeing Eye?*, 'Looking at Things' series, BBC Broadcasts to Schools, aired 21 September 1951, quoted in *Brochures from the BBC for the School Broadcasting Council for the United Kingdom* (London: BBC, 1951), p. 3.

33 See Sparke, *As Long As It's Pink*, p. 215.

34 G. Russell, 'Design in Industry: Today and Tomorrow', in COID, *Design in the Festival*, p. 11.

35 For a discussion of the link between Utility, Ruskin and Morris in terms of the 'ethical dimension' of design, see N. Whiteley, 'Utility, Design Principles and the Ethical Tradition', in J. Attfield (ed.), *Utility Reassessed: The Role of Ethics in the Practice of Design* (Manchester and New York: Manchester University Press, 1999), 190–202.

36 P. L. Garbutt, 'Domestic Appliances', in COID, *Design in the Festival*, p. 31.

37 General Lord Ismay and R. S. Edwards, 'Foreword', in COID, *Design in the Festival*, p. 10.

38 Unfortunately, according to Jose Manser, Hugh Casson's biographer, '"very Festival of Britain" entered the national vocabulary, and it was generally used pejoratively' after 'sub-Festival products began to appear and continued to do so for many years': J. Manser, *Hugh Casson: A Biography* (London and New York: Viking, 2000), pp. 147, 146.

39 W. Feaver, 'Festival Star', in Banham and Hillier (eds), *A Tonic*, 40–55, p. 54.

40 Samuel, *Theatres of Memory*, Vol. I, p. 55.

41 Donoughue and Jones, *Herbert Morrison: Portrait of a Politician*, p. 492. Both Morrison and Barry had previously called for improvements on the South Bank. For example, Max Nicholson's National Plan, launched by Barry in February of 1931 as a supplement of the *Week-end Review*, included a proposal to clear away the 'wasted south bank between the Thames, Vauxhall, the Oval and Elephant and London Bridge'. See Waters, 'In Search of Sir Gerald Barry', p. 40.

42 S. Lambert, *Architects' Journal*, May 1951, quoted in 'Everything from Townscape', *Architects' Journal*, 179 (27 June 1984), p. 92.

43 H. Casson, as quoted by Manser, *Hugh Casson*, p. 146.

44 Edward Mills in an interview with Louise Brodie in 1997 for the National Sound Archive's National Life Story Collection for 'Architects' Lives', British Library Online Information Service.

45 Ralph Tubbs, as quoted by D. Cruickshank in 'The Dome of Discovery', *Architectural Review*, 197:1175 (1995), 80–5, p. 81.

46 R. Tubbs, as quoted by Cruickshank, 'The Dome of Discovery', p. 84.

47 R. Tubbs, as quoted by Cruickshank, 'The Dome of Discovery', p. 83.

48 Cruickshank, 'The Dome of Discovery', pp. 83–4.

49 *The Official Book of the Festival*, p. 6.

50 Moya, as quoted by Cruickshank, 'The Dome of Discovery', p. 80.

51 Sir P. Powell, '"No visible means of support": Skylon and the South Bank', in Harwood and Power (eds), *Twentieth Century Architecture*, 81–6, p. 85.

52 Powell, '"No visible means of support"', pp. 84–5.

53 Aldiss, 'A Monument to the Future', in Banham and Hillier (eds) *A Tonic*, p. 176.

54 Oddly, the outside of the building was labelled 'telekinema', but it was often referred to as the 'telecinema' in the Festival literature.

55 Dilys Powell, *The Times*, 1951, as quoted by National Film Theatre, *Forty Years, 1952–92* (London: National Film Theatre, 1992), p. 5.

56 J. D. Ralph, 'The Telekinema: Planning the Exhibition', in British Film Institute, *Films in 1951: A Special Publication on British Films and Film-Makers for the Festival of Britain* (London: Sight and Sound for the British Film Institute, 1951), 43–5, p. 43.

57 National Film Theatre, *Forty Years*, p. 5.

58 Ralph, 'The Telekinema', p. 43.

59 *Ibid.* and National Film Theatre, *Forty Years*, p. 5. For more on the films made for and shown at the Festival, see S. Easen, 'Film and the Festival of Britain 1951', in I. MacKillop and N. Sinyard (eds), *British Cinema of the 1950s: A Celebration* (Manchester: Manchester University Press, 2003) and D. Robinson, 'Films in 1951', in Harwood and Powers (eds) *Twentieth Century Architecture*, 87–94.

60 *The Official Book of the Festival*, p. 9.

61 Forty, 'Festival Politics', p. 34.

62 On the Butler Education Act of 1944, see, for example, D. Bourn, 'Equality of Opportunity? The Labour Government and the Schools', in Fyrth (ed.), *Labour's Promised Land?*, 163–80; R. G. Burgess, 'Aspects of Education in Post-war Britain', in Obelkevich and Catterall (eds), *Understanding Post-war British Society*, 128–40; and Addison, *The Road to 1945*, pp. 237–9.

63 *The Official Book of the Festival*, p. 9. On the NHS, see, among many, S. Iliffe, 'An Historic Compromise: Labour and the Foundation of the National Health Service', in Fyrth (ed.), *Labour's Promised Land?*, 132–45; and Addison, *The Road to 1945*, pp. 42, 178–81, 239–42 and 247.

64 O. Gavin and A. Lowe, 'Designing Desire – Planning, Power and the Festival of Britain', *Block*, 11 (1985–86), 65.

65 Cox, *The South Bank Exhibition*, p. 75.

66 *The Official Book of the Festival*, p. 7.

67 *The Official Book of the Festival*, p. 6.

68 Feaver, 'Festival Star', p. 51.

69 B. Taylor, quoted by Feaver, 'Festival Star', p. 51.

70 PRO, Work 25/21, 'Festival of Britain, 1951', 1 April 1948, p. 2.

71 Labour Party, *Labour and the New Social Order: A Report on Reconstruction* (London: Labour Party, 1918), p. 21. See subsequent statements in: *Labour and the Nation* (1928) and *What Socialism Will Really Mean to You* (1935), as cited by J. Minihan, *The Nationalization of Culture: The Development of State Subsidies to the Arts in Great Britain* (New York: New York University Press, 1977), p. 185.

72 J. Bronowski, *The Common Sense of Science* (1951, revised 1960), quoted in W. Eastwood, *A Book of Science Verse: The Poetic Relations of Science and Technology* (London: Macmillan, 1961), p. 271. In 1948 Bronowski presented a five-part series by the same name on the BBC Third Programme. On this, see Carpenter, *The Envy of the World*, p. 80.

73 SCNE 71 (1942–43), 4.8.43,139, as quoted by A. Calder, *The People's War: Britain 1939–1945* (London: Jonathan Cape, 1969), p. 457.

74 Calder, *The People's War*, pp. 462–9.

75 Committee on Scientific Manpower, as cited by G. Werskey, *The Visible College: A*

Collective Biography of British Scientists and Socialists of the 1930s (London: Free Association Books, 1988), pp. 274–5.

76 Sir Alan Barlow's *Committee Report on Scientific Manpower*, 1945, as cited by T. Wilkie, *British Science and Politics Since 1945* (Oxford: Basil Blackwell, 1991), pp. 46–7.

77 There were even those in the Labour Party who believed that capitalism inhibited scientific exploration and discovery and that only socialism could allow for optimal conditions for the growth of scientific and 'technical' knowledge. The best-known advocate of such ideas was Aneurin Bevan, who from 1945 to 1951 was Minister of Health, with a brief time as Minister of Labour in the first four months of 1951. Much earlier, in 1937, Bevan had argued that: 'The earlier Socialists put their case on moral grounds. The modern Socialist reinforces this by pointing out that private enterprise is now an active deterrent to improved technical and scientific changes': J. Campbell, *Nye Bevan: A Biography* (London: Hodder and Stoughton, 1994), pp. 149–51, 223, quote p. 88.

78 Wilkie, *British Science*, p. 46.

79 Wilkie, *British Science*, p. 57.

80 S. Forgan, 'Festivals of Science and the two cultures: aspects of science, architecture and display in the Festival of Britain', unpublished paper, 14 July 1995, 'The Visual Culture of Art and Science from the Renaissance to the Present' Conference, the Royal Society, London, p. 14.

81 PRO, Work 25/7, Gerald Barry, speech at the Inauguration of the Festival Committee, held at the Royal Society of Arts, London, from the Minutes of that meeting, 31 May 1948.

82 The leftist-dominated Association of Scientific Workers, the trade union of practising scientists, supported the work of the 'Visible College' of scientists who were committed socialists and who led thinking on the relationship of science and the state in the 1930s. Bernal, a crystallographer and communist, was one of the leading members, according to Wilkie, *British Science*, p. 45.

83 Herbert Morrison, Speech to the Association of Scientific Workers, 1946, as cited by Werskey, *The Visible College*, pp. 274–5.

84 P. Reilly, 'The Role of the Design Council: Before, During and After the Festival of Britain', in Banham and Hillier (eds), *A Tonic*, 60–1.

85 Reilly, 'The Role of the Design Council', p. 61.

86 M. Hartland Thomas, as quoted by Reilly, 'The Role of the Design Council', p. 61.

87 *Land Travelling Exhibition Official Souvenir Guide*, 'Material and Skill', Display Designer: Richard Levin; Theme Convener: Roy Innes, p. 11.

88 Kathleen Lonsdale, as quoted by D. Mellor in 'The Pleasures and Sorrows of Modernity: Vision, Space and the Social Body in Richard Hamilton', in Tate Gallery, *Richard Hamilton* (London: Tate Gallery, 1992), p. 30.

89 RI Bragg, Ms, 50B/157, Thomas to W. I. Bragg, 18 May 1951, as quoted by Forgan, 'Festivals of Science', p. 5.

90 Mellor, 'The Pleasures and Sorrows', p. 29. According to Mellor, Lonsdale's 'scientific document' 'became crucial to the genesis of the centre of his vision in his painting "Particular System", 1951'.

91 *Ibid.*

92 *Ibid.*

93 For a sense of the complexity of D'Arcy Thompson and his work, please see: the editor's introduction by John Taylor Bonner to the Canto edition of D. Thompson, *On Growth and Form* (Cambridge: Cambridge University Press, 1961), xiv–xxiii.

94 *Ibid.*

95 R. Hamilton, as quoted by Mellor, 'Pleasures and Sorrows', p. 29.

96 Mellor, 'Pleasures and Sorrows', p. 30.

97 *Ibid.*

98 *Ibid.*

99 Kathleen Lonsdale, as quoted by Mellor, 'Pleasures and Sorrows', p. 30.

100 Both quotations from an article in *Architectural Review* originally published in August of 1951 as republished in '1951', in *Architects' Journal*, 179 (27 June 1984), 92–9, p. 94.

101 Forgan, 'Festivals of Science', p. 14.

102 *Ibid.*

103 Science Museum, Exhibition Road, Box 8390 Pt. 1: Folder therein labelled: 'Copy of final chapters of draft Guide to Sc. Exhibitions'. Note that here the Festival organisers revealed their roots rather more than they did in the actual published souvenir catalogues and brochures. Those former officers and members of the Ministry of Information and War proclaimed that the ordinary person should be provided in the Science Exhibition with 'the tactics and strategy of science'.

104 Aldiss, 'A Monument to the Future', p. 177.

105 'H. M. S. Campania, Sea Travelling Exhibition', p. 27. Emphasis in the original.

106 J. Bronowski, 'The Story the Exhibition Tells', Introduction to the guide-catalogue for the Science Exhibition at the Science Museum, South Kensington, Science historian, Caption writer for the Science Exhibition, as excerpted in Banham and Hillier (eds), *A Tonic*, p. 144.

107 Light, *Forever England*, especially p. 154.

108 PRO, Work 25/230, originally 230/31/8, *Science Exhibition, Festival of Britain, 1951, Souvenir Brochure*.

109 *Ibid.*

110 It is curious that the planners chose to represent this educable child as a girl. Was this a conscious attempt to interpolate women and girls into a story that had often been male-dominated? Or was it merely a case of Englishness in which Carroll's Alice was the child most quickly thought of – one who had conveniently shrunk and grown as well?

111 'Industrial Power at Glasgow', in *The Story of the Festival of Britain*, p. 27.

112 'Industrial Power at Glasgow', p. 10.

113 Anonymous, 'Exhibition of Industrial Power, Glasgow, Festival of Britain, 1951', in Banham and Hillier (eds), *A Tonic*, p. 152.

114 *Ibid.*

115 'Glasgow's Hall of Power', *Glasgow Herald*, 1 May 1951, p. 3. See also: Ebong, 'The Origins', p. 425; 'Festival Exhibitions Review', *Architectural Review*, 110 (August 1951), pp. 194–5 and *The Official Book of the Festival*, pp. 22–4.

116 'Industrial Power at Glasgow', p. 27.

117 Anonymous, 'Exhibition of Industrial Power', p. 154.

118 *Ibid.*

119 K. Willis, 'The Promotion of Nuclear Power in Britain 1945–1960', unpublished paper presented at the North American Conference on British Studies, Vancouver, October 1994.

120 PRO, Work 25/3, 'Final Report, The Festival of Britain in Northern Ireland', January 1952.

121 Ebong, 'The Origins', p. 444.

122 See: PRO, Work 25/230, *1951 Exhibition Ulster Farm and Factory, Belfast Northern Ireland, Festival of Britain Catalogue* (London: HMSO, 1951); 'The Festival of Britain in Northern Ireland', *Architects' Journal*, 114 (26 July 1951), p. 110; Ebong, 'The Origins', pp. 444–7.

123 'The Festival', *Architects' Journal*, p. 116; *1951 Exhibition Ulster Farm*.

124 Samuel, *Theatres of Memory, vol. I*, p. 52.

125 *Ibid.*

126 BBC, Written Archives, Caversham, HOLT 214 Film no. 214, Script Library Talk Scripts, GOS Tues. 12 June 1951, 17.00. Curiously, *A Tonic to the Nation* does not mention the Dolhendre Scheme or list 'Wales', 'Dolhendre', 'hillside farming', 'farming', etc. in its index. This is probably explained by the fact that that commemorative volume stresses architecture and design and this project was not focused on either. Also, the records I have used extensively at the Public Record Office at Kew were still closed in 1976.

127 BBC Written Archives, HOLT 214. Also see: PRO, Kew, Work 25/54, 'FBC (49) 4th Meeting, Minutes of a Meeting of Welsh Committee, held in Cardiff, on 6 December, 1949'.

128 BBC Written Archives, HOLT 214.

129 *Ibid.*

130 *Ibid.*

131 *Ibid.*

132 *Ibid.*

133 The significance of George Lansbury and the Labour connections to Stepney, East London, as well as the importance of 'the cockney' to the national imaginings represented in the Festival are explored in Chapter 5.

134 Labour Party, *Festival*, pp. 6–7; National Sound Archive, London, BBC Radio Broadcast 16931, 'Exhibition of Architecture, Lansbury at Poplar' and *The Official Book of the Festival*, p. 13.

135 *The Official Book of the Festival*, p. 13.

136 *Ibid.* A history of post-war new towns and their celebration in the 1951 events and discourses is beyond the scope of this book and deserves one of its own. For a brief overview of the policies and character of the new towns, see A. Saint, 'New Towns', Chapter four and J. Rykwert, 'Architecture', Chapter nine of Ford (ed.), *The Cambridge Guide to the Arts in Britain, Vol. 9, Since the Second World War*.

137 *Ibid.*

4 ✧ The Festival's representations of the past

ROBERT HEWISON has argued that 'the optimistic, technological vision promoted by the South Bank was at odds with the neo-romanticism associated with the prevailing ideas of Land and People'. He rightly identifies that the 'the Land and the People' were 'comfortably democratic words from a lexicon of wartime propaganda that created a space within which to explore the way the nation had shaped its environment and been shaped by it'.[1] But, the Festival's imaginings of the future and the past were not 'at odds'; rather they were mutually reinforcing. Particular representations of the past bolstered particular representations of the future and vice versa. Modernism has often combined with the most traditional imaginings of Englishness or Britishness.[2]

The Festival's evocations of the past were chosen for their appropriateness to the post-war New Jerusalem, an imagined world of equality and freedom for all. As such, some versions of the past were unsuitable, such as the Victorian era, which was generally perceived as too laden with associations of capitalism, imperialism and class conflict. The rendition of the past most fitting for a post-war, Labour-led Britain was one based on timeless traditions, reminiscent of Orwell's appraisal of 'English civilisation'.[3] Orwell wrote in 1941 that the essence of English character was rooted in traditions and an appreciation of the simple pleasures of everyday life, such as 'solid breakfasts', 'green fields and red pillar boxes'. He stressed, 'moreover it is continuous, it stretches into the future and the past, there is something in it that persists, as in a living creature ... And above all, it is your civilisation, it is *you*'.[4] As previously stated, the Festival was designed to be 'the autobiography of a nation' – the story the nation told about itself, the narrative created by the British people about the British people.[5] The role of history in this project was to illustrate great universal truths about the British people. These 'truths' were ones like those spelt out by Orwell, such as the 'all-important English trait: the respect for constitutionalism and legality, the belief in "the law" as something above the State and above the individual'.[6]

The Festival portrayed the past not in the sense of history as a chronicle or analytical description, but rather as a series of traditions imbued with trans-class and trans-historical qualities. Tony Bennett has argued that beginning in the mid-nineteenth century with the discoveries made by geologists, palaeontologists and anthropologists, galleries, museums and (by extension) exhibitions, adopted an understanding of 'universal time' 'in which the different times of geology, biology, anthropology and history were connected' in their displays.[7] Ironically, this adoption of a deep past, embedded in 'universal time' was the hallmark of these new disciplines founded by the Victorians. The 1951 Festival employed this sense of 'universal time', which incorporated both the past and the present. But building on Bennett, we need to explain specifically *which* allegedly trans-historical and trans-class narratives were in play in the Festival's representations of 'universal time'. Eley and Suny have asserted that nations are idealised communities because they have ' "recovered" the history they need to bring diverse elements into a single whole' while they have simultaneously 'concealed the actual inequalities, exploitations, and patterns of domination and exclusion inevitably involved'.[8] Particular 'histories' are 'recovered' at particular moments in the creation and re-creation of national stories. The Festival's 'timeless' narratives primarily presented the British people as independent, freedom-loving, humble, steadfast and fair. Such notions of 'patriotism' and 'independence' had been invoked by Radicals, Owenites and Chartists to construct their arguments for the extension of rights.[9] The late eighteenth century's list of the constitutive rights of English liberty included 'Freedom from absolutism (the constitutional monarchy), freedom from arbitrary arrest, trial by jury, equality before the law ... some limited liberty of thought, speech and of conscience, the vicarious participation in liberty (or in its semblance) afforded by the right of parliamentary opposition and by elections'.[10]

A similar set of national virtues had been powerfully revived in the Second World War. J. B. Priestley's very popular wartime, wireless 'Postscripts', for example, conjured up images of 'the people', rather than 'the nation' of Britain, downplaying 'imperial kinds of patriotic appeal ... and replacing them with ... British landscape, history, political traditions and "character"'.[11] In 1940, when the country was standing alone against tyranny and 'its very existence was suddenly in question', 'the spirit and framework of British institutions' were celebrated in pamphlets and lectures by the Army Bureau of Education, which came to be known as 'the British Way'.[12] In them it was announced that the British people were naturally committed to freedom, with an ' "innate dislike" of compulsion and a predilection to voluntary effort'.[13] British liberties were proclaimed as part of 'our national heritage', Westminster was 'the mother of parliaments and the birthplace of democracy. The right to trial by jury 'was the envy of the world', and the rule of law was evidenced by the society's commitment to fair play.[14] Similarly, in January of 1940, Sir William Beveridge chaired *This Freedom*, a discussion series on the BBC asking 'what we should lose if the Nazis had their way in Britain and the rest of the world'. The series answered its question by addressing freedom of thought, religious belief, Parliament and the press.[15] Samuel points to similar discourses in 1940s films, as well as in George Orwell's essays, in which the English were portrayed as kind, modest, tolerant and sportsmanlike.[16]

The role of the past in the 1951 Festival was to illustrate how the British people were unified, yet diverse, 'cemented together' by character, tradition and ancient origins, no matter what their contemporary class position or geographical location. In the words of one of one of the Festival's official guide-catalogues, the exhibitions and events 'aimed to tell the story of the Land and the People – not to present a gallery of portraits'.[17]

The versions of the past most relevant to the Festival were those 'already known' to the educated, middle-class technocrats who organised it. Tony Bennett has argued that 'as educative institutions, museums function largely as repositories of the *already known*. They are places for telling, and telling again, the stories of our time, ones which have become *doxa* through their repetition'.[18] In *The Birth of the Museum* Bennett often applies his discussion of the institutional origins and purposes of museums to other 'exhibitionary complexes', such as exhibitions. The Festival of Britain served to tell the stories of its time. Its time was the immediate post-war period and, as such, the stories on which the Festival planners could most easily draw were those told during the war. Some of the Festival planners, like the Festival's Director of Science, Ian Cox, had been members of the Ministry of Information (MOI), some even working in their exhibitions unit. During the war the MOI, explicitly committed to '"the dissemination of truth to attack the enemy in the minds of the public"', believed that the essence of propaganda on the home front was an appeal to the '"great British virtues" of democracy, freedom and fair play … as the antithesis of Nazi Germany (i.e., tyranny, aggression and perfidy)'.[19] A memorandum outlining the MOI's plans for film propaganda in May 1940 reads very much like a Festival of Britain planning document. Under the heading 'What Britain is fighting for' a list outlined the 'main objects of feature films':

(i) British life and character, showing our independence, toughness of fibre, sympathy with the under-dog, etc.

(ii) British ideas and institutions. Ideals such as freedom and institutions such as parliamentary government can be made the main subject of a drama or treated historically. It might be possible to do a great film on the History of British Liberty and its repercussions in the world.[20]

As we shall see, this portrayal of the past via 'British life and character' and 'British ideas and institutions' dominated the Festival of Britain. In addition, certain particular histories or pasts were deemed inappropriate and, as such, excluded or quickly glossed over, while others were celebrated for the very reason that they were relevant to the 1951 'autobiography of a nation'.

Who the organisers were supplies a further explanation of why the past was represented in terms of these 'mass produced traditions', rather than history.[21] For one thing, as we have seen, the Festival's planning committees were dominated by journalists, including Gerald Barry.[22] Bevis Hillier has argued that: 'The journalistic strain ran ... strongly through the Festival team'.[23] Barry, was, of course, the editor of the *News Chronicle*, but Casson and Tubbs had also written regularly for the paper. 'The journalistic habit of eliciting from an involved story a headline and captions was also valuable in making the complex narrative of the South Bank assimilable', according to Hillier.[24] More critically, we might say that what is now known as the 'sound bite' was the approach the Festival organisers took towards the past; it was evoked, yet not really explored – it was something that was 'already known'.

Additionally, Barry himself was highly sceptical of the past's appeal for 'common folk'. He wrote in the spring of 1949 to Cox, the man behind the idea to organise the South Bank exhibitions around the dual themes of 'the Land' and 'the People', warning that he feared Cox's plan was 'too serious, too scholastic'.[25] Barry explained to Cox that his conception of the exhibitions 'places somewhat undue emphasis on the past at the expense of the future'. Elaborating, Barry wrote:

> I know there is the Dome of Discovery to come, but this too will include the past. The whole weight and emphasis of the Festival Theme is to thrust forward into the future, to show not only what we have been and are, but what we can yet be; moreover, it is my belief that common folk are much more likely to be interested in, and excited by, 'possible worlds' (fairy land, if you like) than by panoramas of the past, some of which will seem infinitely remote even with the brightest treatment, though some, admittedly, can be highly entertaining.[26]

Barry's opinion seems to have triumphed over Cox's. 'Panoramas of the past' were conspicuously absent from the Festival exhibitions. Moreover, in a series of exhibitions that repeatedly used specialist script-writers, with such people representing design, archaeology and various sciences, it is surely significant that no professional historian was employed by the Festival.[27]

Finally, a central problem for the Festival planners was that in order to represent the past in terms of timeless traditions, it was necessary to paper over the all-too-obvious class tensions of the inter-war, if not the post-war, period.[28] In 1921, for example, the Newbolt Report, *Teaching of English in England*, had blamed the Industrial Revolution for 'the lamentable state of the nation'. Specifically, in this case it was responsible for Great Britain's class-based society as evidenced by the great chasm between highbrow and populist pursuits.[29] Thirty years later the Festival sought to overcome this chasm. Humphrey Jennings, in his Festival film, *Family Portrait*, referred to the inequalities created by industrialisation as 'rifts in the family we are still having to repair'.[30] But, while Jennings at least acknowledged the existence of inequality, Harold Nicolson did away with such differences in favour of an idealised British 'people'. Nicolson explained in *The Listener* in 1951 that the Festival's 'first motive was to dissipate the gloom that hung like a pea-soup above the heads of the generation of 1951'. The planners intended to do this by highlighting the British people's common 'history', 'character' and 'traditions'. He wrote of the Festival planners:

> Let us, they said ... emphasize our unity. Let us show the world that we are after all a people, cemented together by the gigantic pressures of history ... One thing, an indestructible thing, we all have in common, whether capitalist, bourgeois or proletariat: we have the same sort of character underneath. We are an ancient people, formed of many obscure strands. We take a pride in our ... wonderful fusion of tradition and invention ... of uniformity with eccentricity. Surely that also was one of the motives of the Festival to remind us that we were very, very old and very, very young.[31]

Nicolson did refer to different classes in terms of 'capitalist, bourgeois or proletariat', but overall he aptly summed up the role of the past in the Festival. It was used to illustrate how the British people were unified, yet diverse, 'cemented together' by character and tradition and ancient history, no matter what their class position. Or, in the words of one of the Festival's official guide-catalogues, the exhibitions and events 'aimed to tell the story of the Land and the People – not to present a gallery of portraits'.[32] The Festival was focused on the British people as a whole, rather than as individuals.

Representing the past in the official Festival exhibitions

Gerald Barry, himself, stated: 'One mistake we should *not* make, we should not fall into the error of supposing we were going to produce anything conclusive. In this sceptical age, the glorious assurance of the mid-Victorians

14 1851 Centenary Pavilion on the South Bank, designed by Hugh Casson

would find no echo'.[33] Yet, on the other hand, one representation of the
past most people would have expected to see in the 1951 exhibitions was
one designed to mark the centenary of the Great Exhibition of 1851. The
anniversary of that earlier celebration of British achievement, housed in
the extremely innovative Crystal Palace, was one of the primary justifications
for the 1951 festivities.[34] And when the Festival officially opened on
London's South Bank on a rainy day in May, there was indeed a miniature
display of the Crystal Palace, designed in glass and steel, like the original
by Joseph Paxton. At either end of the '1851 Centenary Pavilion', as it
was called, were slowly rotating displays, surrounded by ostrich feathers,
featuring dioramas of different views of the Great Exhibition (Figure 14).
The centrepiece was a model of the opening of the Exhibition featuring
Queen Victoria, Prince Albert, the royal children, the Princess Royal and
the Prince of Wales, as well as the Queen's ministers, prelates, courtiers,
gentlemen-at-arms and beefeaters. Through loudspeakers the visitors heard
the actual words spoken and music performed at the opening ceremony
on 1 May 1851.[35] There was also a simple backdrop model of the Crystal
Palace behind a fireworks stand at the Battersea Pleasure Gardens further
down the Thames.

But, in actuality, according to the Festival's planners, the Great Exhibition was really no more than a pretext. Stressing the centenary

commemoration allowed Herbert Morrison to enlist the support of the King and Queen, who were convinced that patronising the 1951 exhibitions and events would demonstrate the monarchy's continuing patronage of the arts and sciences. Monarchical support in turn helped to cool the vociferous opposition to the Festival mounted by some Conservative politicians and the Beaverbrook press. Rab Butler, for example, informed Lord Woolton that if the King and Queen were endorsing it, then the Conservative Party had no option but to do so as well.[36] Yet, the real proof of how little the Great Exhibition mattered to the Festival planners is that late in the planning stages James Gardner accidentally realised that there were no designs in the Festival's blueprints for anything marking 1851. Gardner recalled in 1975 that: 'Everyone had forgotten that we must have something, or should have something, about 1851'. He had been doodling one evening and came up with the idea for a miniature Crystal Palace building and when Gerald Barry saw it, he proclaimed: '"Oh, it's marvellous ... We must have that!"',[37] even though there was no money budgeted for it. And so they did.

The BBC's Third Programme 1851 Week, and The World We Have Lost[38]

Interestingly, the BBC, unlike the Festival's official planners, highlighted the Festival's origins in the Great Exhibition of 1851. According to Barry, the corporation had two roles to play in the Festival. It was to 'help to create a sense of community ... throughout the United Kingdom' by broadcasting the Festival's main events. And it was also to serve as 'a potent vehicle for expressing the national spirit' via its wireless programming. Because they were 'part of the life-stuff of the British people', regular BBC programmes such as *The Archers* and John Arlott's Test Match commentary were dubbed 'Festival of Britain Specials'.[39] In all there were 2,700 Festival-related broadcasts.[40] Some of these were programmed especially for the Festival. That perceived arbiter of (upper-)middle-class taste, the BBC Third Programme, actually listened to by many people from other backgrounds as well, broadcast music played at the Festival in the summer and commissioned a new translation of Virgil's *Aeneid* by C. Day-Lewis, presented in twelve instalments, as well as W. H. Auden's translation of Cocteau's *Knights of the Round Table*, and other high-brow dramatic performances.[41] Yet, the Third's unique contribution to the Festival celebrations was its 1851 Week, commencing on Sunday 22 April.[42]

This well-received week was conceived by Cambridge historian Peter Laslett, who, while a Junior Research Fellow at St John's College, also worked as BBC Talks producer in London. The opening announcement explained that 'During this week all the material in the Third Programme will be taken from the year 1851. Our first broadcast is the Address delivered on the occasion of the Opening of Parliament on February 4th, 1851, by Her Majesty Queen Victoria.'[43] Although some people found the week's format confusing – one machine-tools apprentice reported to a listener research survey that the 'atmosphere was brilliantly achieved', to such a degree that his father 'thought that the 1851 news item was *Today in Parliament*, till mention was made of the Rt. Hon. W. E. Gladstone' – a wide array of listeners praised the week's programming as: 'a splendid idea (Factory Manager's wife)', 'an unqualified success (Police Officer)', and as 'instructive, interesting, amusing and entertaining by turns, and sometimes all at once (Mail Order Clerk)'.[44] The 1851 Week's offerings included: a dramatisation of Henry Mayhew's study of poverty in London; a recon-struction of a Philharmonic Society concert held in 1851; 'Victorian versions of two Light Programmes series: *Listen with Mama* and *A Pot-pourri for the Edification and Instruction of Ladies at Home* – in other words *Woman's Hour*'; readings and speeches originally written by George Eliot, Thackeray, Ruskin, Berlioz, Carlyle, Browning, Disraeli, Charles Kingsley, Herbert Spencer, and Dickens.'[45] Laslett wrote in the *Radio Times* (20 April edition):

> Everything you will hear this week in 1951 was heard in England during 1851 ... All the musical items have been taken from concert programmes belonging to that year ... For the plays, we have chosen from the London successes of the 1851 season ... The features are likewise part and parcel of the year in question ... The news will be the news which was printed in the 1851 newspapers and the talks will be spoken versions of pronounce-ments made in 1851 by the eminent talkers of that generation.[46]

His aim, he said, was 'to use the wireless to recapture the aesthetic atmosphere of the Great Exhibition year'.[47] In an interview in 1998, Laslett was adamant that the 1851 Week was not concerned with people remem-bering or editorialising the past, rather 'it was letting the past address us with no intermediaries at all'.[48] The agenda he brought as a young scholar to this 1851 Week was clearly complicated. On the one hand, there is the naïve methodology of letting the past speak for itself, and, on the other, Laslett did not include much material on 'ordinary lives' in mid-nineteenth-century England. In fact, he was frank in explaining that the week was programmed by the educated for the educated – it was not intended to educate, but instead as a sort of middle-class assertion of their right to have access to the cultural output of their ancestors: 'it was their values we tried to represent', he said.[49] Nevertheless, Laslett was attempting to represent on the wireless *The World We Have Lost* – to give his listeners of one hundred years later a sense of the issues and concerns of the earlier period.

Schools' contributions

Rather similarly to the 1851 Week, the official Festival organisers and the
Ministry of Education encouraged schools and teachers across the United
Kingdom to plan programmes and pageants that compared 1951 to 1851.[50]
A Ministry of Education Circular in December 1950 explained that: 'Most
schools will find in their local history, geography, arts and crafts, architecture, industries and natural history, a rich accumulation of treasures and
achievements that could properly be celebrated as part of a national festival
of thankfulness and legitimate pride'.[51] Social and economic history projects
were the result in most schools, focusing on comparisons of life one
hundred years before the Festival. Children were broadly enlisted in acts
of historical imagination imbued with a Whiggish belief in historical
progress, but one which conveniently erased class conflict and the inequalities created by the Industrial Revolution. For example, in the imagined
nineteenth century there were horses rather than cars and children laboured
in either urban or rural drudgery, rather than enjoying the privilege of
attending school. One extreme example of the erasure of controversial
politics and pasts came from the award-winning school project, chosen for
inclusion in the Secondary Schools Classroom Exhibition on the South
Bank, 'Coleraine 100 Years Ago'. This Northern Irish school's project,
'presented' and 'contrasted' 'the social, industrial and economic background
of Coleraine with that of the present day'.[52] According to the *Belfast
Telegraph*: 'Features include[d] a large-scale model of the borough years
ago with a surround of social studies, painting, maps and written pamphlets'.[53] The specific stories relevant to the history of Northern Ireland and
its relationship to Great Britain were entirely absent.

Not Victorian: appropriate historical architecture for the post-war world

But, apart from these somewhat perfunctory references, what is striking is
the way in which the history of the last century was excluded from the
Festival's main exhibits. Victorian architecture was generally seen as preten-
tious and fussy, as it had been by various critics since at least the 1880s.
By contrast, Georgian architecture, advocated by middle-class architects and
planners since the 1930s, was considered to be both refined *and* popular;
modern yet stable.[54] In the Festival Arts Centres across the UK, themselves
noted and praised for their architecture, the past that was chosen was one
deemed relevant to the post-war moment. Barry Curtis has argued that
Victorian architecture stood accused of having 'brutalised' Georgian buildings by 'laissez-faire industrial capitalism', its designs reeking of 'intrusive
individualism' and 'tainted from the beginning with Imperial projects'.
Such associations, along with those of 'clutter, scale and gloom' made

Victoriana the 'villain in the "story" of democratic design' (even though
enthusiasm for it was growing and within two years it would be reclaimed
in the name of the New Elizabethan Age of Queen Elizabeth II).[55] Even
in 2000, Festival architect H. T. Jim Cadbury-Brown exclaimed in an interview that if you look at the Great Exhibition, 'you can see how horrible
much of the design was in 1851'.[56]

Across Britain twenty-three towns and cities were selected to act as
Festival Arts Centres and given additional funding from the Arts Council.[57]
Existing festivals incorporated into the Festival of Britain included events
at Aldeburgh, Bath, Brighton, Canterbury, Edinburgh, Swansea, and the
International and Royal National Eisteddfods in Wales, while arts festivals
newly created for the Festival of Britain were held in Aberdeen, Bournemouth, Dumfries, Inverness, Liverpool, Norwich, Perth, St David's and
York.[58] In these officially sponsored festivals, most of the cities featured
that were not cathedral towns were celebrated for their Regency and/or
Georgian architecture. For example, Bournemouth was the only official
exhibition site featuring Victorian architecture as 'proof of the confident
and prosperous expansion of the town'. Bournemouth's festival planners
chose to 'celebrate this aspect of its character in a number of special
exhibitions', including one exploring its history as a seaside resort, one on
'Victorian Taste and Fashion', and another representing 'the Pre-Raphaelite
Brotherhood' in mid-nineteenth-century drawing and painting.[59]

But places with the option of revelling in an older architectural style
did so. Bath, Brighton, Norwich and York (the last also venerated for its
medieval architecture and re-invented Mystery Plays) were all written into
the Festival of Britain's 'official' story as exceptional examples of Georgian
or Regency architecture. *The Official Book of the Festival* described Bath, for
instance, as a 'gracious city' – 'the finest memorial to the genius of our
Georgian architecture'. 'In no other place is it easier to appreciate the
virtues and values of the 18th century', the text proclaimed.[60] Norwich was
said to present 'a splendid anthology of architecture' including 'its Georgian
and Regency Houses', while Brighton was proclaimed 'Regency England by
the Sea'.[61] *The Official Book of the Festival* celebrated 'The shining stucco
and the elegant ironwork of Brighton's Regency square and terraces, the
onion domes and minarets of the Prince Regent's pleasure Pavilion, this
architectural elegance and fantasy is a strangely appropriate background
for one of England's gayest seaside resorts'.[62] Finally, York was cited for
its medieval architecture, as well as 'the custom of fine building [which]
persisted through the 17th and 18th centuries'.[63]

An explanation of why the eighteenth and early nineteenth centuries'
architectural styles, commonly known as Georgian and Regency, were
considered the most appropriate to be celebrated in the optimistic days of

1951 is offered by four sources. The *How to Write a Parish Guide* booklet, published in the Festival summer by the National Council of Social Service as part of its 'Local History Series', encouraged its readers in a section outlining how to research and write about the 'History of the Church and Other Buildings of Interest' to: 'Remember that English architecture did not end with the Georges and a church by Soane or a vicarage by Butterfield is worthy of note'.[64] Such a statement clearly indicates that the authors were concerned that many people believed English architecture after the Georgian period was not worthy of comment. A quite different indication of the appreciation of Georgian architecture in the late 1940s comes from Peter Mandler's *The Fall and Rise of the Stately Home*. According to Mandler, 'the Georgian fad of the 1930s, put firmly in an urban planning context, finally reached a popular audience' with the arrival of John Summerson's *Georgian London*, published in 1945, and called by Mandler 'perhaps the most influential work of architectural history published at this time'.[65] As we have seen, the Festival's planners were by and large professional men who had come of age in the early 1930s or, in other words, the perfect advocates of the merits of Georgian architecture.[66] Moreover, writing specifically on the Festival, Barry Curtis has explained that: 'Georgian has a long history of deployment in the terms of a negotiated British modernism' acting as 'a paradigm of stability'. And, in particular, 'Georgian was capable of holding, in productive tensions the ubiquitous antinomies of the Festival – it was: pragmatic *and* visionary; urban *and* rural; international *and* national, and most importantly – refined *and* popular.'[67] Finally, science fiction writer, Brian Aldiss, in his reminiscences of the Festival, reminds us that:

> The cities of England in 1951, not least the capital, were dominated by gloomy nineteenth-century buildings and bomb sites. Today we may be fond of Victorian architecture because it no longer appears to menace us with its funereal-and-marzipan pomposity ... I'm sure a trip in a time-machine would re-awaken a hatred for the overdressed pretensions of Victoriana.[68]

As Curtis has argued, this was not architecture appropriate to the post-war era's imagining of Britain as more egalitarian, yet elegant, or any of the other diametrically opposed notions the Festival planners wished to evoke in their celebrations. And, of course, the 'Pleasure Gardens' at Battersea (the subject of Chapter 8) imaginatively referenced the eighteenth century as the time Pleasure Gardens offered elegant, yet 'not too refined', demotic 'amusement', 'particularly adapted to the taste of the English nation', in the words of Dr Johnson.[69]

British traditions and virtues: the relevant part of the past

However, the Festival's predominant imaginings of the British past were those embedded in 'universal time', imagined as trans-historical and trans-class. These included notions of the British character and tradition, presented as rooted in the pre-history of the British people's ancestors or 'our heritage'. The best examples of such imaginings in the Festival come from the Festival's official film, Humphrey Jennings' *Family Portrait*, and the South Bank's 'The Lion and Unicorn Pavilion' and 'The Land and People' exhibition.

Family Portrait: *a film on the theme of the Festival of Britain, 1951*

Commissioned by the Festival, *Family Portrait* was the work of Humphrey Jennings, one of the three founding members of Mass Observation, who had made documentary propaganda films during the war for the Crown Film Unit as part of the Ministry of Information.[70] The title shot of the resulting film showed the official Festival of Britain symbol, a revised, modernised version of Britannia, resting on a star. This symbol was created by Abram Games, who had, amongst other things, designed posters for the Army Bureau of Current Affairs' September, 1942 poster campaign 'Your Britain – Fight for it Now'. That series depicted 'futuristic housing developments and health centres juxtaposed against scenes of bomb damage and destitution', a contrast which still resonated in 1951.[71]

The film commenced with a male voice informing the viewer that this was 'a film on the theme of the Festival of Britain, 1951'. Music by John Greenwood provided the background to a picture of a hand opening a photo album and the male voice-over explained that: 'Perhaps because we in Britain live on a group of small islands – we like to think of ourselves as a family, and, of course, with the unspoken affection and outspoken words that families have'.[72] The narrator was Michael Goodliffe and in his received pronunciation he read the entire script of the film in the first person, plural.[73] He continued, 'And so the Festival of Britain is a kind of family reunion. So let us take a look at ourselves, to let the young and the old, the past and the future, meet and discuss. To pat ourselves on the back, to give thanks that we are still a family, to voice our hopes and fears, our faith for our children.'[74] This was a rendering of English or British democracy presented by Orwell in his 1941 essays, *The Lion and the Unicorn: Socialism and the British Genius*. There he asserted that England 'resembles a family, a rather stuffy Victorian family ... [with] its private language and its common memories, and at the approach of an enemy it closes its ranks'.[75] Individualistic and reserved, but united against invaders and sharing a common past – this was the imagined community of British people.

As images of bomb sites, a symbol of triumph – St Paul's – and the white cliffs of Dover appeared on the screen, the narrator told the audience of Drake, the Armada and of how the British 'nearly all came as invaders': 'Saxon Jutes, Vikings and Saxons', 'a very mixed family ... but who together resisted invasion for over 1,000 years'. He then informed the audience that there was great 'diversity of nature in this small space' to 'match the diversity of the people'. He spoke of the British people not as heroes, 'but individual people with souls of their own', and here in the film are alternating shots of a man in a pub drinking a pint and of industrial factories. Repeatedly the text of the film stressed that British accomplishments and traditions were a mixture of 'poetry and prose'.[76]

The inequalities and discrepancies, described as created by the Industrial Revolution, were referred to as 'rifts in the family we are still having to repair'. Images of a brass band represented coal-mining life, and the audience was told that 'the first locomotives in the world were Welsh'.[77] In this statement diverse class, work and national histories were incorporated into a simplified whole.[78] The narrator continued, stressing 'What a mixture we are of muddle and orderliness, dingy and open-air', and then asked: 'How to reconcile the farm and the factory?'. Some help was offered 'in our paradoxes' by Lewis Carroll and Edward Lear, according to the narrator. 'So we admire innovations and also love tradition. So we like sitting quiet at home and we like pageantry'.

But in this version of Britain even pageantry on the scale of the opening of Parliament was deemed democratic. Goodliffe explained that: 'Pageantry in Britain, believe it or not, is not put on by a sinister power to impress anyone nor just to have fun, it's part of the pattern of life! ... The secret is we created these things ourselves, gradually'. Great Britain was nothing like fascist Germany or Italy where 'pageantry' represented 'sinister power'; in Britain 'pageantry' was normal, and natural. To illustrate this, the next images were those of the things which made up 'the pattern of life': rowing, rugby, and National Mineworkers' marches. 'We were lucky to learn the trick of voluntary discipline', the audience was told, and here they were offered images of Westminster, miners and male students, as well as the opening of Parliament, once again. Whatever their class background, the British people knew it was 'voluntary discipline' that made a democratic society possible.

'But for the most paradoxical part, compare Britain with the rest of the world', the narrator proclaimed. This declaration was accompanied by of an image of a white-haired, middle-class woman carefully tending her rose garden. The narrator told the cinema-goer that Britain was 'small, varied and restrained', and yet that British people have ventured 'to the violent ends of the earth ... Cape Town, Cairo and Canada'. Scottish bagpipes played as the audience was reminded that: 'We have been to the poles and every time the return has brought us back food and food for machines'. Yet this imperial exploration had also 'brought us experience and responsibility'.[79] This is one of the most direct references to Empire in the Festival of Britain, replete with the version of British imperialism represented as paternalistic and conscientious.[80]

The narrator of *Family Portrait* went on, explaining that: 'we must plan', 'what to preserve, what to exploit' and 'compromise again between one use and another'. So, according to the film, this led to the question of how the 'individual fits into all this'. The farmer and the scientist and the rural and the urban were juxtaposed as 'two sides of the family' – 'the farmer learning to trust, the scientist learning to accept – accept the richness and subtlety of nature, not as error to be corrected but as part of the truth to be understood.' Nature and science need to be reconciled.[81] 'We should pray for these two to agree, our bread and butter depend on it', the audience was told.

Next, there was a statement about the importance of 'the free exchange of knowledge' which 'itself is in danger': 'Tolerance in Britain is linked to the Royal societies ... [and] the free exchange of knowledge.' Intellectual freedom was evoked here, as elsewhere in the Festival, as a British tradition. Then Goodliffe explained to the viewer that 'In the end most of the family faces look back to Scandinavia, Germany, France; our ideas, our faith have their roots in Italy, Greece and Israel'. This was a version of Britain as an amalgam of other European counties, not exactly the same as the ancestry evoked in the South Bank exhibitions, described below. Yet, in all cases, those Britons who hailed from elsewhere, including Ireland and the former colonies, were almost never spoken about in the Festival of Britain.

The subsequent image projected on the screen was one of a woman scientist conducting an experiment. 'We have just had the knack of putting prose and poetry together and now we also belong to a community across the Atlantic ... We are too small, too crowded to stand alone.' As was often perceived as the most practicable foreign policy in post-war Britain, *Family Portrait* argued that Britain should have closer ties with Europe and also act as mediator with the rest of the world.[82] The film then asked: 'For all we have received from them and from our native land, what can we return to them?' The answer, according to the script, was: 'Perhaps the very things that make the family, the pattern possible. Tolerance, courage and faith, the will to be disciplined and free together.' These are the recurring imaginings of Britishness in the 1951 Festival. The film concluded with images of the pageantry of the Mace of the House of Commons, 'the monarchical guarantee of constitutional democracy, borne in procession'.[83] Once again, Parliament was evoked as the essence of British society, 'disciplined and free together'.

There are more imperial references in *Family Portrait* than in most of the Festival offerings. But, otherwise, it is very much in keeping with other Festival portrayals of what it meant to be British in the post-war world: freedom-loving, fair, tolerant, disciplined, etc. Yet not everyone felt comfortable with Jennings' representation of Britain and Britishness in 1951. Although he was impressed by Jennings' work, fellow film-maker Lindsay Anderson was disappointed that it showed: 'only too sadly how the traditionalist spirit was unable to adjust itself to the changed circumstances of Britain after the war'. Anderson criticised *Family Portrait* for presenting the past not as a source of inspiration, but as a 'refuge'. He felt that by 1951 'the "family" could only be a sentimental fiction, inhabiting a Britain dedicated to the status quo'.[84] One shudders to think of what Anderson made of the South Bank exhibitions' portrayals of the past.

The Lion and Unicorn Pavilion

The South Bank's The Lion and Unicorn Pavilion was designed to 'symbolise two of the main qualities of the national character: on the one hand, realism and strength [the Lion], on the other fantasy, independence and imagination [the Unicorn]'[85] (Figure 15). The Lion, denoting the 'might, dignity, power and prestige of the Empire', had been the symbol of Britain in 1924 when the British Empire Exhibition was staged at Wembley to help people focus on the glories of Empire after the disturbing events of the First World War.[86] But the Lion alone was not appropriate for the era following the Second World War; it needed to be balanced by the fanciful, even whimsical, Unicorn.[87] Or as the words above the handcrafted figures gracing the entrance to the pavilion explained: 'We are the Lion and the Unicorn. Twin symbols of the Briton's character. As a Lion I give him solidity and strength. With the Unicorn he lets himself go ...'[88] (Figure 16). 'The Lion was speaking', according to the designers, 'because the Unicorn was otherwise engaged. He was up to his tricks straight away. He had a rope in one front paw [sic] which lifted the latch of a colossal rattan birdcage hanging from the roof and released the great flight of doves'[89] (Figure 17). One of the official guide-catalogues explained that 'the British character is as easy to identify, and as difficult to define, as a British nonsense rhyme: The lion and the unicorn/Were fighting for the crown;/The lion beat the unicorn/All round the town./Some gave them white bread/And some gave them brown;/Some gave them plum cake/And sent them out of town.'[90]

This exhibition's gallery was devoted to a celebration of the English language 'with principal sections on the translation of the Bible into English;

15 The Lion and the Unicorn Pavilion, the South Bank

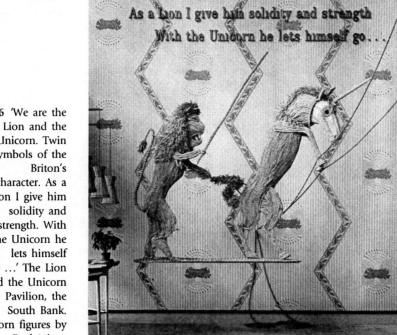

16 'We are the Lion and the Unicorn. Twin symbols of the Briton's character. As a Lion I give him solidity and strength. With the Unicorn he lets himself go ...' The Lion and the Unicorn Pavilion, the South Bank. Corn figures by Fred Mizen

the works of Shakespeare; and idiomatic usage of the present day'.[91] So here the present was clearly linked to a very long sense of the past. There is an imperialistic tone to the way the English language was described in the accompanying guide-catalogue. It stated: 'Through the English language, once upon a time, a huddle of British Islanders founded a mother tongue. Through it, to-day, two hundred and fifty million people can converse together.'[92] How this occurred was tactfully not explored. It continued by crediting 'English penmanship and the pick of English words' with the English Bible, 'still the great beacon for the language' and out of which 'came a resonance and a radiance which has suffused our later literature and speech'.[93] 'Then, there was Shakespeare', according to the guide, who 'enshrined his mother-tongue in monumental plays.' Poets 'long before Shakespeare and long after him ... have been at work with English words'. English prose writing was also praised through evocations of Defoe, Swift, Sterne, Carlyle, Dickens or Lewis Carroll. The text told the visitor that he 'may care to assess for himself how much of lion, how much of unicorn, has gone into the making of such' writers. 'But, the British do not simply leave the development of their language to the professionals of literature',

17 Interior of the Lion and the Unicorn Pavilion, the South Bank

the visitor was told. 'The Cockney has added a local vocabulary to the national one; and every British county has contributed a proverb, or a telling phrase'.[94]

The next section of the pavilion was dedicated to 'another characteristic of the British people' – 'their love of eccentric fantasy'.[95] This was 'presided over by a lifesize figure in white plaster of Lewis Carroll's White Knight whose spirits were lifted by' the sound of 'his own voice uttering a continuous stream of quiet self-congratulation and encouragement'.[96] And in the 'Eccentrics' corner' there were odd inventions, such as an egg roundabout, a violin and mandolin made of used matchsticks and a smoke-grinding machine.[97]

When and where the stereotype of the English or British eccentric originated seems to be unknown, but, the Cambridge political scientist Sir Ernest Barker (who wrote a number of books between 1927 and 1948 on the national character, with titles such as *Britain and the British People* (1942)) referred to this notion of English eccentricity in his 1947 work, *The Character of England*. Barker explained there that 'foreign observers have generally noted in the character of England ... *eccentricity*', but that such 'idiosyncrasy' was hardly noticeable to the English, because 'if all are eccentric, eccentricity will be so normal that it is commonplace'. He argued that 'eccentrics' were generally referred to as 'characters' by their co-patriots and that 'we generally lament they are disappearing – and not least from our Universities, where they once had a way of flourishing'. If Barker is to be taken as representative, his description of English eccentricity served to balance the diametrically opposed national tendencies such as 'a horror of publicity', an attachment to inconspicuous houses and 'old grey clothes'. In his words, 'most of us are mixtures, unreconciled mixtures, and that elements of freakishness, disconcertingly mixed with the element of form, can make disconcerting appearances'.[98]

Next in the Lion and Unicorn Pavilion, the appearances of objects and landscapes were offered as 'clues to the British character'. First was a section featuring British craftsmanship, which included displays of 'old furniture' and fine tailoring. 'There is something deeply revealing, too, about the British view of nature as it has been expressed in landscape painting from the time of Gainsborough and Constable until the present day.'[99] What was revealed was neither explored nor explained. Yet, there was also a section on 'Country Life' and taken together they seem to resonate with one of the clichés of Britishness from the Second World War, identified by Samuel as a 'romantic attachment' to the '"unchanging beauty" of the English countryside'.[100]

And even less surprising than the countryside as essentially British was the Lion and Unicorn Pavilion's claim that 'the instinct of liberty' was a peculiarly British trait.[101] The Constitution, the judicial system, freedom of the press, the right to Roman Catholic worship, female suffrage, the Magna Carta, and the Tolpuddle 'farm-hands' who 'broke down the last fence of resistance to the freedom of labour' all featured in this section.[102] As they did in the Army Directorate of Education, *The British Way* pamphlets, the Tolpuddle martyrs stood in the pavilion as an example of the British tradition of 'Freedom of Association' and the right of trade unionism.[103] These specific versions of British liberty seem inspired by Labour. In addition, recent research reveals what a fragile and invented tradition the evocation of the Tolpuddle martyrs was in 1951.

The Tolpuddle Martyrs: 'representing the growth of freedom in British history'

The story of the Tolpuddle Martyrs came to be one of twelve scenes 'representing the growth of freedom in British history', featured in the Lion and Unicorn's display of 'British character and tradition'.[104] The Trades Union Congress (TUC) was eager to be represented by the Amalgamated Engineering Union, whose centenary fell in the Festival year, and who wished to illustrate 'by means of sketches, drawings and other exhibits, the development of the engineering industry during the past 100 years and the lives of the British people engaged in it'.[105] However, this was not to be since the Festival Office decided early on that 'Because each Festival Exhibition *tells a story* ... no space will be let to industries or individual firms'.[106] The TUC's Secretary of Research and Economic Development, Mr Fletcher, acknowledged this decision and accepted that it was 'clear from this and the letter from the assistant to the Director of Exhibitions that ... the Festival organisers would be unable to accept any such display as that suggested by the A. E. U.'[107] Mr Fletcher told the organisation that perhaps the British Industries Fair, scheduled to run concurrently with the Festival, might be a better place for the engineering displays.[108] This left the TUC to be represented by the Tolpuddle Martyrs, six farm workers who in February 1834 in Tolpuddle, County Dorset, were arrested and marched seven miles in chains to stand trial in Dorchester.[109] They were charged with 'administering an illegal oath in the course of an initiation ceremony', the only possible charge in relation to their formation of a 'Friendly Society of Agricultural Labourers', since the repeal of the Combination Acts in 1824 meant trade unions were no longer illegal. The father and son, Thomas and John Stanfield, the brothers George and James Loveless, along with James Brine and James Hammett had formed the Society 'in response to a cut in farm wages from nine shillings to seven shillings a week, with further reductions threatened'. They were all found guilty and sentenced to transportation to Australia for seven years. After public protests, they only served two years and all six men were returned to Britain. However, all but one of these men chose to emigrate to Canada within a few years of their return.[110]

Today this may seem a standard choice in the search for a symbol of 'the growth of freedom' in Britain. However, Clare Griffiths' work on the commemoration of this incident reveals that the real origins of the Tolpuddle story as an example of 'one of the most dramatic incidents in the long fight to legalise Trade Unions' lay in the inter-war Trade Union movement.[111] Griffiths has shown that:

> The way in which Tolpuddle is remembered ... is the product of the most influential commemoration of the story, on the centenary in 1934, when the General Council of the TUC ... organized a huge effort to turn the movement's eyes on that part of the country, and to inspire the contemporary labour force to follow the lead of the brave men of a hundred years before.[112]

Before the centenary celebrations, the TUC claimed that this incident inspired Chartism, while the Webbs in their History of Trade Unionism (1920) called it the 'best-known episode in early Trade Union history'.[113] Yet, such endorsements were not always accompanied by historical clarity. For example, the 1922 Trade Union Congress resolved to mark the centenary in that year, while an earlier Independent Labour Party pamphlet dated the arrest of the martyrs as 1835.[114] And even the place of the event was at times in question: in the summer of 1933 one of the chief proponents of the 1934 commemoration stated that 'Not one person in a thousand ever refers to them as the Tolpuddle Martyrs', claiming instead that all of the textbooks and trade union history books he could find called the men 'Dorchester Labourers'.[115] Griffiths convincingly argues that the way the story of the Tolpuddle Martyrs was subsequently told in British history was constructed in the conscious acts of commemoration in 1934, when the TUC chose to use the opportunity to raise morale, and 'to provide more enduring resources of influence and inspiration' for the movement.[116] Thus, the Tolpuddle Martyrs, standing as a symbol of the timeless tradition of British liberty, was in fact an invented tradition of less than twenty years' vintage. But it also reveals once again the smoothing over of difference and the exclusion of class in the Festival's representations. The story of the 'real world' of the trade unions and capitalism, generally, was not included in the South Bank's exhibitions, with the possible exception of the displays in the Power and Production pavilion.[117] There one found a series of dioramas designed by Roger Hopkin of the Cockade design group incorporating 'scale models of an ideal factory layout, as employed by Courtaulds; a typical assembly line for tractors at the David Brown plant; and the use of colour and lighting in the cloth-raising department of Hervey Rhodes factory'.[118]

But, generally, such things seem to have been deemed more appropriate
for the concurrently held British Industries Fair, rather than in a post-war
celebration of British 'contributions'.

Official exhibitions of 'The Land and the People': relying on ancient ancestry

Invented traditions calling on much more ancient pedigrees were also
utilised in the Festival. 'The Land of Britain' section of the official sea
travelling exhibition, designed to be a miniature version of the South Bank,
evoked a history based on the prehistoric geology of Britain. The exhibition
included discussions of 'The Origins Of The Island' and 'The Minerals of
the Island'. 'The Origins of the Island' told the story of the geology of the
British Isles, beginning 'about a thousand million years' ago.[119] However,
the essence of this section was not only to make visitors aware of how
old the earth upon which they walked daily was, but also to remind them
that 'For the British people this land still offers materials ready to hand
to challenge their skill; still offers a coastline for seamen, a climate for
farmers and a landscape of extraordinary variety'.[120] Similarly, the following
section on minerals concluded by celebrating 'Coal', 'the prize gem: and
steel, the development of which is of course, a British achievement, in its
own right'. 'Coal and metals provide the basic food for our factories', the
guide told its readers.[121] As in other exhibitions, the relationship between
the land and the people of Britain was evoked as a strong, symbiotic one.

The official text for 'The People of Britain' introductory section of the
Festival Ship *Campania*, attributed to Ian Cox, carried this relationship of
the British land to the British people even further. It commenced:

> You come upon our story just as our ancestors came upon this island –
> by sea. Our forebears made their entries in a number of different rolls [*sic*];
> but, whether they came as conquerors or peaceful settlers, all of them had
> to cross the sea to get here. We are a much-mixed race, and the clue to
> our way of life and achievement lies in this blended ancestry.[122]

The assumptions here about who the British were are quite striking. They
were people of the past and present who were all organically, naturally
connected to the land and had been residing in the British Isles for
generations and generations.[123] Just how many generations became clear
as the reader continued: 'The first comers arrived about five thousand years
ago in dug-out craft, hewn by stone tools from a single trunk ... these
Stone Age colonists were our first farmers; it was they who initiated the
marriage between the people of Britain and the land.'[124] The text carried
on, explaining that 'the next arrivals, warlike people, ... brought with them

the knowledge of metals ... and they were the first to draw upon the mineral wealth of Britain and to found trade upon it'.[125] After the Bronze Age, the Celts came in bands, bringing 'better boats and much more effective agriculture; then the Romans, who gave us our first taste of civilisation'. The Anglo-Saxons came next, according to the brochure, 'as pirates' and then were attacked by the Vikings 'who added a masterly skill in shipbuilding to our inheritance'. 'Relics of all this past are now part of our island', it explained, listing 'tools, weapons, ornaments, the dead still buried in the soil, Avebury ring, great tombs of the Stone Age, the hill forts of the Iron Age Celts, the churches of the Saxons and the Normans' and then adding, 'they are part of Britain'.[126]

The brochure then argued that 'though the ancient dead are buried, it is the very blood they brought here that runs in us'. However, it was quick to point out that 'whether they came as conquerors or men of peace' all of these people had to adapt to what they encountered here. 'They were absorbed into the life that was here before them, and themselves became islanders of a land that moulded the thoughts, feelings, the behaviour of them all into a whole which is our British way of life and our tradition'.[127]

The official Festival's understanding of who was British is clear – those people whose ancestors came here as Normans, Saxons, Iron Age Celts, Romans, Vikings, or as Stone Age 'colonists'. These were the people who melded their thinking, emotions and actions to construct 'our British way of life and our tradition' and only those who had the blood of these ancestors running in their veins were truly British. This conception of Britishness, as reaching back to the Normans and before, clearly excluded Black British subjects, as well as the most significant groups of people to immigrate to Britain before the late 1940s: the Irish and the Jews from many nations for generations.[128]

In addition, Owen Gavin and Andy Lowe have illustrated how these imaginings of the ancestry of the British people in the Festival were highly gendered, and as such acted to exclude women, too. Gavin and Lowe have shown how, at least in some of the official literature, Britishness was gendered masculine and male in the Festival.[129] The first passage in the souvenir-guide-catalogue, *The South Bank Exhibition, a Guide to the Story it Tells* quoted by Gavin and Lowe reads:

> The land is the beginning of the story, and Britain was a ready-made island when our fore-bears stepped ashore. They were practical men with their feet on the ground; but they were also pioneers, men with feet sensitive to the nature of the ground – feet that soon grew so familiar with it that they came to act as roots, exploring it downward and bringing up from it the nourishment and profit that lies beneath. They were pioneers; but they

were also craftsmen, and a craftsman's mind follows his hand and feet. So the stones thrown up by these pioneers from their deep workings have been cracked open and studied like pages torn from a buried book, until now we know the birth pains and the growth of this motherland of ours, and how much wealth lies latent in her still.[130]

Gavin and Lowe note how 'excessive' the language was, calling it 'almost prodigal in the way it insists on the relationship of body to land'.[131] Indeed, it was more extreme than some of the other Festival texts, such as the one above, which stressed the symbiotic relationship between people and land, but not in the same way the language here does. The authors explain that: 'The earth's store of wealth, becomes productive only when joined to the body of the people'. They further point out that if the British land was fertile 'it is also a "mother" earth whose wealth is accompanied by birth pains – or as the diagrammatical "way round" that accompanies this text put it, "the earth in labour"'. In Gavin and Lowe's appraisal: 'The fertility of this feminised nature is something quite gratuitous. There is something almost sacrificial about it'. It was in an entirely different domain, they argue, from 'the practical, utilitarian domain of the male which makes the land productive'. And yet it was 'the sacrificial excess of natural wealth, in respect of this union which makes production sacred in turn, which makes it a source of obligation, duty and national heritage (not that these terms would have been unfamiliar in the age of Austerity'.[132] What now to some of us seems sexist language, many – perhaps, most – people in early 1950s Britain would have perceived as gender-neutral when it came to its linking of 'our forebears' with 'practical men'. Yet, the lines about 'the motherland' and 'birth pains' must surely have been striking even then. The passage suggested that the ancestors of all Britons in 1951 were these 'practical men', 'pioneers' and 'craftsmen' who discovered the island, and then dug into the land. All of these characters in the story were gendered male, whereas the earth itself, explored downward, literally through these men's 'urge to penetrate', was gendered as female as well as maternal.

The imaginings of the true ancestors of the British people as craftsmen and pioneers 'exploring downward' 'this motherland of ours' does make us question the gendered nature of the national imaginary in immediate post-war Britain. How women were constructed as citizens during the war and just after, a generation after they had secured the right to vote, is a perplexing, complicated question. During the war, the Army Bureau of Current Affairs 'reported that many women did not even know they had the vote'. But the Army Bureau revealed their own prejudices in the same sentence stating, 'that trying to run classes for them was like meeting a "wall of deafness" or "wall of dumbness"'.[133] In the immediate post-war period government reports, commissions and speeches, according to Sarah Benton, show that women's imagined role in the New Jerusalem was motherhood, redefined as in most welfare states as a civic responsibility. The Labour Party did not authorise inquiries into equal pay or civic education for women, instead they set up commissions to report on the shortage of domestic servants and on the declining birth-rate, 'responding to fears that both servants and motherhood – the ingredients of a man's household – were in terminal decline'.[134] Benton has shown that although the common notion that women were forcibly returned to the domestic sphere at the end of the war is a complete myth, by 1947 'the treatment of the domestic sphere as part of the [imagined, new, post-war] republic was ended'.[135] The settlements of the new society rested on the assumption that the goal was to make new citizens 'out of the civic virtue of brotherly manliness' and reward the men who had sacrificed so much in the war. The welfare state institutionalised the domestic realm 'as the private protectorate of individual men, not the protectorate of the state, although this was provisional'. When a man was absent, 'morally or physically', the state would provide for the women and children. According to Benton, in Britain's New Jerusalem its 'paradoxical foundation was the welfare state itself, which implicitly treats citizens as in need of state protection – as part of a protectorate under the care of kindly fathers (patriarchy) rather than as citizens (a republic, fraternal or otherwise)'.[136] As a growing body of feminist literature has illustrated, it was often the Conservatives, in the form of organisations such as the British Housewives' League, who were better at addressing the female citizen and her real issues in the immediate post-war world.[137]

Conclusion

The shifting constitutive components of post-war national identity in Britain incorporated numerous representations of the past, but most of these relied on timeless notions of British traditions and character, evoking the 'already known' past, invented traditions and imagined ancient ancestry. A few representations of 1851 were included in the Festival, but the Victorian era was generally perceived as too 'capitalist' and class-riven for the post-war moment. Georgian and Regency architecture, a high-brow fad of the 1930s, was presented as an appropriate architectural history for a new, demotic Britain in 1951. Other versions of the past rested on very long trajectories and excluded significant groups such as the Irish, the Jews, Black Britons, Britons residing anywhere in the Commonwealth or former Empire, and, in some ways, even women. With the exception of a few references in Jennings' Festival film, *Family Portrait*, particular pasts, most notably the war just ended, were basically absent from the Festival as well. As Calder has written in *The Myth of the Blitz*, 'the Myth could not accommodate acts, even would-be-acts, of killing of civilians and domestic destruction initiated by the British'.[138] Six years after the end of the war and the resultant dreariness of daily life in war-weary Britain, the Festival, like the participants of the Second World War, was mostly 'silent' on the topic.[139] In addition, the harmonious modernist vision of a future mastered by scientific planning and reconciling the disparate fields of art and science was produced through the exclusion of the recent past. This is one reason why we should be asking *which* pasts were represented in the Festival, rather than engaging in the now old argument as to whether Britishness was (and is) backward-looking or forward-looking.[140] Sarah Benton convincingly argues that in post-war, Labour Britain 'it was part of the contradictory nature of inventing new Britain that alongside the myth of founding a new society was the myth of the ancestor'.[141] Surely, in the immediate post-war period, if not always, British national identity was 'Janus-faced', looking to the past and the future for explanations of who and what it was.[142]

Notes

1 Hewison, *Culture and Consensus*, p. 59.

2 B. Schwarz, 'Englishness and the Paradox of Modernity', *New Formations*, 1 (spring 1987), 147–53, p. 152.

3 Unfortunately, Orwell wrote of England and Englishness rather than Britain and Britishness. In Bernard Crick's appraisal this is a 'general fault of his argument … [in that] he fails to consider how much the English character has been shaped by the multi-national culture and politics of the United Kingdom', and that instead Orwell 'shows deplorable anti-Scottish and anti-Irish prejudices': B. Crick, 'Introduction', in Orwell, *The Lion and the Unicorn*, 7–30, p. 9). But, even in light of such serious shortcomings, Orwell is a relevant source of notions of national identity in Britain during the Second World War, not least because it was considered in the 1950s one of the few 'pamphlets, tracts and exhortations, which the war produced … [worth] re-reading': Arthur Koestler, *The Observer*, 29 January 1950, as quoted by Crick, 'Introduction', p. 7.

4 *Ibid.*

5 As Raphael Samuel has written, 'traditions … are not inherited: they are a name given to something which is constantly being made': Samuel, *Island Stories, Theatres of Memory, Vol. II*, p. 275.

6 Orwell, *The Lion and the Unicorn*, p. 44.

7 T. Bennett, *The Birth of the Museum: History, Theory, Politics* (London and New York: Routledge, 1995), p. 39.

8 G. Eley and R. Suny, 'Introduction: From the Moment of Social History to the Work of Cultural Representation', in Eley and Suny (eds), *Becoming National*, 3–37, p. 24. The authors, of course, acknowledge their indebtedness to Benedict Anderson.

9 E. P. Thompson, *The Making of the English Working Class* (New York: Vintage Books, 1966), pp. 78–9. See also: Stedman Jones, 'Rethinking Chartism', in *Languages of Class*, pp. 90–178 and Hugh Cunningham, 'The Language of Patriotism 1750–1914', *History Workshop Journal*, 12 (autumn 1981), 13–21.

10 E. P. Thompson, *The Making of the English Working Class* (New York: Vintage Books, 1966), pp. 78–9.

11 Nicholas, *The Echo of War*, p. 233.

12 Samuel, *Theatres of Memory*, Vol. I, p. 218. See also Directorate of Army Education, *The British Way and Purpose: Consolidated Edition of B. W. P. Booklets 1–18, with Appendices of Documents of Post-War Reconstruction* (London: The Directorate of Army Education, 1944).

13 *Ibid.*

14 *Ibid.*

15 Nicholas, *The Echo of War*, p. 23.

16 Samuel, *Theatres of Memory*, p. 218.

17 A. Hippisley Coxe, 'The Seaside', in I. Cox, *Festival Ship Campania: A Guide to the Story it Tells* (London: HMSO, 1951), p. 31.

18 Bennett, *The Birth of the Museum*, p. 147.

19 Ministry of Information (MOI), as quoted by Nicholas, *The Echo of War*, pp. 2 and 229.

20 MOI, 'Programme for film propaganda', *Documentary Newsletter* (1940), as reprinted in J. Giles and T. Middleton (eds), *Writing Englishness 1900–1950: An Introductory Sourcebook on National Identity* (London and New York: Routledge, 1995), 141–6, p. 142.

21 'Mass-produced traditions' is Hobsbawm's phrase: E. Hobsbawm, 'Mass-Producing Traditions: Europe, 1870–1914', in Hobsbawm and Ranger (eds), *The Invention of Tradition*, 263–307.

22 PRO, Work 25/21, Letter from Gerald Barry, the Director General to Ian Cox the Director of Science, 'Theme Paper – Part II', p. 1, dated 26 April 1949.

23 Hillier, 'Introduction', in Banham and Hillier (eds), *A Tonic*, 10–19, p. 14.

24 Hillier, 'Introduction', p. 15.

25 Letter from Gerald Barry, 'Theme Paper – Part II'.

26 *Ibid.*

27 Although numerous scientists were used, the reasoning for employing an archaeologist is less than clear. It may have had more to do with *who* she was than *what* she was. The South Bank's 'Theme Convener' for 'The Land and the People' strand was Jacquetta Hawkes, who was an archaeologist. Hawkes wrote a book on the theme shortly after the Festival, which also referred to the 'relics of the past' and 'the ancient dead', but no particular expertise in archaeology seems to have been necessary for her work on the Festival. It is thus relevant to note that she was, in addition, a poet who had worked in the Post-War Reconstruction Secretariat and the Ministry of Education. She later became 'Archaeological Correspondent' for *The Observer*, which seems to indicate that the field was of a broader interest than than it is today. Also, in 1953, having divorced Christopher Hawkes, she married J. B. Priestley. So, not only was she involved in politics and journalism, but she was also involved with that important voice of populism in war-time Britain,

Priestley, who was so enthusiastic about the Festival that he wrote a 588-page novel about it, *Festival at Farbridge* (1951). J. Hawkes, *A Land* (Harmondsworth: Penguin Books, 1959), back cover.

28 However, even the post-war period and the Festival itself experienced such tensions. For example, the South Bank was the site of strikes and the offer of an official visit from the Pearly Kings and Queens to the South Bank was rejected by the Festival Executive Committee. (See, for example, M. Black, 'Architecture, Art and Design in Unison', in Banham and Hillier, *A Tonic*, pp. 85, 89.

29 J. Giles and T. Middleton, 'Culture and Englishness: Introduction', in Giles and Middleton (eds), *Writing Englishness*, 149–53, p. 151.

30 H. Jennings, *Family Portrait 1951: A Film on the Theme of the Festival of Britain, 1951*, a Wessex Film Production, 1951.

31 H. Nicolson, *The Listener* (1 November 1951). See also Weight, 'Pale Stood Albion', p. 158.

32 Hippisley Coxe, 'The Seaside', p. 31.

33 G. Barry, as quoted by Frayn, 'Festival', p. 336.

34 See, for example, Hillier, 'Introduction', p. 12.

35 '1851 Centenary Pavilion', Architect: Hugh Casson, Display Designer: James Gardner, OBE, in Cox, *The South Bank Exhibition*, p. 85 and T. W. Hendrick, 'The achievements of "Cockade"', in Banham and Hillier (eds), *A Tonic*, 163–4, p. 164. See also '1851 Centenary Pavilion', *Architectural Review*, 109 (1951), p. 266.

36 See, for example, Hillier, 'Introduction', pp. 13–14; Frayn, 'Festival', p. 341; Hewison, *Culture and Consensus*, p. 58 and Conservative Party Archive, Festival of Britain, Additional File II, Butler to Woolton, 18 May 1950, as cited by Weight, 'Pale Stood Albion', p. 143.

37 James Gardner (1975), as quoted by Hillier, 'Introduction', p. 12.

38 Peter Laslett's three talks on the Third Programme in April, 1960 about 'the social order before the coming of industry' formed the basis of his highly influential book, *The World We Have Lost* (London: Methuen, 1965): Carpenter, *The Envy of the World*, p. 191.

39 Gerald Barry, *Radio Times*, 27 April 1951.

40 Frayn, 'Festival', p. 349.

41 Carpenter, *The Envy of the World*, pp. 107–8.

42 BBC Written Archives Centre, Caversham, R51/131/1 and /2, 'Talks Eighteen Fifty One Week', 1950–51.

43 'Talks Eighteen Fifty One Week'.

44 BBC Written Archives Centre, Caversham, R9/9/15, 'The Third Programme 1851 Week', 5 June 1951, as quoted by Carpenter, *The Envy of the World*, p. 109. According to Carpenter, 'a Listener Research survey into the "character" of the Third's audience, completed in the spring of 1952' revealed that, in *The Economist*'s words, 'the Third Programme has a far bigger market among the supposedly philistine than among the cultured', with a larger number than imagined of 'poorly educated people' listening at least once a week (Carpenter, *The Envy of the World*, p. 109). Yet, although the audience was more diverse than thought possible, the Third had been losing listeners for years. For example, in 1949, 'the average winter evening audiences for the Light Programme and Home Service were 5½ million and 3¼ million people

respectively, the Third was "in the neighbourhood of 90,000."' The numbers listening to the Third in 1951 are presumed to have been even lower (Carpenter, *The Envy of the World*, pp. 109–10).

45 Carpenter, *The Envy of the World*, p. 108.

46 Peter Laslett, *Radio Times*, 20 April 1951, as quoted by Carpenter, *The Envy of the World*, p. 108.

47 *Ibid.*

48 Dr and Mrs Peter Laslett, Trinity College, Cambridge, interview with the author, 26 May 1998. Although he did subsequently say that there was, of course, editorialising involved in 1851 when *The Times* – the key source for these programmes – selected what would be published.

49 *Ibid.*

50 Anonymous, 'Regions of Britain', series run in conjunction with the Festival of Britain, first issue, *Times Education Supplement* (13 April 1951) and PRO, ED 142/4, Ministry of Education, 'Circular 231', 15 December 1950, Curzon Street, London, W1.

51 Ministry of Education, 'Circular 231', p. 2.

52 Anonymous, 'Coleraine 100 Years Ago: Intermediate Schools' Exhibition Opened by the Minister', *Belfast Telegraph*, 5 April 1951, p. 3.

53 *Ibid.*

54 Mandler, *Fall and Rise of the Stately Home*, p. 330 and Curtis, 'One Continuous Interwoven Story', p. 51.

55 Curtis, 'One Continuous Interwoven Story', pp. 51–2.

56 Cadbury-Brown, 'A Good Time', p. 60.

57 As previously stated, the various Festival official souvenir guide/catalogues describe anywhere from twenty-two to twenty-four arts festivals. In an electronic mail message of 28 September 2001, Charles Plouviez, Assistant to the Director of Exhibitions, explained that he thought 'we really muddled things up so nobody would know what was "official" and what not. The confusion over the arts festivals is even worse'.

58 PRO, Work 25/130/E1/A2/1, *The Festival of Britain 1951*, p. 7.

59 'The Arts at Bournemouth', in *The Official Book of the Festival*, p. 33. Some of these are discussed in the chapter on local festivals.

60 'The Bath Assembly', in *The Official Book of the Festival*, p. 30.

61 'The Arts in a Country City', in *The Official Book of the Festival*, p. 38 and 'Regency England by the Sea', in *The Official Book of the Festival*, p. 46.

62 'Regency England by the Sea', p. 46.

63 'Choral Music and Medieval Drama', in *The Official Book of the Festival*, p. 34.

64 The National Council of Social Service, *How to Write a Parish Guide*, no. 7 in the 'Local History Series', published for The Standing Conference for Local History, London, June 1951, p. 11.

65 Mandler, *The Fall and Rise of the Stately Home*, p. 330.

66 See Chapter 2 for a fuller description of the Festival's architects and planners.

67 Emphasis in the original. Curtis, 'One Continuous Interwoven Story', p. 51.

68 Aldiss, 'A Monument to the Future', p. 178.

69 Dr Johnson on the Vauxhall Pleasure Gardens, as quoted by A. Hippisley Coxe, 'It Sprang from Spring Gardens', in *Festival Pleasure Gardens Battersea Park Guide*, 44–8, p. 44.

70 Mass Observation was founded by Jennings, along with Tom Harrison, an anthropologist, and Charles Madge, a poet and journalist. Mass Observation's aim was to record the daily lives of 'ordinary' people and their thoughts. They did this through a variety of methods, which included enlisting about 300 volunteers to keep regular 'observers'' diaries: A. Calder and D. Sheridan (eds), *Speak for Yourself: A Mass Observation Anthology 1937–49* (London: Cape, 1984). Due to his tragic accidental death, *Family Portrait* was to be Jennings' last film.

71 Nicholas, *The Echo of War*, p. 228.

72 Jennings, *Family Portrait*.

73 See also Hewison, *Culture and Consensus*, pp. 63–4.

74 Jennings, *Family Portrait*.

75 Orwell, *The Lion and the Unicorn*, p. 54.

76 Jennings, *Family Portrait*.

77 *Ibid.*

78 See, for example, T. Bennett, *The Birth of the Museum*, p. 149; Eley and Suny, 'Introduction', p. 24.

79 Jennings, *Family Portrait*.

80 See Chapter 7 on the virtual absence of representations of Empire in the Festival for a fuller exploration of this point.

81 See also Hewison, *Culture and Consensus*, p. 63.

82 Hewison, *Culture and Consensus*, p. 64.

83 *Ibid.*

84 Lindsay Anderson, as quoted by Hewison, *Culture and Consensus*, p. 64.

85 'The Lion and the Unicorn', Commentary: Laurie Lee, in Cox, *The South Bank Exhibition*, p. 67. There is no overt acknowledgement that I have seen of Orwell's book on *Socialism and the English Genius*, titled *The Lion and the Unicorn*, but all of the planners and many of the visitors must have been aware of this reference.

86 Strong, 'Prologue: Utopia Limited', p. 7.

87 I explore in Chapter 7 why I think the Empire is not an entirely appropriate 'British contribution to civilisation' in 1951.

88 R. D. Russell and R. Goodden, Designers of the Lion and Unicorn pavilion, South Bank, 'The Lion and Unicorn Pavilion', in Banham and Hillier (eds), *A Tonic*, 96–101, p. 100.

89 Russell and Goodden, 'The Lion and Unicorn Pavilion', p. 97.

90 'The Lion and the Unicorn', p. 68.

91 Russell and Goodden, 'The Lion and Unicorn Pavilion', p. 97.

92 'The Lion and the Unicorn'. The subtly imperialistic tones struck in other Festival exhibitions are explored in Chapter 7.

93 'The Lion and the Unicorn', p. 68.

94 *Ibid.* On the Festival's imaginings of the 'cockney', see Chapter 5.

95 *Ibid.*

96 Russell and Goodden, 'The Lion and Unicorn Pavilion', 96–101, p. 98.

97 *Ibid.* and C. Plouviez, 'A Minor Mannerism in Art History', in Banham and Hillier (eds), *A Tonic*, 165–6, p. 166.

98 Sir Ernest Barker, *The Character of England* (1947), as reprinted in Giles and Middleton (eds), *Writing Englishness*, 55–63, pp. 60–1.

99 'The Lion and the Unicorn', p. 68.

100 Samuel, *Theatres of Memory*, Vol. I, p. 218.

101 'The Lion and the Unicorn', p. 68.

102 *Ibid.*

103 Directorate of Army Education, *The British Way and Purpose*, p. 219.

104 Modern Records Centre, University of Warwick, Coventry, TUC file MSS. 292/509.3/6, Letter from Cecil Cooke, Director of Exhibitions, Festival of Britain, 1951, to E. Fletcher, Secretary of the Research and Economic Department, Trades Union Congress, dated 20 April 1951.

105 Modern Records Centre, University of Warwick, Coventry, TUC file MSS. 292/509.3/6, Letter from B. Gardner, General Secretary, Amalgamated Engineering Union, to H. V. Tweson, General Secretary, Trades Union Congress, dated 16 January 1950.

106 Modern Records Centre, University of Warwick, Coventry, TUC file MSS. 292/509.3/6, Information Survey No 4, Festival of Britain Office, p. 10, as cited in Trades Union Congress, Inter-Departmental Correspondence, Department: Research, from E. Fletcher to Mr George Woodcock, Subject: Festival of Britain, 1951, dated 17 March 1950.

107 *Ibid.*

108 *Ibid.*

109 C. Griffiths, 'Remembering Tolpuddle: Rural History and Commemoration in the Inter-War Labour Movement', *History Workshop Journal*, 44 (autumn 1997), 145–70, p. 146.

110 *Ibid.*

111 Letter from B. Gardner to H. V. Tweson, 16 January 1950.

112 Griffiths, 'Remembering Tolpuddle', p. 146.

113 S. and B. Webb, *The History of Trade Unionism* (rev. ed. 1920), p. 144, as quoted by Griffiths, 'Remembering Tolpuddle', p. 147.

114 Griffiths, 'Remembering Tolpuddle', p. 147.

115 Walter Citrine to F. C. James, 12 July 1933, MSS 292/1.91/23, Modern Records Centre, as cited by Griffiths, 'Remembering Tolpuddle', p. 155.

116 Griffiths, 'Remembering Tolpuddle', p. 151.

117 According to *The Official Book of the Festival of Britain 1951*, 'the structure and working of British industry itself' was exhibited in relation to 'the conquest of power' in The Power and Production Pavilion: *The Official Book of the Festival*, p. 8.

118 T. W. Hendrick, Production Manager, Cockade, 'The Achievements of "Cockade"', 163–4, p. 164. It is noteworthy that so many of the artists, designers and craftspeople employed by Cockade who worked on the Festival's interior displays were women.

Some of the names listed by Hendrick are Elizabeth Corsellis, Grace Bryan-Brown, Marie Hill and Margot Burry.

119 K. Chapman, Theme Convener, 'The Origins of the Island', in Cox, *Festival Ship Campania*, p. 10.

120 *Ibid.*

121 S. Withers, Theme Convener, 'Minerals of the Island', in Cox, *Festival Ship Campania*, pp. 11–12.

122 J. Hawkes, Theme Convener, 'The Land of Britain: Coming Aboard', in Cox, *Festival Ship Campania*, p. 9.

123 Nicos Poulantzas has argued that the modern state 'establishes a unique relationship between time and space, between history and territory, in organising the unity of the nation in the form of a *"historicity of a territory and territorialisation of a history"'*: Poulantzas 1980: 114, as quoted by Bennett, *The Birth of the Museum*, p. 141.

124 Hawkes, 'The Land of Britain', p. 9.

125 *Ibid.*

126 *Ibid.*

127 *Ibid.*

128 David Feldman, for example, has shown that in 1880 there were over 40,000 Jews in London alone, and that 'between 1871 and 1911 the Russian and Russian Polish population in London, a modest indicator of the Jewish immigrant presence, grew from 5,000 to 63,000'. D. Feldman, 'Jews in London, 1880–1914', in Samuel (ed.), *Patriotism: The Making and Unmaking of British National Identity*. 3 vols. *Volume II: Minorities and Outsiders*, 207–29, pp. 208–9.

129 Gavin and Lowe, 'Designing Desire', *Block*, 11 (1985–86), p. 64. It is important to note that Gavin and Lowe rely exclusively on one souvenir guidebook-catalogue of the South Bank and on articles in the contemporary *Architectural Review*, when there were actually numerous different souvenir guides and brochures produced and available for purchase. The one they chose, *The South Bank Exhibition, a Guide to the Story it Tells*, authored by Ian Cox, is clearly the most extreme in its masculinist analogies. That said, Cox was one of the primary London Festival organisers and his text must have been approved by a battery of officials and individuals. As such, Gavin and Lowe's observations on it make an intriguing, and seldom commented upon point about at least one official version of 'Britishness' promulgated by the Festival of Britain.

130 Cox, *The South Bank Exhibition*, pp. 11–12, and reprinted in Gavin and Lowe, 'Designing Desire', p. 64.

131 *Ibid.*

132 *Ibid.*

133 Army Bureau of Current Affairs, as quoted by S. Benton, 'The 1945 "Republic"' (review essay), *History Workshop Journal*, 43 (spring 1997), 249–57, p. 257, fn. 14.

134 Benton, 'The 1945 "Republic"', p. 254.

135 Benton, 'The 1945 "Republic"', p. 256. See also P. Summerfield, 'Women in Britain since 1945: Companionate Marriage and the Double Burden', in Obelkevich and Catterall (eds), *Understanding Post-War British Society*, 58–72.

136 *Ibid.*

137 Benton makes this point (p. 254), but does not cite the most important contributor to the field, Ina Zweiniger-Bargielowska. See, for example, her 'Rationing, Austerity and the Conservative Party After 1945', *Historical Journal*, 37:1 (1994), 173–97, and 'Exploring the Gender Gap: The Conservative Party and Women's Vote, 1945–1964', in Francis and Zweiniger-Bargielowska (eds), *The Conservatives and British Society, 1880–1990*, 194–223. For an exploration of who was included and excluded from wartime notions of citizenship, see S. Rose, 'Sex, Nation and Citizenship in World War II Britain', *American Historical Review*, 103:4 (October 1998), 1147–76.

138 A. Calder, *The Myth of the Blitz* (London: Pimlico, 1991).

139 P. Fussell, *Killing in Prose and Verse and Other Essays* (London: Bellow, 1990).

140 This debate commenced with Martin J. Wiener's *English Culture and the Decline of the Industrial Spirit 1850–1950* (Cambridge: Cambridge University Press, 1981). See also Colls and Dodd (eds), *Englishness*; P. Wright, *On Living in an Old Country* (London: Verso, 1985); and P. Mandler, 'Against "Englishness": English Culture and the Limits to Rural Nostalgia, 1850–1940', *Transactions of the Royal Historical Society*, 6th series, 7 (1997), 155–75.

141 Benton, 'The 1945 "Republic"', p. 253.

142 The term 'Janus-faced' is, of course, borrowed from T. Nairn, *The Break-up of Britain* (London: New Left Books, 1977), specifically Chapter 9, pp. 329–63.

III
PLACE

Introduction: why place? This section's conceptual framework

The next section of this book considers representations of Britishness rooted in notions of place, with subsections focusing on the metropole; what were called 'the regions', but were Wales, Northern Ireland and Scotland (both covered in Chapter 5); local cities, towns and villages (the topic of Chapter 6); 'the place that was virtually absent' in the Festival's representational repertoire – the Empire or Commonwealth (Chapter 7); and some of the representations at the Battersea Pleasure Gardens – 'the place of escape and edification' (Chapter 8). To some (perhaps, most) people the obvious, logical corollary to a section headed 'Time' would appear to be one entitled 'Space'. Not so to the many geographers who are impatient with those of us in adjacent fields whom they find just interested enough in their work to attempt to write or speak about 'space', but not interested enough to try to comprehend the distinction they make between 'space' and 'place'.[1] Their frustration seems warranted once one realises that the distinction can be a simple one: for example, 'place is space to which meaning has been ascribed'.[2] Thus, 'it is not spaces which ground identifications, but places', according to Erica Carter, James Donald and Judith Squire in their introduction to *Space and Place: Theories of Identity and Location*.[3] Clearly then it is 'place' and not 'space' which is the category under investigation in these next examinations of the representations of Britain and Britishness in the Festival. The metropole, the region and the locale all exist in 'space', of course, but their significance to the celebrations of victory and renewal which were the Festival was as meaningful 'places', as was true in different ways of the Empire and the Battersea Pleasure Gardens, too.

Notes

1 At the Historical Geographers' seminar held at the Institute of Historical Research, University of London, one of the liveliest and most wide-ranging of the seminars in the time I regularly attended (1993–95), I often heard (and overheard) those

geographers present complain about how this speaker or that questioner did not understand the difference between the concepts of 'space' and 'place'.

2 E. Carter, J. Donald and J. Squire, 'Introduction', in E. Carter, J. Donald and J. Squire (eds), *Space and Place: Theories of Identity and Location* (London: Lawrence & Wishart, in association with *New Formations*, 1993), p. xiii.

3 *Ibid*. See also collected essays by Doreen Massey, *Space, Place and Gender* (Cambridge/ Oxford: Polity Press, in association with Blackwell Publishers, 1994).

5 ✧ London-based representations of the metropole and 'the regions'

London's official exhibitions

THE 'ex-officers and gentlemen' who constituted the most influential planning committees of the Festival, the Festival Committee and the Presentation Committee, tackled the task of representing various places within Britain to the British people and their foreign visitors.[1] The Festival Headquarters inhabited the entire building located at 2 Savoy Court, the home of the 'recently defunct Electricity Commission'. (A spring 1948 memorandum from Gerald Barry called this situation 'One of the fortunate by-products of the nationalisation of electricity'.[2]) From these offices came the conceptions, blueprints, structures and language for not only those exhibitions sited in London – the South Bank's 'Combined Exhibition', the Battersea Pleasure Gardens,[3] the Science Exhibition held at the Science Museum in South Kensington, and the Exhibition of Architecture and Town Planning in Poplar, East London – but also the land and sea travelling exhibitions, and the three 'regional' exhibitions: the Dolhendre (Wales) Exhibition of Hillside Farming, the Ulster Farm and Factory Exhibition, and the Glasgow Exhibition of Industrial Power. The planners chose to construct exhibitions and accompanying discourses that emphasised the uniqueness of these places.

The Festival of Britain's 'programme should be nation-wide and would therefore differ radically from previous great exhibitions and fairs which have been held on a single site in a single large centre', according to the Minister of Works' Report to Parliament.[4] In practice this meant that every town and village in the UK was encouraged to hold a festival event of some kind, but, it also meant that the centrally planned exhibitions included travelling versions of the South Bank designed to take the displays to what the organisers called 'the provinces'. In addition, the London planners organised exhibitions in what they called the 'regions' of Wales, Northern Ireland and Scotland, indicating a clear tendency to subordinate other national identities to England. Even so, it is a tribute to the Festival organisers that the 1951 festivities were conceived as multi-sited, unlike earlier fairs and exhibitions or the Labour Millennium celebration – the Millennium Dome. Britain's 'unity through diversity' was one of the themes of the Festival and these travelling and 'regional' exhibitions were attempts to simultaneously construct and bolster that notion.[5] This chapter starts by placing London in the imagined British community and then examines the travelling and 'regional' exhibitions.

The metropole: London's place in the Festival's imagining of Britishness

One Thomas Cook Travel Service brochure, specially designed for the Festival summer, commenced with Samuel Johnson's famous claim that: 'when a man is tired of London, he is tired of life, for there is in London all that life can afford'.[6] London was written into the story of the 'auto-biography of a nation' in predictable terms – the metropole was both assumed and asserted to be the 'capital of the Commonwealth and Empire', as well as 'the centrepiece' of the Festival.[7] The British people were encouraged to travel to London for the Festival. Advance advertising posters read: 'Book your tickets *in advance*. 5/– all days except Tuesdays. 10/– Tuesdays. *Make sure of getting in*.'[8] And this injunction to travel to the capital was extended to schoolchildren who needed to see the South Bank because it was 'designed as the central feature of the Festival, to display in story form British achievements in science, technology and industrial design'. In addition to the importance of the Festival's content, the Ministry of Education circular outlined all the details for school parties, covering transportation and accommodation options, which included the possibility of sleeping in the Clapham South Deep Shelter or 'a tented camp'.[9]

London was the centre of the Festival and the capital of the United Kingdom. Raphael Samuel has written that in the immediate post-war period London was a source of 'symbolic capital', representing not only 'the capital of England, and of the British Empire', but 'the greatest city in the world', in the language of *Whitaker's Almanack*.[10] Additionally, in the Festival publications the capital was the home of the monarchy and St Paul's Cathedral, and it was on the steps of St Paul's that the King and Queen opened the Festival of Britain. Surrounded by red, white and blue bunting, the King declared the Festival 'a symbol of Britain's abiding courage and vitality'.[11] As a part of the Festival, St Paul's had already been treated to a new permanent garden 'planted with the help of voluntary labour as a memorial to the city's resistance to bombing'.[12] The symbolism of the cathedral behind the King was surely clear to those who had planned the event, along with the crowd. For most people St Paul's had become the 'icon of wartime survival', evoked repeatedly in Ministry of Information (MOI) films.[13] For some, the Cathedral had come to stand for a more democratic, enlightened future as well. Filmmaker Humphrey Jennings, for example, used the Cathedral as a symbolic transmitter of Enlightenment ideals and 'resurgent socialism'.[14] By 1951, St Paul's had acquired a multiplicity of meanings, old and new, and the choice of it for the opening of the Festival – a celebration of British achievements past, present and future – was an astute one.

The symbol of St Paul's may have been one of a more enlightened future or 'resurgent socialism' for Jennings, but first and foremost it was a cathedral and therefore a symbol of the Church of England.[15] Kenneth Thompson has written in relation to British national identity that 'In Britain, a variety of discourses, and sets of differences, have been rearticulated to construct the imagined community of the British nation at different times. Some of the most interesting are those in which religious and political discourses were combined in attempts to produce an ideologically unifying nationalism'.[16] Religious and political discourses were subtly combined in the Festival of Britain's official literature. One souvenir guide asserted that: 'Britain is a Christian Community. The Christian Faith is inseparably a part of our history. It has strengthened all those endeavours which this Festival has been built to display'.[17]

Barry had written to Archbishop Fisher in February of 1950 to say that 'everything the church can do to emphasise that the Festival is not a stunt but a solemn act of national reassessment will be of very great help'.[18] The Archbishop had responded by issuing a special Form of Divine Service to be used in Anglican churches across the country during the Festival season, and by the end of the summer he concluded in a speech broadcast on the Home, Light and General Overseas programmes of the BBC that '"a brightening up of the family home" had been carried out'.[19]

In London, Festival religious events included: Saturday night 'community hymn singing', services or meetings in the Royal Festival Hall, daily performances at Matins and Evensong in Westminster Abbey, an exhibition in St Paul's Cathedral's crypt illustrating 'the influence of the Christian Faith upon the life of the nation', and an evangelical exhibition at the Central Hall Westminster.[20] There was even an official Festival of Britain church, the Church of St John. Situated in Waterloo Road, adjoining the South Bank exhibition, it was specially rebuilt for the Festival. There visitors could find daily prayerbook services and 'a different choir each day to sing Evensong'. Weekly, they could partake in the liturgies of Scotland, America, South Africa and Australia, which had 'sprung from the English prayer book'.[21] These different services were clearly intended to illustrate another 'British contribution to civilisation'. Perhaps there was a touristic agenda as well, with the organisers hoping to please their foreign, English-speaking visitors by providing them with the opportunity to attend familiar church services in the middle of London and all the awe-inspiring, yet tiring, exhibitions on the South Bank.

London: the capital of the arts

Not surprisingly, one of London's celebrated achievements was its role as a 'traditional' home to 'the arts'. The Festival featured the London Season of Arts in May and June organised by the Arts Council. The official souvenir of the arts season presented London as the 'producer' 'of artists in plenty', the provider of 'opportunities to artists from other parts of the country', and the extender of 'hospitality to guest talent from overseas'.[22] 'London has never lacked artists, both creative and interpretative or patrons of the arts', it declared.[23] But, more importantly in the post-war moment, the Arts Council's souvenir explained that their Festival arts season stemmed from: 'a democratic conviction which has been growing steadily through the years that good art is enjoyable art and should be appreciated by all and sundry, whatever their incomes may be'.[24] Underscoring this point, the brochure explained how the Arts Council had been given a Treasury grant 'not only to extend the knowledge and practice of the arts and to maintain and improve their standards, but also to make them accessible to the people throughout the country'. The Council translated this agenda into a variety of offerings which they listed as: 'music hall, musical comedy and revues as well as operas, ballets and plays, with brass bands as well as symphony orchestras, with dancing and fireworks as well as exhibitions'.[25] Explaining their choices further, the brochure stressed that: 'we can be gay as well as serious. All this is being presented within the battered but novel framework of London herself: *"The flower of cities all."* However difficult the times, we need the solace and stimulus of the arts.'[26]

The Council's goal for its Festival season was to extend the motto of its predecessor, the Council for the Encouragement of Music and the Arts (CEMA), 'the best for the most' into these times of national recovery.[27] The Council's Chairman stated that: 'We readily agree that nothing is good enough but the best; but we always bear in mind that the arts cannot be made truly popular unless they are attractive'.[28] In the Festival summer, if at no other time, it seems that the Arts Council was attempting to navigate a path between giving 'the people' the traditional music hall owner's dictum of 'a bit of what you fancy' and Lord Reith's belief in offering the public 'slightly better than it now thinks it likes'.[29] But, as has often been the case, the Council did in the end give the most money to the most expensive arts. The chief beneficiaries were classical music, opera and ballet. Arts Council commissions included Sir Arnold Bax's and

Sir Arthur Bliss's orchestral and choral music, Benjamin Britten's opera *Billy Budd*, and *Tiresias*: a new ballet by Constant Lambert with choreography by Frederick Ashton for Sadler's Wells at Covent Garden. On a smaller scale, Alicia Markova and Anton Dolin established their small ballet company as the Festival Ballet and a Wagner season was funded at Covent Garden.³⁰ In its Annual Report, retiring Chairman, Pooley, celebrated the Art Council's Festival achievements, putting them in the context of the Korean War: 'Dangers and anxieties continue to beset Great Britain, yet in this year of so many shadows, there has been more good art and music to be seen and heard in this country than ever before. The public has shown, in its hundreds of thousands, that it has a keen and growing appetite for the serious pleasures'.³¹ Pooley considered the West End contributions to the Festival season and he claimed that London's patronage of the arts was part of its identity within the nation. A very different identity was, however, celebrated in the East End. In Chapter 3 we saw that the 'Live Architecture Exhibition' in Poplar, East London, was represented as an example of the brighter, better future Britain would soon see. But, it was represented as a unique *place* in the Festival's story of Britain and Britishness, as well.

Poplar, East London and the Festival's Lansbury estate

The site of the Lansbury estate, Poplar, was represented as a special area of London and written into the Festival narrative as a unique place – unique for its kind of people as well as its industry. The official catalogue of the 'Live Architecture Exhibition' offered a 'Background to Lansbury' – this new planned 'neighbourhood' or 'community' whose buildings were funded and sped up to serve as educational examples of the importance of good planning and 'scientific' building.³² The catalogue explained that 'Within and to the north of the sudden loop in the Thames which almost encircles the Isle of Dogs, close to the heart of London's busy docklands, lies Poplar – part of the East End home of the traditional Londoner, the cockney ... For more than fifty years Poplar has been one of the metropolitan boroughs ... But long before it became a borough, Poplar was a firmly established community, rich in historical associations and with its own local loyalties, traditions and customs, which have endured to the present-day.'³³ As a 'historical' place, Poplar was defined by its inhabitants, along with its industry.

Gareth Stedman Jones has argued that, in the 1940s, Labour discourses 'subtly transformed' previous imaginings of the 'cockney' and were able to harness them 'to the language of Labour' and 'the notion of "the common people"', patriotism and democracy.³⁴ This was the notional 'cockney' evoked for the Festival, coupled with a perhaps more conservative ideal of the East Ender as 'plucky' and imbued with that 'carry on spirit', as it was called during the Blitz.[35]

Stressing its industrial capacities, the Festival catalogue related the history of Poplar over the previous three hundred years. Poplar was central to the story of 'London as a port, and Britain as a maritime nation'. Then, the passing of sailing ships and 'the development of iron-built ships' had led to a gradual decline in shipbuilding on the Thames, with this industry almost dying out. 'But the docks still remained, for their importance as a terminal and distribution point was as great as ever, and the population of Poplar to-day is still largely dependent on the fortunes of the shipping industry'.[36] As we will see, defining places by their industries was a common trope in the Festival narratives. Poplar was featured in the Festival story because of its innovative, planned housing estates, constructed quickly to be symbols, as well as examples for the Festival of Britain. It is not at all clear how many of the inhabitants of these estates engaged in any sort of trade related to shipping. The East End was also, of course, famous for its small-scale production of furniture and clothing.[37] Yet its location near the port was accentuated as an accessible way of designating Poplar as a unique area of the national cartography, just as the uniqueness of its people – 'the cockneys' – was imagined as an important component of this chapter of 'the autobiography of a nation'.

On a very different point, in keeping with Herbert Morrison's pronouncement that the Festival not be party political, significant 'characteristics' of Poplar were never mentioned in the Festival literature.[38] Poplar had been a Labour stronghold since the 1920s to such a degree that historical geographer, Gillian Rose, proclaims 'voting Labour' was 'one of Poplar's habits'.[39] She also describes the radicalism of George Lansbury, the Christian Socialist and 'Poplar's leading politician for fifty years', for whom the estate was named.[40] This too was not elaborated in most of the Festival literature. The only guide-catalogue to mention George Lansbury specifically was the one intended for the Exhibition of Architecture (as opposed to the more general guides covering all of the official events). In that publication George Lansbury was identified as a Leftist, but certainly not a radical. The souvenir explained that: 'For forty years he served Poplar as a member of the old Poplar Borough Council. He was its first Labour Mayor in 1919 and again held this office seventeen years later. From 1910–1912 and from 1922 till his death in 1940, at the age of 81, he was Labour Member of Parliament for one of the Poplar Divisions. He devoted his life to working for a better world and a new Poplar.'[41] So, if a visitor did go to the Exhibition of Architecture and buy this souvenir guide, then he or she might have thought about the connections to Labour that this exhibition implicitly evoked. But, otherwise, references to Labour were generally suppressed in the Festival literature.

Finally, it may have struck some visitors that the East End's long-term economic problems had been a priority for Herbert Morrison in his role as Chairman of the London County Council.[42] In the early 1930s, Poplar was such a poor area that it was included in a study conducted by the London School of Economics (LSE) committed to updating Charles Booth's investigations of London's slums published in the 1890s. In the LSE report, one quarter of Poplar's population was shown to be living below a 'very demanding definition of poverty'.[43] Nevertheless, neither the Labour Party's connections, generally, nor Morrison's commitment were stated in the official Festival literature.

The Festival planning documents reveal that the Architectural Council recommended 'without reserve that the site for the "Live" Architectural Exhibition' be 'within the area covered by Neighbourhood Units Nos. 9 and 10' in the Stepney–Poplar area and that the Ministry of Town and Country Planning and the London County Council were 'in complete agreement'.[44] The reasons given for this overwhelming support included the site's close proximity and convenient transport to central London, its feasibility in regard to developing it in time for the Festival (this decision was made in September of 1948), as well as the 'great importance' attached 'to the advantages which river access [gave] to all future planning'.[45] Had people really forgotten, not only the roles which Lansbury and Morrison had played in the area, but also that Prime Minister Attlee had been Stepney's councillor and then Mayor after his service in the First World War?[46] For those who did know these histories of Labour involvement in the East End, the significance of choosing Poplar as the site of the Live Architecture exhibition and its concomitant reconstruction of the area would not have gone unnoticed.

Through the Festival, London was represented as the home of the cockney, the arts, a more democratic future, the monarchy, and the capital of the United Kingdom. Although traditions were sometimes highlighted, it was more often London's forward-looking and modern characteristics that were stressed in the 1951 festivities. At least one influential Festival organiser feared that events held locally might not share the London exhibitions' orientation towards the future. Travelling and 'regional' exhibitions were planned to take London's Festival messages to the British people.

The travelling exhibitions

The Festival's planners designed land and sea travelling exhibitions in order to transport miniature versions of London's South Bank exhibition to 'the provinces'. Housed on a fleet of lorries and a decommissioned aircraft carrier, these exhibitions were arranged so that 'the story told on the South Bank', considered 'fundamental to the expression of the Festival theme', would 'reach the main centres of population throughout the country'.[47] Gerald Barry also expressed the hope that these exhibitions would contribute to a feeling that the 1951 Festival was 'as widely spread over Britain as possible'.[48] He explained in a memorandum written in April of 1948 that the travelling exhibition would be 'pitched and struck on suitable sites in the centre or on the edge of towns up and down the Kingdom, rather in the manner of a travelling circus'.[49] And in this way it would function 'to some extent satisfying local demand and at the same time acting as a valuable "trailer" or magnet for the central exhibitions in London'.[50] About a month later he explained to the first Festival Council meeting that 'in order to fulfil the Government's wish that the Festival should be as widely spread as possible over the country ... there should be a small mobile exhibition, containing replicas of what is best and most suitable in the large combined exhibition, which shall tour the provinces'.[51] In the end there were two separate travelling exhibitions – one by land and one by sea.

Barry's may sound like a very straightforward explanation of the purpose of these exhibitions, yet other sources reveal that the Festival planners actually had divergent ideas about the best way to articulate regional and local identities in relation to the London Festival. For example, the souvenir guide-catalogue produced to accompany the sea travelling exhibition suggests that at least its author, Ian Cox, viewed the local festivities as potentially problematic chapters in the national story. He was concerned that the local festivities might portray images or promulgate ideas about Britain or Britishness that would need to be countered by the centre. He repeatedly insisted on the necessity of using the Festival ship to diffuse more metropolitan notions:

> The Exhibition in the Festival Ship, Campania, is part of something far larger – the Festival of Britain ... It was always intended that the Festival should be nationwide and that the lead given in planning the official events might encourage independent organisations all over the country to contribute to it in ways of their own choosing. This has, in fact, happened in full measure, and the summer of 1951 will see a wonderful display of the many facets of our national life. These independently organised events naturally centre round subjects of particular local interest or prestige *and most of them are some distance away from the Festival's centrepiece – the South Bank*. Now, the story told there is fundamental to the full expression of the Festival theme, so it was decided to create special versions of this Exhibition that could bring the story to the main centres of population throughout the country.[52]

The organiser, Cox (also the Director of Science for the Festival), feared that the 'distance' between the South Bank exhibition and the local, 'independently organised events' might be too great. The travelling exhibitions would serve as a bridge between London's central, official representations and the local festivities Cox anticipated would present different stories of local interest.

We should remember though that rather early in the planning of the Festival Barry expressed his worry that Cox was too preoccupied with the 'scholastic' aspects of the exhibitions and that he felt it was imperative that Cox keep in mind that no one would attend the exhibitions if they were not fun.[53] Yet, Cox's concerns seem to have provided at least partial impetus for the land and sea travelling exhibitions.

Of course, it is also true that many of the London-based planners had gained considerable expertise during the war, putting on travelling exhibitions that toured the country aiming to entertain, inform and educate the British citizenry. Ralph Tubbs, one of the Festival architects, designed the 'Living in Cities' exhibition for the Architect's Reconstruction Committee, for example.[54] Others, such as Cecil Cooke, James Holland, Misha Black and Richard Levin, were members of the MOI or CEMA, both of which organised travelling events and displays.[55] In December 1942 alone, for example, the Ministry of Labour and the MOI showed 478 films in 149 factories or construction sites.[56] CEMA created its own theatrical circuit with fourteen touring companies in 1942. At the same time, a team of '"music travellers" worked with local professionals and amateur groups and the Rural Music Schools Council to organise a nation-wide series of concerts. Nine CEMA travelling companies were launched to take plays to Royal Ordinance [sic] Factory hostels'.[57] In addition, the Council orchestrated the impressive travelling art exhibitions known as 'Art for the People', generally held in factory canteens and shops, and sometimes in libraries, with a clear educational purpose.[58] Originally founded by the voluntary organisation, the British Institute of Adult Education (BIAE) in 1935, the extraordinarily successful 'Art for the People' exposed many people to art for the first time. According to Janet Minihan, 'The truckloads of pictures, displayed in small towns and rural areas lacking public collections, were on loan almost exclusively from private owners'. Each exhibition lasted about a month and admission was free.[59] CEMA began contributing financially to 'Art for the People' in the late 1930s, and thanks to that funding the annual number of touring exhibitions increased from a pre-war 4 or 5 to 18 in 1941, 30 in 1942, and 42 by 1944. CEMA then began to mount its own exhibitions, which numbered 37 by 1944. In total, in that year, the BIAE and CEMA exhibited in 208 art galleries and 522 other venues.[60] With the success of these ventures, the appropriateness and importance of taking versions of the South Bank Festival to 'the people' must have been obvious to the London planners.

Furthermore, when you examine where the land and sea travelling exhibitions were sent, it seems possible that they had a more specific political purpose than merely the cultivation of a people 'rich in culture'.[61] Most of the cities visited by the travelling exhibitions had a population of over 100,000.[62] But not every city of that size or larger received an official Festival exhibition, so there must have been additional criteria for selecting these places. It is interesting to note that all of the cities that played host to the travelling exhibitions, bar one, were bombed by the Germans during the war, some of them quite badly.[63] The one not bombed, Dundee, had endured high unemployment and depression, at a time when most of the country experienced full employment.[64] Thus, these sites were more in need of a post-war 'tonic' to boost morale. It is possible that the visit of a travelling exhibition may have been a reward for Labour loyalty, as well. The 1950 election revealed, for example, that 'the Labour party held its vote in areas for whom the inter-war years and the image of the "depressed areas" had significance'.[65]

In addition to being morale boosters and rewards, the travelling exhibitions were at the centre of the Festival's agenda to diffuse knowledge throughout Britain. Clearly, the best way to bring the most information to the most people is to take that information to the places most populated. It is especially in the travelling exhibitions that we can see a concerted attempt by the Festival organisers literally to transport middle-class education, information and tastes to 'the people' of Britain, whoever and wherever they might be. The themes explored in these two exhibitions ranged from science and health care to interior design and fashion. The director of the Council of Industrial Design at the time of the Festival, Paul Reilly, considered the Festival a 'turning point in public taste'.[66]

The Land Travelling Exhibition

Richard Levin, chief designer of the Land Travelling Exhibition, explained at the time that 'The theme of the Land Traveller is similar to that of the South Bank Exhibition, but because it is visiting the industrial towns of the Midlands, the emphasis has been placed more on industrial design'.[67] This exhibition visited Manchester, Leeds, Birmingham and Nottingham between the beginning of May and the beginning of October of 1951.[68] As we shall see, this focus on linking the places' industrial resources to the contents of the exhibition was something the Land Traveller had in common with the 'regional' exhibitions held in Wales, Northern Ireland and Scotland.

'Designing the world's biggest-ever travelling exhibition will not go

down in the books as "my favourite assignment"', said Levin.[69] One of
the less amusing aspects of designing this exhibition was that in Manchester
and Birmingham it went into existing halls, while in Leeds and Nottingham
it had to go 'into an enormous tented structure especially built for it'.[70]
Levin spelled out the situation further, stating that the 'first complication
was that three different sets of layouts had to be prepared for all the
Exhibition halls'.[71] The solution he arrived at was a structure constructed
from welded tubular steel supporting a canvas covering. In the end the
exhibition covered about 40,000 square feet (12,000 square metres).[72] The
entrance façade was made of steel and laminated, transparent plastic
measuring 120 feet (36.6 metres) long by 50 feet (15.3 metres) high and
flanked by a grouping of plaster statues representing 'industry', 'communication' and 'effort'. Twenty-one ex-naval red, white and blue searchlights
with an output equivalent to forty million candles lit the exhibition,
containing three thousand objects arranged in six sections.[73] These sections
were: 'Materials and Skill', 'Discovery and Design', 'People at Home', 'People
at Play', 'People at Work', and 'People Travel'.[74] Clearly, British people's
lives were the primary concern of the Land Travelling Exhibition.

According to the official brochure, the 'Materials and Skill' section
dealt with 'the development of Man's skill in handling materials throughout
the ages'.[75] This would have been a fitting topic in the Festival's celebration
of British achievements in 1951, as the British had developed numerous
new materials during and just after the war ranging from plastics to
plywood.[76] 'Discovery and Design' displayed 'how today in a world of
machines the traditions of British craftsmanship have been supplemented
by scientific knowledge and new techniques in the production of such
things as domestic equipment and the objects made from plastics'.[77] The
next section, 'People at Home', illustrated 'in all the rooms of an ordinary
house', how 'the designer and the scientist combine to solve many domestic
problems', while 'People at Play' was 'devoted to our sports and pastimes',
which ranged from field sports and camping to hobbies and even included
a display of 'clothes for leisure wear'.[78] Over half of the Land Travelling
Exhibition was devoted to home and leisure – places and times when the
British people relaxed and enjoyed themselves, but also realms in which
questions of taste might be said to be at the fore. The fourth section,
'People at Work', was organised rather differently: the invention of the gas
turbine engine by Sir Frank Whittle, along with its development and
production was to act as 'a symbol of the enterprise of our industries, the
skill of our engineers and the scientific research which lies behind their
efforts'.[79] 'People Travel' was the final section, tying into the former section
with an exhibit on 'how the gas turbine engine is being applied to other
forms of transport as a prelude to the final section'.[80] This end-point

focusing on travel illustrated 'the comfort of modern air travel, the story of passenger travel by rail from 1830 to the present day, with a full-size model of a designer's idea of the passenger coach of the future'.[81] Also included was 'the story of the omnibus and of our achievement in every form of ocean travel from liners to yachts'.[82] The past was mentioned, but recent achievements and visions of the future dominated the 'Land Traveller': the invention of the gas turbine, the development of new materials and scientific solutions to domestic problems were key to this exhibition's story.

Campania, *The Sea Travelling Exhibition*

The Festival ship, *Campania*, was 16,000 tons of decommissioned aircraft carrier, which did 'not convert very readily into a showboat', according to James Holland, the resident designer at the Festival Office. Holland had been in the MOI and was then Chief Designer of Exhibitions and Display at the Central Office of Information.[83] He and the other Festival planners knew they had to consider themselves very lucky to acquire any ship at all for their exhibition at a time when 'anything that floated was still in demand for bringing basic cargoes to Europe'.[84] 'Large as the hull appeared, the flight deck could carry little weight additional to the necessary lifeboats. But white paint, skeleton masts and plentiful bunting transformed a rather graceless hulk into the semblance of a floating fairground', declared one of the official Festival brochures.[85] Once all decked out, the *Campania* visited the ports of: Southampton, Dundee, Newcastle, Hull, Plymouth, Bristol, Cardiff, Belfast, Birkenhead and Glasgow (in that order), between 4 May and 6 October 1951. The ship docked for a period of between ten days and two weeks in each port.[86]

The Sea Travelling Exhibition's themes were similar to the Land Traveller's – 'The Land of Britain', 'Discovery' and 'The People at Home'. The first section explored 'how this country came to have such a diversity of landscape and natural resources, and shows how these have been developed by its people'.[87] There followed exhibits on agriculture, mining, steel and 'the conversion of raw materials into usable products, all of a high standard of design'.[88] In the words of one official guide-catalogue: 'from here, the theme develops into the stories of power, transport, and finally, sea and ships'.[89] The 'Discovery' section of the exhibition detailed the story of 'terrestrial exploration and the development of overseas territories by the application of new scientific techniques', along with discoveries in biology and physical and chemical science, and the exploration of 'outer space itself'.[90] The elliptical reference to the Empire here is typical of the lack of direct reference to Britain's imperial past, yet the simultaneous impossibility of completely ignoring it.[91] Even the word 'discovery' is evocative of imperial conquest, as well as scientific breakthroughs. The final section, 'People at Home', commenced with a Homes and Gardens display 'where the visitor is offered a number of solutions to contemporary problems of lack of space in the home'.[92] Next there were displays presenting 'British contributions to health, medicine, surgery and nursing'.[93] Finally, the visitor walked through exhibitions on a rural scene and the seaside. The catalogue underscored how the Seaside section explored not only 'pleasure resorts but the ports and harbours which are our gateways to the world'.[94] The final description of this exhibition explained how, 'All through the Exhibition, it emerges how closely our history, our achievement and our destiny are linked with the sea. On the way out, the visitor is given an opportunity to salute some of the men who in very diverse ways, have added to our marine tradition'.[95] As with the industrial focus in the Land Traveller, the planners adapted the themes of the exhibition to its context, a decommissioned warship visiting ports. The places visited were designated unique because of their close proximity to the sea, and then in turn the sea was used as a defining characteristic of the places themselves. Their other characteristics, such as their shared experiences of bombing during the Second World War, were not mentioned explicitly, much less explored.

The unrealised 'Festival Tours of Britain'

Interestingly, in addition to the land and sea travelling exhibitions, there was an unrealised London-based scheme to sponsor official 'Festival of Britain, 1951 "Tours of Britain"'.[96] According to Festival Council records, one of the 'objects' of these tours was to provide the visitor with 'a comprehensive and balanced view of the land of Britain in all its variety, [and] of the varied people that inhabit and work in it and what they are doing'.[97] Another aim was to 'demonstrate this theme in action', clarifying that 'the theme of the Festival is the live story of British achievement and the environment from which it has been won'.[98] The 1949 records are accompanied by a map, and the plans reveal that the organisers envisioned England divided into four 'regions', containing within them twelve areas'.[99] Laid out for each area were the 'foci of movement', which were not dissimilar to what could be called the 'foci of movement' for the South Bank exhibition, in which the official guide-catalogue writers included 'the way to go round' that exhibition. The legend on the 'sketch map' explains that these 'regions' and 'areas' were suggested 'for coverage of England in five and a half day tours'. Ian Cox later pointed to the Tours of Britain scheme as an example of the flexibility of the overall Festival theme, for which he was responsible. He claimed that this 'scheme ... could have told the same story but "on the ground" if we finally failed to get an adequate site or accommodation for the Combined Exhibition [known later as the South Bank exhibition]'.[100] The 1949 document also explained, for those who were thinking this plan only addressed England, and not all of Britain, that: 'England has been taken for example only; Scotland and Northern Ireland would, of course, be included in the complete plan'.[101] Moreover, we know that the London-based Council asked the Northern Irish Festival Committee to appoint a member to serve on the Tours Panel.[102] Not only does this unactualised project support my earlier contention that the Festival was partially conceived as a tourist event designed to encourage visitors to travel around Britain, spreading hard currency across the British Isles, but it also illustrates the London committee's visions of the United Kingdom as a diverse, yet united, land.

According to Cox, 'all that survived of this scheme was a series of guidebooks that made use of the approach we had worked out for the tours themselves'.[103] In the planning documents, the books were dubbed 'a very important feature both in the Tours themselves and in the Festival plans as a whole'.[104] The resulting series of thirteen books, entitled *About Britain*, were published for the Festival of Britain Office by Collins.[105] As their inside covers declare, they were designed as 'guides to the living Britain, covering the whole country, England, Wales, Scotland and Northern Ireland'. 'Each is a guide to a well-defined district, planned to give you the fundamental facts ... Tours, too, are suggested (and illustrated by road maps, drawings and notes) to enable you to explore each district in a short time by car or bicycle'.[106] These convenient, inexpensive guidebooks costing 3/6 came with beautiful relief maps of each area printed on their covers. The final line of the inside cover statement reads: 'Not everyone has ten shillings or fifteen shillings to spend on a fat topographical volume. Here are 94 pages of lively matter including upwards of 50 illustrations for a reasonable price'.[107] This democratic approach to information is consistent with most of the Festival's schemes, as I have discussed in other chapters – schemes that sought to distribute knowledge across class lines as well as the geographical areas of the United Kingdom.

Overall, like the other London-planned exhibitions, the travelling exhibitions stressed the uniqueness of the British places where they went, with the Land Traveller emphasising industrial design 'because it is visiting the industrial towns of the Midlands' and *Campania* illustrating the link between British achievements and the sea for its visitors in Britain's ports.[108] As explored in the next section, the uniqueness of the so-called 'regions' of Britain – Wales, Northern Ireland and Scotland – was the focus of the Festival exhibitions held in these places, as well. These constructions of uniqueness generally relied on rather unimaginative conceptualisations, such as a place's industrial capacities, as opposed to more contentious options such as differences in languages or cultural traditions.

'The Regions': representing Britain and the British as regionally diverse

David Lowenthal has written that 'icons of identity are not confined to nation states. They are just as crucial to ethnic or other groups whose autonomy is partial or residual – Scots and Welsh, Basques and Bretons'.[109] His point is that, even though this is true, national history in Britain is really English history, not British history, and that 'in schools the regional past scarcely figures'.[110] Yet in the Festival of Britain the representations of the British nation were bound up with those of Wales, Northern Ireland and Scotland. In the Festival, the imagined community of Great Britain calmly incorporated these other places into the larger conception by labelling them 'the regions'. Stories of conquest and struggle over these nations were generally absent in the official exhibitions. However, the identities of these places were portrayed as both integral to the identities of their residents and to the central story being told in the Festival about Great Britain as a united yet diverse whole. As I suggested earlier, this may have been a sort of compensatory move in which the focus of national identity was quietly shifted from the diminishing Empire or Common-wealth to the coherent British Isles.

There was a constant refrain in the Festival of Britain resoundingly stressing the vast variety of this island nation. Even when presented as only England and not Britain (the latter being the more prevalent and certainly, the 'official' conception during the Festival and its planning), the nation was portrayed as a widely heterogeneous place, with great regional diversity. Thus, for example, an article in April 1951's *Times Educational Supplement*, appearing as part of a series on the 'Regions of Britain', a teaching tool to prepare students for their visits to the Festival, stated: 'England owes much of her unity to her lack of uniformity'.[111] 'Unity in diversity' was an actively promoted imagining of Britain in the Festival.[112]

An illustration of this underlying conceptualisation comes from an early Festival planning meeting held in September, 1948. At this meeting the group known as the 'Presentation panel' discussed all their ideas thus far for the organisation of the South Bank Exhibition. Their suggestions were displayed on 'the chart', which one of the members had devised.[113] In the minutes there is a section headed 'The Chart, Its Sections and the Exhibition', and according to them, the following was agreed to be essential to the Festival's theme:

(i) Origins of the British People
... through examples based on results of archaeological research, this section should show how and why we are *a mixed race*. The characteristics

and achievements of the various peoples that settled in Britain would be demonstrated and it would be seen that these persist as the basis of present-day regional differences ...

(ii) Expressions of Regional Character which offers scope for the demonstration of *dialects, physical types, differences in way of life* and other material of this sort recommended by our expert advisors.[114]

From the early planning stages, then, it is apparent that the Festival was to represent the British as 'a mixed race' whose regional differences in speech, appearance and ways of life could be traced to very early history. By the time the *Official Book of the Festival of Britain, 1951*, sold as a souvenir at the exhibitions, was published, the discourse in some ways had changed little: 'We are a people of mixed ancestry and here ... is the story of how our different forebears came to Britain', it declared.[115] However, it also seems that by 1951 the planners had settled on a story of regional diversity linked most directly to industrial production. So, for instance, instead of Scotland being celebrated for its fine architecture, heavy engineering was the theme of the official Scottish exhibition. Or instead of Wales' festivities focusing on the Welsh language, they accentuated agricultural innovation. Perhaps dialects and physical types came to be considered too contentious, whereas a series of exhibitions which sought to announce national recovery as well as to stimulate national renewal found their logical linking theme in productive capacities.

The events considered in this chapter as 'regional' are those orchestrated by London planners in association with the Festival of Britain committees in Cardiff, Belfast and Glasgow. The London planners were committed to presenting official exhibitions in each of Britain's 'regions', which they considered to be Wales, Northern Ireland and Scotland. These exhibitions were substantially financed by the Government, while those 'independently organised events [which] naturally centered around subjects of particular local interest or prestige' were provided with no government funds.[116] These latter festivities are not the subject of this chapter, but the next.

London-based discourses on Britain's 'regions'

Regional identities were central to a new story of Britain in the post-war world. These 'regions', as construed by the 'centre', were characterised (some might say caricatured) most often by their productive capacities. This does not seem inappropriate at a time when all over London there were billboards proclaiming 'Export or Die'.[117] The Festival was clearly designed to be an announcement of national recovery, as well as an attempt at renewal. The nation's industrial capacities were key to its survival. London's official Festival planning committee repeatedly employed this narrative device of defining a place and its importance in terms of its unique, productive contributions to the nation. That committee had primary responsibility for organising three 'regional' exhibitions: the Dolhendre (Wales) Exhibition of Hillside Farming, the Ulster Farm and Factory Exhibition, and the Glasgow Exhibition of Industrial Power.[118]

The wider context: regional planning

According to historical geographer Dennis Hardy, 'The idea of the region, and its applicability in a policy context, gained ground in the interwar years – moving from largely unexplored territory on the periphery of political and economic debate, to occupy a more focal point of interest in British political life'.[119] Labour had really led the way in these discussions of regional planning and it makes sense that the left-leaning Festival planners would have been sympathetic to such ideas.[120] As early as 1919 Neville Chamberlain, in his role as Minister of Health and Chair to the committee originally known as the Slum Areas Committee, later dubbed the Unhealthy Areas Committee, led governmental inquiries into slum clearance and rebuilding.[121] In its Interim Report in 1920, this committee recommended planned dispersal and 'the development of self-contained garden cities, either round an existing nucleus or on new sites'.[122] Herbert Morrison, future 'Lord Festival', but at this time Secretary to the London Labour Party, as well as a former resident of the first garden city, Letchworth, strongly advocated similar schemes for the Greater London Area.[123] Thus, there emerged between 1919 and 1921, both within and beyond government, plans to divide England into 'regions' and 'subregions'. One such scheme, outlined by G. D. H. Cole in his *The Future of Local Government* (1921), proposed a division of England into nine provinces as the basis of a new system of local government.[124]

Ten years later, in 1931, the Labour Minister of Health set up a Departmental Committee with the remit of considering the numerous planning proposals and reports produced by joint local authority committees and then to make recommendations. 'Hopes were expressed that the Committee would "discover that regional planning, now so well established as an idea, can be brought into action to the general advantage of the country and the employment of labour"'.[125] But, unfortunately, this Committee suffered from the changing political situation and was only convened on five occasions.[126] With the fall of Labour, 'the potential of this initiative was blunted before it started', according to Hardy.[127] By 1936 there was, however, public as well as governmental agitation for regional planning and relocation of industries in an effort to address the 'differential plight of regions'.[128] With the worst of the depression over, in 1936 the Government compiled a list of places to be prioritised for the allocation of official contracts. Among the places that appeared on this list were: Glasgow, Dundee, Liverpool, and Portmadoc in North Wales.[129] While in London in 1932, for example, only about one worker in eight was unemployed, in 1937 one Scot in six and one Welsh person in four were out of work.[130] In Angus Calder's words, 'coal, steel, heavy engineering, shipbuilding, textiles had grown up together and were going down together as their export markets shrivelled. [Although] Clydeside, Tyneside, Lancashire, South Wales had made Britain "Great" ... The buoyancy had gone; the meanness of the houses, the arduousness of the conditions, and the defiled landscape endured'.[131]

Then, in October 1937, the Royal Commission on the Geographical Distribution of Industrial Population chaired by Sir Montague Barlow first sat.[132] Clement Attlee, in a speech the following March, called for a 'national organization to say where particular industries are to be located, where the land is to be kept free for residential development, and where there are to be parks and other open spaces'.[133] Attlee's proposal was supported by a number of Labour and Liberal politicians.[134] The need for the 'fundamental reorganization of Britain's economic and physical structure' was made completely clear by the advent of total war and the aerial bombing of essential and greatly populated urban centres.[135] Civil servants and politicians thus gained 'practical experience in the economic management of labour and physical resources' in the war – 'an encounter with a form of planning that was destined to leave an indelible mark upon post-war thinking and practice', according to Wayne Parsons, author of *The Political Economy of British Regional Policy* (1988).[136] Town planning and regional planning, as well as the redistribution of industry, were firmly established during the Second World War as important practical and political issues. By 1945, Hugh Dalton, acting as the President of the Board of Trade, was determined to do more for the depressed areas so, in spite of its Conservative majority, he pushed through the War Cabinet the Distribution of Industry Act of 1945. Under this act the pre-war 'special areas' (later called 'development areas') were extended from 8.5 per cent of the population to 13.5 per cent and tighter central-government control was imposed.[137]

Historian Peter Hennessy has argued that the first two years after the war, with Labour in power, were 'impressive' in this respect. For instance, he explains that 'the "development areas" contained some ten per cent of the country's population, but between 1945 and 1947 they received fifty per cent of new building investment. As a result of such targeting, and what had gone before in the war, unemployment in these localities fell from an average figure of twenty-two per cent in 1937 to single figures'.[138] Hugh Dalton regarded the Labour government's regional policies as one of its greatest achievements. In the notes to his 1946 Budget Speech, Dalton wrote: 'The battle for the Development Areas is not yet won, but we mean to win it. We mean to wipe out the evil heritage of mass unemployment in these areas, due to long years of political neglect and private enterprise ... I have told my colleagues that I will find, and find with a song in my heart, whatever money is necessary'. These words were underlined in red ink in his original notes.[139] By the autumn of 1948 [140] when the Government published its White Paper outlining its successes in lowering unemployment and redistributing industries to the depressed or 'special areas', Dalton proclaimed privately that: 'All this was victory indeed ... My dreams of twenty years ago ... were all coming true at last. Now at last mass unemployment was on the way out. Now I could rest content in deep joy'.[141] In the short term, at least, Dalton's joy was justified. And some of the Labour-leaning Festival planners must have wanted to highlight these achievements – to spread this joy, so to speak.[142] The redistribution of industry and the lessening of poverty in the depressed areas were Labour issues, as was regional planning. The Festival organisers were surely aware of this and the regional exhibitions, like the travelling ones, provided opportunities to both highlight the nation's industrial diversity and provide further regeneration across the UK.

The Festival of Britain in Wales

Unfortunately, we have only final reports of the meetings of the Welsh Committee of the Festival of Britain, but they do include the early meetings held at the end 1949 in Cardiff with the City Council acting as the Welsh Festival Committee.[143] These extant records tell us that the official, London-based Festival Committee, meeting in Cardiff on 6 December 1949, clearly stated their desire to see a 'national exhibition' held in that city in the summer of 1951.[144] We do not, however, have records of what occurred when the Lord Mayor convened the meeting to consider this suggestion, but the outcome was reported to the Welsh Committee of the Festival in March of 1950 by Leonard Crainford, who stated: 'Unfortunately, owing to unavoidable causes, the meeting was very thinly attended, and no indication was given during the proceedings that Cardiff was prepared to do anything to further the project of a National Exhibition'.[145] He continued by clarifying that 'he left the meeting with a feeling that no indication had been given that there would be response in respect of a national undertaking, he could assure the Committee, however, that Cardiff would put on a very good local programme, sponsored by themselves'.[146] What precisely transpired at that 'thinly attended' meeting, we may never know. But, for some reason, the City Council of Cardiff and whoever else was present, decided not to hold a 'national exhibition' in Wales. Was this some sort of protest against the Festival's politics or its London-centredness? We can only speculate. We do know, though, that, according to Parsons, the Welsh Labour group in the House of Commons pressed in the spring of 1949 for something to be done about the 'worsening unemployment problem in Wales and other regions', while also addressing 'the inadequacy of administrative machinery and the necessity of some kind of Regional Planning Authority for Wales'. And, 'the demands of the Welsh MPs, led by James Griffiths, for new structures of regional government and planning were consistently opposed and ignored by the leadership of the party'.[147] Such rifts might well explain Cardiff's refusal to hold an official, 'national' Welsh Festival celebration.

The ramifications of this decision meant that the Welsh contributions to the Festival were limited to the Pageant of Wales and the St Fagan's Folk Festival in Cardiff; the St David's music festival; the National Eisteddfod held in Llanrwst; the International Eisteddfod in Llangollen; an art and music festival in Swansea; the travelling exhibition of Welsh books; the Dolhendre Hillside Farming Scheme; and small local festivals.[148] Cardiff also received a visit from the Festival ship, *Campania*. *The Official Book of the Festival of Britain*, a souvenir catalogue of events, explained that 'unlike the National Eisteddfod', the International Eisteddfod was 'a young festival', for which 'choirs and dancers come from all parts of the world to compete in the various contests'.[149] During the Festival summer, Cardiff was the host to numerous musical and theatrical productions including a schools music festival, a combined Male Voice Choir, the Welsh National Opera, the National Orchestra of Wales, the Cardiff Shakespeare Players, and a Welsh Historical Pageant, 'telling the story of Wales throughout the ages'.[150] The Festival Headquarters in London provided almost £10,000 for the Pageant of Wales, and funded restoration work on several buildings belonging to the National Museum of Wales.[151] Representing other interests in Cardiff there was the Welsh Industries Fair, an Exhibition of the Rural Industries, a photographic exhibition, along with exhibitions of scientific and artistic interest, and sporting events including hockey, international soccer, seven-a-side rugger, the Cardiff Horse Jumping Show, national and international inter-varsity sports competitions, archery tournaments, swimming competitions, and cricket tournaments, all held in the name of the Festival of Britain in the summer of 1951.[152]

The Dolhendre (Merioneth) Hillside Farming Scheme

One of the only Welsh events fully funded by the British government was the Dolhendre Hillside Farming Scheme in North Wales. Listed as an 'other exhibition' in the Ministry of Works Report to Parliament and as a 'feature of the Festival' in the *Official Book of the Festival*, this contribution had more in common with the 'Live Architecture Exhibition' at Poplar than any other official Festival event. Like the Poplar exhibition, it created real housing for 'ordinary people', and illustrated new building techniques, offering no other thrills or surprises to the visitor.[153]

As discussed in Chapter 3, the Dolhendre scheme originated in a Government decision to renovate farms in Wales that had become Government property due to death duties.[154] Minutes taken in March 1950 at a Festival of Britain Welsh Committee meeting held in London announced that the Treasury had approved £10,000 to be spent on the 'Hillside (Dolhendre) Farm Scheme'.[155] They explain that 'the scheme covers the rehabilitation and modernisation of three hill farmsteads and of a cottage, and the erection of a group of four cottages which the Forestry Commission proposes to put up'.[156] One committee member expressed his belief that the project should be called the Dolhendre Farm Scheme because 'He felt that Dolhendre was a simple name which could easily be pronounced by Englishmen'.[157] It appears that the original idea for such a scheme's inclusion in the Welsh Festival of Britain celebrations was as part of a 'Welsh Exhibition of Rural Life'. *The Official Book of the Festival* informs the reader that 'this scheme presents the work done in recent years to improve the living and working conditions of hill farmers and small holders and to raise their level of production. Model farmsteads and outbuildings, new cottages, and improvements in road approaches are being shown together with a plan for co-ordinating forestry and agriculture.'[158]

The context for this seemingly strange contribution was the highly successful County War Agricultural Executive Committee (CWAEC), commonly called the 'War Ags'. The Ministry of Information claimed that the CWAEC was 'perhaps the most successful example of decentralization and the most democratic use of "control" this war has produced'.[159] CWAEC had been created in the First World War to help carry out government plans to cultivate two million extra acres of land in Britain.[160] Part of their efforts during the Second World War was the compilation of what was known as 'a modern Domesday book', chronicling every farm in England and Wales. In order for the CWAEC to do this, each farm was visited by a trained observer 'who noted (or should have noted), the types of soil, state of the buildings and cartroads, and so on'.[161] The farms were then rated on a scale of 'A' to 'C' and the few farms rated as 'C' (according to Calder, twelve out of twenty farms were rated as 'A') were generally offered help from committee members. But, in extreme cases the 'C' rating led to farmers being deprived of their land.[162] Each committee was made up of eight to ten men and one woman from the Women's Land Army, all appointed by the minister. Below them were district committees of four to seven local residents, who worked voluntarily. These were overwhelmingly farmers who were eager to advise others on how to improve their techniques.[163] Four hundred thousand acres in England and Wales were taken over by the Government in this way by the end of 1943. Calder explains that 'most cases of dispossession involved non-resident occupiers, parts of farms, or formerly non-agricultural land. Less than one-tenth of ten thousand cases recorded involved a farmer having to quit his house or a complete holding'.[164] Half of this land was rented to tenant farmers, while the other half was farmed by the War Ags themselves.[165]

The War Ags were well known and well praised by the MOI. It seems then that some of the Festival planners, many of whom had been in the Ministry of Information, as we have seen, felt that a scheme to improve and modernise farming in Wales would be a fitting contribution to the Festival of Britain, especially in light of the fact that no one in Cardiff took up their offer for that city to host an official Festival exhibition along the lines of Belfast's or Glasgow's.

Northern Ireland and the 'Ulster Farm and Factory Exhibition'

'The Festival was one for the United Kingdom of Great Britain and Northern Ireland; it was not the intention that it should be over-centralised in London and the Council expected Northern Ireland to play a part in the arrangements comparable to that of either Scotland or Wales', asserted Gerald Barry at a November 1948 meeting in Belfast of the Festival of Britain Committee for Northern Ireland.[166] The ultimate result of Barry's rousing speech was the Ulster Farm and Factory Exhibition, planned by the Northern Ireland Festival Committee, with the assistance of the Ministries of Agriculture and Commerce and the financial backing of the Government of Northern Ireland.[167] This arrangement differed from that of Scotland and Wales, where 'the executive responsibility for carrying out projects and proposals in these two countries [was] the responsibility of the main Festival of Britain organisation' (in London). In Belfast 'the executive responsibility' rested on the Northern Ireland Committee.[168]

Even so, the London planners felt it within their remit to instruct the Northern Irish committee to 'lay a magnifying glass upon an important section of the South Bank Exhibition and develop it in detail'.[169] 'This would be much more significant than an exhibition of a general character that embraced all the industries of Northern Ireland', according to the London committee.[170] And although the Northern Ireland Committee did not take up London's suggestion that the Ulster Festival focus on 'flax', they did decide to develop the theme of 'farm and factory'.[171]

During the war years, half of the population in Northern Ireland still worked at jobs directly or indirectly related to the land. And, although about one-fifth of Ulster workers were employed in the linen industry before the war, during the war the Germans occupied the Low Countries, thus severing Northern Ireland from its flax supply. This led to the expansion of ship and aircraft building in the country during the Second World War. Thus 'farm and factory' must have described the working environments of the vast majority of immediate post-war workers in the Six Counties of Northern Ireland.[172]

The Festival of Britain Committee for Northern Ireland was headed by the Rt Hon. Sir Roland Nugent,[173] whose foreword to the Ulster exhibition's guide-catalogue stressed that this was a unique event in Northern Ireland and that its goal was 'to demonstrate the craftsmanship and productive skills of Northern Ireland's factories and farms as aspects of the pattern of British industry and agriculture'.[174] Willy de Majo was the co-ordinating and chief designer and H. Lynch-Robinson was the architect for the farm buildings and the adviser to the Festival Committee.[175] The exhibition was held in a government industrial estate located at the foot of the Castlereagh Hills on the edge of Belfast. New factory premises there were specially adapted for the exhibition.[176] Inside the factory building there were narrative displays of industry and agriculture, while outside were the old and new farmsteads, set near each other for comparison.[177] The interior 'Industry' exhibition featured displays on rayon, cotton, poplin, shirtmaking, wool, shipbuilding, whiskey, mineral waters, tobacco, rope, machinery, packaging, aircraft, nylons, pottery, tabulating machinery,[178] and 'pioneers of Ulster Industry' or 'some of the men who laid the foundations of Ulster industry'.[179] The second large section, 'Agriculture', was divided into a historical subsection, telling 'what we were, what we did, and what we have become', along with exhibits of eggs and poultry, potatoes, milk, fruit, food processing, machinery, livestock, country life, and distribution.[180]

The exhibitions in the grounds featured a farm of 1851, in replica, with attention to period details, down to the farm implements. Juxtaposed to this was 'the farm of the future'.[181] Clearly, Ulster's agricultural and industrial capacities were at the centre of the story told in the Festival about Northern Ireland.

Mary Banham's 1976 interview with Willy De Majo, the co-ordinating and chief designer of the Ulster exhibition, reveals that that exhibition was very different from the one on the South Bank. For instance, there were labour disputes and at least one strike on the South Bank site. But De Majo stated in 1976 that:

> I brought over from London a selection of frankfurters, continental sausages and cheeses, rye bread and so on. I also had 'muzak' piped in; in those

days it was unusual for workers to be allowed to have that. And if anyone said, 'I'm tired and I want to go home,' I'd say, 'Come on, have something to eat, have a glass of beer, and off you go.' And I think that's why, unlike other Festival building sites, I had no strikes. That is probably why it was the only Festival exhibition which was ready to the last letter. And I was very proud of that.[182]

For the visitors it seems it was different from the South Bank in a similar way. The amenities were better, including the food (we must not forget that rationing still existed in 1951). De Majo told Mary Banham in the interview:

we were very lucky and people came and *really* enjoyed it. I organised a special caterer, I insisted on that kind of detail right round. If I had to be in charge I wanted to choose the cutlery, I wanted to select the dresses of the waitresses and all that, and, in fact, the menus too. But it was great fun, because people really came, as I'd hoped, to enjoy, to eat and to have a day out.[183]

Compare this to what one visitor recalled as her strongest memory of the South Bank exhibition. Twenty-five years after the Festival, Margaret Bean, remembered:

The slatternly waitress with a dirty dishcloth over her arm took our order, and an enormous helping was dumped on our plates. An order for wine caused consternation. 'Wine!' she said in horror and went away to confer with a higher authority, returning with news that nothing was available except British sherry or (I think) someone's Invalid Port. She was disappointed when we turned them down. Afterwards she wrote out the bill and stuck the pencil behind her ear, and we paid at the desk. The furnishings and tableware for this meal embodied a novel system of decorative pattern, derived from the diagrams made when scientists map the arrangement of atoms in crystals studied by X-ray methods. The occasion was luncheon at the Regatta Restaurant on the first day of the 1951 South Bank Exhibition. The odd contrast between the building, designed by a distinguished modern architect, and the elegant fittings, and the catering, let out to a north-country firm with old fashioned ideas, is one of my clearest memories.[184]

Perhaps it was de Majo's attention to detail that made the Ulster exhibition such a success, visited as it was by 156,760 people – twice as many as was originally estimated.[185]

Glasgow's 'Exhibition of Industrial Power'

Unfortunately, the Festival offering for Scotland planned in London was not as successful. The theme of the officially sponsored exhibition in

Glasgow was Scotland's industrial capacities, with heavy engineering its focus. The Festival's planners must have thought this appropriate since 20 per cent of the Strathclyde population worked in heavy industry in 1951 – a percentage equal to its 1871 figure.[186] A number of new industries had moved into the area due to the war, as well, including shell and explosive works, aircraft components factories, optical glass, and gun manufacturing.[187]

As explored in Chapter 3, 'The exhibition of Industrial Power at Kelvin Hall, Glasgow, was to demonstrate the harnessing of the sources of power on which all industry ultimately depends'.[188] Or as the 1976 twenty-fifth anniversary edition recounts: 'it was concerned not only with machines, but with the men who made them and the people who used them. It set out to show British inventiveness and the effect it had had on the world. Against this background was shown the outstanding products of British heavy engineering at the time of the exhibition'.[189]

Thus, Scotland's resources and capacities were illustrated as more than the important machinery manufactured in the region, but as the people involved in the production and use of the equipment as well. Distinct in its calls for Home Rule, which had been supported by the Labour Party for years but which became marginalised once Labour were in government, Scotland may have seemed especially important to represent as a unique yet essential chapter in the Festival's 'autobiography of the nation'.[190]

The Glasgow exhibition was planned by Mr Alistair Borthwick.[191] 'Like the other Festival exhibitions, this was a narrative exhibition and not a trade fair.'[192] The co-ordinating architect, Basil Spence, created an exhibition covering 100,000 square feet (9,300 square metres), laying out the subject matter in two parallel sequences: coal and water.[193] These sequences then led to 'a grand finale, a spectacular presentation of the power source of the future – atomic energy'.[194]

The visitor's journey through this narrative exhibition commenced with 'The Hall of Power', which was a large oval chamber, 60 feet (18.3 metres) long, 56 feet (17 metres) wide and 35 feet (10.7 metres) high. After the Hall of Power, the visitor explored the Hall of Coal, the Hall of Steel, Power for Industry, the Hall of Electricity, the Hall of Hydro-Electricity, the Hall of Civil Engineering, the Hall of Shipbuilding and Railways, and then, finally, came to the Hall of the Future, focusing on atomic energy, as discussed in Chapter 3.[195]

The surviving images of these halls show impressive murals and exhibits, the entrance exhibiting a symbolic sun created by a 'stroboscopic' flash contained in a perspex sphere opening on to the huge relief sculpture of 'God the Creator' by Thomas Whalen.[196] This sculpture was considered 'one of the many remarkable features' of the exhibition by the reporters who toured prior to its opening.[197] In addition, Whalen's sculpture was alleged to be 'the largest piece of sculpture executed in Scotland', measuring 105 feet (32 metres) from end to end.[198]

Yet, regardless of this fine piece, which would have looked at home in a hall of heroic workers in the contemporary Soviet Union, the London-based Festival of Britain planning committee felt that the attendance at the Glasgow exhibition was 'disappointing'. Its final report stated: 'Those best qualified to judge regarded it as an excellent exhibition – perhaps the best of all the Festival exhibitions. Yet in three months it attracted only a little over 280,000 people, about a third of the estimated figure.'[199] The report then outlined 'various explanations' for the disappointing turn-out. These included the speculation 'that the story of industrial power lacked feminine appeal, that admission prices were too high, that Glasgow saw sufficient of engineering products in its everyday life without wishing to see an exhibition on the subject alone'.[200] These conclusions are especially interesting to those of us currently attuned to gender concerns, as the discourses of this exhibition's official brochures were overtly masculinist. For instance, the description of the Hall of the Future states: 'Above is a shining cone rising from the floor, its tip pulsating and throwing off great crackling flashes of lightning to a night sky which curves above it in a twinkling hemisphere – the limitless future.'[201] The phallic nature of this description must not have evaded everyone and might just have alienated some of the women who did venture into the exhibition. But equally compelling is the speculation that Glaswegians 'saw sufficient of engineering products' in their daily lives. It makes one pause and question why the London-based planners did not consider such a possibility in advance. If in 1951 one-fifth of the population worked in heavy industry, why would they want to pay to see representations of this industry in their leisure time? It seems to indicate that the planners in the case of Glasgow were more concerned with their theme of unity through diversity than they were with putting on an entertaining exhibition for the people who lived and worked in this 'region' of Britain.

Conclusion

The Festival planners, predominately based in London, declared regional diversity and 'lack of uniformity' to be defining characteristics of the United Kingdom.[202] As such, they staged exhibitions in what they considered to be 'the regions' of Wales, Northern Ireland and Scotland, stressing their unique contributions to the national story, as well as to national survival. Overwhelmingly, the industrial and labour capacities of these places were the leitmotifs of these exhibitions' buildings, machinery and objects, as well as their more abstract portrayals in captions and catalogues. Clearly, this is only one of many possible ways the post-war British nation could have been imagined.

Emphasising the 'common wealth' of its various component areas and nations underscored the recovery and renewal of badly wounded yet victorious *Great* Britain. This imagining also opened up a space for an implicit message that the post-war Labour party was responsible for Britain's recovery, and that they were the party which would lead the British people into a better future. As we shall see, locally organised and executed versions of the Festival of Britain often featured similar stories of industrial strength and recovery told in somewhat different ways.

Notes

1 Bevis Hillier called the Festival organisers and architects 'ex-officers and gentlemen' in Hillier, 'Introduction', p. 14. Please see Chapter 2 for a further explanation and Appendix 1 for a complete listing of the members of these committees.

2 PRO, Work 25/44, Gerald Barry, 'Statement by Mr. Gerald Barry, Director-General, at the first Council Meeting on 31st May, 1948, Annex B', p. 3.

3 The Battersea Pleasure Gardens are the subject of Chapter 8.

4 Minister of Works to Parliament by Command of Her Majesty, *Festival of Britain 1951* (London: HMSO, July 1953), Cmd. 8872, p. 3.

5 Anonymous, 'Regions of Britain I: The Staffordshire Potteries', *Times Education Supplement*, 13 April 1951, p. 277.

6 Thomas Cook Travel Service, *Holidays in London, During the Festival of Britain, 1951, Travelling by Express Day Coach Service, arranged by Cook's World Travel Service, in association with Crosville Motor Services Ltd. Chester*, p. 7.

7 The South Bank was repeatedly referred to as the 'centrepiece' of the Festival. See for example, Cox, *The South Bank Exhibition*; the second quotation is from Sir Ernest Pooley, *Official Souvenir Programme London Season of the Arts 1951: May–June*, p. 4 (PRO, Work 25/232/E1/B2/6). In the *About Britain Guides*, produced in conjunction with the Festival, London was called 'the gateway to the world': R. S. R. Fitter, *Home Counties: A Portrait of London and the South-East*, vol. 3 of the *About Britain Guides*, 13 volumes, gen. ed. Geoffrey Grigson (London: Published for the Festival of Britain Office by Collins, 1951), p. 7.

8 Emphasis in the original. Festival advertising poster, 1951, as cited by Feaver, 'Festival Star', p. 52.

9 PRO, ED 142/4, Ministry of Education, 'Circular 231', 15 December 1950, Curzon Street, London, W1: pp. 3–4.

10 *Whitaker's Almanack*, 1945, p. 663, as quoted by Samuel, *Island Stories, Theatres of Memory, Vol. II*, p. 41. Even though the Empire/Commonwealth was generally downplayed in the Festival, as elaborated in Chapter 7, the official souvenir programme for the London Season of the Arts, referred to London as 'the capital of the Commonwealth and the Empire': Pooley, 'Introduction', p. 4, PRO, Work 25/232/E1/B2/6.

11 King George VI, Speech, May 1951, as quoted by Barry, 'The Festival of 1951'. See also Weight, 'Pale Stood Albion', p. 145.

12 *The Official Book of the Festival*, p. 64.

13 Hewison, *Culture and Consensus*, p. 63.

14 S. Daniels, *Fields of Vision: Landscape Imagery and National Identity in England and the United States* (Cambridge/Oxford: Polity Press, 1993), p. 34.

15 *Ibid.*

16 K. Thompson, in Bocock (ed.), *Modernity and Its Futures: Understanding Modern Societies, Book Four* (Cambridge: Polity Press, in association with Blackwell Publishers and the Open University Press, 1992), p. 343.

17 *The Official Book of the Festival*, p. 20.

18 Letter, Barry to Fisher, 13 February 1950, Fisher Papers, 85/51, Lambeth Palace Archive, as quoted by Weight, 'Pale Stood Albion', p. 145.

19 Archbishop of Canterbury, 30 September 1951, Home, Light and General Overseas Broadcast, reprinted in *The Listener*, 46:1179 (4 October 1951).

20 *The Official Book of the Festival*, p. 20.

21 *Ibid.*

22 Pooley, 'Introduction', p. 4.

23 *Ibid.*

24 Pooley, 'Introduction', p. 5.

25 *Ibid.*

26 *Ibid.* Emphasis in the original.

27 CEMA was a wartime, government-funded organisation.

28 Pooley, 'Introduction', p. 5.

29 Lord Reith, as quoted by McKibbin, *Classes and Cultures*, p. 460.

30 A. Sinclair, *Arts and Cultures: The History of 50 Years of the Arts Council of Great Britain* (London: Sinclair-Stevenson, 1995), p. 82.

31 E. Pooley, Chairman, *The Annual Report of the Arts Council*, as quoted by Sinclair, *Arts and Cultures*, p. 83.

32 PRO, Work 25/230/E1/A1/4, *1951 Exhibition of Architecture Poplar, Festival of Britain* (inside title page reads: *Guide to the Exhibition of Architecture, Town-planning and Building Research*, edited by H. McG. Dunnett) (London: HMSO, 1951), pp. 6–9.

33 *1951 Exhibition of Architecture Poplar, Festival of Britain*, p. 6.

34 Stedman Jones, 'The "cockney"', p. 315.

35 Stedman Jones, 'The "cockney"', p. 313. However, Stedman Jones points out that in actuality 'the reaction of the "cockney" to the Blitz was anything but cheerful. As Harold Nicolson noted in his diary on 17 September, "everybody is worried about the feeling in the East End ... There is much bitterness. It is said that even the King and Queen were booed the other day when they visited the destroyed areas".': p. 314.

36 *Ibid.*

37 On this see M. P. Fogarty, *Prospects of the Industrial Areas of Great Britain* (London: Methuen, 1945), pp. 351, 435.

38 Forty, 'Festival Politics', p. 34. Forty states that Morrison 'turned down the requests of some of the left-wing members of the Labour party for more attention to be drawn to the Government's achievements since 1945'. See Chapter 2 for my opinion of how genuine Morrison was when he made such statements.

39 G. Rose, 'Locality, Politics, and Culture: Poplar in the 1920s', *Environment and Planning D, Society and Space*, 6 (1988), 151–68, p. 164.

40 Rose, 'Locality, Politics', p. 156.

41 *1951 Exhibition of Architecture, Poplar, Festival of Britain*, p. 6.

42 On poverty in Poplar, see P. L. Garside, 'London and the Home Counties', in F. M. L. Thompson (ed.), *The Cambridge Social History of Britain, 1750–1950. Volume 1: Regions and Communities* (Cambridge: Cambridge University Press, 1990), 471–539, p. 538.

43 Rose, 'Locality, Politics', p. 153.

44 PRO, Work 25/44, G. Barry, 'Confidential, F. B. C. (48) 12, The Council of the Festival of Britain 1951 Site for the Live Architectural Exhibition. Memorandum from the Executive Committee', 18 September 1948, p. 2.

45 *Ibid.*

46 Adelman, *British Politics*, p. 75.

47 *The Official Book of the Festival*, p. 62.

48 PRO, CAB 124/1334, Gerald Barry, 'Confidential F. B. (48) 8, 5th April, 1948 Festival of Britain, 1951 Executive Committee Scope and Organisation of Exhibitions, Memorandum by the Director-General', 5 April 1948, p. 1.

49 Barry, 'Confidential F. B. (48) 8, 5th April, 1948 Festival of Britain', p. 2.

50 *Ibid.*

51 Barry, 'Statement by Mr. Gerald Barry, Director-General, at the First Council Meeting on 31st May, 1948', p. 5.

52 Emphasis added. Cox, 'The Story the Exhibition Tells', pp. 1–2.

53 Letter from Barry to Cox, 'Theme Paper – Part II', p. 1.

54 'Living in Cities', *Liverpool Council Social Services, Wartime Bulletin*, 70 (1 January 1942), 59–60.

55 J. Holland, 'Festival Ship Campania: Britain in Festive Guise', in Banham and Hillier (eds), *A Tonic*, p. 150.

56 T. Haggith, 'Citizenship, Nationhood and Empire in British Official Film Propaganda, 1939–45', in R. Weight and A. Beach (eds), *The Right to Belong: Citizenship and National Identity in Britain, 1930–1960* (London and New York: I. B. Tauris, 1998), 59–88, p. 74.

57 A. Croft, 'Betrayed Spring: The Labour Government and British Literary Culture', in Fyrth (ed.), *Labour's Promised Land?*, p. 199.

58 See PRO, EL1/6 '15th Meeting of the Council for the Encouragement of Music and the Arts Held at the Offices of the Board of Education at 5 p. m. on Wednesday, May 27th, 1942' and '13th Meeting of the Council for the Encouragement of Music and the Arts held at the Offices of the Board of Education at 2.30 p. m. on Tuesday 17th, February, 1942'; Croft, 'Betrayed Spring', p. 209 and N. M. Pearson, *The State and the Visual Arts: A Discussion of State Intervention in the Visual Arts in Britain 1760–1981* (Milton Keynes: Open University Press, 1982), 48–50.

59 Minihan, *The Nationalization of Culture: The Development of State Subsidies to the Arts in Great Britain* (New York: New York University Press, 1977), p. 183.

60 Pearson, *The State and the Visual Arts*, pp. 49–50.

61 Labour Party, *Labour Believes in Britain* (London: Labour Party, 1949), p. 3.

62 Please see Appendix 2 for a list of cities and towns arranged by population with a corresponding description of their centrally funded Festival events.

63 See for example: Calder, *The People's War*, pp. 202–27.

64 In the autumn of 1941, for example, when the national unemployment average was 1.5 per cent, Dundee reported 6 per cent: Calder, *The People's War*, p. 322. See also Fogarty, *Prospects of Industrial Areas of Great Britain*, p. 138.

65 W. Parsons, *The Political Economy of British Regional Policy* (London: Routledge, 1988), p. 89.

66 P. Reilly as quoted by Banham, 'The Style: "Flimsy … Effeminate"?', p. 194. But such attitudes did not go unchallenged. John Berger, for example, was critical of attempts to foist middle-class standards of taste on all British people: Banham discussing Berger's views in same, pp. 194–5.

67 R. Levin, Chief designer of the Land Travelling Exhibition, 'Land Travelling Exhibition', description written in 1951, as reprinted in Banham and Hillier (eds), *A Tonic*, p. 148.

68 *The Official Book of the Festival*, p. 63.

69 Levin, 'Land Travelling Exhibition', p. 148.

70 *Ibid.*

71 *Ibid.*

72 *Ibid.*

73 PRO, Work 25/230/E1/A1/7, *1951 Exhibition Birmingham, Leeds, Manchester and Nottingham*. See also: Ebong, 'Origins and Significance', p. 406 and Levin, 'Land Travelling Exhibition', pp. 148–9.

74 *The Official Book of the Festival*, p. 63.

75 *Ibid.*

76 For an accessible account of such developments, see J. E. Gordon, *The New Science of Strong Materials or Why You Don't Fall Through the Floor* (Harmondsworth: Penguin Books, 1976), especially pp. 154–206.

77 *The Official Book of the Festival*, p. 63.

78 *Ibid.*

79 *Ibid.*

80 *Ibid.*

81 *Ibid.*

82 *Ibid.*

83 Holland, 'Britain in Festive Guise', p. 151.

84 Holland, 'Britain in Festive Guise', p. 150.

85 Holland, 'Britain in Festive Guise', p. 151.

86 *The Official Book of the Festival*, p. 63.

87 'The Festival of Britain, 1951', p. 62.

88 *Ibid.*

89 *Ibid.*

90 *Ibid.*

91 The absent presence of the Empire/Commonwealth in the representations produced by the official exhibitions is the theme of Chapter 7.

92 *The Official Book of the Festival*, p. 62.

93 *Ibid.*

94 *Ibid.*

95 *Ibid.*

96 PRO, Work 25/44, 'Confidential FBC (49) 4. The Council of the Festival of Britain 1951. Tours of Britain' and attached 'Sketch Map'. Signed by Gerald Barry and dated 27 January 1949.

97 *Ibid.*

98 *Ibid.*

99 *Ibid.*

100 I. Cox, 'Three Years a-Growing: Recollections of the Festival Before the Turnstiles Opened', in Banham and Hillier (eds), *A Tonic*, p. 65.

101 *Ibid.*

102 PRO, Work 25/54, 'FBC N. Ireland (49) 6th Meeting, F of Britain Comm for Northern Ireland, Mins of the Seventh Meeting of the Comm for Northern Ireland held in the Conf Room, Law Courts Bldg, Belfast, on Thurs., 29th Sept, 1949 at 2.30 pm'; 'Committees for N. Ireland, Scotland and Wales'. At a meeting in Belfast held on 29 September 1949, the Committee for Northern Ireland discussed the 'Tours Panel', and the Chairman, Major the Right Honourable Sir Roland Nugent, 'informed the committee that he had been asked to nominate a Northern Ireland representative to a Tours Panel set up to advise on policy in regard to Festival Tours of Britain. He had approached Professor E. Estyn Evans'. Evans is the author of the Northern Ireland volume (no. 13) of the *About Britain* guide book, gen. ed. G. Grigson (London: Festival of Britain Office, Collins, 1951).

103 Cox, 'Three Years', p. 68.

104 Barry, 'Confidential FBC (49) 4', p. 3. PRO, Work 25/44, 'Confidential FBC (50) 8 The Council of the Festival of Britain 1951 Festival of Britain Guide Books Memorandum from the Director-General', signed by Gerald Barry, dated 3 March 1950. The latter document explains that the Brewers' Society had been 'considering production of a series of somewhat different character, independently', and that it had been agreed for the Society to fund a twelve-volume series (excluding Northern Ireland, but attempting to locate the funds for that volume from elsewhere) of guidebooks, 'produced under the full editorial control of the Festival Office free of all cost to the Festival'.

105 See, for example, Evans, *About Britain*, no 13 *Northern Ireland*.

106 *Ibid.*

107 *Ibid.*

108 Levin, 'Land Travelling Exhibition', p. 148.

109 D. Lowenthal, 'European and English Landscapes as National Symbols', in D. Hoosen (ed.), *Geography and National Identity* (Oxford: Blackwell, 1994), 15–38, p. 15.

110 Lowenthal, 'European and English Landscapes', p. 16.

111 Anonymous, 'Regions of Britain I: The Staffordshire Potteries', p. 277.

112 See, for example, PRO, EL6/23, 'Festival of Britain: Purpose and Approach to Theme', August 1948, pp. 2–3.

113 PRO, Work 25/47, 'FB PRESENTATION PANEL (48) 4th Meeting, Festival of Britain 1951 Presentation Panel, Minutes of a meeting of the Presentation Panel held at Shepherd's House, the Sands, near Farnham, on Tuesday 14th September, Wednesday 15th September and Thursday 16th September, 1948', p. 1.

114 *Ibid.* Emphasis mine.

115 *The Official Book of the Festival*, p. 9.

116 Cox, 'The Story the Exhibition Tells', pp. 1–2 (emphasis mine).

117 According to Brian Aldiss, 'under the Bovril advert in Piccadilly Circus there was at that time a dramatic sign which read "Export or Die"': Aldiss, 'A Monument to the Future', p. 177.

118 Scotland's exhibition of 'industrial power' in the early versions was called a 'heavy engineering exhibition'. Northern Ireland's was originally to be an exhibition of 'Flax'. PRO, Work 25/21, 'Letter dated 11th April, 1949 from the Industrial Division Copy to Mr. Ian Cox, Letter to H. A. Howard, Esq. Ministry of Commerce, Directorate of Scientific Development, 20 College Gardens, Belfast from M. Hartland Thomas, Chief Industrial Officer'. On page 2 of that letter, Hartland Thomas states: 'The obvious subject is, of course, Flax'.

119 D. Hardy, 'Regionalism in Interwar Britain: The Role of the Town and Country Planning Association', in P. Garside and M. Hebbert (eds), *British Regionalism 1900–2000* (London and New York: Mansell, 1989), 77–97, p. 77.

120 Historians of regional planning, such as Urlan A. Wannop, have stressed that the Conservatives were uninterested in regional planning between 1948 and 1962: U. A. Wannop, *The Regional Imperative: Regional Planning and Governance in Britain, Europe and the United States* (London: Jessica Kingsley, 1995), pp. 8–9. For a sense of the historiography of regional planning, see P. Garside and M. Hebbert, 'Introduction', in Garside and Hebbert (eds), *British Regionalism*, 1–19, and Parsons, *The Political Economy of British Regional Policy*. See also: J. B. Collingworth and V. Wadin, *Town and Country Planning in the United Kingdom* (London: Routledge, 1997); R. J. Bennett, 'Regional Movements in Britain: A Review of Aims and Status', *Government and Policy*, 3 (1985), 75–96; M. Keating, 'The Debate on Regional Reform', in B. W. Hogwood and M. Keating (eds), *Regional Government in England* (Oxford: Clarendon Press, 1982), 235–54; B. Smith, *Regionalism in England, Regional Institutions – A Guide* (London: Acton Society Trust, 1964) and his *Regionalism in England 2: Its Nature and Purpose 1905–1965* (London: Acton Society Trust, 1965); G. E. Cherry, *Cities and Plans* (London: Edward Arnold, 1988), 'Interwar Regional Planning Schemes in Britain', *Planning History Bulletin*, 2 (1980), 14–16, and G. E. Cherry (ed.), *Pioneers in British Planning* (London: Architectural Press, 1981); M. Hebbert, 'The Daring Experiment: Social Scientists and Land-use Planning in 1940s Britain', *Environment and Planning B: Planning and Design*, 10 (1983), 3–17; H. W. E. Davies, 'Regional Science and Planning in Britain', *Journal of the Town Planning Institute*, 48:10 (1962), 315–16; F. B. Gillie, *Basic Thinking in Regional Planning* (London: Mouton, 1967); E. C. Willatts, 'Geographers and their Involvement in Planning', in

R. W. Steel (ed.), *British Geography 1918–1945* (Cambridge: Cambridge University Press, 1987); J. Banks, *Federal Britain? The Case for Regionalism* (London: Harrap, 1971); and P. Garside, 'The Failure of Regionalism in 1940s Britain: A Re-examination of Regional Plans, the Regional Idea and the Structure of Government', in Garside and Hebbert (eds), *British Regionalism*, 98–114. For some of the important early texts, other than Abercrombie's well-known plans, see: Association for Planning and Regional Reconstruction, *The Delimitations of Regions for Planning Purposes: The Concept of a Functional Region* (broadsheet, 1942, reprinted 1943) and their *Regional Boundaries of England and Wales: An Examination of Existing and Suggested Boundaries* (broadsheet 1943, reprinted 1946) and W. Isard, 'Regional Science: the Concept of Region and Regional Structure', *Papers and Proceedings of the Regional Science Association*, 2 (1956), 1–11.

121 Hardy, 'Regionalism in Interwar Britain', p. 79.

122 'Chamberlain Committee'(1920, 1921), *Principles to be followed in dealing with Unhealthy Areas* (London: Ministry of Health), as quoted by Hardy, 'Regionalism', p. 79.

123 Hardy, 'Regionalism', p. 80.

124 Hardy, 'Regionalism', p. 81. Hardy cites G. D. H. Cole, *The Future of Local Government* (London: Cassell, 1921).

125 *Garden Cities and Town Planning*, 21:2 (February 1931), p. 27, as quoted by Hardy, 'Regionalism', p. 85.

126 Hardy, 'Regionalism', p. 85.

127 Hardy, 'Regionalism', p. 86.

128 Hardy, 'Regionalism', p. 88. Interestingly, the term 'place' entered the discourse on the issue of regional planning and relocation of industries. 'In the middle of what was a contentious debate, the issue of the "depressed areas" emerged to a new level of political saliency in the columns of *The Times*. Three articles entitled 'Places Without a Future' (March 1934) drew attention to the plight of a typical Durham mining village … *The Times*' editorial was to introduce into political debate for the first time the notion that there was a distinct and separate problem in the existence of the "depressed" or, as it chose to call them, "derelict" areas; a problem which required the introduction of special measure of central intervention in the economy for the direct benefit of hard struck areas': Parsons, *The Political Economy of British Regional Policy*, 10–11.

129 Calder, *The People's War*, p. 27.

130 *Ibid.*

131 *Ibid.*

132 Hardy, 'Regionalism', p. 89.

133 Clement Attlee, from a symposium of views, in *Town and Country Planning*, 6:23 (March 1938), pp. 25–30, as quoted by Hardy, 'Regionalism', p. 89.

134 Hardy, 'Regionalism', p. 89.

135 Garside, 'The Failure of Regionalism in 1940s Britain', p. 98.

136 Parsons, *The Political Economy*, p. 49.

137 Hennessy, *Never Again*, p. 210.

138 Hennessy, *Never Again*, p. 211.

139 Hugh Dalton, as quoted by Parsons, *The Political Economy*, p. 99.

140 By this time Sir Stafford Cripps had replaced Dalton at the Board of Trade, but it is Hennessy's opinion that Cripps 'inherited a tried and tested system': Hennessy, *Never Again*, p. 211.

141 H. Dalton, *High Tide and After, Memoirs 1945–60* (Frederick Muller, 1962), pp. 310–11. See also Hennessy, *Never Again*, p. 211.

142 Wayne Parsons repeatedly stresses the great distance between particular commissions' recommendations and socialist plans for intervention into planning industry versus the actual policies implemented by the Coalition and Labour governments. He is very critical, as is apparent in the title of his Chapter 4: 'Administering Capitalism: The Labour Governments 1945–51'. I, on the other hand, am less interested in assessing the radicalism or the failures of Labour on this front than I am in ascertaining the context for the decisions taken as to where the Festival exhibitions would visit and how Britain would be represented in the official Festival events. Therefore, what someone like Dalton *thought* he had achieved seems just as relevant as what later appraisals might say he did or did not accomplish.

143 For a complete list of the members of the Welsh Committee of the Festival of Britain, please see Appendix 1.

144 PRO, Work 25/54, 'FBC (49) 4th Meeting, Festival of Britain 1951 Welsh Committee Minutes of a meeting of the Welsh Comm held at City Hall, Cardiff, on 6 December, 1949 at 10.30 am'.

145 PRO, Work 25/54, 'FBC Welsh (50) 1st meeting Festival of Britain 1951 Welsh Committee Minutes of a meeting of the Welsh Committee held at 2 Savoy Ct WC2, on March 3rd at 10.30 am'. The local newspapers and the Festival of Britain papers in the National Library of Wales in Aberystwyth did not shed any further light on the situation.

146 *Ibid.*

147 Parsons, *The Political Economy*, pp. 86, 94.

148 *The Official Book of the Festival*, pp. 54–5, 27–8, 45, 52, 60 and 61, and *South Bank Exhibition*, p. 95.

149 'The International Eisteddfod', *The Official Book of the Festival*, p. 52.

150 'The Festival in Cardiff', *The Official Book of the Festival*, p. 28.

151 Minister of Works to Parliament, *Festival of Britain 1951*, pp. 7, 6.

152 See Welsh Festival of Britain files in PRO, Work 25/54, as well as Ebong, 'The Origins', p. 448.

153 Minister of Works to Parliament, *Festival of Britain 1951*, p. 7; *The Official Book of the Festival*, p. 61; BBC Written Archives, Caversham, HOLT 214.

154 BBC Written Archives, Caversham, HOLT, 214.

155 PRO, Work 25/54, 'Committee Minutes of Northern Ireland, Scotland and Wales': blue folder containing 'Welsh Committee Proceedings and Papers 1948–1949 and 1951' (this is an error: it states the 1950 minutes are missing, but they are contained herein as well). 'FBC Welsh (50) 1st Meeting of Festival of Britain 1951 Welsh Committee Minutes'. Hillside (Dolhendre) Farm Scheme.

156 *Ibid.*

157 *Ibid.* This statement reveals that the imagined centre of the nation clearly resided in England. This is not surprising in 1951, of course. *Whitaker's Almanack*, for

example, lists 'the Principality of Wales and Monmouthshire'. It was also agreed that £10,000 be retained as a contingency against any damages which might emerge before 1951. 'FBC (49) 4th Meeting, Minutes of a Meeting of Welsh Committee'.

158 *The Official Book of the Festival*, p. 61. Williams and Boyns' 1977 article, 'Occupations in Wales, 1851–1971', states that the proportion of the working population engaging in agriculture was 8.2 per cent in 1951, which was considerably higher than the UK average. So, although it was not a particularly creative imagining, representing Wales as rural was not inappropriate: L. J. Williams and T. Boyns, 'Occupations in Wales, 1871–1951', *Bulletin of Economic Research*, 29 (1977).

159 Ministry of Information, *Land at War*, p. 12, as quoted by Calder, *The People's War*, p. 427.

160 Calder, *The People's War*, p. 420.

161 Calder, *The People's War*, p. 426.

162 *Ibid.*

163 Calder, *The People's War*, pp. 425–6.

164 Calder, *The People's War*, pp. 426–7.

165 Calder, *The People's War*, p. 427.

166 PRO, Work 25/54/A5/I–1, 'Minutes recording a speech by Gerald Barry', 'Confidential FBCN Ireland (48) 1st meeting Festival of Britain 1951 Committee for Northern Ireland Minutes of the First Meeting of the Committee for Northern Ireland held at the City Hall, Belfast, on Tuesday, 23rd November, 1948 at 2.30 pm', p. 2.

167 PRO, Work 25/3, 'Final Report, The Festival of Britain in Northern Ireland', January 1952; *1951 Exhibition Ulster Farm and Factory*; and 'The Festival of Britain in Northern Ireland', *Architect's Journal*, 114 (26 July 1951), p. 110. See also, PRO, Work 25/44, 'Minutes of the 13th Meeting of the Council of the FoB 1951, held at 2, Savoy Court, WC2, on Thurs. May 4, 1951 at 10.30 am', 'Northern Ireland Committee – Final Recommendations FB. C. (50) 14'. For a list of the complete membership of the Northern Ireland Committee of the Festival of Britain, please see Appendix 1.

168 PRO, Work 25/54/A5/I–1, 'FBC N. Ireland (49) 4th meeting, Festival of Britain, 1951, Committee for Northern Ireland, Minutes of the Fifth Meeting of the Committee for Northern Ireland, Held in the Conf Room, Law Courts Bldgs, Belfast on Thurs., 19th of May, 1949, at 2.30 pm', p. 3.

169 Hartland Thomas, 'Letter dated 11th April, 1949 from the Industrial Division Copy to Mr. Ian Cox, Letter to H. A. Howard'.

170 *Ibid.*

171 *Ibid.*

172 Calder, *The People's War*, p. 414.

173 *Story of the Festival of Britain, 1951* and *The Official Book of the Festival*, p. 72. For a complete list of the membership of the Northern Ireland Festival of Britain Committee, please see Appendix 1.

174 Anonymous, 'Ulster Farm and Factory Exhibition, Belfast', in Banham and Hillier (eds), *A Tonic*, p. 155.

175 Willy de Majo, 'The Professionals v. the Amateurs', interview by M. Banham, in Banham and Hillier (eds), *A Tonic*, pp. 156–8.

176 *Ibid.* See also Ebong, 'The Origins', p. 441. In the foreword to the guide-catalogue, Sir Roland Nugent states that 'the main building itself, a new factory on an industrial estate, is symbolical of future developments': PRO, Work 25/230/E1/A1/8, Foreword by Sir Roland Nugent, Chairman of the Festival of Britain Committee for Northern Ireland in *1951 Exhibition Ulster Farm and Factory* (London: HMSO, 1951), p. 5.

177 Anonymous, 'Ulster Farm and Factory Exhibition, Belfast', p. 155.

178 PRO, Work 25/230/E1/A1/8, J. D. Stewart, 'Ulster Farm and Factory: A Guide to the story it tells', in *1951 Exhibition Ulster Farm and Factory*, pp. 8–29.

179 Stewart, 'Ulster Farm and Factory', p. 17.

180 Stewart, 'Ulster Farm and Factory', pp. 19, 21–8.

181 Please see Chapter 3 on the Festival's representations of the future for a discussion of this.

182 De Majo, 'The Professionals v. the Amateurs', p. 158.

183 De Majo, 'The Professionals v. the Amateurs', p. 157.

184 M. Bean, 'Almost Surreal Confusion', in 'Visitors and Abstainers', Banham and Hillier (eds), *A Tonic*, p. 183.

185 'Final Report, The Festival of Britain in Northern Ireland'.

186 T. C. Smout, 'Scotland, 1850–1950', in Thompson (ed.), *The Cambridge Social History of Britain, 1750–1950. Volume 1: Regions and Communities* (Cambridge: Cambridge University Press, 1990), 209–80, p. 214, Table 3.3. Incidentally, this table reveals that the nearby region constituted by central Scotland and Fife had 26 per cent of its population engaged in heavy industry in 1951. See also, Fogarty, *Prospects of the Industrial Areas of Great Britain*.

187 Fogarty, *Prospects of the Industrial Areas of Great Britain*, pp. 158–9.

188 'Industrial Power at Glasgow', in *The Story of the Festival of Britain, 1951*, p. 10

189 Anonymous, 'Exhibition of Industrial Power, Glasgow', pp. 152–4.

190 On Scottish nationalism and the Labour Party, see, for example, K. Alexander, 'Lessons from Scotland', in Fyrth (ed.), *Labour's High Noon*, 195–213, and M. Keating and D. Bleiman, *Labour and Scottish Nationalism* (London: Macmillan, 1979). See also: D. Young, 'Scotland: Time for Decision', *Tribune*, 5 May 1950, p. 11.

191 *The Story of the Festival of Britain, 1951*, p. 27. For a complete list of the members of the Scottish Festival of Britain Committee, please see Appendix 1.

192 *Ibid.*

193 *Ibid.*

194 *Ibid.* Please see Chapter 3 on the 'future' for a discussion of 'The Hall of the Future' and perceptions of the role to be played by atomic energy in Britain's future.

195 Anonymous, 'Exhibition of Industrial Power, Glasgow', p. 152.

196 *Ibid.*

197 PRO, Work 25/230, Anonymous, 'Glasgow's Hall of Power', *Glasgow Herald*, Tuesday, 1 May 1951, p. 3, column b. See also Ebong, 'The Origins', p. 425; *The Official Book of the Festival*, pp. 22–4; and 'Festival Exhibitions Review', *Architectural Review*, 110 (August 1951), 194–5.

198 *Ibid.*

199 *The Story of the Festival of Britain*, p. 27.

200 *Ibid.*

201 'Hall of the Future', from the guide-catalogue: Anonymous, 'Exhibition of Industrial Power Glasgow, Festival of Britain, 1951', p. 154.

202 Anonymous, 'Regions of Britain I: The Staffordshire Potteries', p. 277.

6 ✧ The role of 'the local' in the Festival

Metropolitan discussions of the role of 'the local' in the Festival

ON 8 JUNE 1949, Gerald Barry, Lord Ismay and the Lord Mayor of London convened the first meeting of civic heads since 1916. Inviting the mayors and chairmen of all local authorities in England and Wales to the Guildhall, the order of business was to explain 'the objects of the Festival and the part which local authorities could play'.[1] Similar meetings were arranged in Wales and Northern Ireland and further plans were made for involving local authorities in Scotland. In the Guildhall, Barry proceeded to tell those assembled that the participation of their communities was fundamental to the success of the 1951 Festival of Britain. He explained that this could mean anything from 'the removal of an eyesore to the ... planting of trees, the cleaning of public buildings' or just the completion of public works already begun.[2] As the words of *The Story of the Festival of Britain* made clear, 'This local activity would provide an opportunity not only for ephemeral celebrations but also for permanent improvement of the amenities of the neighbourhood'.[3] The Festival representatives stressed that although there would be no government funding available, it was essential that 'the Festival should not be confined to London but should cover as much of the country as possible'.[4] From its inception the Festival had been imagined as a 'national event' celebrating the British people and their 'industries, trades, crafts ... local traditions and entertainments, their practice and appreciation of the arts, their sports and hobbies'.[5] In 1951 the Festival was to be 'an act of national autobiography' and the people of every town and village with their 'local events' and the 'spontaneous expression of their life and interest' were encouraged to meet the 'challenge' and 'to write the year into their memories'.[6] Of course, Barry and his team were making a virtue of necessity; there were no funds budgeted for local events. One official brochure explained that:

It is hoped that every town and village will share in the Festival by contributing its own independent festivities in ways most suited to itself. The Festival organisation does not intend to try to plan such local celebrations in any way; it firmly believes that British communities can be left to devise their own means of enjoying themselves, either singly or in collaboration one with another.[7]

For the Festival of Britain to be what the planners envisaged the entire nation needed to participate. The BBC had been willingly enlisted in the task of helping 'to create a sense of community' 'throughout the United Kingdom' through its broadcasts of the Festival's main events, along with its own special programming.[8] However, local initiative was key. According to an early planning document, Festival preparations were to be announced to the nation by 'a Royal' who should stress 'that the Government has given a lead, the central features are already being planned, but the Festival stands or falls on the enthusiasm of the people to show their neighbours and the world that we are *still* a creative people, that we have every reason to be proud of our country.'[9]

This sense of the centrality of the local festivities to the success of the Festival, as well as the insinuation that provincial civic pride and participation were not really what some London leaders felt they should be, was echoed in an article written by Barry in the autumn of 1949. In this article for a local arts newsletter, he asserted that:

> the motives that inspire the Festival … can only be fully translated into action if the whole country takes part. We have a right to some pride in our past, but equally we have a duty to the future – to quicken the sense of civic pride and of responsibility to succeeding generations (*a sense which is less vigorous today than it should be*), and to equip ourselves to solve successfully the many problems of readjustment occasioned by *our changing position in the world*.
>
> It is hoped that the Festival of Britain, by providing an outlet for creativeness after years of austerity and frustration, and by stimulating the people to fresh endeavour, will make some modest contribution to the life of the nation.[10]

As we have seen, Britain was a country attempting reconstruction and recovery after world war and austerity; thus it was necessary for people everywhere to participate and illustrate their 'pride in our past', 'duty to our future', as well as 'civic pride' and 'responsibility'. Such phrases would have been very familiar to people; it was the language of the 'people's war'. The nation depended on everyone to make a contribution, however 'modest'. The Festival was offering people across the British Isles the opportunity to help to reconstruct Britain. Additionally, the people could assist in Britain's 'readjustment' to the new post-war world in which Britain was less central than it once had been. As we will see, 'the people' responded enthusiastically, organising reconstruction projects, historical pageants, religious choral concerts, sporting events, and other celebrations. And in the local celebrations we find stories and genealogies similar to those presented in the official Festival events, such as the stress on a long past, the bright future, and production. However, there were also places which used such recognisable stories to tell different tales. This was especially true in the few places, predominately in the 'Celtic fringe', where communities participated in the Festival of Britain while emphasising how different they were from the rest of Britain.

Before we turn to the efforts organised by an array of local communities in the name of the Festival, it is important to look at how the central Festival organisers in London saw such events and their role in the overall the plan.

Metropolitan assumptions and anxieties about the cultures and traditions of the 'provinces'

Barry's language in the 1949 local arts newspaper article reveals that, among other concerns, some of the Festival planners felt a sense of malaise about the local festivals. Barry was worried that local, civic pride and energy were lagging and that the Festival celebrations outside of London and 'the regions' would simply not occur. For him the threat to local identities was internal; the towns, cities and villages might not respond his to call for rejuvenation and celebration. As we saw in chapter 5, for Ian Cox, Director of Science and organiser of the travelling exhibitions, the threat was quite the opposite. Cox worried that the local celebrations might portray Britishness in a way that diverged from the story told on the South Bank.[11]

For Jacquetta Hawkes, the 'theme convener' for the South Bank's 'The People of Britain' 'circuit', the source of the threat to local cultures was internally located, as it was for Barry. But, it did not originate in 'the people' themselves. According to her Pelican paperback, published in the Festival year, it was not her 'intention' 'to pass judgements', and thus, she explained that her assertions were 'simply ... murmurings representative of a consciousness subjected to the conditions of the year A. D. 1949'.[12] What followed, though, was a polemic strikingly at odds with the rest of her text. These 'murmurings' of Hawkes focused on her serious concern over what she perceived as the loss of local cultures in Britain. She claimed that in post-war Britain 'intellectual control' originated 'from a distant centre' and imposed 'plans alien to the local community'.[13] Hawkes blamed this state of affairs not on the post-war government, but on the Industrial Revolution that had left Britain with:

an urban culture which is highly complex, yet not creatively embodied in the people themselves. Everything is supplied for them from outside, whether by the State, the merchant or the purveyor of entertainment. The individual, especially the man, does not possess culture, cannot express it, but merely receives a doubtful mixture in a spoon, paid for from his purse.[14]

The local cultures and traditions that seemed potentially troubling to Cox were, according to Hawkes, already lost. For Hawkes, 'the poetry of a people delicately adjusted to varied surroundings, finding their new but always fitting responses, must blur into a grey uniformity'.[15] In her book Hawkes was calling for a revival of local culture to stem the tide of standardisation and encourage people to once again 'live in some direct and creative relationship with the land from which they have come'.[16] In Hawkes' imagining the problem with local cultures was not rooted in the immediate post-war moment, as it was for Barry, but rather it stemmed from a much longer history, harking back almost 200 years, to the Industrial Revolution and the urbanisation of Britain.

Wider discussions of the imaginings of the role of the 'local' or 'provincial'

Interestingly, however, Hawkes' call for an end to standardisation and a renewal of local customs, arts and celebrations was not based on that familiar fear, evoked repeatedly at least since the inter-war period – the fear of Americanisation – yet that concern must surely have haunted some of the Festival planners. Discourses on the importance of 'authentic', often 'provincial', representations of Britishness and Englishness (whether British or English varied in different renditions) especially in combating the detrimental effects of popular (commercialised/garish/contaminating/in-authentic) American culture, were widely circulated in the 1930s, 1940s and 1950s. As Andrew Higson has written of mid-1930s British cinema: 'Britain's late and post-imperialist crisis over national identity ... [was] worked out ... in terms of "the potential danger of the Americanization of the world", or the fear of losing an organic national identity and authentic cultural values to standardized mass culture.'[17] At other times anti-Americanism was combined with anti-metropolitanism. For example, in much of *The Uses of Literacy*, written in the early to mid-1950s, Richard Hoggart bemoaned the disappearance of what he considered the signposts of indigenous working-class culture, such as pub-going and pigeon fancying. He worried that such 'authentic' pursuits had been replaced by lurid 'American'-style sex and violence novels and milk bars with their 'nastiness of ... modernistic knick-knacks' and 'their glaring showiness'.[18]

Similar views on the authenticity of local British culture, as opposed to the corrupting nature of Americanisation, were expressed by John Maynard Keynes in his July 1945 speech aired on the BBC's Third Programme. Acting as chair of the newly formed Arts Council, Keynes mused:

> How satisfactory it would be if different parts of the country would again walk their several ways as they once did and learn to develop something different from their neighbours and characteristic of themselves. Nothing can be more damaging than the excessive prestige of metropolitan standards and fashions. Let every part of Merry England be merry in its own way. Death to Hollywood! [19]

Geoff Eley has rightly pointed out that such a statement from Keynes was disingenuous; 'it's hard to imagine anyone more of a metropolitan intellectual than Keynes'.[20] Nevertheless, it is true that, from its inception, the Arts Council emphasised that it intended to bolster local arts. Keynes explained in the same speech that the Arts Council was 'greatly concerned to decentralise and disperse the dramatic and musical and artistic life of the country, to build up provincial centres and to promote corporate life in these matters in every town and country'. He stressed that the Council aimed to 'collaborate with local authorities and to encourage local institutions and societies and local enterprise to take the lead'. 'We look forward to the time when the theatre and the concert-hall and the gallery will be a living element in everyone's upbringing', Keynes announced.[21]

It is ironic, however, that by the time the Festival opened in 1951 the Arts Council was no longer committed to decentralisation, having actually consolidated most of its energies and funds on London productions and performances. In its 1951 report the Arts Council took the first step towards its later 1950s policy of funding 'few but roses' in its assertion that it was shifting its priorities from 'spreading' cultural production and participation to '"raising" artistic standards'.[22]

Nevertheless, the London-based Festival planners did work within the Arts Council's original remit, encouraging local festivities, co-sponsoring at least twenty-two arts festivals, and organising regional and travelling versions of the official Festival of Britain. The planners' conceptions of 'the local' were similar to those expressed in the special reconstruction issue of the *Architectural Review* (1941).[23] The editorial in that issue stressed that 'each locality will naturally express itself in its own way and in relation to its traditional background. It is reasonable and natural that people should want the places they are familiar with to retain their distinctive character'.[24] What guided the Festival planners' resolution to encourage local participation seems to have been a very mixed sense of what local cultures and traditions meant and what they would offer by way of chapters to the Festival's 'autobiography of the nation'. Further reasons for their decision to stress the essential nature of Britain as 'united, yet diverse' through local events may lie in wider Labour agendas for the renewal of local government involvement in the everyday lives of British citizens.[25]

'The local' as part of a larger Labour plan

At the opening of the South Bank exhibition in May of 1951, the President of the Festival, Herbert Morrison, proclaimed 'I want everyone in Britain to see it, to take part in it, to enjoy it. I want to see the people happy. I want to hear the people sing.'[26] Yet this was more than Morrison's personal desire: Labour Party policies and legislation reflected its efforts to 'promote and co-ordinate the cultural activities of local authorities'.[27] The Town and Country Planning Act of 1947 required government approval of councils' plans for recreation in their communities and the Local Government Act of the following year encouraged, among other things, local authorities to provide entertainment for their citizens.[28] Aneurin Bevan had pushed that part of the Act through the Commons hoping it would lead to more support for local artists and arts. But many party members felt that 'Democracy, to be virile, must be local democracy'.[29] Their belief that daily contact with the activities of the local authority 'is the embryo of the new democratic technique which will make the citizen conscious of the vital part, the living part he has to play as a citizen in a real democracy' provided one of the primary motives for the Local Government Act.[30] Finally, such a version of decentralisation in the provision of arts and leisure also helped Labour to stress that their vision of social democracy was not statist in the way that Russia's was. Local government and voluntary association were British traditions to be held on to and celebrated.

'The local' as an ancient British tradition

However, an emphasis on the importance of the locality was no monopoly of the left. Winston Churchill wrote in the preface to his *A History of the English-Speaking Peoples Volume I, The Birth of Britain*, published in 1956, but begun twenty years earlier: 'Parliament, trial by jury, local government by local citizens, and even the beginnings of a free Press, may be discerned, at any rate in a primitive form, by the time Christopher Columbus set sail for the American continent'.[31] Like Churchill, the Festival's organisers considered local government and local participation as key items on the long list of British traditions and achievements that were worthy of celebrating in 1951. For example, *The Official Book of the Festival of Britain*, a souvenir guide, concludes:

> Throughout the country, in great cities and the smallest of our villages, men and women have been meeting during the past year or two to plan

this Festival. They have considered what is most worthy to be remembered and celebrated in our local and national history … This country was among the first to recognise and protect the freedom of individual towns, and the form which the Festival of Britain has taken is a further proof that only through remembering this ancient principle have we been able to present in 1951 the Autobiography of our Nation.[32]

The individualism and 'freedom' of towns were evoked as ancient British rights, but this was also used to explain why it was imperative for every village, town and city across the UK to do something – however 'modest' – to mark 1951 as a special year. The local Festival of Britain celebrations were left alone to represent 'their distinctive character[s]'.[33] The result was a bewildering profusion of 'tidying up schemes', as well as more elaborate exhibitions, events, pageants and weeks.

Representing 'the local' from the places themselves

Despite the anxieties of the London organisers and the lack of financial support, Barry's exhortations were heeded.[34] According to one official brochure, 'the response to the appeal to the country was so enormous that a separate branch of the Festival organisation had to be created to deal with events throughout the country and the enquiries that flowed in by every post'.[35] Twenty-five years after the Festival, Antony Hippisley Coxe, a key member of its planning committee, reminisced in the anniversary volume, *A Tonic to the Nation*. There he explained that:

> The key to the real meaning of the Festival is in a green-covered booklet of some 160 pages listing the 'Events and Activities arranged by Local Authorities and Local Festival Committees throughout the United Kingdom.' Here you will find lavish, but ephemeral historical pageants; and simpler but more lasting projects such as re-gilding the face of the church clock. Some are strictly utilitarian – 'New Sewage Scheme'; some are just for fun – 'Bonfire and Fireworks'. Then there are those jobs which until then nobody had got round to doing, for example 'Tidy up bomb site' (as if the mess was due to the children leaving their toys lying about.) Re-reading the list I was pleasantly surprised at the number of places which celebrated 1951 by planting trees.
>
> That is what the Festival was really all about. It gave the people a goal and a deadline. For too long we had been saying 'Britain can take it'. That had been proved. Now we had to bestir ourselves and hold our heads high.[36]

So, for Hippisley Coxe, as well as Barry, the locally planned and executed Festival celebrations were what 'the Festival was really all about'.

Barry had stressed at the meeting of civic heads in 1948 that 'the Festival should not be interpreted as an excuse merely to reiterate the nation's past glories, but that permanent improvements and amenities, whether they took the form of playing fields or gardens, or new or restored buildings, were as much a part of the Festival idea as exhibitions, concerts and pageants.'[37] Many places planned religious events which, as you would expect, took the form primarily of choral concerts, special services and Sunday school pageants.[38] A number of local communities marked the Festival summer of 1951 with their 'tidying up schemes'; while others illustrated their community's past or future through exhibits, pageants, plays, balls and parades. Some towns decided to celebrate their industrial contributions to the nation. And a few places, primarily in the 'Celtic fringe', chose to emphasise that their local identities were different from a perceived hegemonic Englishness – or even Britishness in one case. What follows is a selection of these varied events.

Local 'tidying up schemes' as contributions to the Festival

Early official Festival correspondence between Barry and the Arts Council's Mary Glasgow reveals these two hammering out their 'approach to the country'. One such memo juxtaposed 1851's Great Exhibition with the Festival of Britain: 'When the turnstiles of the Great Exhibition were closed, the exhibits from the Crystal Palace were returned to their owners and ... for the great majority, the Exhibition was over and that was that.' 1951's exhibition was to be very different. The 1951 events were to be 'of a less ephemeral nature'. According to the memo, every town and village should be exhorted to remove 'an eyesore', plant some trees, create an arts centre, a new playing-field or a public garden from a bomb site and thus 'contribute to its own and the nation's enrichment'.[39] The point is clear: 1851's was an elitist exhibition to which 'the people' were invited. When it closed, it returned to its owners. By contrast, through local efforts, the 1951 Festival would leave permanent improvements across the UK. The Victorian elites were smug and self-satisfied, but in the 'New Britain' of 1951 everyone knew it was time to take the initiative and 'tidy up' after an exhausting and devastating war. The Festival organisation itself 'sponsored a scheme, administered by the National Association of Parish Councils, for tidying the neglected corners of the countryside'.[40] Many local authorities took up Barry's patriotic call to action by sprucing up their town halls. Through the volunteer labour offered by 'children as well as adults', trees, flowers and shrubs, 'presented as gifts', had 'tidied up' numerous communities. The language of 'tidying' was cosy and domestic, in line with the greater imaginings of Britishness in the period. The official souvenir guide announced that these efforts had indeed resulted in the improved appearance of many places in 1951, which would 'no doubt be setting a standard for years to come'.[41]

'Local limitations – not the least being financial – did not permit of Bermondsey taking an active part in the wider aspects of the Festival of Britain, 1951', according to the 'Resumé of Council's Plans and Progress to August, 1951', submitted by the 'Metropolitan Borough of Bermondsey'.[42] Yet the report reveals that the Borough Council did see the Festival as an 'opportunity' to be 'grasped' to 'tidy and brighten up' the Borough in every possible way. It stated that 'The Council's main concern was the bombed sites (numbering nearly 300 and covering an area of approximately 60 acres [24 hectares]) and the Council were determined to draw upon numerous resources and the enthusiasm of everyone in the Borough to play their part in its restoration, improvement and beautification'.[43]

Such a report to the official Festival planners may not provide useful evidence for assessing exactly what was 'tidied and brightened up' in Bermondsey in the name of the Festival, but it does act as an acknowledgement that the Festival's planners accomplished one of their goals – to motivate local councils to marshal local labour and materials. It also serves as a useful reminder of just how badly damaged much of England remained in the summer of 1951.

The borough of Tottenham and Edmonton, in addition to educational and cultural activities, transformed 'many Edmonton bomb sites into gardens and flower-beds', making the residents 'glad to be rid of these grim reminders of war'.[44] An article in the Festival summer from the *Tottenham and Edmonton Weekly Herald* explained that 'Where once stood houses and then the rubble of people's homes, left in a tangled mess after enemy bombing, now grow sweet scented flowers and lawns in well laid-out gardens. The town has a new facade. The people are pleased.'[45] The article also described the improvement of 'the corner of New-road and St. George's road. Regarded as a black spot for accidents, and not helped by the high advertisement hoarding'. This area had been transformed 'into a lovely sunken garden'. Their Town Hall was also given a new life that summer through new 'paving surrounds' and 'flowers in specially-constructed walls'.[46]

Birmingham's Town Hall was also renovated and its council made improvements in lighting across the city as part of their Festival. Birkenhead's Festival Committee allocated £4,000 for local festivities, primarily centred around the return of the Festival ship, *Campania*, to its home dock.[47] They also pledged to 'to improve the appearance of the roundabouts' and the city's flowerbeds were laid out 'and planted with bulbs'.[48]

Local Festival efforts in some instances offered large-scale community improvements like 'the restoration of the Colston Hall in Bristol, or the restoration of the Walker Art Gallery in Liverpool, or, on a smaller scale, a children's playground, seats and litter bins in the village of Abinger in

Surrey'.⁴⁹ Many, many places built playing fields for their communities. Penshurst Parish built 'seats with suitable inscriptions at Bus Stops', Sussex East County Council rebuilt the walls of their Lewes Castle, and King's Lynn restored the 'ancient St. George's Guildhall'.⁵⁰

In Suffolk, in 'the ancient Borough of Aldeburgh,' the 'permanent reminder of this wonderful year' was the renovation of a different sort of structure. That community chose to update its war memorial. The Mayor of Aldeburgh explained in his Festival report, that the names 'had been inscribed by raised lettering on the Portland Stone and had become much worn.' It was decided that the old panels should be removed and that new panels should be put in their place – 'Westmoreland grey green stone [inscribed] with the names of the heroes in both World Wars'.⁵¹

And a war memorial of another kind was planned in Tewkesbury, in the Cotswolds, as their Festival offering. In December of 1950, as part of his series on the Festival of Britain, William Holt featured Tewkesbury on the wireless. Holt's words are worth quoting at length, as they provide us with the flavour of an actual BBC Festival broadcast. Holt explained in the programme that:

> During the war a large number of American soldiers were stationed near Tewkesbury and in 1944 they streamed through the town towards the ports of embarkation for the beaches of Normandy, so the inhabitants of Tewkesbury thought it would be a good idea to build, as a permanent memorial to the Festival of Britain, an Anglo-American Garden of Remembrance and Riverside Walk. The idea is to clear some old buildings away from part of the river bank and plant trees, and lay out this garden.⁵²

Local people volunteered and set about demolishing old buildings, but the overall scheme was estimated to cost £30,000. It is not clear from the documents how far this project progressed, but it provides an interesting counter-example to the wide-ranging anti-Americanism of some of the metropolitan cultural critics discussed earlier. Unlike most of the centrally planned Festival offerings, the recent war was the focus of a number of local events.

Taken together, these examples may on some level seem mundane but, in a sense, that is the point. The Festival's organisers sought to bolster local reconstruction efforts and they succeeded. Clearly, this was in pragmatic terms an important goal in cash-strapped, war-scarred Britain, but it may also have been an impressive understanding and imagining of the crux of belonging to a nation – of being British. As Eley and Suny have argued, 'national identification is clearly a matter of sensibility ... something transmitted from the past and secured as a collective belonging, something reproduced in myriad imperceptible ways, grounded in

18 Trowell, the official Festival village, celebrated 1851 in its Festival celebrations

everydayness and mundane experience'.[53] By encouraging local regeneration, the Festival and its planners were also encouraging national identification and a belief in a better future, rooted in the places where the British people actually lived.

The 'local' versions of the past and the future in 1951

Local, like national, identity often relied on a sense of 'something transmitted from the past'. Many communities represented their understanding of the uniqueness of their town or village in terms of its received collective history. That historical chapter often glossed over in the South Bank's displays, the Second World War, was the focus of a Festival event in Swansea. *An Account of Swansea's Contribution to the National Celebrations* describes a performance of a 'tale of Dunkirk set to music for tenor and baritone solos with men's voices and brass band'.[54]

Trowell, on the Nottingham–Derbyshire border, was the official Festival village, chosen 'not for its beauty, but as an example of what a small community has done to celebrate the Festival and make itself a better place to live'.[55] This village, whose population numbered 2,000, working in 'the huge Stanton ironworks as well as the surrounding farmlands', organised a Festival week of children's sports, which featured a cricket match 'played in the dress of a century ago' (Figure 18). They also hosted an exhibition in the parish hall describing the village's longer history.[56] The Victorian past, generally eschewed in the official Festival exhibitions and events, was often celebrated locally, it seems.

Nottingham hosted 'the pageant of Women Through the Ages', 'presented in twenty episodes by 600 performers'.[57] And, in keeping with the official Festival's displays of ancient British traditions, 'the original

Royal charters and other documents illustrating the history of Nottingham from 1155' were on display at the Guildhall.[58]

With three tented exhibitions and a programme running all summer, Bristol's efforts meant that they were voted best festival outside of London. Their festivities stretched from folk theatre to looks through a 12-inch (30-centimetre) telescope with astronomical society members on hand to explain what you saw, and from the Bristol's Shakespeare Society's production of *Much Ado About Nothing* to a civic commerce display, featuring tobacco, chocolate and much more.[59] In its official souvenir brochure, Bristol, like Nottingham, chose to emphasise its ancient historic character as the key to its Festival celebrations, but the past they celebrated was quite a contrast to the one presented in the South Bank exhibitions. The foreword of Bristol's official souvenir programme, penned by the Lord Mayor, Alderman R. F. Lyne, OBE, began 'Whether we like it or not, this is clearly one of the great moments of Destiny; we either go forward and upwards or backwards and decay ... No city in this country has taken a prouder and more honourable share in our national success and reverses than Bristol; it must and will continue to do so.'[60] Lyne explained that Bristol will do this by 'drawing sustenance from ancient experience'.[61] The particulars of this 'ancient experience' were left to the next section of this souvenir guide, authored by C. M. MacInnes, Professor of Imperial History at the University of Bristol.[62] His piece was tellingly titled, 'From the Beginning', and asserted that: 'Bristol was already an important trading centre in Anglo-Saxon times'.[63] The Anglo-Saxon origins of all Britons were evoked in the official Festival displays and discourses, as we have seen, but from there MacInnes' story of Bristol diverged from the official narratives. Unlike the South Bank's version of the history of the British nation, MacInnes did not downplay Bristol's history of commerce or colonisation. He positively celebrated it, explaining that before 1500 Bristolians went in search of new markets and fisheries with 'John Cabot ... the last of a number of Bristol captains sent out on this quest, but unlike his predecessors, sought a continent, not a non-existent island, and so was successful.' Then, in the sixteenth century, 'while the rest of England ... ceased to concern itself with overseas exploration, Bristol's interest never flagged'. We are told that the first Englishman in the West Indies was from Bristol and that during the reign of Queen Elizabeth, many expeditions 'sailed from the Avon to prey upon the Spaniards, to search for gold and to develop trade'. However, it was after 1604 that 'the city's greatest period opened.' Bristol 'colonised Newfoundland ... New England and Virginia ... dispatched Captain James to discover a northwest passage; ... founded Surat; her merchants bought slaves in Africa which they exchanged for sugar in the West Indies and for tobacco in Virginia'.[64] Curiously, even the triangle slave trade, seldom celebrated by historians today, was a source of pride for MacInnes in 1951.

MacInnes then went on to show that Bristolians did have other past achievements in addition to imperialism. Such histories were more in keeping with the Festival's official version. He pointed to the fact that during the Civil War the city was divided in its allegiance to King and Parliament, that great mansions were built in Bristol in the sixteenth, seventeenth and eighteenth centuries, and that in that last century Bristol became a popular spa visited by Pope and Cobbett, among others.[65] Even so, MacInnes' writing of Bristol into the national 'autobiography' of 1951 illustrates the kind of divergence from the official story that Ian Cox had feared.

In an article entitled 'Leeds gets the spirit of the Festival', appearing in the midst of the Festival summer, Derrick Boothroyd compared Leeds' version of the Festival to York's. The striking differences between the festivities in the two cities were not missed by this correspondent to the *Yorkshire Post*. Boothroyd called on the relative ages of these two cities to underscore how very different they and their Festival celebrations were from one another. He wrote: 'The guide to the Leeds Festival of Britain celebrations says that Leeds is a city in which the present outweighs the past. "Its vigour", it declared, "is more noticeable than the intimations of a past age"';[66] 'Leeds, you see, is a vigorous boy, whereas York is a dear old lady'.[67] The gender connotations are obvious, but the generational analogy is even more striking. The language throughout his article is extremely telling. Boothroyd informed his readers that: 'The *motif* of the York celebrations was the traditional glories of the past. There were Mystery Plays revived from the dust of four centuries and a Georgian Ball in which costumed participants danced the minuet.' For this journalist the 'York Plays of the Creation and Redemption of Man and the Life of Christ',[68] not performed since 1572, were not 'a kind of antiphon to the austerities of post-war Britain', as Raphael Samuel argued, but merely, 'revived from the dust'.[69] Boothroyd continued by explaining the particulars:

> In Leeds there was none of this. Instead of Mystery Plays there was the University rag-procession, with a mobile atomic-bomb factory exploding its way hilariously down Woodhouse Lane and bevies of Hawaiian maidens pirouetting in the Headrow and threatening very seriously to take policemen's minds off their business. And instead of a Georgian Ball there was a mammoth display of fireworks in Roundhay Park, with set-piece elephants wagging both their tails and their trunks and set-piece battleships sending up showers of shot and shell. And because it was Leeds it was equally successful.[70]

Clearly, a celebration featuring models of atomic bombs, fireworks, battleships and scantily clad women was more focused on the present, or at least the very recent past, than one that presented Mystery Plays, a Georgian Ball and the minuet.

Another Festival project stressing the future more than the past was one of Liverpool's special exhibitions and schemes. Echoing London's, Liverpool organised a 'Live Architecture' exhibition held at the Speake Estate. A newspaper article at the time claimed that 'housewives who visited it with their children in the afternoon, took their husbands in the evening to point out improvements which could be made at home with the latest appliances displayed'.[71] The exhibition included 'two newly-built flats', with 'built-in cupboards', and 'maps, photographs and plans illustrating the City Council central redevelopment scheme to accommodate some of the applicants still on Liverpool Housing Register'. The exhibition showed visitors 'how attractive Council flats can be when care and thought are taken with their furnishing'.[72] This 'Live Architecture Exhibition' was a very timely and important portrayal of the future in Merseyside and North Wales. There were still many people without adequate housing in the city and the region, as the article stated, and concrete examples of liveable, 'modern' flats were hopeful representations of life tomorrow for 'ordinary' people. They were also, obviously, projects of recovery and renewal, as the official Festival had hoped. Liverpool's representations of its 'industrial importance' looked to the future, as well.

Festival of Britain celebrations that stressed a place's industrial capacities

There were many local communities who, in keeping with the official Festival narratives, chose to stress that their uniqueness lay in their industrial capacities. Liverpool boasted some of the most impressive Festival events, and their open-air exhibition focusing on the city's industrial importance represented a significant contribution.[73] The Liverpool Festival Director, Mr Alfred Francis, declared the 'Daylight on Industry Exhibition' to be 'one of several events which would make the Liverpool Festival distinctive in the national scheme'.[74] The exhibition was planned to be one 'of a style to measure up to the high standards set for music and the arts of theatre, and the designer's plan was so boldly conceived that widespread attention would be focused on Merseyside's industrial schemes'.[75] It was held on a blitzed site in the centre of the city measuring 4.5 acres (1.8 hectares), making it simultaneously a display and a reconstruction project.[76] 'Daylight on Industry' aimed both 'to interest the non-technical visitor by showing the varied nature of industry in the region, and to demonstrate the less familiar uses of basic materials so that those with a specialised interest in industry may see new possibilities in local manufactures'.[77] The 'varied nature' of Liverpool's industries was one of the points of pride of this exhibition. An early section of the exhibition's souvenir brochure, authored by Alderman A. Ernest Shennan, Chairman of the Lancashire and Merseyside Industrial Development Association, explained that 'To look at the industries of Merseyside and South West Lancashire is indeed to look at what amounts to the industrial structure of England, for here more than anywhere can be found the life-blood of the nation's trade'.[78] Alderman Shennan argued that most industrial areas are linked to specific industry, but 'Here it is different, for within a radius of twenty miles of the Liverpool Town Hall can be found virtually every trade and every process on which the economy of the nation depends'.[79]

Like on the South Bank, none of the items displayed was to be for sale and they were exhibited in a unique way. Mr W. L. Stevenson, vice-principal of the Liverpool College of Art, designed 'Daylight on Industry' in such a way that the industrial projects were grouped so 'that their nature [was] demonstrated, functionally', or in other words, 'so that material used for both construction and display, such as flooring, scaffolding, awnings, and glass [were] themselves exhibits'.[80] The reason for such an innovative exhibition technique was 'to show a wide variety of products with the liveliest effect, in a form understandable not only by the technical expert, but also to the man-in-the-street'.[81] The Liverpool Festival Council agreed to take initial responsibility for this exhibition and pledged £1,000. But, ultimately, 'Daylight on Industry' was intended to be self-supporting with receipts from entrance fees and sales of a 'comprehensive catalogue'.[82] Liverpool's proud industrial heritage and current contributions to the national economy were the essence of its largest exhibition and act of regeneration.

Nottingham, in addition to their historical representations, planned their own nine-day trade fair 'designed to demonstrate to visitors the standard of achievement attained by Nottingham craftsmen in the first half of the century and give some indication of the improvements and developments which may be expected to be produced by British skill and imagination in the future'.[83] The Land Travelling exhibition also included 'the Hall of Textiles, in which Nottingham's selected products' were displayed when the one hundred lorries with their '5,000 exhibits ranging from a complete railway carriage and gas turbine engines to thimbles, pins and needles' came to town.[84]

Similarly, Stroud in the Cotswolds decided that its most distinctive characteristics lay in its manufacturing. Hence, Stroud had planned to hold an industrial exhibition, featuring open days in the factories so that visitors could see the manufacturers.[85] Acting as a real reminder of the dire straits still facing Britain in the early 1950s, 'the association of Stroud and district industries' decided by Christmas of 1950 that 'an exhibition and the opening of works to the public might interfere too much with the production drive, and they now say that "the essential needs to the country must be foremost in these very critical times"'. Because of this, the town leaders decided simply to display Stroud's industrial products in its shop windows, instead.[86] They also settled on projects of renewal and 'planning useful things', such as new playing fields, bus shelters, and trees, as their contributions to the Festival.[87] But, if Stroud's Festival displays and activities were a reminder of the recent war and continuing austerity, those of the Rhondda in South Wales were a reminder of a time just as dark for some places – the Industrial Revolution.

The Festival and other Britishness: the 'Celtic fringe'

The ravages and inequalities resulting from industrialisation, generally side-stepped in the South Bank's exhibitions, were acknowledged and even celebrated as the core of the Rhondda's identity. The official Festival souvenir brochure for the area explained, somewhat defensively that:

> The first impression of visitors to the Rhondda will be one of industrially scarred valleys, but without seeking to excuse this unfortunate state of affairs, it is pointed out that the Rhondda has concentrated within its borders one of the most intensive and highly populated mining communities in the country, and we venture to suggest that, despite the ravages of industrialism, the Rhondda still retains traces of its ancient beauty, with nooks here and there showing shades of once green and wooded valleys.[88]

Rhondda's souvenir brochure made a virtue of its valleys' scars, writing of the community as key to both Wales and Great Britain due to its coal production. 'Coal mining continues to be of major importance in South Wales and Great Britain, whose future prosperity is bound up with the maintenance of adequate supplies of this basic material', it stressed. Also, in language foreign to the official Festival, Rhondda's discourses recognised the 'notorious fluctuations to which it has been subject with alternating periods of boom and depression'.[89] It seems that there was no way to ignore the fact that coal mining had brought with it economic uncertainty. However, the brochure stressed that the people of the Rhondda were proud of the role that their labour and their production of coal contributed to the 'future prosperity' of the nation.

In an article written in connection with the Festival and published in the *Glamorgan County Magazine*, the editor, Rowland Harris, celebrated what he believed to be the other characteristics of the inhabitants of this coal-mining community. Harris highlighted the friendliness of the people, emphasising how 'many doors are open' and how 'a cup of tea is never very far away at any hour of the day!'[90] He then outlined the 'community sympathy, unpretentious, practical, spontaneous' which 'swelled' and 'flowed' whenever a family experienced a mining tragedy.[91] Once again, in a narrative quite removed from the South Bank and its comparatively anodyne story of ancient traditions, Harris revealed a disturbing story of industrialisation.

Other Britishness

In 1951 some communities chose to represent themselves as distinct from Britishness or, perhaps more accurately, what they perceived as hegemonic versions of Englishness. The official Festival attempted to smoothly incorporate the four nations of Great Britain into a unified whole. At times its planners did this by presenting all Britons as the same, thanks to centuries of the melding of traditions and ways of life, as in the case of descriptions in 'The People of Britain' exhibition. There, as we have seen, Jacquetta Hawkes wrote of 'our ancestors [who] came upon this island – by sea ... We are a much-mixed race, and the clue to our way of life and achievement lies in this blended ancestry.'[92] Other facets of the official exhibitions, including the travelling exhibitions, and the 'regional' ones, stressed the continuing diversity of the people and places of Britain as a source of strength and pride. And, at times, even cultural traditions were called upon to represent this diversity: for example, in the inclusion of the International Eisteddfod in Llangollen and the National Eisteddfod in Llanrwst, both celebrated as components of the official arts festivals. But, when we look at the representations produced by the places themselves, we see that at times some places decided to stress their diversity as an example of their separateness rather than unity. Welsh communities often signalled this difference through their rugby playing. The Isle of Man, Liskeard in Cornwall and Dumfries in Scotland were among the places that presented their local identities as different from Englishness and, as such, as also different from anything we have seen represented in the official London-planned displays.

As discussed in Chapter 4, 'sportsmanlike' behaviour[93] and the 'great British virtues of democracy, freedom and fair play' were presented as timeless features of Britishness in the official festivities.[94] The Festival's South Bank included a Sports Pavilion and the accompanying souvenir guide-catalogue, cleverly eschewing any direct reference to imperialism whilst inadvertently acknowledging it, proclaimed: 'we have devised many of the world's sports and excelled in not a few of them'.[95] Sport was an important part of Britishness, as well as a 'British contribution to civilisation'.

In 1947 for an anthology entitled *The Character of England*, Vita Sackville-West wrote that 'the love of games with its attendant character-building qualities of fair play, team-spirit, generosity in victory, cheerfulness in defeat, respect for the better man, and all the rest of the platitudes is in fact responsible for many of the less offensive traits in our national make-up'.[96] With such notions in circulation in the post-war period, as well in our own, it would be foolish to ignore the role of games and sport in constructions of Britishness, as well as more local identities. In much of the United Kingdom, games and sport act as sources of a place's identity. Masculine identification with an urban area or a city or town often derives from the sports played there and the resulting rivalries between regions and communities.[97]

Social historian Richard Holt argues that 'Cricket was supposed to bring together the classes in a uniquely English way ... [and] despite differences in the way the game was interpreted north and south of the Trent, it remained the true national sport of the English'.[98] Yet cricket was mentioned in only a small number of the random sample of local celebrations here discussed. For example, in a description of 'The Bristolian Today', written for the Festival celebrations, the fact that the average Bristolian's 'cricket allegiance is divided, roughly by the turgid-breathing Avon, between Gloucestershire and Somerset', was meant to serve as an illustration of his moderation and lack of partisanship.[99] Leeds included in its Festival report that 'a Cricket Match was played at Headingley on 20th and 21st June between Yorkshire Past [and] Yorkshire Present, and on July 1st, a match was played at Roundhay Park between Appleyard's XI v. West Indians'.[100] And, Cardiff's schedule of Festival sporting activities listed the Glamorgan County Cricket Club's six matches at the Cardiff Arms Park, 'including one against the South African Touring Team at Whitsun'.[101]

Welshness and rugby

However, the clearest connections between communities' identities and the sports they played are found in relation to Welshness and rugby.[102] Holt explains that 'Instead of being a middle-class game cut off until recently from popular sentiment, rugby in Wales has been thoroughly democratised and is patriotic to the point of chauvinism'.[103] In the face of the 'invasion of English sports, the Welsh took the winter-game of the English public schools and turned it into a vehicle for their own brand of "Celtic nationalism"'.[104] Finally, and according to Holt most importantly, Welsh Rugby Union played a crucial cultural role in Wales' swift transformation from a predominately rural to urban, industrial place.[105] He elaborates:

> 'Welshness' had to be created amongst the migrants who flocked to the coalfields from Ireland and the west of England in the forty years before

the First World War, giving Wales the highest immigration rate outside the United States. The one and a half million or so workers clustered around the southern industrial region knew little or no Welsh; the legends and literary traditions of the ancient Britons passed them by.

It was rugby, Holt argues, that 'took its place alongside chapel choirs, self-education, and socialist unionism in the new canon of Welshness'. In Wales, rugby 'became "the one great pastime of the people"'. It was more unifying than politics or religion, in Holt's opinion, 'drawing together coal-heavers and coal-owners in a common passion for the national side'. The game 'became a new Welsh myth, a unifying belief; a strand in the national character that gained strength from being so tightly entwined with the idea of ancient liberties reborn of a rich and independent culture'.[106]

And, as if to illustrate Holt's point, every Welsh community I have evidence for listed rugby games as part of its Festival celebrations. Cardiff's festivities, for example, included May's games of 'seven-sided rugger' and Swansea reported that its thirty-five-member planning committee included a representative of Swansea rugby.[107] The Rhondda Festival brochure extolled the virtues of its rugby fields, found in parks and funded by 'the Miners' Welfare Scheme and the Local Authorities'.[108] In these communities, rugby was central to their Festival celebrations of Welshness and its difference from Englishness.

The Isle of Man, Cornwall and Dumfries

The Isle of Man's Festival of Britain celebrations stressed that the most important aspect of this place's identity was its separateness and difference from Britain.[109] The authors of its official Festival brochures chose to stress the Isle of Man's independence from the rest of the United Kingdom, rather than its clearly semi-dependent status.[110] Their programmes described the Isle of Man as 'the western world's smallest nation' and a place 'with a longer history of democratic government than anywhere else in the British Commonwealth of Nations, including England'.[111] One of its souvenir brochures proclaimed that 'The Isle of Man will play a noteworthy part in the Festival Celebrations on both a local and a national scale ... The opportunity afforded by the Festival Year is being taken by every town, village and parish to stage a host of special attractions.' These 'special attractions' were to 'range from the revival of old customs to the inception of modern social developments'.[112] But the major contribution that Festival summer was a 'series of open-air pageants illustrating the outstanding events in the Island's centuries of history'.[113] The programme explained that:

> Scenes from the Celtic and Norse periods, and, in more recent times, from the Derby regime down to the present day, will be brought vividly to life:

and, symbolic of the record numbers of early season visitors from Scandinavia, under King Orry, who, a thousand years ago, gave the Island its
unique constitution, will be realistically portrayed ... with the co-operation
of strong local casts in period costume, the pageants will Provide never-to-
be-forgotten spectacles in the four quarters of the Island.[114]

The Isle of Man's Festival history pageants accentuated that place's difference
from the rest of Britain.

Another place which figured itself in its Festival literature as both
historically significant and somewhat separate from England was Cornwall.
'The Borough of Liskeard Festival of Britain 1951 Programme of Events'
commenced by describing 'the county of Cornwall' as 'a narrow peninsula
eighty miles [129 kilometres] long, thrust out into the Atlantic at the
south-westernmost extremity of Britain' with 'an area of 868,167 acres
[351,328 hectares]' and a population at the time of the 1931 census of
317,968.[115] But, after describing the landscape and demography, the programme asserted the unique characteristics of the Cornish people
themselves. Under the heading 'East Cornwall: Land and People' it explained that 'The Cornish people like to regard themselves as a nation
apart from the English, and it is held that the characteristic Cornish
colouring – swarthy skin and black hair – marks a survival of the earliest
stock of whom we know anything: the Seafaring Iberians who spread the
cult of great stone monuments and the first use of metal up the western
coasts of Europe some two thousand years before Christ'.[116] Evoking a very
long history, this passage figured Cornwall and the Cornish as 'a nation
apart from the English'. James Vernon has written of how Cornwall lies
on 'the margins of Englishness, both a county of England and a foreign
country'.[117] He suggests that a 'definition of an authentic Cornwall rooted
in its primitive but pure folk – which of course relied upon a deeply
romantic imagination' was promulgated between the mid-nineteenth century and the inter-war years.[118] In Liskeard's Festival programme, penned
by a Cornish person, similar assumptions and ideas about the 'authentic'
nature of the Cornish people were perpetuated.

The Liskeard programme continued with an explanation of East Cornwall's early history: 'About the time of the Roman's withdrawal the Cornish
became Christians ... After the Anglo-Saxons came Danish raiding parties,
and after them the Normans, last successful invaders of this island. In 1337
King Edward settled the Dukedom of Cornwall on his young son, later called
the Black Prince, and by this Charter the eldest son of the King of England
has borne this title ever since'.[119] East Cornwall's major sources of identity
seem to have been rooted in a very long history, struggles with invaders,
and a sense of being separate and unique from England and Englishness.
Similar imaginings were at play in the Festival celebrations in Dumfries.

Seldom within the Festival-related records does one find evidence of a community so freely mixing and inventing traditions as in the Dumfries celebrations. The ritual celebration of Dumfries' naming as a Royal Borough in the twelfth century smoothly added on a ride to the Castle and the unfurling of the flag to symbolise 'the first blow in the battle for Scotland's independence' in 1306.[120] The Queen of the South's ride on the river referenced a pagan rite of spring, yet she wore a Tudor costume. And the ritualised riding of the marches had by 1951 incorporated the laying on of wreaths at the Dumfries and Maxwelltown War Memorials.[121]

For one week in June the town of Dumfries celebrated the Festival of Britain by linking it with the annual Guid Nychburris, or 'Good Neighbours', Week.[122] The biggest day was Thursday when, in view of the Duchess of Gloucester, 'thousands of visitors from all parts of the south-west', and 'the citizens' of Dumfries witnessed the beginning of the day's events at 7:30 a. m. 'with the time-old ceremony of riding the marches'.[123] This ceremony referred to 'earlier occasions when the town's magistrates rode out to re-establish the borough's boundaries'.[124] The riding of the marches segued into 'an interesting ceremony ... at the Castledykes, where the Cornet, Lynors and Pursuivant, with the cavalcade, entered and unfurled the flag on the site of the Castle captured by King Robert the Bruce in 1306', being 'the first blow in the battle of Scotland's independence'. Then 'at 9:30 a.m. the Queen of the South elect, Miss Gladys Rennie, a pupil of Dumfries High School, with her attendants left Crindau port in the royal barge'.[125] 'The Queen of the South' was dressed in 'a Tudor costume of bright purple', according to the Festival souvenir brochure.[126] It informed its readers and visitors that this annual event marked a pagan ritual anticipating 'the coming of spring and the May Queen, here in the Lowlands called "The Queen of the South"'.[127]

The brochure continued, explaining that 'The subsequent programme aimed at a re-enactment of the stirring events which took place in the town in the far-off days, for it was in the twelfth century that Dumfries was raised to the status of Royal Burgh by a gift from King William the Lion'.[128] The ceremony symbolised 'the incorporation of Dumfries as a Royal Borough by the gift of the Standard, the Charter and the Seal, brought by the Pursuivant who is greeted at the borders of the town by the Cornet and his escort'.[129] The Provost received the charter, seal and flag, and after the singing of the song of Dumfries and three cheers of 'the burgh's motto', Provost Bell made a speech.[130] In addition to welcoming the Duchess of Gloucester and expressing the town's joy in the fact that 'the Duke of Gloucester came to the south of Scotland to choose his bride', the Provost declared the town's loyalty to 'the Royal House'. He concluded his speech, stating 'As I look down on the vast concourse of loyal citizens with pride, I am conscious of the spirit of independence which was once born in the streets of Dumfries. That alone entitles us to a place as empire-builders. May the characteristics of the people of Dumfries continue to grow in strength and favour.' [131]

Dumfries' imperial spirit was different from Bristol's: in Dumfries it incorporated pride in Scotland's struggle for independence. Invented traditions mixed references to the pagan past with ones from the twelfth, fourteenth and twentieth centuries. But, in addition to Dumfries' sense of an extraordinarily long history, Scottishness was the essence of Dumfries' self-representation. And the struggle for Scottish independence, not surprisingly omitted from the South Bank's exhibitions, featured in Dumfries' Festival celebrations. The uncomplicated sense of 'unity through diversity', so central to the official Festival's sense of Britishness, was not always apparent in the local Festival exhibitions and events.

Conclusion

First, by way of conclusion, we need to address the initial questions raised in this chapter. As we have seen, the London organisers did not agree on the role of the locally planned festivities in the national celebration. For example, Jacquetta Hawkes worried that British culture was created by elites, not by 'the people themselves',[132] while Ian Cox believed that local imaginings needed countering by his land and sea travelling exhibitions, which carried the official Festival messages from the central offices in London.[133] Still other elites must have agreed with Keynes that the enemy of 'the people's' culture was a combination of metropolitanism and Americanisation. Or, in other words, the anxieties represented by the Festival's London planners centred around issues which could broadly be described as metropolitan versus provincial, centre versus periphery, and authentic versus American. But these anxieties may have masked a larger, underlying concern. Surely, if during the Second World War the centre of imagined British national identity had shifted, as McKibbin has argued, making the true bearers of Britishness no longer the 'modernized middle class', but the 'organized working class', this was enough to give London elites pause.[134] If post-war narratives of democracy and Britishness were to be promulgated by 'provincial' (upper-) working-class people (or more likely, lower-middle-class people), it was important to help them to get their stories straight. Class anxieties, consciously or unconsciously, may have been manifested in terms of these other less-troubling categories. According to Philip Dodd, the issue of 'core/periphery' was discussed even by Matthew Arnold in terms of 'metropolitan' versus 'provincial' cultures, and the *Oxford English Dictionary* cites Arnold in one of its definitions of 'provincial'. There the term is defined as 'wanting the culture and polish of the capital'.[135] Dodd writes of the elites' recognition in the early twentieth century of the necessity of British national identity being 'secured at the cultural as well as – or indeed as an alternative to – the political level'.[136] In the aftermath of the Second World War that struggle must also have been present. With the extraordinary changes wrought by the war and the post-war 'settlement', some middle-class 'experts', despite their left leanings and good intentions, may well have felt embattled.

We have seen a variety of possible responses to the (barely) perceived threat to their cultural hegemony. Someone like Hawkes chose to romanticise the pre-industrial world as the site of authentic, local cultures.[137] Conversely, Cox opted for the idea that metropolitan ideas and culture could triumph, presenting 'the people' with genuine, appropriate representations of their past and future. While those like Keynes favoured the opinion that inauthentic, commercial culture stemmed from America, particularly its film industry, and was then perpetuated by London, but that this situation could be halted if the cultures of true, 'Deep England' exerted themselves. However, as both McKibbin and LeMahieu have convincingly argued, at least before 1951, British culture 'tended to "smooth out" overt Americanization ... either by domesticating it, or by assimilating it to a familiar common Anglo-American culture'.[138] The local festivals show that 'England had no common culture, rather a set of overlapping cultures'.[139] This statement by McKibbin explains why we see in the local celebrations familiar tropes from the national Festival events, such as the stress on a long past, the future, production and to a lesser degree, the role of sport, but why we see them sometimes used to tell different stories. Overall, the Festival organisers seemed to get it right; the Britain of the post-war moment was generally unified yet diverse, held together by narratives of the past and the future most vociferously announced in the Second World War. But, as Ian Cox anticipated, how the local organisers of the unsupervised, local Festival events chose to represent these broad, nebulous notions was often quite different from the London version.

The local 'chapters' created by the cities, towns and villages of Great Britain as their contributions to 'the autobiography of the nation' illustrate that there is no aggregate of 'representative' forms of local identities to be gleaned from a sampling of the local Festival celebrations. Nor was there an uncomplicated, uniform sense across the United Kingdom of being British in the post-war world. Places chose to represent themselves through their celebrations in a wide variety of ways from the home of rugby to the place of coal and from ancient to youthful. In addition, the majority of communities stressed their unique contributions to the United Kingdom as a whole, while a few exceptions, particularly from the 'Celtic fringe', emphasised how very different those places were from England, if not Britain. More of 'the actual inequalities, exploitations, and patterns of domination and exclusion' that were 'concealed' or 'enfolded' into a single story in the centrally planned exhibits were apparent in the local Festival events.[140] And as we have seen, in the case of the Rhondda, for example, at times they were even incorporated into a new narrative of celebration as essential qualities of specific places. These wide-ranging examples support the idea that post-war Britons conceived of themselves as hailing from both Great Britain and also a town or city, or even a smaller country, such as Wales, Northern Ireland or Scotland.[141] This may seem a very obvious, even banal conclusion but, as Linda Colley has pointed out, Britishness has often been conceived of as a '"blending" of the different regional or older national cultures contained within its boundaries' or 'in terms of an English "core" imposing its cultural and political hegemony on a helpless and defrauded Celtic periphery'.[142] Yet the examples in this chapter support Colley's important contention that 'identities are not like hats. Human beings can and do put on several at a time'.[143] The superimposing of British identity did not entirely eradicate the more local identities of people residing within the British isles. Conversely, certainly in the period immediately following the 'People's War', in which the nation was conceived as '"all in it together"', local identities did not overwhelm or extinguish national pride in most cases.[144] In 1951 in most places in the UK, the British people seem to have proudly and contentedly lived with a combination of identities.

Notes

1 *The Story of the Festival of Britain*, p. 4.

2 PRO, CAB 124/1221, Speech by Gerald Barry, Festival of Britain Meeting of Mayors and Chairmen of Local Authorities. See also Weight, 'Pale Stood Albion', p. 151.

3 *The Story of the Festival of Britain*, p. 4.

4 PRO, EL6/2, 'Festival Executive Committee, 1948' 'The Arts Council of Great Britain', 'Notes on the Possible Organisation of the Festival of the Arts in 1951,' p. 2 (handwritten at bottom 'No date–Jan. 48?').

5 *Official Book of the Festival*, p. 68.

6 *Ibid.*

7 PRO, Work 25/230 (originally labelled WKS 25/130/E1/A2/1), 'The Festival of Britain, 1951' (London: HMSO, 1951), p. 9.

8 Gerald Barry, *Radio Times*, 27 April 1951, as quoted by Weight, 'Pale Stood Albion', p. 152.

9 PRO, Work 25/21, 'Conf FBC (48) 7: The Council of the Festival of Britain in 1951, Outline of Theme and Programme', p. 2 (emphasis added).

10 PRO, EL6/23, 'Article for the *Chichester Quarterly*, September 1949, The Festival of Britain 1951 by Gerald Barry' (located in a folder labelled 'F. O. B. Correspondence with the Director General, April 1948–August 1950). Emphasis added.

11 Cox, 'The Story the Exhibition Tells', pp. 1–2.

12 Hawkes, *A Land*, p. 187.

13 Hawkes, *A Land*, p. 188.

14 *Ibid.*

15 Hawkes, *A Land*, p. 189.

16 Hawkes, *A Land*, p. 190.

17 *Kine Weekly*, 31 January 1924: 35, as quoted by A. Higson, *Waving the Flag: Constructing a National Cinema in Britain* (Oxford: Clarendon Press, 1995), p. 19.

18 R. Hoggart, *The Uses of Literacy* (New Brunswick: Transaction Publishers, 1992). On novels, see pp. 196–209 and on milk bars, pp. 189–90.

19 J. M. Keynes, 'The Arts Council: Its Policy and Hopes', *Listener*, 34 (12 July 1945), p. 32. See also J. Donald, 'How English Is It? Popular Literature and National Culture', in Carter, Donald and Squire (eds), *Space and Place*, 165–86.

20 G. Eley, 'How is "History" Represented?', unpublished essay, 1996, n.p. Note also that the quotation is: 'Let every part of Merry *England* be merry in its own way'. This may not be merely habit, but may reveal condescension towards the rest of the British Isles. We know, for instance, that Keynes expressed rather obnoxious views about Scotland in his correspondence with Arts Council Secretary, Mary Glasgow. In a letter dated 30 July 1945 from Keynes to Glasgow, he agreed that Scotland could have a separate Scottish Committee of the Arts Council 'as long as they do not require the Chairman to wear a kilt at one meeting out of 10' (PRO, EL2/40).

21 Keynes, 'The Arts Council', *Listener*, 34 (12 July 1945), p. 32. See also, Minihan, *The Nationalization of Culture*, p. 232.

22 Croft, 'Betrayed Spring', p. 211.

23 For example, note architectural critic Reyner Banham's assertion that 'the Festival Style' was 'undoubtedly' the 'common triumph' of 'all those salaried spokespersons of the Council of Industrial Design, the editorial "We" of the *Architectural Review*, and other former officers and gentlemen' (whom he 'warily' dubbed the 'British Establishment'). Banham, 'The Style: "Flimsy … Effeminate"?', p. 190.

24 *Architectural Review*, Special Issue on Reconstruction, 1941. I thank Peter Mandler for bringing this article and its discourses to my attention.

25 'Festival of Britain: Purpose and Approach to Theme', pp. 2–3. For another discussion of this 'favourite Festival concept' and its relationship to Morrison and the Parliamentary Labour Party, see Burstow, 'Modern Sculpture in the South Bank Townscape', p. 105.

26 H. Morrison, Festival of Britain opening speech, May 1951, as quoted by Forty, 'Festival Politics', p. 36.

27 Fielding, Thompson and Tiratsoo, 'England Arise!', p. 139.

28 *Ibid.*

29 Editorial, *Fact*, 1949, as quoted by Fielding, Thompson and Tiratsoo, 'England Arise!', p. 107.

30 G. Hodkinson, *Coventry Evening Telegraph*, 12 June 1945, as quoted by Fielding, Thompson and Tiratsoo, *'England Arise!'*, p. 108. The use of the term 'virile', in reference to democracy, is not commented upon by Fielding *et al.*, but it should not go unnoticed. As discussed in Chapter 4, at times it seems many Labour leaders and activists had trouble comprehending how to incorporate women into their new, imagined citizenry.

31 W. S. Churchill, *A History of the English-Speaking Peoples Volume I, The Birth of Britain* (London: Cassell, 1956), p. xvii.

32 *The Official Book of the Festival*, p. 70.

33 'The Festival of Britain, 1951', p. 12.

34 *Ibid.*

35 *The Story of the Festival*, p. 4.

36 Hippisley Coxe, 'I enjoyed it more than anything', p. 90.

37 *Ibid.*

38 The best source for all of these events, but especially for the religious ones, is *The Festival of Britain Catalogue of Activities throughout the Country* (London: Festival of Britain Office, 1951).

39 'When the 1851 Exhibition closed, it was finished, but 1951 ...', from a memo entitled: 'Suggested headings for article in *Chichester Quarterly*'. At the end of the paragraph quoted above appear the words '(GUILDHALL SPEECH)'. This memo is not signed or dated, but, because of other letters in this file, it seems to have been written in mid-August, 1949. Ellipsis in the original.

40 *The Official Book of the Festival*, p. 65.

41 *Ibid.*

42 PRO, Work 25/4, 'Metropolitan Borough of Bermondsey', 'Resumé of Council's Plans and Progress to August 1951'.

43 *Ibid.*

44 PRO, Work 25/4, Newspaper clipping dated 'Friday June 29th, 1951', from the *Tottenham and Edmonton Weekly Herald* clipping book.

45 *Ibid.*

46 *Ibid.*

47 Liverpool Local History Department, Liverpool Library (hereafter LL), 'Festival of Britain in Liverpool, vol. 1, 22nd July to 12th August, H F394 5 FES' (Cuttings book), Pressmark 352 CLE/CUT 3/8, p. 13; '£4,000 Festival Scheme', *Liverpool Daily Post*, 5 January 1951.

48 *Ibid.*

49 Forty, 'Festival Politics', p. 36.

50 *The Festival of Britain Catalogue of Activities throughout the Country*, n.p.

51 'Aldeburgh Festival of Britain report'.

52 BBC Written Archives, Caversham, 'On the Job: Getting Ready for the Festival of Britain'.

53 Eley and Suny, 'Introduction', p. 22.

54 Morris, 'County Borough of Swansea Festival of Britain, 1951', pp. 4–7.

55 *The Official Book of the Festival*, p. 67; and E. Harwood, 'Trowell, Festival Village', in Harwood and Powers (eds), *Twentieth Century Architecture*, 163–4, p. 163. Harwood explains that in *A Tonic to the Nation* Trowell is said to be in Buckinghamshire and in the Festival Committee's final report its location is given as Northamptonshire.

56 *The Festival of Britain, 1951*, p. 67.

57 'Book I FOB Land Travelling Exhibition Nottingham'; Anonymous, 'Something for Everyone at Nottingham Festival', *Nottingham Guardian*, 18 July 1951.

58 *Ibid.*

59 'Frank Buckley looks back at the celebrations he organised for the Festival of Britain in Bristol', *Bristol Times* (online edition), 144 (24 April 2001).

60 British Library, London, Alderman R. F. Lyne, OBE, Right Honourable the Lord Mayor of Bristol, 'Foreword', 'City and County of Bristol, Festival of Britain June 25th to July 28th, 1951, Souvenir Handbook', n.p.

61 *Ibid.*

62 C. M. MacInnes, 'From the Beginning', in R. F. Lyne, 'City and County of Bristol', n.p.

63 *Ibid.*

64 *Ibid.*

65 *Ibid.*

66 'Leeds Gets the Spirit'.

67 *Ibid.*

68 *The Festival of Britain*, p. 35.

69 Samuel, *Theatres of Memory, Vol. I*, p. 93.

70 'Leeds Gets the Spirit'.

71 Anonymous, 'Modern Flats on View', *Liverpool Daily Post*, 25 July 1951.

72 *Ibid.*

73 *The Festival of Britain, 1951*, 'The Port, the City and the Arts', p. 51.

74 LL, 'Festival of Britain in Liverpool, vol. 1', p. 8; Anonymous, 'Industry's Products in Striking Form', *Liverpool Daily Post*, 24 September 1950.

75 *Ibid.*

76 LL, *Liverpool Festival, 1951 Daylight on Industry Exhibition, 23rd July–11th August* (brochure), 'General Description of the Daylight on Industry Exhibition', p. 8, published by the Liverpool Festival Society.

77 *The Festival of Britain, 1951*, p. 51.

78 Anonymous, 'Industry's Products'.

79 *Ibid.*

80 *Ibid.*

81 *Ibid.*

82 *Ibid.*

83 'Book I FOB Land Travelling Exhibition Nottingham'; Anonymous, 'Something for Everyone at Nottingham Festival', *Nottingham Guardian*, 18 July 1951.

84 Anonymous, 'Something for Everyone at Nottingham Festival'.

85 BBC Written Archives, Caversham, 'On the Job'.

86 *Ibid.*

87 *Ibid.*

88 PRO, Work 25/240, 'Rhondda, Festival of Britain June 4th to 9th Brochure/Souvenir Programme' (both on the cover), p. 2.

89 *Ibid.*

90 PRO, Work 25/240, R. Harris, 'The Rhondda has Many Faces', *Glamorgan County Magazine.*

91 *Ibid.*

92 J. Hawkes, Theme Convener, 'The Land of Britain: Coming Aboard', in Cox, *Festival Ship Campania*, p. 9.

93 Samuel, *Theatres of Memory, Vol. I*, p. 218.

94 MOI, as quoted by Nicholas, *The Echo of War*, pp. 2, 229.

95 *The Official Book of the Festival*, p. 9. See Chapter 7 for a fuller discussion of the virtual absence of representations of empire in the Festival.

96 V. Sackville-West, 'The Outdoor Life', originally published in E. Barker (ed.), *The Character of England* (Oxford: Clarendon, 1947, 410–11), as reproduced by Giles and Middleton (eds), *Writing Englishness 1900–1950*, p. 167.

97 Of course, there are women who are interested in sports and support their local clubs, and so on, but even with the increased numbers of female football fans, this form of identification with a place is still overwhelmingly male. A historian of British sport, Richard Holt, states: 'The history of sport in modern Britain is a history of men ... women figure only fleetingly ... sport has been so thoroughly identified with masculinity': R. Holt, *Sport and the British: A Modern History* (Oxford: Clarendon Press, 1989), p. 8. See also: C. Brackenridge and D. Woodward, 'Gender Inequalities in Leisure and Sport in Post-war Britain', in Obelkevich and Catterall (eds), *Understanding Post-War British Society*, 192–203.

98 Holt, *Sport and the British*, pp. 265–6.

99 British Library, London, E. Buston, 'The Bristolian Today', *The Western Daily Press and Bristol Mirror*, from *City and County of Bristol, Festival of Britain June 25th to July 28th, 1951, Souvenir Handbook*, Pressmark: YA. 1991. b. 7066.

100 PRO, Work 25/4, 'Leeds – Festival Of Britain' (three-page typed document, in a folder marked 'Leeds'). It is noteworthy that the two teams in the first match were named 'Yorkshire Past' and 'Yorkshire Present'. As we have seen, this sense of the past *versus* the present appeared in a newspaper report of Leeds Festival festivities. This example once again refers indirectly to Britain's imperial past by mentioning that a British team was scheduled to play a West Indian team, with cricket being one of many imperial legacies in that country.

101 *The Festival of Britain, 1951*, 'Cardiff', p. 28.

102 The most important historian of Welsh rugby is Gwyn Williams. See his: '"How Amateur was my Valley?": Professional Sport and Amateur Identity in Wales 1890–1914', *British Journal of Sports History*, 2 (December 1985); 'From Grand Slam to Grand Slump: Economy, Society and Rugby Football in Wales during the Depression', *Welsh History Review*, 11 (June 1983); and 'From Popular Culture to Public Cliché: Images and Identity in Wales', in Magan (ed.), *Pleasure, Profit and Proselytism* (London: Frank Cass, 1988). Holt says similarly interesting things about

the role of football in the making of a different sort of Scottish identity (distinct from the kilt-wearing type) in the industrial areas near Glasgow: see Holt, *Sport and the British*, p. 254, for example. Unfortunately, the material I have on Glaswegians does not cover their football allegiances and enthusiasms. On football more generally, Holt asserts that 'Football was the property of industrial workers, rugby of the middle class': Holt, *Sport and the British*, p. 266. I have only a few references to football. These are not at all representative samples, but within this sample, for instance, Leeds reported that as part of their Festival celebrations: 'Football Matches were played at Elland Road between Leeds United v. Rapide (Austria) on 9th May, and Leeds United v. Holland on 14th May': 'Leeds – Festival Of Britain'.

103 Holt, *Sport and the British*, p. 246.

104 Holt, *Sport and the British*, pp. 246–7.

105 Holt, *Sport and the British*, p. 249.

106 Holt, *Sport and the British*, pp. 249–50.

107 *The Festival of Britain 1951*, 'Cardiff,' p. 28; 'County Borough of Swansea Festival of Britain, 1951'.

108 PRO, Work 25/240, 'Rhondda Urban District Council Festival of Britain Music Festival' (three-fold paper brochure with the national Festival symbol).

109 Curiously, 'Man' was also spelled 'Mann' in their own Festival literature.

110 For a lucid explanation of the status of the Isle of Man, see R. Quayle, 'The Isle of Man Constitution', in V. Robinson and D. McCarroll (eds), *The Isle of Man: Celebrating a Sense of Place* (Liverpool: Liverpool University Press, 1990), pp. 123–32.

111 Manx Museum Library, Isle of Man, 'Isle of Man Festival of Britain 1951', Official Programme of events, London: Issued by the Isle of Man Publicity Board, n.p., pressmark F64/2X; and 'Souvenir Programme, Isle of Man, Festival of Britain 1951, National Pageants,' p. 2, 'Message from the Author', L. du Garde Peach, Manx Museum Library, Acc. no, 15668, Class: C252/12q.

112 *Ibid.*

113 *Ibid.*

114 *Ibid.*

115 PRO, Work 25/239/E2/A-L, 'Borough of Liskeard Festival of Britain 1951 Programme of Events', n.p.

116 'Borough of Liskeard Festival of Britain 1951', n.p.

117 J. Vernon, 'Border Crossings: Cornwall and the English (imagi)nation', in Cubitt (ed.), *Imagining Nations*, 153–72.

118 Vernon, 'Border Crossings', p. 160.

119 'Borough of Liskeard Festival of Britain 1951', n.p.

120 PRO, Work 25/4, *FESTIVAL Souvenir 30th June, 1951 Galloway News*, p. 1, in Dumfries files.

121 *FESTIVAL Souvenir*, p. 2.

122 *FESTIVAL Souvenir*, p. 1 and *Festival of Britain*, 'Guid Nychburris Week', p. 44.

123 *FESTIVAL Souvenir*, p. 1.

124 *The Festival of Britain, 1951*, p. 44.

125 *FESTIVAL Souvenir*, p. 1.

126 *Ibid.*

127 *The Festival of Britain, 1951*, p. 44.

128 *FESTIVAL Souvenir*, p. 1.

129 *The Festival of Britain, 1951*, p. 44.

130 *FESTIVAL Souvenir*, p. 3.

131 *Ibid.*

132 *Ibid.*

133 Cox, 'The Story the Exhibition Tells', pp. 1–2.

134 McKibbin, *Classes and Cultures*, p. 533.

135 P. Dodd, 'Englishness and the National Culture', in Colls and Dodd (eds), *Englishness*, 1–28, p. 12. Dodd's emphasis in the use of these terms is in relation to the 'Celtic fringe' rather than a broader question of 'local' versus metropolitan cultures, but I think the comparison holds.

136 Dodd, 'Englishness and the National Culture', p. 15.

137 No doubt such notions of the importance and authenticity of pre-industrial Britain influenced her decision to study archaeology.

138 McKibbin, *Classes and Cultures*, p. 526; and LeMahieu, *A Culture for Democracy*, p. 82.

139 McKibbin, *Classes and Cultures*, p. 527.

140 Eley and Suny (eds), *Becoming National*, p. 24; and Bennett, *Birth of the Museum*, p. 149. According to Bennett, 'the very concept of national heritage is, of necessity, demotic; its *raison d'être* is to enfold diverse histories into one'.

141 Please see the section in Chapter 2 on Britishness as belonging rather than othering.

142 Colley, *Britons*, p. 6.

143 *Ibid.*

144 Fielding, Thompson and Tiratsoo, '*England Arise!*', p. 19.

7 ✧ The place that was almost absent: the British Empire

O TODAY's sensibilities, it seems surprising that in the 1951 Festival – 'a national display of British contribution to civilisation, past, present, and future'[1] – there were very few representations of the Empire or the Commonwealth. According to Robert Hewison, 'imperial echoes sound[ed] only in the celebration of British explorers in the Dome of Discovery'.[2] Hewison has explained this absence of empire by arguing that, 'aware of Britain's indebtedness to the United States, the government had no wish to lay undue emphasis on the Empire'.[3] While Hewison displaces all of the anxieties about the Empire, and by implication even decolonisation, on to the Americans, various sources suggest a more complex story. For example, they tell us that the British were struggling with the question of how to reconcile the discrepancy they had faced, at least since the Second World War, between being the bearers of freedom in opposition to the 'barbarism' of the Germans and their own history of colonisation and empire-building. Hewison is correct in maintaining that the Americans were not well disposed to Britain's Empire or Commonwealth. Particularly between 1944 and 1947 British policies in relation to Palestine, for example, were a great cause of friction between the two countries.[4] Britain acknowledged it needed American assistance in order to create and maintain its place as 'the bridge between the Western and Eastern Hemisphere', in addition to needing its financial support.[5] However, a close examination of the official Festival planning documents, as well as other contemporary and historical sources, reveals that Hewison's appraisal is too simple.[6] First, there were more references to Empire than merely those in the Dome, as Hewison suggests. Second, the reasons for the near absence of representations of Empire – or the Commonwealth, as it was more frequently called in official circles after Indian independence in 1947 – in the Festival are more complicated than the explanation that Hewison offers.[7]

For one thing, recent developments in imperial politics made the Empire/Commonwealth a politically sensitive and ambiguous topic. True, for some, the British withdrawal from India, Ceylon and Burma was seen as a point of pride – as the fulfilment of Labour's promises of decolonisation. But, for many others, such events indicated a loss of British power and prestige in a period already filled with disappointment and uncertainty, particularly in the case of India – 'the jewel in the crown'. The financial follies and political disturbances in most of Britain's remaining colonies, including Ghana, Southern Rhodesia, Zambia, Malawi and Malaya, concerned others.[8]

However, neither Herbert Morrison nor the Festival Executive Committee cited external or internal political pressures as the reason for excluding the Empire/Commonwealth from the 1951 festivities. The Festival organisers' official explanation for the absence of these representations was a simple one; it was merely a matter of resources. (Of course, although this was not publicly articulated, it could be argued that limited resources were the reason that the Attlee governments supported the retreat from Empire, as well.) But some people, including Members of Parliament, protested against this decision.[9] In a Memorandum from the Director-General, Gerald Barry, written in June 1949, Barry acknowledged that some members of the Festival Council had 'expressed the view that the purpose of the Festival would be lost if the foundation of the British Empire – Britain's greatest contribution to civilisation – was not demonstrated'.[10] This document reveals that some influential Britons were devoted to the idea that in an exhibition of 'British contributions to civilisation' the Empire was an essential component. It is important, however, to remember that the Festival Council, which was made up primarily of politicians and famous people in the arts, was not the body that actually planned and organised the Festival.[11] As explained in Chapter 2, it was the members of the Executive Committee who were chiefly responsible for the Festival's buildings and representations.

Herbert Morrison laid down the official line on this issue in the summer of 1949 in his dual roles as 'Lord Festival' and Lord President of the Council. Morrison argued that 'Owing to shortages of manpower and materials, the Festival of Britain, 1951 ... has, unfortunately, had to be limited to putting on show the contribution of the United Kingdom to civilisation. It is not, therefore, possible to invite Commonwealth Governments and administrations to arrange for pavilions or other displays in the exhibitions.'[12] Yet the combination of political sensitivity and pragmatic concerns is surely insufficient to explain the decision to do so little with the issue of the Empire/Commonwealth in the Festival. This chapter explores what few representations of Empire or Commonwealth there were in the Festival, as well as the reasons why they were so heavily edited out of its representational repertoire.

The official Festival exhibition of the National Book League portrayed the English language and literature as 'missionaries'; 'The Earth' exhibition on the South Bank featured 'minerals from the Commonwealth'; and the Sport Pavilion there made small allusions to imperialism in its rendition of 'the British at play'.[13] In fact, the original conceptions for the Dome of Discovery explicitly referred to the 'British race' 'projecting themselves abroad' and 'opening up the Dark Continent'. But, by 1951, the Dome's actual representations were much more muted, featuring science, rather than imperialism, as the motor of discovery. Perhaps most importantly, the Festival also counted the Imperial Institute's offering, the 'Traditional Art and Sculpture from the Colonies' exhibition, amongst its recommended London events.[14]

The paucity of imperial representations suggests that most people, not surprisingly, conceived of Great Britain in the immediate post-war period as an all-white nation. In the midst of Black British immigration from the West Indies to the British Isles, for instance, the Lord Chancellor publicly maintained that there was a distinction 'between our own people and the people for whom we are trustees'.[15] This is a further explanation for the relative absence of imperial references in the Festival; for many people in Britain at the time the Empire and the Commonwealth were irrelevancies, as we shall see. Another comes from political stands taken by some of the key Festival planners in the 1930s.

Political and Economic Planning (PEP) and Empire Free Trade

Charles Plouviez, the Festival's assistant to the director of exhibitions, explained in 2001 that he did not remember the issue of representing the Commonwealth or the Empire ever being mentioned, but he also said he did not recall thinking that it should have been.[16] According to historian Raphael Samuel, during the period in which most of the Festival's planners would have attended school – the inter-war years of 1918–39 – the British Empire disappeared from the history syllabus.[17] This meant that the planners did not see the Empire as an integral part of British history and as such would not have thought it necessary to represent it in the Festival's displays. However, Plouviez also wrote that 'the *Daily Express*, when it wasn't slanging the Festival, was promoting Beaverbrook's favourite idea of "imperial preference". So the Empire was a real political issue, and whatever way we had approached it it would have been immensely unpopular with about half our audience. Which would have been a good enough reason for ignoring it I guess.'[18]

Here we get a glimpse into a little-remembered debate from the 1930s, which sheds light on the politics of some of the Festival's key planners in relation to questions of Empire. Gerald Barry and Max Nicholson's political stands in response to Beaverbrook suggest why references to the Empire and the Commonwealth were muted in the 1951 exhibitions. Max Nicholson, who was Morrison's under-secretary and a key member of the Festival Committee, gave a fuller, although extremely cryptic explanation for ignoring the Empire and Commonwealth in a letter of 1 November 2001. He wrote:

> I think I can answer the profound question which is troubling you about the Festival of Britain's attitude to the British Empire.
>
> That Empire had been created almost unintentionally. Not until late Victorian times was there any serious British response to the strong German challenge, leading to World War I. That war led thoughtful people, especially young serving officers, to question such a scenario. Among these was Gerald Barry, who as the young editor of the Establishment weekly, the *Saturday Review*, was confronted, through its abrupt sale early in 1930 to a pal of the Canadian press tycoon Lord Beaverbrook. He accepted the challenge to reject the imposed policies of Empire Free Trade and to stand for broad modern principles of politics and economics. Despite ensuing upheavals for Britain, this prevailed especially among the young.
>
> The post-war opportunity of a centennial celebration of the Great Exhibition of 1851 was eventually entrusted by Deputy Prime Minister Herbert Morrison to me as head of his office, enlisting Gerald Barry and his mature group to create the Festival of Britain, which it duly did. This brought over to the Festival the mature scepticism and comprehensive background knowledge of the team. The Festival, thus fully briefed, carried a message about the British Empire which the ensuing half-century's record has done nothing to invalidate.[19]

From Nicholson's remarks it appears that it is a little-remembered chapter in 1930s political history that heavily influenced the decision to downplay the Empire and Commonwealth in the 1951 Festival.

As Nicholson hinted in his letter, Gerald Barry had resigned from the *Saturday Review* in 1930, taking with him most of his staff, in protest of the new owner's use of the paper to publicise Lord Beaverbrook's United Empire Party. He objected to a publication being used as a vehicle of propaganda, as well as opposing Beaverbrook's idea that there should be within the Empire a free trade policy that excluded Europe.[20] This, in turn, fuelled Beaverbrook's dislike for the Festival twenty-odd years later. Beaverbrook believed that Britain needed new markets and that they should come from the British Empire.[21] Historian A. J. P. Taylor, in his 1972 biography of Beaverbrook, claimed that 'all memory of' the 'Empire Crusade', as he called it:

> was washed away by the great depression, and it seems in retrospect a trivial episode hardly worthy of record. Yet, it was in its time an astonishing

achievement. Beaverbrook had no standing in the Conservative Party. He had never been a member of the Conservative government. Yet he came nearer than any other single man has ever done to unhorsing the accepted leader of a great political party.[22]

Beaverbrook decided it was 'the duty of his newspapers to tell only the news of the Empire Crusade'.[23]

By contrast, Nicholson and Barry were founding members of the Labour think-tank, Political and Economic Planning or PEP.[24] PEP had been formed as a direct result of the *Weekend Review*'s National Plan, issued as a supplement to the paper on 14 February 1931. The National Plan was in many ways in direct opposition to Beaverbrook's Empire Crusade. The Plan was described as 'a manifesto for a radical change in how to govern a nation', proposing the reorganisation of the workings of government and a series of state-controlled organisations. Its aim was to 'replace "the present chaotic economic and social order with a national planned economy, capable of working with other planned economies both within the Empire and abroad."'[25] The National Plan, aside from opposing Beaverbrook's campaign, was a response to the economic depression and high unemployment facing the MacDonald government of 1931. Barry not only called for a planned economy mixing state control with responsible self-government and the streamlining of bureaucracy, interestingly, he also proposed in the Plan that a London Planning Commission should solve the problem of the 'wasted south bank between the Thames, Vauxhall, the Oval, Elephant and London Bridge'.[26] The 1951 Festival of Britain offered Barry a solution – an opportunity to transform London's South Bank. The National Plan might seem a long way from the question of the Empire and the Festival, and yet the proposals by PEP represent a rejection of Beaverbrook's ideas of special preference for the Empire, and reflect a set of left-wing political concerns, including planning and streamlining, much evidence of which can be found in the 1951 exhibitions. Max Nicholson, in his 2001 letter, argued that the Empire 'had been created almost unintentionally' and in this way he seems to insinuate it was really an irrelevance when it came to displaying 'British contributions to civilisation'. Given the defeat of Germany and the humiliation of France, it seemed to Nicholson and Barry that Britain was the country left to defend true European values and culture. This was Britain's proper place, rather than in the midst of a far-flung Empire or Commonwealth, they believed.

Plans and displays of the Empire and Commonwealth in the Festival

But not everyone on the Festival's Executive Committee agreed with Barry and Nicholson's ideas about the Empire or the Commonwealth. As we have already seen, some people argued that imperial representations should be included in the 1951 exhibitions. Planning documents from 1948 and 1949 for Festival exhibitions, as well as some actualised displays, suggest that some Festival planners were keen to represent attempts to re-negotiate the relationship between the Empire/Commonwealth and Great Britain as its centre. For example, a summer of 1948 'Report by the Director General' states:

> From the combination of this variety of race and of natural resources results – British history. From the impact of the one on the other has developed the kind of life we have made for ourselves and the kind of contributions we have made to human progress. The first has given us our thought, our literature and other arts, our science, our games, our exploration, our Empire-building. These can be exhibited in their practical end-results ... If we take one of our chief British attributes – love of adventure, for example, we see how from it have stemmed innumerable achievements both great and small, from an Empire to the design of a solar tepee (the second made necessary by the acquisition of the first).[27]

In this early draft of a souvenir brochure for the South Bank exhibition, the Empire was evoked as both an achievement and as evidence of the adventurous and inventive nature of the British. But by the summer of 1951 the language actually used in the official Festival literature made no such obvious mention of British imperial inclinations. Instead, there were rather subtle references to the imperial past and to the possibility of these nations' future independence. For example, 'The Land' section of the South Bank's Dome of Discovery included a display entitled 'Commonwealth links'. There the Commonwealth of Nations was described as 'the great witness to British exploration by land'. The 'strongest binding force' of the Commonwealth in 1951 was proclaimed to be 'common ideas and ideals, and visual evidence of this is the vast communications system which came into being as a result of British enterprise – sea lanes, air routes, railways, cables, and now radio. Speech is the most intimate of all ways of communications.' The radio system was announced as both a British achievement and a tool to allow the British people to speak with 'our sons and daughters' who 'have left Britain and set up their own homes overseas', as well as 'our adopted children ... coming into their own estates'.[28] In the Dome, 'Commonwealth Agriculture' was celebrated for providing the world with food, rubber and wool. The visitor learned that in terms of world exports, the Commonwealth produced 'two thirds of its butter, half its cheese, much of its wheat, nearly half its tinned meat', and 'about half the world's wool supply'. The tropical areas contribute a very large percentage of the world's supply of sisal, sugar, cocoa, palm oil, rubber and tea', the display stated.[29] This Dome display implied that British imperialism had offered the world the means to access such important goods through technology and transportation. The display, 'Minerals from the Commonwealth', which exhibited 'part of the well-founded riches of the Commonwealth countries', relayed a similar message.[30] Adventurous British 'sons and daughters', impressive agriculture, and rich minerals resided in the Commonwealth, according to this exhibition. Unlike in the earlier planning document where the language was overt and the connections between 'Empire-building' and 'innumerable achievements both great and small' were clearly laid out, in the actual displays the messages were more muted.

Other Festival exhibitions, in addition to those in the Dome of Discovery, resounded with 'echoes' of Empire, to loosely borrow Hewison's phrase. For example, the Sport Pavilion quietly referred to imperialism in its presentation of the British at play. The guide explained:

> The British relish sport for its own sake and for the sake of its open air setting. They are possessed of inventing their own games and for adapting other people's ... Once they have got a game codified, they have carried it with them overseas, where the people of other nations have found themselves solemnly playing according to British rules.[31]

In the Sport Pavilion's text, how people in 'other nations' had come to play 'according to British rules' went unexplained; any direct explanation would have had to engage overtly with the difficult issue of imperialism. The imperial tones are apparent, although subdued, with the reference to these other people *finding* 'themselves solemnly playing' by the British rules. In this move Britain was re-cast as the great *umpire*, rather than *empire*, regulating the rules of the game worldwide. Great Britain was now the rule-giver rather than the ruler of the world.

In the Second World War this was the imagined British mission in Europe, to force the Nazis to abide by the rules of law and fair play. As we saw earlier in this book, the late Raphael Samuel argued that during the Second World War, in contrast to the First World War imaginings, the British conceived of themselves as 'a domestic people rather than a master race, home-lovers rather than conquerors'.[32] He showed how a wide range of discourses – including popular cinema, J. B. Priestley's widely heard BBC radio 'Postscripts', and George Orwell's essays – portrayed the British as kind, modest, tolerant and sportsmanlike.[33] Sian Nicholas has shown how images of the British Empire were 'progressively played down by the B.B.C. as an explicit feature of "national propaganda" during the Second World War'.[34] Thus, most paternalistic notions of Britain vis-à-vis its colonies had been downplayed in the war and by 1949 the most prevalent imaginings of Britishness – proud, but not boastful, fair, honest, and dedicated to the rule of law – would have understandably excluded overt references to the Empire/Commonwealth. In keeping with this, in the Festival the British were primarily represented as dedicated to fairness and justice.

But some publications during the Second World War had explained that it was the British people's responsibility to help more 'primitive' peoples to learn the rule of law. This argument was at the core of *You and the Empire*, the Army Bureau of Education pamphlet published in March of 1944. The Army Bureau of Education produced eighteen educational pamphlets between 1942 and 1944, designed to be used by instructors in hourly courses, held thrice weekly for troops. When the scheme was first discussed in the autumn of 1942 it was recommended that at least one hour per week should be 'devoted to education in citizenship' and these pamphlets were the resulting suggested texts.[35] Many of them were widely distributed among both soldiers and civilians. Whether they were read or taken to heart is questionable, but they reveal how one important British institution answered the question of how Britons *should* feel about the issue of 'Ruling Over Others?'. Under the larger heading, 'What Does the Empire Mean to You?', *You and the Empire* told its readers that 'To many people nowadays the very word "Empire" has a nasty sound. It reminds them of Nazi ideas of a master-race ruling others. Perhaps the empire means to you the idea of Britain ruling over coloured people in Africa, Asia and the Pacific Islands'.[36] The pamphlet asked 'Do you think these people could govern themselves?', and answered 'Maybe you think some of them could, but obviously not all. Then if they are to be protected and helped, and governed according to better standards than their primitive ideas, it is our business as the Power in charge to see that they get the best government that we know and can afford'.[37] The negative associations of empire and its connotations of a Nazi 'master-race ruling others' had to be countered in the minds of British soldiers. According to the Army Bureau of Education, the British were a responsible people whose role was to offer more 'primitive', 'coloured people' 'protection and help' in learning to govern themselves.

This altruistic justification of the Empire/Commonwealth was one of the most prevalent in the post-war rhetoric promulgated by the Labour government, as well. For example, a 1946 government pamphlet for schools, *Britain and the Colonies*, explained to British children that today 'even the critics of empire now begin to appreciate that the maintenance and strengthening of the British Commonwealth is no sinister imperialism in the worst sense, and that all of us who have a common loyalty to the Throne are honestly trying to create a better world not only for ourselves but for mankind generally'.[38] This is the sort of imperialism for which the

British often claimed they were famous – concerned and paternalistic. Such a notion also lay at the heart of the representations of Empire/Commonwealth in the National Book League's Festival exhibition.

'Our language as missionary': the National Book League's exhibition

One London Festival event, the National Book League's exhibition at the Victoria and Albert Museum in South Kensington, featured oblique references to Britain's imperial attitudes and activities. English literature and the English language itself were represented as 'missionaries' rather than conquerors, paternalistic rather than pugilistic. The first page of the special Festival of Britain issue of *Books*, the League's journal, was boldly headed 'Our Language as Missionary'.[39] The entry began by quoting a letter written by Gerald Barry and his oft-repeated statement that 'The underlying purpose of the Festival is to demonstrate – to our own people no less than to our visitors from abroad – the contributions which the British nation has been able to make to the common welfare of mankind, and something of the ideas and traditions which have shaped them'.[40] Barry then turned to the role of English Literature 'in fulfilling such a purpose'. He asserted that 'Literature' 'naturally assumes a place of honour' because 'Not only are its glories recognised throughout the world; it is also the vehicle by means of which many of the most potent and subtle ingredients of the British character and British habits of thought are conveyed, and have influenced the minds of other peoples'.[41] Or, in the words of the title, English language and literature had acted as 'missionaries'. Such a reference is unmistakably, either consciously or unconsciously, related to Britain's imperial endeavours and the belief that it had a role to play in 'influencing' 'the minds of other peoples'. Barry concluded, proclaiming that 'The Festival of Britain, while reminding us of our heritage from the past, is designed to display no less vividly our thought for the future, the manifold ways in which our continuing vitality is still contributing to the common store. In fulfilling this purpose the English language is itself perhaps our most persuasive missionary'.[42] The English language was not only charged with the task of reminding the British of their collective past. It was also meant to exhibit to everyone from Britain and beyond that the British people were continually – to use the Festival's own terms – 'contributing' to world culture or 'civilisation'.

Alan Bott, Representative of the National Book League Festival Committee on the Executive Committee of the Festival Office and Joint Chairman of the League's Exhibition Sub-Committee, authored the next piece in this special Festival edition of *Books*. Bott described the exhibition's layout and explained that the book displays were arranged beneath 'a ceiling composed from the alphabet that conquered the world'.[43] In Bott's text, Barry's 'missionaries' were perhaps more honestly portrayed with truer faces as 'conquerors'. But, either way, they were certainly colonising in a way more compatible with the post-war world – through culture, rather than through force. English literature and the English language were part of the collective British past, as well as key components of the cultural legacy they had passed on to much of the world.

Who 'The People' were in the South Bank exhibitions

One of the central exhibitions on the South Bank site explained how the British came to be a freedom-loving people who spoke English – that mixture of earlier languages. 'The People of Britain' was one of the two organising themes of the overall exhibition. As we saw in Chapter 4, the accompanying official Festival guides proclaimed that 'the British are a nation of many different parts. In appearance, too, they are just as mixed – certainly one of the most-mixed people in the world.'[44] The text carried on, asking the questions 'But who are these British people? What differing breeds of ancestors have contributed to the shaping of such a rare miscellany of faces as confronts the visitor in any London bus? Where did those various ancestors come from? And how did they reach this land?'[45] If one anticipates that the answers to these questions incorporate some recognition of the impact the British Empire had had on Great Britain, *per se*, one is disappointed. For the answers to these questions lay in pre- and early history, according to the souvenir guide: first 'primitive hunting and fishing men, equipped with flint and bone, were the only people here ... The first newcomers were farming folk, long-headed and lightly built ... After Stone, Bronze. Bronze was the speciality of a tough and warlike people who invaded England and Scotland nearly four thousand years ago'.[46] Each group who came to Britain contributed something to 'human progress' – stone, bronze, agriculture, etc. The next stage of this story of development came when 'the incoming Celts ... gave a fresh impulse to agriculture. They were people from Northern France looking for new land'. Unfortunately, the narrative continued, 'the Celts could not resist a war; and their intertribal feuds made things easy for the Romans, when in A.D. 43, they came, and conquered'. Then, 'less than two hundred years after the Anglo-Saxons settled in, St. Augustine's mission brought a new infusion of Christianity to Britain. Their Anglo-Saxon converts mingled with those of the Celtic peoples'. 'The last invaders' were the 'Norse and Danish Viking sea-raiders', who the British people and land 'accommodated' and 'absorbed', 'as it had absorbed so many invaders in the past, and as it was destined to absorb the conquerors of the future – the Normans.'[47]

The guide summed up this story of accommodation and progress with the assertion that 'though the ancient dead are buried, it is the very blood they brought here that runs in us ... They were absorbed into the life that was here before them, and themselves became islanders of a land that moulded the thoughts, the feelings, the behaviour of them all into a whole which is our British way of life and tradition'.[48] The assumption that ran throughout the London-produced Festival guides and catalogues was that the British were a people who had been born and bred in the British Isles for generations and generations – more generations than anyone could count, in fact.[49]

This story of the ancient origins of the British 'land and people' excluded thousands of immigrants past and present, but perhaps just as importantly, it also explained British exceptionalism. Its narrative of Britain as an island nation was driven equally by old stories of British sturdiness and adaptability, and by Britons' innate refusal to accept unfair authority in the form of Popery, Continental absolutism and, most recently, German fascism. This particular rendering of a presumed common past explained how the British came to be a people who played fairly, had a judicial system that 'was the envy of the world', and spoke a polyglot language.[50] Taken together, it was an imagining of an all white, self-contained British nation residing in the British Isles. 'The People of Britain' section of the South Bank site did not include imaginings of British people's encounters with people of colour in lands the British had conquered over centuries, nor did it engage in the sticky issue of people from those places who considered themselves British.

Once again, it is possible through the official documents to glimpse the earlier thoughts behind the planning of the South Bank exhibition. A Festival Presentation Panel's preliminary memo from April 1949 described the Dome of Discovery as 'demonstrating' 'the British contribution to world civilization ... in its most heightened form', with the 'key word' being 'INITIATIVE'.[51] 'The theme throughout the section is the success with which the British have been able to project themselves – whether physically or mentally – beyond the immediate confines of everyday experience'.[52] The 1949 document also spoke of 'how much of the world has been made known to civilisation by British explorers', suggesting that 'one or two areas in particular ... should be selected for detailed treatment', with 'the opening up of the Dark Continent' constituting a special section. But by 1951 this idea, along with references to 'the British race', were not as prominent as they were in the earlier planning document. In addition, the document from 1949 stressed that in the Dome 'reference should be made ... to the British way of life as expressed in our attitude towards the more backwards peoples of these overseas areas'.[53] 'The British way of life' and the mention of 'our attitude' helped to construct an imagined unitary, white audience and implied British citizenry – 'in opposition to the primitive otherness of conquered peoples'.[54] This overtly racist tone was missing from the actual Festival in 1951, but rather similar binaries were evoked in the Imperial Institute's exhibition, the 'show of traditional sculpture and craft work from the Colonies'.[55]

'A show of traditional sculpture and craft work from the Colonies'

The Imperial Institute's catalogue for its 1951 temporary exhibition, 'Traditional Sculpture from the Colonies', made a conceptual move not generally seen in London's Festival events. The catalogue's author, William Fagg, chose the stark differences between 'Europeans' and 'primitives' as his starting point in unravelling the mysteries of 'traditional sculpture from the colonies' for his imagined audience.[56] First, Fagg attempted to disabuse the exhibition's visitors of what he believed would be their predilection for judging 'works of art in the first place by whether they are lifelike'.[57] He explained to his audience that:

> The European who seeks to 'understand' what is usually called 'primitive' art, to cultivate a state of mind and heart receptive to its strange forms and rhythms, must begin by divesting himself of some of the assumptions which are so fundamental in modern European thought that he is probably unconscious of the part which they play in forming his own reactions to art and to life.[58]

Fagg's use of quotation marks around the word primitive suggests that he did not consider himself guilty of such assessments of African art, yet he was concerned that most of his viewers would suffer from such ignorant appraisals. He informed his audience that Western culture – or what he called 'modern industrial civilization' – was underpinned by 'mathematical and philosophical ideas ... laid down for us about the sixth century before Christ by the Ionian philosophers'.[59] And that 'we may take as a symbol of this civilizing revolution its most fundamental idea, the intellectual concept of the straight line, "the shortest distance between two points"'.[60] This, Fagg argued, was at the core of Europeans' 'subconscious acceptance of the "collective representations" of our society (as the sociologists call them)'. In other words, this was why 'Europeans' had come to expect their sculptures and paintings to look 'lifelike'.[61] However, he suggested that 'Negro Africa and other tribal areas which are represented never underwent the philosophical and scientific revolution' described above.[62] As such, he continued, 'We may perhaps say that their categories of thought tend to be "poetic" – with emphasis on analogy, metaphor and symbolism – rather than scientific'.[63] This creation of a dichotomy between 'European' and 'traditional' art and between Europeans ('us') and Africans ('them') reveals Fagg's assumption that his visitors would be primarily both white and unfamiliar with the colonies. The binary also extended to 'categories of thought'. According to Fagg, the 'African' was 'poetic', while the 'European' was 'scientific'. The dichotomy then was also 'irrational' versus 'rational', which were clearly racialised terms in the immediate post-war period. Such notions of race constructed a stark division between the white viewer and the imagined 'traditional' creators of the works before them, even as Fagg attempted to widen his audience's understanding. The viewer was part of the white 'we', united in their comprehension (or lack of comprehension) of the non-European 'primitive' art and, by extension, people. Here we see another example of the idea that Britain could be the leader of other less-fortunate people – that the British could act as cultural 'missionaries'. Colonised people were not irredeemably inferior, they were 'poetic' because they lacked the advantages that the scientific revolution had offered Europeans. With Britain's help, these Africans and others could learn to master scientific knowledge and learn to make art that would be considered less 'primitive' in Europe. Though the gap might be bridged, Fagg's explanation of the exhibition illustrates that white British people in this period implicitly accepted that a vast gulf separated them from the people of colour who resided in the British colonies and former colonies. 'The colonies' were places of radical otherness.

Britishness and whiteness

Fagg's binaries provide us with one of the most compelling explanations of why the Empire/Commonwealth was virtually absent from the Festival of Britain celebrations. As we have seen, for some of the Festival's planners the Empire was irrelevant because it was inappropriate and situated Britain in the wrong context. For many of them, schooled in the inter-war period, it was just not an important chapter in British history. But there is also the simple idea that, as Paul Rich has explained, in 1951 Britain was 'a society still unused to the presence of black people in its midst, certainly outside of London and the major cities'.[64]

Although the Empire was beginning to come home, there were still only relatively small and concentrated populations of Black people in Britain in the 1940s and early 1950s.[65] For example, in inter-war Britain there were only a few thousand Black people, settled almost exclusively in the port cities of London, Liverpool, Bristol, Manchester, Glasgow, Swansea, Cardiff, and South Shields. But 800 West Indians migrated to Britain between December 1947 and October 1948, and then 2,000 arrived annually between 1948 and 1951.[66] And in July of 1950 an *ad hoc* committee of Ministers appointed to consider legislation on immigration control estimated that Britain's Black population numbered 30,000, with 10,000 in Merseyside, 5,000 in London, 5,000 in Cardiff and 2,000 in Tyneside.[67] There is evidence of public discussion of Black immigration from the former colonies, though. One example comes from a *Picture Post* article published in July 1949, entitled 'Is there a BRITISH COLOUR BAR?'. The newspaper was surprised when it discovered that the answer was affirmative. The *Picture Post* informed its readers that all 'colonial coloured people', regardless of class or origin, had been raised to think of Great Britain as 'the Mother Country' and themselves as British. Because of this, these people were likely to experience much emotional distress, possibly leading to bad behaviour, if they were to encounter attitudes and situations to the contrary.[68] The *Picture Post* article was at pains to explain to its readers that these 'colonial coloured people' were British and needed to be treated as such when they came to these shores. Such colonial British subjects, were, of course, not represented in the 1951 Festival. As we have seen, the only major London exhibition focusing on the Empire or the Commonwealth was a display of 'primitive', 'traditional' art, primarily from Africa, and it was planned by the Imperial Institute, not the Festival Executive Committee.

Tony Bennett has written that within 'the exhibitionary complex' generally 'the space of representation' 'permitted the construction' of a 'totalizing' order of things and people.[69] For Bennett, that order 'organized the implied public – the white citizenries of the imperialist powers – into a unity', which erased other divisions between the population by construct-ing a united white 'we'. This white citizenry was unified 'in opposition to the primitive otherness of conquered peoples' through the exhibitions.[70] This is true in the case of the Festival of Britain's exhibitionary complex. As we have seen, for a variety of reasons the Empire/Commonwealth was no longer thoroughly presentable in the immediate post-war world. The Festival represented Great Britain as an island nation inhabited by a diverse array of people from many lands, but those people, to put it bluntly, were conceived of as exclusively white and having resided on this island for at least a thousand years.

In fact, as we have seen through the Festival's rhetoric and through the statements of planners Gerald Barry and Max Nicholson, the Em-pire/Commonwealth was irrelevant to many British people for various reasons in the immediate post-war period. Writers, journalists and politi-cians in the 1940s and 1950s often pointed out that the British people were extremely ignorant when it came to questions about the British Empire/Commonwealth. For example, Hugh Dalton stated at the time of

Indian Independence in 1947 that 'I don't believe one person in a hundred in this country cares tuppence about [India] so long as British people are not being mauled about out there'.[71] According to Paul Rich, a survey of British attitudes to the colonies in 1951, conducted by the Central Office of Information, 'revealed that many people in Britain were unaware that white settlers lived in British colonies'.[72] And in 1951 the Government's Social Survey Unit found that 59 per cent of the British population could not name a single British colony.[73] It seems clear that for many British people the Empire and the Commonwealth were not relevant to their lives.

This does not mean, however, that ignorance of the Empire and the Commonwealth rendered British imperialism entirely extraneous to how white British people conceived of themselves. As David Lloyd and, more recently, Richard Dyer, have argued: 'racial theories as such and even the aspirational structure of ... imperialism are less crucial to the development of white identity than the attainment of a position of disinterest – abstraction, distance, separation, objectivity – which creates a public sphere that is the mark of civilisation itself'.[74] And as Geoff Eley has argued, 'Notions of British national identity, and of the "Englishness" at their heart, have formed historically around understandings of racial difference, coming partly from the imperial past'.[75] Indeed, no matter how little white British people living in their island nation purported to know about the whats and wheres of the British Empire/Commonwealth, one thing they almost certainly assumed was that it was where Black, 'less civilised' people – 'others' – lived. Lloyd asserts that immigration from the former colonies is especially unsettling because 'it upsets the asymmetrical distribution of humanity into the local (native) and the universal'.[76] Britain was perceived by the vast majority as an all-white nation.

Conclusion

The fight for freedom from fascist imperialism in the Second World War led some people to question how to reconcile Britain's commitment to freedom with its commitment to Empire/Commonwealth. The Festival enabled the British people to reconcile this contradiction by celebrating paternalism, exalting Britain's mission as a cultural one, and perpetuating radical acts of othering. The Festival's representations showed the British of the post-war moment just as they had been seen in the Second World War: as plucky, determined people, residing on the island nation of Great Britain. Such images were not flexible enough to incorporate the British citizenry that lived beyond the UK's shores. There may have been some fears of offending the Americans with imperialistic representations of Britain; there must have been concerns about the ambiguous state of the

Empire/Commonwealth by the late 1940s and there were definitely real pragmatic issues – actual shortages of materials and labour – that curtailed the range of possible representations of Britain and Britishness in the Festival. But, as we have seen, there were also political hangovers from the 1930s and an overwhelming common-sense notion of Britain as an all-white nation.

The 1951 Festival of Britain was a national act of reassessment and reconstruction that in many ways signalled a turning inward, as discussed earlier in this book. Sociologist Stuart Hall stated in a 1997 interview that 'In the 1960s, when it was plain the empire was no longer tenable, people thought the thing to do was pretend it never happened. I think some people may have done it out of the best possible motives: the liberal thing to do was not to come on as an old imperial power, just never refer to it again'.[77] Perhaps even in the early 1950s – when, ironically, Hall arrived in England, in the midst of the Festival of Britain – the liberal thinkers and planners behind the Festival felt that the best way to handle the issue of Empire/Commonwealth was to publicly 'pretend it never happened'. For at least two key planners, Barry and Nicholson, an emphasis on the Empire simply seemed inappropriate for a modern Britain.

Others saw the Empire as a politically charged issue best ignored, as Charles Plouviez indicated. Writing on the twenty-fifth anniversary of the Festival, Plouviez claimed that:

> Where 1851 had been deliberately international, 1951 was deliberately chauvinistic. It might almost be said to mark the beginning of our 'English disease' – the moment at which we stopped trying to lead the world as an industrial power, and started being the world's entertainers, coaxing tourists to laugh at our eccentricities, marvel at our traditions and wallow in our nostalgia.[78]

This may well say more about the anxieties of the 1970s than the realities of 1951. But with hindsight it is clear that Britain was on the cusp of a new era in 1951; it would soon be facing up to the challenge of how to build a multi-racial society. Even though most references to the Commonwealth and the Empire were excluded from the Festival, the actual people from these places could not be excluded from Great Britain. In some ways this representation of a white, self-contained island nation was already nostalgic in 1951, as the people from its former Empire had begun 'coming home' to their 'Mother Country'.

Notes

1 Morrison, 'Proposals Regarding the 1951 Exhibition'.

2 Hewison, *Culture and Consensus*, p. 59.

3 *Ibid.*

4 On Britain's policies towards Palestine, see C. J. Morris, 'The Labour Government's Policy and Publicity over Palestine, 1945–7', in Gorst, Johnman and Scott Lucas (eds), *Contemporary British History*, 169–92; F. Carr, 'Cold War: The Economy and Foreign Policy', in Fyrth (ed.), *Labour's High Noon*, 135–47; A. Sked and C. Cook, *Post-war Britain: A Political History* (London: Penguin Books, 1990), p. 55.

5 General Report of the Committee on European Economic Co-operation, as cited by C. C. S. Newton, 'The Sterling Crisis of 1947 and the British Response to the Marshall Plan', *Economic History Review*, 37 (1984), 395–7, 404. See also: J. E. Cronin, *The Politics of State Expansion: War, State and Society in Twentieth-Century Britain* (London and New York: Routledge, 1991), p. 166.

6 Hewison's notes to *Culture and Consensus* indicate that he did not consult the Festival of Britain records in the Public Record Office.

7 On the shift from Empire to Commonwealth, see, for example, K. Paul, *Whitewashing Britain: Race and Citizenship in the Postwar Era* (Ithaca and London: Cornell University Press, 1997). See also R. Hewison, *The Heritage Industry: Britain in a Climate of Decline* (London: Methuen, 1987), p. 35.

8 For a good overview of the situation, see Childs, *Britain Since 1945*.

9 *Hansard*, 467 (1948–49), col. 13, point 67, Mr Herbert Morrison, written answer to a question by Mr Janner, 12 July 1949.

10 PRO, Work 25/44, 'The Council of the Festival of Britain, 1951, Commonwealth Participation, Memorandum from the Director-General', 'Confidential FB C (49) 20' (16 June 1949).

11 For the full list of the members of both the Council and the Executive Committee, please see *The Official Book of the Festival*, p. 71.

12 *Hansard*, 467 (1948–49), col. 13, point 67. See also: PRO, Work 25/44/A5/A4 'Council Papers 1948', 'Strictly Confidential FBC. (48) 3 The Council of the Festival of Britain 1951, Memorandum by the Director-General, Recommendations for the Executive Committee for which Council Approval is Sought at the Meeting', 'Information from the Executive Committee. Commonwealth Participation', p. 4; PRO, Work 25/21 'General 5/Festival Theme', 'Extract From FB(C) (48) 4th meeting held on 23rd Sept, 1948'; PRO Work 25/44 'The Council of the Festival of Britain 1951, Minutes of the 7th Meeting of the Council held at 2, Savoy Court, WC2, on Thursday, April 7, 1949, at 10.30. a. m., Confidential FB C (49) 2nd Meeting'; PRO, Work 25/44, 'The Council of the Festival of Britain, 1951, Commonwealth Participation, Memorandum from the Director-General', 'Confidential FB C (49) 20' (June 16, 1949); and PRO, Work 25/44, 'The Council of the Festival of Britain 1951, Minutes of the 9th Meeting of the Council held at 2, Savoy Court, WC2, on Wednesday, July 20, 1949 at 10.30 a. m. Confidential FBC (49) 4th Meeting'.

13 PRO, Work 25/232/E1/B3/5, Gerald Barry in *Books: The Journal of the National Book League*, 260 (May 1951), Festival of Britain Issue, p. 97.

14 See *The Official Book of the Festival*, under the heading 'Painting and Sculpture', p. 19.

15 Parliamentary Debates, fifth series (1948), as cited by Paul, *Whitewashing Britain*, p. 22. On immigration, see P. B. Rich, *Race and Empire in British Politics* (Cambridge: Cambridge University Press, 1990), p. 163, and Paul, *Whitewashing Britain*, p. 119.

16 Charles Plouviez, electronic mail message to the author, 29 October 2001.

17 Samuel, *Island Stories, Theatres of Memory, Vol. II*, p. 86.

18 Charles Plouviez, electronic mail message to the author, 30 October 2001.

19 Max Nicholson, CB, CVO, letter to the author, 1 November 2001.

20 Waters, 'In Search of Sir Gerald Barry', p. 39.

21 C. A. McCurdy, *Empire Free Trade: A Study of the Effects of Free Trade on British Industry and of the Opportunities for Trade Expansion Within the Empire*, with an introduction by Lord Beaverbrook (London: Hutchinson, 1930), p. 76.

22 A. J. P. Taylor, *Beaverbrook* (London: Hamish Hamilton, 1972), p. 273.

23 *Ibid.*

24 Waters, 'In Search of Sir Gerald Barry', 41; and Weight, 'Pale Stood Albion', p. 144.

25 *Weekend Review*, 14 February 1931, supplement in BLPES folder no. 46, as quoted by Waters, 'In Search of Gerald Barry', p. 40.

26 *Ibid.*

27 PRO, Work 25/44/A5/A4, 'Report by the Director-General' (Photocopy) 'Confidential FB. C. (48) 5: The Council of the Festival of Britain 1951 Report by the Director', dated 27 July 1948, p. 3.

28 Cox, *The South Bank Exhibition*, p. 43.

29 *Ibid.*

30 Cox, *The South Bank Exhibition*, p. 46.

31 PRO, Work 25/230/E1/A1/2, *1951 Exhibition, London, Catalogue of Exhibitions, Festival of Britain*, p. 158.

32 Samuel, *Theatres of Memory, Vol. 1*, p. 219.

33 *Ibid.*

34 Nicholas, *The Echo of War*, p. 235.

35 'Preface', Directorate of Army Education, *The British Way and Purpose: Consolidated Edition of B. W. P. Booklets 1–18, with Appendices of Documents of Post-War Reconstruction* (London: The Directorate of Army Education, 1944), p. 1.

36 'Third Sequence: Today and Tomorrow. B. W. P. 16. You and the Empire. March, 1944', as reprinted in Directorate of Army Education, *The British Way*, pp. 458–61.

37 'Third Sequence: Today and Tomorrow. B. W. P. 16', p. 461.

38 *Britain and the Colonies* (1946), as quoted by Rich, *Race and Empire in British Politics*, pp. 65–6.

39 PRO, Work 25/232/E1/B3/5, *Books: The Journal of the National Book League*, 260 (May, 1951), p. 97 (actual first page of journal).

40 G. Barry, as quoted in *Books*, p. 97.

41 *Ibid.*

42 *Ibid.*

43 Bott, 'The Festival Exhibition Of Books, Victoria and Albert Museum', in *Books*, p. 98.

44 Anonymous, 'The People of Britain', in Cox, *The South Bank Exhibition*, 63–5, p. 63.

45 *Ibid.*

46 Anonymous 'The People of Britain', in Cox, *The South Bank Exhibition*, p. 65.

47 *Ibid.*

48 *Ibid.*

49 Such assumptions were in no way unique. There was, for example, what Peter Clarke has called 'a strong eugenic undertow to discussion of demographic trends in the twentieth century': Clarke, *Hope and Glory*, p. 217. William Beveridge's 1942 report on social insurance included language about 'the British race' and the 1949 Royal Commission on Population report referred to 'people of British stock'. See, for example, P. Thane, 'Population Politics in Post-War Britain', in Conekin, Mort and Waters (eds), *Moments of Modernity*, 114–33.

50 Samuel, *Theatres of Memory*, Vol. I, p. 218.

51 PRO, Work 25/21, 'Confidential F. B. Presentation Panel (49) 17 – Part II. Festival of Britain 1951. Presentation Panel. The Combined Exhibition Preliminary Memorandum for guidance in presentation of the Combined Exhibition – Part II', dated 27 April 1949, p. 44.

52 *Ibid.*

53 'Confidential F. B. Presentation Panel (49) 17', p. 46.

54 Bennett, *The Birth of the Museum*, p. 79.

55 It is noteworthy that neither the National Book League's Exhibition nor the colonial sculpture exhibition was mounted on the central South Bank site. In the London-planned exhibitions the only overt exhibitions referencing the Empire and colonialism were the Imperial Institute's two temporary exhibitions: 'Focus on Colonial Progress' and 'A show of traditional sculpture and craft work from the Colonies': *The Official Book of the Festival*, p. 61. Unfortunately, I have been unable to locate any extant documents relating to the former.

56 This exhibition received one line in the official Festival of Britain souvenir guide, under the heading 'Painting and Sculpture': *The Official Book of the Festival*, p. 19.

57 W. Fagg, *Traditional Sculpture from the Colonies* (London: Colonial Office, 1951), p. 3.

58 *Ibid.*

59 *Ibid.*

60 *Ibid.*

61 Fagg, *Traditional Sculpture*, pp. 3–4.

62 Fagg, *Traditional Sculpture*, p. 4.

63 *Ibid.*

64 Rich, *Race and Empire*, p. 175.

65 Rich, *Race and Empire*, p. 163; and Paul, *Whitewashing Britain*, p. 119.

66 D. Hiro, *Black British, White British: A History of Race Relations* (London: Grafton Books, 1991), p. 8.

67 Rich, *Race and Empire*, p. 167.

68 'Is there a BRITISH COLOUR BAR?', *The Picture Post*, 2 July 1949, as quoted by Errol Lawrence, 'Just Plain Common Sense: The "Roots" of Racism', in Centre for Contemporary Cultural Studies (ed.), *The Empire Strikes Back: Race and Racism in 70s Britain* (London and New York: Routledge, in association with the Centre for Contemporary Cultural Studies, University of Birmingham, 1992), 47–94, pp. 68–9.

69 Bennett, *The Birth of the Museum*, p. 79.

70 *Ibid.*

71 Hugh Dalton (1947), as quoted by Lawrence, 'Just Plain Common Sense', p. 69.

72 Rich, *Race and Empire*, p. 175.

73 Lawrence, 'Just Plain Common Sense', pp. 69–70. Furthermore, even the chronicler and champion of Black London life in the 1950s, Colin MacInnes, did not really 'fall in love' with his romanticised ideal of Black people, who he believed brought 'an element of joy and fantasy and violence into our cautious, ordered lives', until the summer of 1952 when the US African-American dance troupe, the Katherine Dunham Dance Company, appeared for their London season. Quotation from C. MacInnes, *City of Spades* (London: MacGibbon & Kee, 1957), as cited by Tony Gould in *Inside Outsider: The Life and Times of Colin MacInnes* (London: Allison & Busby, 1993), p. 94. Gould asserts that 'MacInnes's discovery of blacks, his drinking and his homosexuality developed simultaneously': *ibid.*

74 R. Dyer, *White* (London and New York: Routledge, 1997), pp. 38–9.

75 Eley, 'How is "History" Represented?', n.p. See also E. Said, *Culture and Imperialism* (London: Vintage, 1994); P. Gilroy, *'There Ain't No Black in the Union Jack'*; S. Rushdie, 'The New Empire Within Britain', in *Imaginary Homelands: Essays and Criticism 1981–1991* (London: Granta Books, 1991), 129–38; E. Lawrence, 'Just Plain Common Sense'; Sinfield, *Literature, Politics and Culture in Postwar Britain*, Chapter 7; and Dyer, *White*, especially pp. 30–9.

76 D. Lloyd, 'Race under Representation', *Oxford Literary Review*, 13:1–2 (1991), 62–94, p. 70, as quoted by Dyer, *White*, p. 38.

77 S. Hall, 'Les Enfants de Marx et Coca Cola: In the Second of Three Dialogues, Martin Jacques and Stuart Hall Discuss Globalisation, Ethnicity and Cultural Differences', *New Statesman*, 28 November 1997, 34–6, p. 35.

78 C. Plouviez, 'A Minor Mannerism in Art History', in Banham and Hillier (eds), *A Tonic*, 165–6, p. 166.

8 ✧ Escape and edification: the Battersea Pleasure Gardens

RATHER FAR from the issue of representing the Empire in the Festival are the 'conglomeration of thrills, spectacles and a myriad of activity' offered by the Festival's Battersea Pleasure Gardens in South London.[1] More in keeping with the respresentations of the past found in some of the local Festival celebrations than the modern, even futuristic, vistas of the South Bank, the Pleasure Gardens were a 'dreamworld' where 'fantasy was the rule'[2] (Figure 19).

When, twenty-five years after the 1951 events, Bevis Hillier asked architect James Gardner if he had been 'particularly involved in the Festival Gardens', Gardner replied:

> Oh completely, that's when my hair turned white. Barry, the inspiration behind it all, was finding the South Bank rather too clinical for his tastes. Architects and scientists seemed to be running away with it. He wanted a place where people could relax and have fun – elegant fun. Remembering the old pleasure gardens at Vauxhall, he decided we'd have a Festival Gardens. Battersea Park, then given over to allotments and a cricket pitch, was to be the site.[3]

For the Director-General of the Festival, Gerald Barry, 'elegant fun' were the keywords – he wanted to provide the war-weary British people with 'elegant fun'. Yet, although the Battersea Pleasure Gardens were to be a kind of antidote to the serious and more overtly educational exhibitions on the South Bank, this did not mean that they missed their chance to be edifying. Even with American funfair rides, commercial sponsorship – banned on the South Bank – and the consumption that logically followed, improving agendas were prominent at the Battersea site. These seeming contradictions and their sources are explored in this chapter.

The Pleasure Gardens had much in common with the other official 1951 London exhibitions, but there were some striking differences as well. The Battersea site shared a climate of controversy and contention with the entire Festival, and it was unique in allowing corporate sponsorship. For instance, like the Festival as a whole, the Gardens were a political football, with the Beaverbrook press and most Conservative MPs vociferously against the idea. One newspaper, for example, proclaimed on its front page: 'Spend the money on St. Thomas' Hospital', which had been bombed. After initial discussions, the Gardens project was shelved for almost a year, but then given the go-ahead with about half the budget originally estimated as necessary by the planners.[4]

Corporate sponsorship and consumption

With such a small budget, it was obvious to Gardner that they had to 'get the major features sponsored'.[5] Such sponsorship had been barred on the South Bank. Gerald Barry linked this decision to the wider purpose of the Festival, explaining that the Festival's organisational strategy was revolutionary because 'There was to be no space to let. No one would be able to have his goods on exhibit by paying to do so; they would get there by

19 The Funfair Piazza, the entrance to the funfair at the Battersea Pleasure Gardens. Designed by Hans Tisdall. On the right is the Hall of the Centaurs, containing the Nestlé Playground. In the centre is the Hall of the Golden Cockerel, which housed the Fun House

merit or not at all'.[6] By contrast, Battersea's Pleasure Gardens included the Lewitt-Him Guinness Clock,[7] the bronze sculpture of a mermaid sponsored by the Lockhead Hydraulic Brake Company,[8] the Leichner Cosmetics' Ladies Powder Room,[9] the Nestlé Playland (designed by Hans Tisdall, it was actually a crèche facility),[10] the Schweppes Grotto, the Sharp's Kreemy Toffee Punch and Judy Show, and three beer gardens sponsored by the Worshipful Company of Brewers.[11] As a place of fun and fantasy, the Battersea site was seen as more appropriate for sponsorship, advertising and more overt commercialism than the more educative exhibitions created on the South Bank or in the Science Museum at South Kensington, where science was presented as fun and fantastic. By contrast, Battersea offered the hedonistic pleasures of an amusement park – dancing, shopping and eating – in addition to improvement.

In the Ladies' Powder Room and the shops along the Parade, you could 'buy almost anything from perfume to tobacco, from toys to jewellery'.[12] At the Pleasure Gardens the main expertise on offer was provided by 'half-a-dozen expert assistants', centrally located in the Ladies' Powder Room. 'In the dove-grey salon with its twelve mirrored dressing-table [sponsored by Leichner Cosmetics] the ladies, in their pause for beauty, find a full range of powders, lipsticks ..., eye-shadows in all the colours of the spectrum.' Also available were 'cleansing creams and lotions'. The brochure further states that: 'there are special trays of make-up for blondes and brunettes'.[13] This passage reminds us not only of the almost complete absence of cosmetics and creams in wartime Britain, but also of the perceived homogeneity of white Britain with its assumption that British women come in two colours: 'blonde or brunette'!

The further gendered assumptions revealed in the descriptions of the 'small blue-and-white shops designed in the Regency style ... nine here and three more on the south side', are also striking to today's sensibilities. 'Practically everything you can find in Bond Street, and a good many places beside, is here on sale.'[14] The souvenir brochure further informed the visitor that:

Along the Parade [are] to be found ... shops whose very names spell quality and luxury. Here you can find exquisite antiques, figures in porcelain and ivory ... Here, too, are bright adornments for my lady – earrings and necklaces of pearl and brilliants, costume jewellery of every description. And while madam yearns over gems and fine perfumes, elegant slippers and diaphanous underwear, the mere male can comfort himself with the contemplation (and purchase) of pipes, snuff, fountain pens, cameras, watches or electric razors – while younger members of the family gape at miraculous toys, stamps (including the special Festival issue), and other wonders.[15]

If we ignore the gender assumptions, what is most striking is the descriptive language in this brochure: the visitor 'yearns' and 'gapes' for things characterised as 'quality', 'luxury', 'elegant', 'miraculous', 'wonders'. Such language seems extreme today, yet in a period that produced tales of men resorting to shaving with the same razor blade for six weeks, women creatively employing burnt matchsticks to blacken their eyebrows, and everyone rolling their own low-quality, smelly cigarettes, the variety of such goods for sale in such charming shops must have been a welcome relief indeed.[16] In what was an age of austerity so severe that the post-war national industrial design exhibition, named 'Britain Can Make It', was re-dubbed by the press 'Britain Can't Have It', this shopping Parade must have felt like the height of extravagance.[17] It must also have been a good advertisement that Britain could both 'make it' and 'have it' in 1951. Luxury consumption signalled recovery to people at home and abroad – an important message the Labour government and the Festival aimed to relay.

Add the 'luxury restaurant' to this picture and the place surely seemed the epitome of opulence for many British visitors. This most elegant of the Gardens' restaurant offerings was housed in the Riverside Rooms, 'a long low restaurant of West End standard with a Wine Garden ... consisting of little umbrella-ed alcoves of Vandyke brown-and-white behind a white trellis fence, webbed above with fairy lights suspended from a central mast'.[18] The terrace overlooked the Thames and diners could eat inside or out, accompanied by 'music from a small orchestra'.[19] For those less willing or able to indulge in such extravagance, there were six other restaurants, half of which were buffet style, a tea shop, two snack bars, three pubs, a wine garden, a refreshment stand, and two 'refreshment bars', most housed in temporary structures.[20] Catering for 'all tastes, all ages and all pockets', in the Festival's language, was on offer, and in the evenings for all to enjoy 'the most spectacular and unusual' fireworks and illuminations lit the skies.

Battersea as nostalgia

In addition to offering an arena for sponsorship and consumption, the Pleasure Gardens were also seen as a place more appropriate than the South Bank for nostalgic representations of the past. The South Bank exhibitions overwhelmingly stressed progress and modernity, projecting 'the belief that Britain will have contributions to make in the future'.[21] 'The contemporary style', so important to the South Bank's identity, 'had been deliberately eschewed' at Battersea, according to a planning document[22] (Figure 20). In the Battersea Gardens it was possible to find oneself in a beautiful setting far from the realities of post-war Britain – a setting

20 'The contemporary style', so important to the South Bank's identity, 'had been deliberately eschewed' at Battersea. A girl selling flowers, dressed in Victorian costume, at the Battersea Pleasure Gardens

incorporating many architectural styles including that of Regency Brighton and eighteenth- and nineteenth-century London.[23]

Laid out on 37 acres (15 hectares), once containing allotments and a cricket ground, the Gardens offered visitors from Britain and beyond a six-acre (2.5-hectare) amusement park, a children's zoo and pet corner, two theatres (one dedicated to music-hall performances, the other to ballets, revues and marionettes), a fanciful tree-top walk, and a huge tented dance pavilion[24] (Figure 21). A respectable mixture of 'high' and 'low' culture was on offer, furthering the illusion of a classless society. As we have seen, one major aim of the Festival organisers was to diffuse education, ideas and tastes, generally the preserve of elites, to the people of Britain. Selected visions of the past supplied the backdrop at Battersea for this place of fun and fantasy.

21 The tree-top walk at the Battersea Pleasure Gardens

22 Rowland Emett's Nellie locomotive on his Far Tottering and Oystercreek Railway at the Battersea Pleasure Gardens

One of the most popular attractions offered a nostalgic, child-like pleasure in the form of the enchanting railway designed by the cartoonist Rowland Emett. His 'Far Tottering and Oystercreek Railway' appeared regularly in contemporary issues of *Punch*[25] (Figure 22). Battersea's version – a complete miniature railway, 500 yards (547 metres) long – was described in the souvenir brochure as containing 'all his characteristic fantasy'.[26] According to Emett himself:

> The main station, at the western end of the line, was Far Tottering ... There were many nice railway touches about this station: a luggage-crane ... from which hung a wealth of Gladstone bags, leather silk-hat boxes ... A wicker bird-cage containing a depressed sea-gull, was consigned to Oystercreek ... the railway teemed with forbidding notices – 'Do NOT tease the Engines' ... 'Do NOT feed the Bats' ... 'Passengers must NOT cross HERE, so *there!*' And, of course, the one that stated quite simply: 'IT IS FORBIDDEN.' All of these strictures carried the normal penalty of forty shillings.[27]

Between these two stations ran the three cartoon-inspired versions of the train, led by locomotives 'Nellie', 'Neptune 10', and 'Wild Goose', each pulling three or four coaches and conveying passengers from one station to the other. The trains were a favourite amongst Gardens visitors and ran continuously throughout the summer.[28]

The Pleasure Gardens' dance pavilion by James Gardner, modelled after a similar one in a Scandinavian Pleasure Garden, was deemed impressive. For one thing, the Battersea version was the biggest single pole tent ever erected in the world at the time. James Gardner, the co-ordinating designer of the Battersea site, claimed that 'It turned out that the English are too shy to dance in public, so we had to engage tame dancers to start the ball rolling. Then it worked.'[29]

Battersea's funfair with its American rides

Thrilling American funfair attractions were on offer at the Pleasure Gardens, as well. The British people and their visitors were treated to an impressive fair, featuring a Waterfall '25 feet [7.6 metres] high, 65 feet [19.8 metres] wide, pouring up to 7,000 gallons [31,808 litres] a minute ... an exact replica of Niagara Falls, down to the smallest details', the Skywheel, the Bubble-Bounce, and the Flyo Plane.[30] There was also a Water Splash ride, resembling those present-day versions in which cars ascend a steel ramp and then descend 'a slope at ever-increasing speed to splash down in a large pool of water!', and other new American rides developed while the British were understandably too preoccupied with the war effort to spend money and talented labour on fair rides.[31]

The Board of the Battersea Pleasure Gardens had decided that, for the funfair to be as attractive and appealing as they desired, it was necessary to purchase new features from America. Under post-war conditions this was a bold step. The Festival of Britain Council Meeting Minutes from October 1950 state:

> While plans for entertainment were proceeding well, the provision of amusements was causing some anxiety. This was primarily due to the fact that no novelty of the type sought had been introduced into this country during the past 10 years, owing to lack of dollars. The prospect of having any unique and new amusement feature in the Gardens was therefore remote, even though there was now in progress a search which might extend to the United States.[32]

They agreed to apply to the Treasury for £30,000 (at that time the equivalent of approximately $84,000) to facilitate these purchases. This is approximately £500,000 in the year 2000's terms, but its significance was far greater, given the acute shortage of dollars in Britain. Surprisingly, the Treasury agreed, and a date was set for a trip to the States. In an attempt to make this journey seem more practical, the Board recommended that a number of large British funfair operators should accompany the Battersea representatives, and that if these operators decided to purchase new attractions for their own fairs, then the Battersea Company would buy those chosen. The individual operators could then purchase them from the Battersea Company at cost, plus transport costs, eschewing the import duties or purchase tax.[33] Thus, on 16 November 1950, Major Joseph – as the representative of the Battersea Pleasure Gardens, a Board member and the Chairman of the NAC – along with four large funfair operators, set off for America. Not surprisingly, the Pleasure Gardens Company wished to keep all of this quiet, as Lidderdale told Nicholson: 'All concerned should be given a special warning not to make it public. It would be very unfortunate, just when we are at last beginning to get across the serious purpose of the Festival, to have attention focused on this side line'.[34]

However, the money spent on American rides did not go unnoticed by the Beaverbrook press, Conservative backbenchers or the increasingly vocal Nottingham housewives' association. There followed questions in Parliament, *Daily Mail* headlines asking why the Government was about to spend $100,000 on a new roundabout, and a telegram from Nottinghamshire housewives to the Ministry of Food stating 'if no dollars available for purchasing eggs and other food, why use same for funfair equipment – should be all British – we protest strongly'.[35] The *Daily Graphic* featured an article that quoted MP Teeling, Conservative for Brighton, as asking Morrison in the Commons why, if 'the Festival is supposed to show people from overseas what Britain can do, ... it seems we are spending a great deal of money to show what America ... can do?'[36]

Which fantasies on offer? Englishness and otherness

It is a valid question. 'British contributions to civilisation' was the overarching theme of the Festival of Britain, and the range of these on show at the Battersea Pleasure Gardens was certainly rather modest. This is especially striking when we compare the Gardens with the South Bank, where Britishness was so explicitly at the centre that there was even a rule that foreign food should not be served there! Versions of an *English* past were evoked in the Gardens' early Regency architecture, the rendition of the popular elite fashion for the eighteenth-century grotto, the traditional Punch and Judy puppet show, the music hall performances, and the orange girls reminiscent of Nell Gwyn. Raphael Samuel wrote of how follies, 'one of the commonest eighteenth-century forms of holiday architecture, contrived to be both experimental and atavistic, playing on the appeal of antiquities and reproducing them in replica, while at the same time cultivating an appetite for the exotic'.[37] In addition, according to the souvenir brochure, the Battersea Pleasure Gardens strove above all to create a place evocative of the Belvedere Gardens, which resided on the South Bank from 1781 to 1785, and the Vauxhall Gardens, which flourished even earlier, and of which Dr Johnson wrote 'That excellent place of amusement ... is particularly adapted to the taste of the English nation, there being a mixture of curious show, gay exhibition, music, vocal and instrumental, not too refined for the general ear ... and though last, not least, good eating and drinking for those who chose to purchase that regale'.[38] Johnson's demotic references to eighteenth-century pleasure gardens was quoted in the Battersea souvenir brochure as an appropriate description of 'the Festival Gardens today'.[39]

Yet however English these representations, many other nations and styles were on display at Battersea as well. There were the previously mentioned American funfair rides, but there was much more. For example, the popular Tree-Walk sported a Chinese-style dragon. The bronze sculpture of a mermaid, sponsored by Lockhead Hydraulic Brake Company, was allegedly inspired by its creator's time on the island of Bali.[40] The 'Piazza', although not specifically named or written about as Mediterranean beyond that evocative word 'piazza', featured 'shadows painted and the flooring so designed that ... [it] looks half as long again as it really is'. 'Reds and yellows on the facade of the building fade in the distance into pinkish greys and blues', giving the impression that one is in 'The Land of Always Afternoon' with 'deep shadows cut[ting] down the faces of the buildings on the right-hand side'. And, as if this was not exotic enough for the British, rain-soaked visitor ('the first five months of 1951 were the wettest since 1815'[41]), 'the skyline, especially at the end, is an oriental wonderworld of minarets and turrets', and on the roof to the right were 'two mighty Centaurs'.[42] When visitors exited the Grotto and turned left towards the Grand Vista, they walked under 'a curving row of hanging chandeliers in the Chinese taste',[43] and both arcades were 'in the Chinese Gothic style, built of timber and cane with golden roofs'.[44] Finally, although English antecedents were evoked in the official Pleasure Gardens' souvenir brochure, the planners and designers repeatedly remarked that their Gardens were actually modelled after those of Tivoli in Copenhagen.[45]

The Battersea Pleasure Gardens as a site of improvement

William Feaver, the designer of the Festival symbol, called the Gardens a place where 'fantasy was the rule'.[46] Although in many ways the Gardens were no more fanciful than the South Bank, Feaver's appraisal seems apt, and yet improving agendas, such as those found in the more overtly educational exhibitions on the South Bank and in the South Kensington Science Exhibition, were also apparent at Battersea. Two aims: the regulation of 'leisure in socially beneficial directions' and the education of the (female) citizen consumer – both acknowledged goals of the post-war Labour-led settlement – were evident in the Battersea Gardens.[47] A *Tribune* correspondent wrote after Labour's victory in 1945 that 'the time has now arrived when culture should cease to be the hall-mark of the leisured classes and should be available to all'.[48] And, as we have seen, Morrison himself had argued in 1949 at the Labour Party conference that: 'Part of our work in politics and in industry must be to improve human nature ... we should set ourselves more than materialistic aims'.[49] The publication *Labour Believes in Britain*, of the same year, claimed that it was actually the party's duty to stimulate leisure and the arts, as well to establish a state-funded holiday council.[50]

In addition, rational consumption was essential in the imagined New Jerusalem led by Labour. For example, an official Labour publication, *Womanfare*, published in the Festival year, celebrated 'Joan' as:

> the most important woman in Britain today. She is the shop girl ... the factory worker ... the girl who works in the mill, the local store. She is business girl, housewife, teenager and mother. The wise girl knows that she can have a smart wardrobe through wise planning – she knows, too, that some Tories have threatened to do away with the Utility scheme.[51]

Women's planned, rational consumption for all goods was, of course, considered necessary during the war, and it was deemed the only fair way in the post-war world. John Newsom's *The Education of Girls* (1948) included a chapter on 'Woman as Purchaser' in which he 'envisaged education as guiding working-class girls towards middle-class standards of taste'.[52] He wrote:

> Our standards of design, and therefore our continuance as a great commercial nation, will depend on our education of the consumer to the point where she rejects the functionally futile and aesthetically inept and demands what is fitting and beautiful ... Woman as purchaser holds the future standard of living of this country in her hands ... If she buys in ignorance then our national standards will degenerate.[53]

In their *Design in the Festival*, the Council of Industrial Design (discussed in Chapter 3) employed very similar language. In that official Festival publication 'a critical and appreciative public' was deemed necessary if British industries were to achieve a 'high standard of design'.[54] And this new consumer was explicitly gendered as female in Newsom, as well as the Labour Party's *Festival* magazine.

If women were to consume in a restrained, aesthetically pleasing (and by implication, middle-class) fashion, all British citizens were to spend their leisure time in similarly defined pursuits. The Labour agendas outlined above acknowledged the need for leisure and holidays in the same breath as 'the evolution of a people more ... intelligent and rich in culture'.[55] According to Raphael Samuel, socialists from William Morris onwards have tended to 'rebuke the masses for what another great Labour leader, Ernest Bevin, called the "poverty" of their desires'.[56] Like Methodist teetotallers as well as working-class radicals of one hundred years before, post-war Labour leaders wanted 'rational recreation' for the people – 'improving' activities, involving absolutely no alcohol or violence.[57] Labour had identified a 'leisure problem' in 1946 and 1947, which was resulting in 'the failure of the majority of Britain's citizens to enjoy a full life through their leisure pursuits'.[58] Due to their narrowly defined pastimes, such as pub- and cinema-going, British citizens' recreational activities were 'passive', superficial and only temporarily exciting. Labour's leisure policy, according to MP Noel-Baker, needed to help 'the citizens of Britain to live full and varied lives' and facilitate 'a great extension in the horizon of mind and spirit for the men and women of Britain'.[59]

As Gardner said, edifying and improving agendas were so prominent in the London exhibitions that Gerald Barry had begun to worry that 'architects and scientists ... [were] running away with it'.[60] Barry believed that what the British people really wanted and needed was a place where they 'could relax and have fun – elegant fun',[61] but it is important to mark

Barry's words carefully. He wished to provide the British people and their visitors with not just fun, but 'elegant fun'. Fairs have commonly been conceived of as diametrically opposed to museums. Since the late nineteenth century, according to Tony Bennett, museums' advocates have furthered this dichotomy by claiming that the fair not only occupied time and space differently, but also 'confronted' and 'affronted' 'the museum as a still extant embodiment of the "irrational" and "chaotic" disorder that had characterized the museum's precursors', including fairs.[62] But Bennett challenges this appraisal, arguing that the fixed-site amusement park occupies 'a point somewhere between ... the museum and the travelling fair'.[63] Amusement parks are, he argues, 'modern' and committed, 'like the museum, to an accumulating time, to the unstoppable momentum of progress which ... [they] claimed both to represent and to harness to the cause of popular pleasure' through their stress on 'the new', and their inclusion of the latest mechanical rides.[64] As we have seen, the latest American rides were a priority for Battersea's planners – 'the new' was a necessity. The stationary amusement park also represents a negotiation of the perceived dichotomy between museums and fairs by producing regulated and orderly crowds, 'unlike their itinerant predecessors'.[65]

Nevertheless, the traditional view of the fair as the definitive unruly and dangerous place of crowds, disorder and distasteful (working-class) pleasures haunted the middle-class planners of the Festival Gardens who repeatedly stressed that they did not want this place to be known as a fair. As such, they introduced the word 'Pleasure' into the Gardens name as an attempt to get 'away from the idea of a fun fair'.[66] They were, of course, only the latest in a long line of critics of popular, commercial pursuits. In addition to the nineteenth-century advocates of 'rational recreation', Matthew Arnold called anything connected to commerce 'vulgar' and believed the 'populace uncultured'. Later in the 1930s and 1940s, the Leavisite critics argued that 'mass civilisation is by its very nature degraded, and popular tastes, as they succumb to it debased'. In 1934, J. B. Priestley bemoaned many holiday amusements as 'mechanized', 'standardized' and 'Americanized', claiming they thus rendered their visitors 'passive'. Funfairs and amusement parks were similar to 'Hollywood films' or what Priestley dubbed the '"Blackpooling" of English life and leisure'.[67] These activities catered to 'the less intelligent and enterprising', who preferred 'mass entertainment' to 'leisure in quieter places, cycling and walking and playing games in the sun', in his words.[68] Concerns about 'Americanisation' – that shorthand for commercial, crass, cultureless culture – lurked behind most critiques of popular culture, at least from the inter-war period onwards.

Fears of disorder and inappropriate behaviour, especially amongst working-class visitors, were also evident in the Board's concern that the siting of the Pleasure Gardens in Battersea would lead to objections because it was 'a district containing a rougher element among its population'.[69] But in the end the Pleasure Gardens were so elegant that one Gardens Board member, Sir Arthur Elvin, 'questioned whether the general treatment was not too high-class for the tripper element', while another responded that he 'thought that it was appropriate to preserve a reasonably high tone in view of the expectation that a number of Continental and other high-class visitors would attend'.[70]

Such class anxieties, however, were suppressed by the time the Gardens finally opened.[71] The 1950 press release contained only a broad hint: 'The Festival Pleasure Gardens ... will provide facilities for entertainment, refreshment and relaxation to suit all tastes, all ages and all pockets'.[72] By the time one actually entered the Gardens in the summer of 1951, the illusion of equality dominated this fanciful land. The same press release may have explained that 'the pavilions will be an echo of the "follies" and temples that gentlemen built in their parks at the end of the 18th century', but one of the fantasies encouraged by the Pleasure Gardens was that in post-war Labour Britain access to such 'gentlemanly' pleasures was available to everyone.[73]

Generational, gender and class differences in post-war fantasies

The Pleasure Gardens may have been conceived of a classless place, but what sort or degree of fantasy and escape the Battersea Pleasure Gardens afforded, of course, depended on factors such as generation, gender and class. For example, quoting Susan Cooper, Peter Hennessy has striven to impress upon us how:

> For those who remembered the years between the wars, the gradual climb back to prosperity was a long, dispiriting haul, echoing with pre-war memories of better days. For the wartime children, it was different. Those years were ... lit by surprises; between 1945 and 1951 we saw not only the first pineapples and bananas of our lives, but the first washing-machine, the first fountain, the first television set. The world opening up before us was not a pale imitation of one we had lost, but a lucky dip of extraordinary things we had never seen before.[74]

By contrast, as an adult, Cyril Connolly, the editor of *Horizon* and presumably more privileged than most in post-war Britain, wrote in 1950 that: 'As a Londoner I was affected by the dirt and weariness, the gradual draining away under war conditions of light and colour from the former capital of the world'.[75] Queues for rationed goods, housing shortages, and general dreariness were the overwhelming realities of the immediate post-war world in Britain. Thus, for many adults, Battersea and the South Bank represented 'a great looking forward after years of rationing and greyness', in Raphael Samuel's words.[76]

The Pleasure Gardens were a place of fantasy and escape in very different ways for children and adults. Valerie Walkerdine has written of how Freud 'concentrated on the creation of fantasy in the gap between need and wish-fulfillment'.[77] As the Cooper versus the Connolly quotes make clear, for children who had no memory of life before the Second World War, Battersea's pleasures were experienced as novel and exciting, perhaps the stuff of future fantasies, while for the adults who could remember the world before the Second World War, if not even earlier, the Pleasure Gardens was a place assembled to fulfill their current wishes and needs – a place of beauty and elegance far from the grit and shabbiness of much of Britain.[78] Shopping, drinking and dining opportunities, as well as theatres, a dance pavilion, an amusement park, enchanting follies and whimsical attractions offered up a world of fun and fantasy intentionally constructed for them to enjoy. This was also a world that many adult Britons must have felt they deserved after the deprivations and sacrifices of the recent war, which they had won.[79] It is important to remember that the Festival was to be 'a tonic to the nation', and during the war products such as cosmetics were acknowledged as morale boosters. Furthermore, as we have seen, the Festival was to be the major tourist event of the post-war period. This meant that it was important for Britain to appear to have recovered fully, even if this was not yet quite true.[80] Luxury goods for sale and nice restaurants, along with the myriad of other amusements, projected the preferred version of British reconstruction to people from home and abroad.

Battersea's open-air sculpture exhibition

Also presented as on offer to everyone was sculpture, the 'highest' of the fine arts, according to some. Co-sponsored by the Arts Council and London County Council, the Pleasure Gardens featured the second Battersea Park international open-air sculpture exhibition.[81] Festival planning documents state that the first Battersea sculpture exhibition in 1948 proved so successful that the Festival organisers thought a second in 1951 a good idea.[82] The sculptures were chosen by a committee consisting of sculptors and 'arts experts' 'from the work of leading British and European artists of the last fifty years, each of whom will be represented by one piece'. All the British pieces were borrowed from private collections, and included were Henry Moore and Jacob Epstein, then seventy years old.[83] 'About ten' European countries were represented, with contributions ranging 'from famous bronzes by the Frenchman, Auguste Rodin, and the Belgian, Meunier, to a "mobile" by the American, Alexander Calder, and an "abstract" by the Swiss, Max Bill.'[84] The planning document declared:

> For the student, for the art-lover, and even for the many who normally prefer to avoid galleries and museums, the scope of the exhibition will make it one of the most outstanding events of its kind in recent years. Many visitors will find themselves enjoying sculpture as never before. To see these works of art in the open air against a natural background of grass and trees will be a new and vivid experience of beauty.[85]

Those 'who normally prefer to avoid galleries and museums' probably would not have found this exhibition of sculpture – considered by many the most difficult of the visual arts – accessible. It was designed primarily for people who were familiar with sculpture, allowing them to 'enjoy sculpture as never before' in the outdoors. But the Festival planners wanted to believe that all sorts of people on their way to the amusement park would enjoy this exhibition of great British and European sculpture. 'The best for the most' had been the motto of the Arts Council's predecessor, the Council for the Encouragement of Music and the Arts, and this is what the Battersea organisers must have had in mind as well.[86]

Conclusion: *whose* fantasies on offer?

The organisers of the Battersea Pleasure Gardens offered an alternative classless world constructed of a curious combination of architectural styles eclectically borrowed from seventeenth-, eighteenth- and nineteenth-century England, with a cartoon-inspired, whimsical railroad, a Mediterranean piazza, Chinese Gothic arcades, an American funfair, along with 'Bond Street' – standard luxurious restaurants and shops. One may ask what sort of men, for they were almost exclusively men, created this fantasy world of sculpture, the new and exciting funfair, 'the always afternoon' piazza, the grotto, and the wide range of choices in dining, drinking, shopping and powdering one's nose? As previously stated, Gardner remarked a little less than eloquently in 1976 that the Festival Gardens 'did put a moment of dreamworld into a lot of people's lives',[87] but whose dreams were represented at Battersea? The Gardens were the actualisation of a dream created by established architects, designers and planners, established enough to attract the attention of politicians such as Herbert Morrison, as well as Gerald Barry, for whom the Festival Pleasure Gardens represented a special dream – a particular package of 'fun, fantasy and colour' that he wanted to give the British people.[88]

As we have seen, the Festival's planners were overwhelmingly professional men in their forties who would have been students in the early 1930s. These 'radical, middle-class do-gooders' can also be characterised as representatives of the new post-war public sphere dominated by experts – members of a 'technocracy'.[89] Like William Beveridge they were 'obstinately convinced' that their class would have to do the job: 'there must be a revolution; but it must be guided by persons with training and knowledge'.[90] They were 'officers and gentlemen', who were 'steeped in paternalistic philosophy ... determined not only to protect and care for the ordinary man, but ... to make his drab existence worthwhile'.[91]

The vast majority of written historical evidence relating to the Battersea Pleasure Gardens tells us more about the fantasies of escape, pleasure and extravagance of its middle-class planners than about the 'ordinary' British visitor.[92] Those fantasies included a desire to eschew the traditional associations of fairs with disorder and tackiness by creating an 'elegant pleasure garden'. This seems to have been part of a more general Labour-led agenda for encouraging 'improving' pursuits for 'the people' in the hopes of replacing their 'passive', 'superficial' pastimes. Encouraging aesthetically orientated consumption was something the Festival planners shared also with the BBC and the Council of Industrial Design, those middle-class arbiters of taste. James Gardner said of the Battersea Pleasure Gardens in his 1976 interview that 'it is rather nice to meet latter-day friends who found it exciting as children, maybe even got engaged there'.[93] And, democratic or not, a 'real' world of dreams, however ephemeral, must have been worth quite a lot to the British who had had almost nothing *but* dreams since the late 1930s.

Notes

1 This is how Leonard Thompson, the inter-war owner of the Blackpool Pleasure Beach, described it. L. Thompson, as quoted by Bennett, *The Birth of the Museum*, p. 237.

2 J. Gardner, 'Pleasure Gardens Battersea Park, Battersea Pleasures: Interview with James Gardner', in Banham and Hillier (eds), *A Tonic*: 118–22, p. 118; and Feaver, 'Festival Star', p. 53.

3 Gardner, 'Pleasure Gardens', p. 118.

4 Gardner, 'Pleasure Gardens', p. 120.

5 *Ibid.*

6 Gerald Barry, unpublished memoir as quoted by Hillier, 'Introduction', p. 15.

7 Feaver, 'Festival Star,' p. 53.

8 PRO, Work 25/233/E1/D3/6, *Festival Pleasure Gardens Battersea Park Guide, Festival of Britain 1951*.

9 *Festival Pleasure Gardens Battersea Park Guide*, pp. 16, 38.

10 Electronic mail correspondence between the author and Martin Packer, Festival of Britain Society, autumn, 2001.

11 PRO, Work 25/21/A2/A6, 'Confidential, FG Ltd. (50) 8th meeting, Festival Gardens Limited, Minutes of the 8th Board Meeting held at 2 Savoy Court, London, WC2 on Thurs. April 27, 1950 at 2:30 PM', p. 7. Sponsorship was also necessary since the idea of the Gardens had been shelved for ten months due to opposition and then, when it was reintroduced, the co-ordinating designer, James Gardner, was offered a budget which was 'about half' of what he had originally estimated: Gardner, 'Pleasure Gardens', p. 120. For one planning discussion of the merits and appropriate types of sponsorship, please see: PRO, Work 25/21/A2/A6, 'Confidential FG Ltd. (50) 9th meeting, Festival Gardens Limited, Minutes of the 9th Board Meeting held at 2 Savoy Court, London, WC2 on Thurs. May 25, 1950 at 3 p.m.'; 'Sponsorship of Individual Attractions and Features', pp. 5, 7.

12 *Festival Pleasure Gardens Battersea Park Guide*, p. 16.

13 *Festival Pleasure Gardens Battersea Park Guide*, p. 38.

14 *Festival Pleasure Gardens Battersea Park Guide*, p. 16.

15 *Festival Pleasure Gardens Battersea Park Guide*, p. 38.

16 See, for example, P. Fussell, *Wartime: Understanding and Behaviour in the Second World War* (Oxford and New York: Oxford University Press, 1989), 195–228, or R. Harris, *Enigma* (London: Arrow Books, 1996), p. 113.

17 MacDonald and Porter, 'Mid-Century Modern', n.p.; Maguire and Woodham (eds), *Design and Cultural Politics in Postwar Britain*.

18 *Festival Pleasure Gardens Battersea Park Guide*, p. 15.

19 *Ibid.*

20 Gardner, 'Pleasure Gardens', p. 121, and 'Architectural Preview: Festival Pleasure Gardens Battersea Park', *Architectural Review* (April 1951), 230–5, p. 231.

21 Cox, 'The Story the Exhibition Tells', p. 4.

22 'Confidential, FG Ltd. (50) 9th meeting', p. 3.

23 Sue Harper's work on the great popularity of the 1940s Gainsborough melodramas (historical romance films, primarily set in the Regency period) may offer some explanation of why particular centuries were seen as more popular, fanciful and elegant than others. See S. Harper, *Picturing the Past: The Rise and Fall of the British Costume Film* (London: BFI Publishing, 1994). Also, on the popularity of these films, see McKibbin, *Classes and Cultures*, pp. 527–8. He argues that they were 'largely asocial' and 'apolitical': p. 527.

24 *Festival Pleasure Gardens Battersea Park Guide*. See also *The Official Book of the Festival*, pp. 10–11 and Ebong, 'The Origins', p. 390.

25 R. Emett, 'The Far Tottering and Oystercreek Railway', in Banham and Hillier (eds), *A Tonic*, 125–7, p. 125. The railway was originally called 'Far Twittering', 'evocative of birdsong', according to Emett, rather than 'Tottering'. But its name was changed because Gillie Potter, philosopher and radio comedian, said that there was a Little Twittering near where he lived and he did not think its residents would approve: pp. 125–6.

26 *Festival Pleasure Gardens Battersea Park Guide*, p. 16.

27 Emett, 'The Far Tottering', p. 126.

28 Emett, 'The Far Tottering', pp. 125–7. See also Ebong, 'The Origins', p. 396.

29 Gardner, 'Pleasure Gardens', pp. 120–1.

30 *Festival Pleasure Gardens Battersea Park Guide*, p. 24.

31 G. Willis, 'An incident in the Grotto', in Banham and Hillier (eds), *A Tonic*, 180–1, p. 181. See also Ebong, 'The Origins', p. 402. On issues surrounding purchasing American funfair equipment, see: PRO, Work 25/21/A2/A6 (Festival Gardens), 'FBC (50) 4th Meeting October 4, 1950', 8. Festival Pleasure Gardens; PRO, CAB 124/1302, Undated Document on Funfair Equipment; and Ebong, 'The Origins', pp. 399–402.

32 'FBC (50) 4th Meeting October 4, 1950', 8. Festival Pleasure Gardens.

33 Undated Document on Funfair Equipment. See also Ebong's discussion of this in 'The Origins', pp. 399–402.

34 Letter from Lidderdale to Nicholson, dated 7 October 1950.

35 PRO, CAB 124/1302, 'Telegram to Minister of Food from Nottingham Housewives', dated 14 November 1950.

36 Ebong, 'The Origins', p. 401. Quote from Mr Teeling MP, as published in the *Daily Graphic*, 13 November 1950 and as cited by Ebong, 'The Origins', p. 401.

37 Samuel, *Island Stories, Theatres of Memory, Vol. II*, p. 358.

38 Dr Johnson on the Vauxhall Pleasure Gardens, as quoted by A. Hippisley Coxe, 'It Sprang from Spring Gardens', in *Festival Pleasure Gardens Battersea Park Guide*, p. 44.

39 Hippisley Coxe, 'It Sprang from Spring Gardens', p. 44.

40 *Festival Pleasure Gardens Battersea Park Guide*, p. 14.

41 Frayn, 'Festival', p. 344.

42 *Festival Pleasure Gardens Battersea Park Guide*, p. 15.

43 *Festival Pleasure Gardens Battersea Park Guide*, p. 19.

44 *Festival Pleasure Gardens Battersea Park Guide*, p. 21.

45 J. Piper, 'A Painter's Funfair: Interview with John Piper', conducted by Bevis Hillier, in Banham and Hillier (eds), *A Tonic*, pp. 123–4, p. 124; PRO, Work 25/21/A2/A6, 'Memo: Festival Gardens, Battersea Park', from E. W. Swaine and G. A. Campbell, dated 30 March 1949, 'Distribution: Chairman of the Council, Director-General, Secretary, Director of Public Relations, Chairman of the Official Committee, Secretary of the Official Committee, Private Secretary to the Lord President, Members of the Executive'. And, for example, 'The scheme follows the model of the Tivoli at Copenhagen, where high standards of horticulture, catering and so on are maintained and great care is given to details, but provides for more "fun fair" attractions' is the statement in: PRO, Work 25/21/A2/A6, 'Lord President, Festival Gardens in Battersea Park', 'the report of the working party to examine the case for Festival Gardens in Battersea Park submitted to you by the Director-General of the Festival of Britain and by the Clerk of the London County Council in February … Signed E. M. Nicholson, Chairman, Office of the Lord President of the Council 2nd April 1949', p. 3.

46 Feaver, 'Festival Star', p. 53.

47 Hennessy, *Never Again*, p. 310: 'Inevitably in the afterglow of the "People's War" there were attempts by those in authority to regulate leisure in socially beneficial directions especially where it spilled over into culture.'

48 *Tribune*, 17 August 1945, as quoted by Fielding, Thompson and Tiratsoo, 'England Arise!', pp. 136–7.

49 Morrison, in Francis, *Ideas and Policies Under Labour*, pp. 56–7.

50 Labour Party, *Labour Believes in Britain*, p. 3; Francis, *Ideas and Policies*, p. 57.

51 Ellipsis in the original. Labour Party, *Womanfare* (London: Labour Party, 1951), pp. 6–8. On clothing, consumer knowledge and working-class women in the post-war period, see A. Partington, 'Popular Fashion and Working-Class Affluence', in J. Ash and E. Wilson (eds), *Chic Thrills* (London: Pandora Press, 1992), 145–61, and 'The Days of the New Look: Working-Class Affluence and the Consumer Culture', in Fyrth (ed.), *Labour's Promised Land?*, 247–63.

52 E. Wilson, *Only Halfway to Paradise: Women in Postwar Britain: 1945–1968* (London and New York: Tavistock Publications, 1980), p. 36.

53 Newsom, 1948, p. 103, as quoted by Wilson, *Only Halfway*, p. 36.

54 Russell, 'Design in Industry', p. 11.

55 *Labour Believes in Britain*, p. 3.

56 Samuel, *Theatres of Memory*, Vol. I, p. 262.

57 There is a vast literature on nineteenth-century 'rational recreation'. See, for example, R. D. Storch, 'Introduction: Persistence and Change in Nineteenth-Century Popular Culture', in *Popular Culture and Custom in Nineteenth-Century England* (London: Palgrave-Macmillan, 1993); G. Stedman Jones, 'Class Expression versus Social Control? A Critique of Recent Trends in the Social History of Leisure', in *Languages of Class*; E. Yeo and S. Yeo, *Popular Culture and Class Conflict, 1590–1914* (Brighton: Harvester Press, 1984); and J. Walvin, *Leisure and Society 1830–1950* (London: Longman, 1978).

58 Labour Party Archive, Manchester, Research Department Files, RDR 284/March, 1945; P. J. Noel-Baker, 'Facilities for Popular Entertainment and Culture', RD 35/November, 1946; Anonymous, 'A Policy for Leisure', and RD 43/February 1947; Anonymous, 'The Enjoyment of Leisure', as cited by Fielding, Thompson and Tiratsoo, *'England Arise!'*, p. 137.

59 Noel-Baker, 'Facilities for Popular Entertainment and Culture'; Anonymous, 'A Policy for Leisure', as cited by Fielding, Thompson and Tiratsoo, *'England Arise!'*, p. 137.

60 Gardner, 'Pleasure Gardens', p. 118.

61 *Ibid.*

62 Bennett, *The Birth of the Museum*, pp. 1–4.

63 Bennett, *The Birth of the Museum*, p. 4.

64 *Ibid.*

65 *Ibid.*

66 Sir Henry French alerted the Council to the insertion of the word 'Pleasure' into its name for this reason: 'FBC (50) 4th Meeting October 4, 1950, 8'.

67 Samuel, *Theatres of Memory*, Vol. 1, pp. 267–8; M. Arnold, *Culture and Anarchy*, ed. J. Dover Wilson (Cambridge: Cambridge University Press, 1932 [1869]); J. B. Priestley, *English Journey* (London:1934); Q. D. Leavis, *Fiction and the Reading Public* (London: Chatto and Windus, 1932).

68 J. B. Priestley, 'Blackpool', from *English Journey* (1934), reprinted in Giles and Middleton (eds), *Writing Englishness*, 174–7, p. 176.

69 PRO, Work 25/21/A2/A6, 'Office of the Lord President of the Council 2nd April

1949 (next page reads: p. 1, Fest of Britain, 1951, Festival Gardens in Battersea Park, Report to the Lord President').

70 *Ibid.*

71 On the opening of the Pleasure Gardens, please see, Gardner, 'Pleasure Gardens', p. 122.

72 PRO, Work 25/21/A2/A6, 'Gerrard 2842 [telephone number], Release date: Immediate, FG/Press/4/50, Festival Gardens Limited, 5, Sidney Place, New Coventry Street, London, W1, FESTIVAL PLEASURE GARDENS in Battersea Park' (n.d.: April 1950?).

73 *Ibid.*

74 S. Cooper, as cited by Hennessy, *Never Again*, p. 309.

75 C. Connolly, *The Unquiet Grave: A Word Cycle by Palinurus* (London: Hamish Hamilton, 1951), pp. xi–xii.

76 Samuel, *Theatres of Memory, Vol. I*, p. 55.

77 V. Walkerdine, *Schoolgirl Fictions* (London: Verso, 1990), p. 100.

78 In a very different context, Tania Modleski has written impressively about the importance of 'waiting' in the formation of fantasies – especially women's fantasies. And Susan Willis has extended this notion to the pleasures of consumption generally. T. Modleski, *Loving with a Vengeance* (New York: Methuen, 1982); S. Willis, *A Primer for Daily Life* (London and New York: Routledge, 1991).

79 I offer here anecdotal evidence. Shortly after I arrived in the UK to begin the research for this project, in 1994, I was attending a lecture at the University of Warwick. On the way to the lecture I met a visiting female professor of Classics who I believe was in her sixties. She inquired about my research. When asked how I had decided to work on this topic, I answered that as an American I found it extraordinary that in the midst of rationing and reconstruction the government funded the Festival of Britain. The professor replied curtly, 'Well, we had won the war!'

80 PRO, BT 64/4058, 'Draft note on Tourism for inclusion in C. E. P. S. statement for O.E.E.C.', registered on 17 August 1948.

81 S. Ferleger Brades and J. Bernstein, *Symbols for '51: The Royal Festival Hall Skylon and Sculptures for the Festival of Britain*, Designed by Royal Festival Hall/Hayward Gallery Studio, Printed by Trevor-Hobbs, n.d. (exhibition held 2 March–21 April, 1996), p. 9.

82 PRO, Work 25/232/E1/B2/4, 'Open Air Exhibition of Sculpture, Battersea Park London May to Sept 1951'.

83 'Open Air Exhibition of Sculpture'; and Ferleger Brades and Bernstein, *Symbols for '51*, p. 9.

84 'Open Air Exhibition of Sculpture'.

85 'Open Air Exhibition of Sculpture'.

86 See for example, F. M. Leventhal, '"The Best for the Most": CEMA and State Sponsorship of the Arts in Wartime, 1939–45', *Twentieth Century British History*, 1:3 (1990), 289–317.

87 Gardner, 'Pleasure Gardens', p. 122.

88 Gerald Barry, as quoted by Frayn, 'Festival', p. 337.

89 Forty, 'Festival Politics,' p. 37.

90 Beatrice Webb on Beveridge, as quoted by G. Stedman Jones, 'Why is the Labour Party in a Mess?', in *Languages of Class*, 239–57, p. 245.

91 Ebong, 'The Origins', p. 59.

92 The fact that about a million people attended the Gardens in the summer of 1951, with 76 per cent of them being Londoners, implies that the planners got something right: *The Story of the Festival*, p. 32 (three-day survey conducted with the co-operation of the Social Survey Division of the COI between August and December 1951). But it is noted that the figures did not include advance tickets, and therefore probably underestimated overseas visitors. This suggests it may have underrepresented provincial ones as well.

93 Gardner, 'Pleasure Gardens', p. 122.

IV
CONCLUSION

9 ✧ Conclusion: the Festival and its legacy

B Y STRESSING pleasure, fun and a modern future, the Festival underscored the renewal of a badly shaken, but victorious country – a
country that could make a distinctive contribution alongside the
superpowers. By emphasising long, deep 'invented traditions', embedded
in classless, transhistorical time, the Festival portrayed an imagined community of all-white British people progressing together into a more
egalitarian future. The Festival's collective project of imagining also created
a space for an unuttered, yet unmistakable, message that the Labour Party,
in office since 1945, was the force behind Britain's recovery, as well as its
guiding light for the future. A rational and cultured citizenry with greater
access to knowledge would be able to evaluate Labour's contribution.
Unfortunately for Labour, the general election results in the autumn of
1951 revealed that not everyone had heeded the message.

The Festival was one of the Labour government's creations that was
not strong enough to survive the return of the Conservatives. Although
there was discussion of keeping the South Bank site open for a second
season in 1952, the new Conservative Minister of Works, David Eccles,
declared 'I am unwilling to become the caretaker of empty and deteriorating
structures'.[1] Eccles ordered the clearance of the South Bank's 27 acres (10.9
hectares), with the exception of the telekinema (to become the National
Film Theatre, as planned), the Riverside Restaurant, the walk along the
Embankment, and the London County Council's unfinished Festival Hall.[2]
The rest of the site stood empty for the next ten years, until most of it
became a car park. The Minister explained that the immediate demolition
of the Festival's temporary pavilions, cafés and restaurants was necessary
to make way for a garden to be used in the Coronation celebration of
1953.[3] Many British people found in the Coronation Day celebrations a
more reassuring balance of the modern and the quintessentially British
than they had in the Festival.

Historian Ross McKibbin has written that 'The Festival of Britain (1951)
and the coronation of Queen Elizabeth II (1953) were celebrations of what

contemporaries thought was a uniquely harmonious society'.[4] But, although it is true that the Festival planners repeatedly attempted to present a vision of a classless, united society, to say that the version of British society in the Festival was the same as that in the Coronation is to seriously misunderstand the Festival and its intents, not to mention the very different agendas of Labour and the Tories. As Hewison has said, the social democratic vision of '"New Britain" had hardly had time to establish itself when it was replaced by the "New Elizabethan Age"'.[5] This age had been predicted as early as June of 1942 by conservative critic and historian A. L. Rowse in the *Evening Standard*, and that enemy of the Festival, the *Daily Express*, was eager to trumpet the New Elizabethan Age once the Tories were in office.[6] In the Coronation year, the popular journalist Philip Gibbs published a survey of British youth entitled *The New Elizabethans*. In it he revealed how deeply he disliked Labour's vision of 'New Britain'. He wrote:

> Our poets loved the song of the cuckoo heralding the summer – and all the flowers of an English spring and the drowsy days of summer with the ripple of a streamlet nearby, and the song of the lark rising high, and the love song of the nightingale in the dusk of starlight nights and the peace and delight of English fields. They would grieve that so much of English beauty is being defaced and destroyed by the ugliness of sprawling cities, the blight of factories, the utter wantonness of those who grab and invade our heritage of beauty when often they might spare it – these Borough councils and governmental tyrants who do not care a jot for the loveliness of our countryside.[7]

On Gibbs' meanings in this piece, Hewison and I agree; the idea of the 'New Elizabethan Age' was founded primarily on the myth of Deep England. 'The state – meaning the welfare state – is the bureaucratic and industrial enemy of the sweet pastoral of Deep England to which British notions of heritage are so firmly attached'.[8] Yet the greatest paradox of the Coronation was that it also portrayed the monarchy as 'modern' and new. The mood of 1953 has been characterised by Ben Pimlot as a combination of 'the restoration of the *status quo ante bellum* together with an anxious optimism'.[9] *The Twentieth Century*, 'a serious journal, the heir to the reviews of the Victorian era',[10] claimed: 'The quick common sense of the Queen, and the shrewd modernity of the Duke of Edinburgh have already begun to help the nation in its formidable task of transforming itself to take a new place in a new world'.[11] The most 'modern' thing about the monarchy as portrayed in the Coronation was the use of television, not yet an option in 1951. Thanks to television, Elizabeth II was actually the first monarch crowned 'in the sight of all her people', as the ritual commands.[12] According to the BBC, for two and a half hours over twenty million people, or almost half the population of Britain, watched the ceremony on 2,700,000 television sets.[13] Television made the Coronation both a world event and an oddly domesticated public spectacle, consumed for the first time in red, white and blue-festooned living rooms across the nation.[14] The Coronation was portrayed as making a *'return to the future'* – a fresh start, which recalled earlier moments of Britain's national greatness.[15] As we have seen, the Festival relied on notions of heritage and tradition in many of its official and unofficial celebrations. But in the official, London-planned exhibitions, such notions were put to different uses from those of 1953; they were harnessed to a forward-looking agenda committed to a better world for all British people.

Being 'modern' in 1951

Moving between a road-side café, a queue for cakes and a fish-and-chip shop on the eve of the peace, Bernard Newman, a reporter for the Ministry of Information, recorded that he overheard discussions of 'post-war housing, the Bevin boys, ... the second-hand furniture ramp, equal pay for equal work, income tax, the cut in cheese ration, poor quality corsets, holidays away from home, overcrowding in trains and buses, ... [the] shortage of matches, high wages of boys and girls, and the bad distribution of fish.'[16] Post-war housing, consumption, well-designed goods, transport, holidays and leisure were all addressed in the Festival's main exhibitions. In these ways, the Festival attempted to give the people what they wanted, not only the more Reithan idea of giving them what they *needed*, yet did not *know* they wanted.[17]

Encouraging people to partake in 'culture' in their leisure time, improving their tastes and consequently their material surroundings, stimulating the arts, and broadly fostering an 'enlightened' citizenry – these were all goals shared by both the 1951 Festival and the post-war Labour Party. The Festival was planned primarily by left-leaning journalists, architects and designers. These men represented all of the tendencies in the Attlee government – its stress on planning and expertise along with its older ideas of ethical socialism.[18] Technocratic visions of a scientifically planned future literally sat next to older representations of the rule of law, fair play, and 'our Christian heritage' on the South Bank, while downstream there was the imaginary elegance of the Pleasure Gardens' tasteful consumption and leisure for all.

Also, to its credit, the Festival must be acknowledged as the only British national celebration held in the twentieth century committed to presenting the United Kingdom not only as regionally diverse, but also as consisting of four nations. It seems that the Festival planners would have agreed with Hugh Kearney who has written that 'we will be distorting the complexity of our history if we speak of a single "national past" and a single "national image". The "we" and "our" of all this are rather a mixed bunch.'[19]

Comparisons between the Festival and the Millennium Dome

By contrast, the Millennium Dome was nothing if not unselfconsciously metropolitan. Other aspects of the two events reveal few similarities, with the exception of the fact that 'Lord Festival' Herbert Morrison was the grandfather of Peter Mandelson, the initial Labour MP responsible for the Dome. According to Charles Plouviez, assistant to the director of the 1951 exhibitions, 'the biggest difference is that the South Bank was "story led" – the theme was written first, and the buildings designed to carry it, whereas the Millennium Dome was purely "design led" – not only was the Dome designed without any idea what was going inside, but the exhibits were mostly style first, content afterwards.'[20] Or in the more critical words of Iain Sinclair, 'the Dome covered nothing and meant whatever its sponsors said it meant'.[21] The Millennium Dome, more like its 1851 than 1951 predecessor, was reliant on corporate sponsorship. With the exception of Battersea, in the 1951 Festival industries and firms were not allowed to exhibit their wares 'by paying to do so'. In Barry's words, goods 'would get there by merit or not at all'.[22] In the 1990s, the Labour government appeared to have a vision of a new, modern and inclusive country 'based on flexible labour markets, lifelong learning, a transformed welfare state and a devolved Union', as Kevin Davey has written.[23] But it missed the opportunity to proclaim or represent what this new Britain might look like in the national celebration it was handed in the form of the Millennium Dome.

The Great Exhibition was seen in 1851 as a testament to the free-market and voluntarism (although Chartists and protectionists disagreed), while the 1951 Festival of Britain has often been portrayed as 'a perfect piece of Socialism', as Ernest Benn called it.[24] The 1951 Festival was state-funded and centrally planned. A national celebration of 'British achievement' was what Herbert Morrison and his team of experts decided was needed to express national recovery and to enact it as well. As we have seen, the goals of diffusing knowledge, constructing a modern, cultured citizenry, as well as improving 'the people's' surroundings, both in the form of the built environment and everyday objects, were ones that the Festival planners shared with the post-war Labour Party. In a different tone and register, as well as time, the Great Exhibition of 1851 also had the education of 'a substantial portion of British society about ... the importance of art and taste' as one of its central goals.[25] The Millennium Dome, on the other hand, did not aim to influence taste or leave behind any new works of art or design. Neither did it aim to provide useable, liveable buildings as part of its celebration of the Millennium. Not only did the development of the Lansbury estate and the Dolhendre scheme mean that the Festival built new flats and houses for 'ordinary' British people, but even in the competitive, free-market 1851 Exhibition, the Society for Improving the Conditions of the Labouring Classes exhibited Prince Albert's model working-class houses outside the Crystal Palace. These were built to house four families, two on each floor, and with their open staircases, freely circulating air, high ceilings and indoor toilets, they symbolised the exhibition's values of order, economy, social welfare and profits.[26] The Millennium Dome, however, was within sight of the last council-operated, high-rise block, but New Labour built no housing in Greenwich.

Labour's 1951 defeat and the end of the Festival

In October 1951, with an extremely high general-election turn-out of approximately 82 per cent, Labour received more votes than any other party in Britain before or since (13,948,883).[27] But what Peter Clarke has called 'the genius of the electoral system' meant that the Conservatives had gained the majority in Parliament:[28] the first-past-the-post system of British elections proved to be the downfall of the Labour government. Michael Frayn famously dubbed the Festival planners 'the Herbivores or gentle ruminants'.[29] In Frayn's view, the Festival was 'philanthropic, kindly, whimsical, cosy, optimistic, middlebrow, deeply in sync with the Herbivorous philosophy so shortly doomed to eclipse'. The 'Carnivores' – 'the upper and middle classes who believe that if God had not wished them to prey on all smaller and weaker creatures without scruple, he would not have made them as they are' – were to take charge in Britain for the majority of the next decades.[30]

However, despite Labour's defeat, the Festival of Britain is a fondly remembered reminder of the post-war Labour government's achievements. The 1951 Festival was the result of Herbert Morrison's vision of 'a new Britain springing from the old' along with his team of experts headed by Gerald Barry. As we have seen, the Festival's antecedents lay in Stockholm's modernist, social-democratic exhibition of 1930, whose goal was to be 'a great symbol of national regeneration'.[31] The Festival's 'first motive', according to Harold Nicolson at the time, was 'to dissipate the gloom that hung like a pea-soup above the heads of the generation of 1951'.[32] And from all the accounts of people dancing in the rain to big bands on the South Bank and enjoying the imaginary classless 'dreamworld' of the

Battersea Pleasure Gardens, as well as the travelling exhibitions, regional exhibitions and the many, many local schemes, fetes and pageants, it seems to have done just that. On 1 May, the *Daily Mirror's* report of the South Bank read: 'There is an air of gaiety about this exhibition – and flags, score, upon score of them, red and blue cafes, the pavilions, all are exciting just to look at. And inside the hall visitors from home and abroad alike will wonder. Britain has done a great job of work'.[33] On 3 May, when the King and Queen declared the Festival open, 'there was a sense of holiday in the air', and *The Times* carefully observed the people lining the streets to glimpse the royal family. The newspaper declared: 'People in Joyous Mood'.[34] A few days later *The Guardian* exclaimed that a visit to the South Bank 'will be as invigorating as a trip across the Channel, for in its final form the scene is quite as unfamiliar as any foreign seaside resort'.[35] That arch critic of the Festival, the *Daily Telegraph*, grudgingly concluded: 'It may perhaps be likened to a moderately successful party, but one held on the wrong day and at far too great a cost'.[36] On the contrary, in *The Spectator* Harold Nicolson wrote in his inimitable style:

> never shall I quite forget how suddenly it dawned on me that this exhibition differs from all previous exhibitions because it has been conceived in high spirits. I had known that it was intended as the British Council is intended, to express the British way of life; I had foreseen that I should find exhibits illustrating the past history of our Island and the glories of our literature, industry and hygiene; I had been expecting to be reminded of the solid virtues of the welfare state. What I had not counted on was that the master who has inspired this exhibition would have the imagination to see that it was the New Britain we wished to demonstrate not the old ... In place of the cemetery I had dreaded I found a maternity home, gay with pink and blue and resonant with cries and gurgles of the world that it is to be. I returned to the drab outside encouraged and entranced.[37]

The imagined post-war 'new Britain', that curious thing made up of deep, ancient stories of the British people and their traditions melded together with visions of the technologically and scientifically inspired future, was the essence of the official Festival exhibitions, as Nicolson said. And, in the words of the Festival's Director of Architecture, Hugh Casson, 'it made people want things to be better and to believe that they could be'.[38] Unfortunately, the autumn after the Festival summer brought the defeat of the Labour government, leaving them to console themselves with 'Victory in Votes'[39] and offering the Conservatives the opportunity to be forever associated with that stranger combination of ancient traditions and modern technology – that 'return to the future' – the New Elizabethan Age. But from May to September 1951 the British people and their visitors were given a glimpse of a different Utopia.[40]

Notes

1 D. Eccles, Hansard, 1952, as cited by Forty, 'Festival Politics', p. 38. See also Hewison, *Culture and Consensus*, pp. 65–6 and Frayn, 'Festival', p. 352.

2 Forty, 'Festival Politics', p. 38. See also Hewison, *Culture and Consensus*, pp. 65–6 and Frayn, 'Festival', p. 352.

3 *Ibid.*

4 McKibbin, *Classes and Cultures*, p. 535.

5 Hewison, *Culture and Consensus*, p. 66. See also Conekin, Mort and Waters, 'Introduction', pp. 1–2.

6 *Ibid.*

7 P. Gibbs, *The New Elizabethans* (London: Hutchinson, 1953), as quoted by Hewison, *Culture and Consensus*, pp. 66–7.

8 Hewison, *Culture and Consensus*, p. 67.

9 B. Pimlott, *The Queen: A Biography of Elizabeth II* (London: HarperCollins, 1996), p. 202.

10 Hewison, *Culture and Consensus*, p. 66.

11 *The Twentieth Century*, 153:916 (June 1953), p. 404, as cited by Hewison, *Culture and Consensus*, p. 66.

12 H. Hopkins, *The New Look: A Social History of Forties and Fifties Britain* (London: Readers Union, Secker & Warburg, 1964), p. 295.

13 BBC, as cited by Hopkins, *The New Look*, p. 295. See also Conekin, Mort and Waters, *Moments of Modernity*, p. 2. Almost 12 million people, or 32 per cent of the adult population, listened on the wireless. Hewison, *Culture and Consensus*, pp. 67–8.

14 Conekin, Mort and Waters, 'Introduction', p. 2. In *Family Secrets* Annette Kuhn writes of her mother's 'desire to commemorate a special day, a day of national significance' and of how her mother did this by making Annette a Coronation dress and having her photograph taken in it. According to Kuhn, 'my dress and the photography are a tiny part of a grand ceremony of affirmation, of commitment to a larger identity: a sense of national belonging' (pp. 65, 67). For this wonderfully evocative description of one family's celebrations and viewing of the Coronation, see A. Kuhn, 'A Meeting of Two Queens', in *Family Secrets: Acts of Memory and Imagination* (London: Verso, 1995), 59–83.

15 Conekin, Mort and Waters, 'Introduction', p. 1.

16 Bernard Newman, May 1944, recorded in his British Journey (London, 1945), p. 29, as quoted by Fielding, Thompson and Tiratsoo, *'England Arise!'*, p. 39. Oddly, as both John Marriott and James Hinton have pointed out, Fielding, Thompson and Tiratsoo agree with Newman that these are 'selfish', 'parochial' concerns or, in their words, 'relatively trivial personal problems and not the big issues of the day' (p. 39). J. Marriott, 'Labour and the Popular' (review essay), *History Workshop Journal*, 43 (spring 1997), 258–66, p. 262; and J. Hinton, '1945 and the Apathy School' (review essay), *History Workshop Journal*, 43 (spring 1997), 266–72, p. 268.

17 Lord Reith's motto for the BBC was 'Give the public slightly better than it now thinks it likes' (Lord Reith, as quoted by McKibbin, *Classes and Cultures*, p. 460).

18 Francis, *Ideas and Policies Under Labour*, especially Chapter 2.

19 H. Kearney, 'Four Nations or One?', in B. Crick (ed.), *National Identities: The Constitution of the United Kingdom* (Oxford: Blackwell Publishers in association with *The Political Quarterly*, 1991), 1–6, p. 1.

20 C. Plouviez, electronic mail message to the author and Martin Packer, 31 December 2001.

21 I. Sinclair, 'Dome Truths', *The Guardian*, Saturday Review, 30 October 1999, p. 102.

22 Gerald Barry, unpublished memoir, as cited by Hillier, 'Introduction', p. 15.

23 K. Davey, *English Imaginaries: Six Studies in Anglo-British Modernity* (London: Lawrence & Wishart, 1999), p. 16.

24 Ernest Benn, as quoted by J. A. Auerbach, *The Great Exhibition of 1851: A Nation on Display* (London and New Haven: Yale University Press, 1999), p. 229. See Auerbach for a comparison of the Great Exhibition and the Festival of Britain, pp. 220–7.

25 Auerbach, *The Great Exhibition*, p. 94.

26 Auerbach, *The Great Exhibition*, pp. 111–12.

27 Hennessy, *Never Again*, p. 422.

28 P. Clarke, *A Question of Leadership: Gladstone to Thatcher* (London: Hamish Hamilton, 1991), p. 198. See also Hennessy, *Never Again*, p. 422.

29 Frayn, 'Festival', pp. 331, 333. See also Hennessy, *Never Again*, p. 62.

30 *Ibid.*

31 Herbert Morrison, as quoted by Donoughue and Jones, *Herbert Morrison*, p. 492.

32 H. Nicolson, *The Listener* (1 November 1951). See also Weight, 'Pale Stood Albion', p. 158.

33 The *Daily Mirror*, 4 May 1951.

34 Frayn, 'Festival', p. 347.

35 *The Guardian*, as quoted by Frayn 'Festival', p. 347.

36 *Daily Telegraph* (summer 1951), as quoted by Frayn, 'Festival', p. 350.

37 H. Nicolson, 'Marginal Comment', *The Spectator*, 186–7 (11 May 1951), p. 616.

38 H. Casson, 'Period Piece', in Banham and Hillier (eds), *A Tonic*, 76–81, p. 81.

39 'Victory in Votes', as quoted by Fielding, Thompson and Tiratsoo, *'England Arise!'*, p. 209.

40 Gerald Barry wrote in his draft autobiography that his generation or '(what was left of it) were Angry Young Men', but that they 'also believed in Utopia': folder no. 57, draft autobiography, Sir Gerald Barry papers, BLEPS, as quoted by Waters, 'In Search of Sir Gerald Barry', p. 39.

Appendices

1. Membership of Festival committees

Festival Executive Committee

Gerald Barry, Director-General, Chairman
Bernard Sendall, Controller, Deputy-Chairman
George Campbell, Director, Finance and Establishments
Hugh Casson, Director, Architecture
Cecil Cooke, Director, Exhibitions
Ian Cox, Director, Science
Leonard Crainford, Managing Director, Festival Gardens, Limited (also Secretary
   of the Festival Organisation, March 1948 to July 1950)
Denis Forman, Director, British Film Institute
S. Gorden Russell, CBE, MC, Director, Council of Industrial Design
Huw Wheldon, MC, Arts Council of Great Britain
Paul Wright, Director, Public Relations
Howard V. Lobb, Controller, South Bank Construction

Festival of Britain Council Members

General Lord Ismay, GCB, CH, DSO, Chairman; Sir Patrick Abercrombie; Will
Arthur; Sir Alan Barlow, Bt, GCB, KBE; Robin Brook, OBE; The Rt Hon. R. A. But-
ler; Sir Kenneth Clark, KCB; The Rt Hon. Lord Clydesmuir, GCIE, TD; The Rt
Hon. the Earl of Crawford and Balcarres; The Very Rev. A. C. Don, KCVO; Dr
R. S. Edwards; T. S. Eliot, OM; The Rt Hon. Walter Elliot, MC; L. K. Elmhirst; Sir
Henry L. French, GBE, KCB; John Gielgud; Sir William Haley, KCMG; Miss
Florence Hancock, CBE; Kenneth Lindsay; Lady Megan Lloyd George; Howard
V. Lobb; Mrs Jean Mann; The Rt Hon. Sir Roland Nugent; Sir Ernest Pooley,
KCVO; Sir Robert Robinson, OM, PRS; Sir Malcolm Sargent; Sir Wynn Wheldon,
DSO; The Rt Hon. Lord Wilmot; Gerald Barry, Director-General.

The Welsh Committee

Sir Wynn Wheldon, DSO, Chairman; Will Arthur; Alun Oldfield Davies; Sir
William Llewelyn Davies; Sir Leonard Twiston Davies, KBE; H. T. Edwards; Idris
Evans; Sir Herbert Hiles, MBE; The Rev. A. E. Jones, CBE; Lady Megan Lloyd
George; R. H. R. Lloyd; Morgan Nicholas; Miss Myra Owen; J. D. Powell; Emlyn

Williams; Dr W. J. Williams; Clough Williams-Ellis, MC; A. G. Pyrs-Jones, OBE, Secretary.

The Northern Ireland Committee

The Rt Hon. Sir Roland Nugent, Chairman; Denis Rebbeck, Vice-Chairman; D. H. Alexander, OBE; James Alexander; A. G. Algeo, CBE; The Countess of Antrim; L. Arndell; R. W. Berkeley; S. Clarke, MBE; Professor E. Estyn Evans; E. T. R. Herdman; A. J. Howard; J. Keating; Mrs J. A. Mackie, OBE; J. Nelson McMillen; Professor J. Morrison; Councillor J. H. Norritt; Major F. A. Pope, CIE; A. Stewart; A. A. K. Arnold, Secretary-Controller.

The Scottish Committee

The Rt Hon. Thomas Johnstone, Chairman; W. M. Ballantine; Lord Bisland, MC; The Rt Hon. Lord Clydesmuir, GCIE, TD; The Rev. Dr Nevile Davidson; Lady Dollan, MBE; Frank Donachy; The Rt Hon. Walter Elliot, MC; Sir Hector Hetherington, KBE; Sir Alexander King, CBE; A. B. Mackay; R. A. Maclean; Mrs Jean Mann; Sir Hector McNeill; Sir Frank Mears; Sir Andrew Murray, OBE; Sir Victor Warren; Dr James Welsh; Sir John Handford, CB, OBE, Secretary.

Festival Gardens Limited, Board of Directors

Sir Henry L. French, GBE, KCB, Chairman; I. J. Hayward; Alderman D. H. Daines; Sir Howard Roberts, CBE; The Rt Hon. Lord Latham; G. J. Hill; Major H. L. Joseph; Sir Arthur Elvin, MBE; Sir Giles Loder, Bt; Gerald Barry; B. C. Sendall; G. A. Campbell; Cecil Cooke, Leonard Crainford, Managing Director.

Source: *The Official Book of the Festival of Britain, 1951* (London: HMSO, 1951), 71–2.

2. Population analysis of places hosting the fifty-five principal Festival events

This analysis of the structure of the Festival of Britain ranks the places by size of 1949 population (descending) and then shows the fifty-five principal Festival events against each city or town.

London: 8,203,900 South Bank/Science/Architecture/Books/1851 Centenary/
    Festival of Films/Battersea Pleasure Gardens
Birmingham: 1,107,200 Land Travelling Exhibition
Glasgow: 1,105,000 Industrial Power/Contemporary Scottish Books
Liverpool: 802,000 Arts Festival (plus the Festival Ship *Campania* visited nearby
    Birkenhead)
Manchester: 700,700 Land Travelling Exhibition
Leeds: 505,400 Land Travelling Exhibition
Edinburgh: 490,300 Living Traditions/Arts Festival/Eighteenth-century Books/
    Gathering of the Clans

Belfast: 452,100 Ulster Farm and Factory/Festival Ship *Campania*/Arts Festival
Bristol: 439,840 Festival Ship *Campania*
Nottingham: 301,240 Land Travelling Exhibition
Newcastle-upon-Tyne: 295,240 Festival Ship *Campania*
Cardiff: 243,500 Pageant of Wales/St Fagan's Folk Festival/Festival Ship *Campania*
Plymouth: 209,960 Festival Ship *Campania*
Aberdeen: 189,700 Arts Festival
Southampton: 180,930 Festival Ship *Campania*
Dundee: 180,500 Arts Festival/Festival Ship *Campania*
Swansea: 160,300 Music and the Arts
Brighton: 155,350 Arts Festival
Birkenhead: 141,460 Festival Ship *Campania*
Bournemouth: 139,400 Arts Festival
Norwich: 119,000 Arts Festival
Oxford: 107,100 Arts Festival
York: 107,100 Arts Festival
Cambridge: 90,590 Arts Festival
Bath: 77,450 Arts Festival
Cheltenham: 64,150 Arts Festival
Worcester: 62,020 Arts Festival
Perth: 40,900 Arts Festival
Kingston-upon-Hull: 40,660 Festival Ship *Campania*
· Inverness: 28,239 Arts Festival
Dumfries: 27,100 Arts Festival
Canterbury: 26,490 Arts Festival
Stratford-upon-Avon: 14,050 Arts Festival
Llangollen: 3,003 Arts Festival
Llanrwst: 2,555 Arts Festival
Aldeburgh: 2,500 Arts Festival
St David's: 800 Arts Festival
Dolhendre: n.a. * Welsh Hillside Farm Scheme

* It can be safely assumed that Dolhendre had a small population as well.

Information compiled and analysed by Martin Packer of the Festival of Britain Society.

3. A note on sources

It is a testament to how important the planners believed the Festival to be that they requested that all local, as well as official, planning documents be deposited in the Public Record Office. As such, there are hundreds of files in the Public Record Office at Kew relating to the Festival. Although there are relevant documents in EL, CAB, BT and INF, the vast majority are in Work 25. The reader of this study may notice some discrepancies in how I have referred to archival sources in this classification. This is due to the fact that over the period of seven years in which I researched this book the files at Kew were reorganised. If the researcher uses the PRO's finding guides, he or she comes upon a classification in Work 25 that reads, for example, 'Work 25/233/E1/D3/6'. In the first three years I used these documents I was told to request a document with such a classification by asking for simply 'Work 25/233'. This generally produced a large box file. However, in the following two years, Work 25 was re-examined and reorganised and the researcher was then instructed to use the entire classification. The result of which was that sometimes he or she is brought only a single piece of paper or brochure.

When I was able to find my original notes where I had listed the entire six-part classification number, or in the case of documents I have requested since the reorganisation, I have noted the entire classification. But in cases where I saw the document earlier in my research, especially when I photocopied the document, the only reference I have is the three-part classification and this is how the document is referred to in this book. Any researcher desperate to locate the exact documents I used is welcome to write to me. Finally, it may be helpful to know that the PRO allows 'bulk ordering' in advance, which facilitates the viewing of entire classifications at a time.

Select bibliography

Primary sources

Public Record Office, Kew
Cabinet Series (CAB) CAB 21/2203, CAB 124/1220, CAB 124/1221, CAB 124/1252, CAB 124/1302, CAB 124/1332, CAB 124/1334
Colonial Office Series (CO) CO 1032/119
Office of Public Work Series (Work) Work 25/1–3, Work 25/4, Work 25/6, Work 25/7, Work 25/12, Work 25/15, Work 25/17, Work 25/19, Work 25/21, Work 25/23, Work 25/24, Work 25/25, Work 25/44, Work 25/46, Work 25/47, Work 25/54, Work 25/57, Work 25/188–9 (plans and drawings), Work 25/199–220 (photographic records), Work 25/230 (official catalogues), Work 25/232, Work 25/233, Work 25/235, Work 25/239, Work 25/248, Work 25/250
Ministry of Education Series (ED) ED 142/4
Information Office Series (INF) INF 1/962, INF 12/255, INF 12/302, INF 12/350, INF 12/486, INF 12/584, INF 12/587, INF 12/591, INF 12/594, INF 12/620
Board of Trade Series (BT) BT 64/246, BT 64/4050, BT 64/4058
CEMA and Arts Council Series (EL) EL1/6, EL4/6, EL6/1, EL6/8, EL6/20, EL6/21, EL6/23, EL6/133
Foreign Office Series (FO) FO 800/655

Victoria and Albert Archive of Art and Design (23 Blythe Road, London W14)
AAD 5/1–1979 to 5/44–1979 (Information Office files), AAD 5/121–1979 to 5/134–1979

National Art Library, Victoria and Albert Museum
'Great Britain. Festival of Britain. Misc. Catalogues. 1951', 77. G. B.

Modern Records Office, University of Warwick
TUC (Trade Union Congress) file MSS. 292/509.3/6

Liverpool Record Office and Local History Department, City Library, Liverpool
'Festival of Britain in Liverpool', volumes 1 and 2 (cuttings books), H F 394 5 FES, *Liverpool Festival, 1951 Daylight on Industry Exhibition, 23rd July–11th August* (brochure).

Interviews
Dr and Mrs Peter Laslett, Trinity College, Cambridge, 26 May 1998

Correspondence
Max Nicholson, London, autumn 2001; Charles Plouviez, London, autumn/winter 2001

Government publications and Command Papers
Hansard, Parliamentary Debates, fifth series, Command 8277 *Documents Relating to the Festival Gardens Limited*

Private papers
Papers of J. D. Bernal, Add. 8287, Box 85, J. 146, Correspondence with H. D. Megaw: Cambridge University Library, Department of Manuscripts and University Archives; Papers of J. D. Bernal, Add 8287 Box 84, J. 128, Correspondence with Kathleen Lonsdale, Cambridge University Library, Department of Manuscripts and University Archives

Films
Ministry of Information Films viewed at the Imperial War Museum, London: *Dangerous Comment* (1940), *Men at the Lightships* (1940), *Britain at Bay* (1940), *An Airman's Letter to His Mother* (1941), *Citizens' Army* (1941), *Salvage with a Smile* (1940), *The Dawn Guard* (1941), *Tyneside Story* (1943), *Coalminer* (1944), *Builders* (1942), *Jane Brown Changes Her Job* (1942), *They Keep the Wheels Turning* (1942), *For This our Heritage* (1944), *USA The Land and Its People* (1944)
Humphrey Jennings Films viewed at the National Film Theatre, London: *A Diary for Timothy* (Crown Film Unit, 1944–45), *Heart of Britain* (US title: *This is England*) (Crown Film Unit for the Ministry of Information, 1941), *Listen to Britain* (Crown Film Unit for the Ministry of Information, 1942), *London Can Take It!* (GPO Film Unit, for the Ministry of Information, 1940)
Humphrey Jennings, *Family Portrait 1951: A Film on the Theme of the Festival of Britain, 1951*, a Wessex Film Production, 1951. Viewed at the British Film Institute, London, on a steamback

Museum of London
Later London History, Festival of Britain Objects and Ephemera Collection: four boxes of booklets, leaflets and assorted pamphlets; three boxes of posters; objects and costumes

Boy Scout Archives, South Kensington, London
Two files relating to the Festival of Britain, 1951

Original BBC broadcasts
Attlee, Clement, 'Speech given to the BBC 1949 at the laying of the foundation stone of the Royal Festival Hall', the National Sound Archives, London: BBC 14097
'The Festival of Britain, The South Bank Exhibition – A Microphone Visit with Wynford Vaughan Thomas and a team of BBC Commentators', an eleven-part series (nine sides in existence) the National Sound Archives, London: B. 2485
'A Tonic to the Nation', British Library, National Sound Archive, Tape T 10993, WR, Track W, copies of three BBC transmissions, BBC # T52334, played on the BBC on 28 November, 1976 (recorded on 23 November).

BBC Written Archives, Caversham (transcripts of contemporary broadcasts)
'HOLT 214 Film no. 214, Script Library Talk Scripts, GOS Tues. June 12th, 1951, 17.00', consulted in BBC Written Archives, Caversham, November 1994
R51/131/1, 'Talks Eighteen Fifty One Week', 1950–51, BBC Written Archives Centre, Caversham
R51/131/2, 'Talks Eighteen Fifty One Week', 1950–51, BBC Written Archives Centre, Caversham

R51/684 'From: Chief Producer, Talks Department, Subject: The English Theme or
Heritage, Copy to: Mr. Newby; Mr. Langford; Mr. Stewart; Miss Kallin; Mrs. Smith',
18 September 1950, BBC Written Archives Centre, Caversham

R51/684, 'From Overseas Talks Manager, Room 305, Langham, Subject: "The Heritage
of Britain" – Transcription Figures, To: C. O. S., A. C. O. E. S., G. O. S. O., Mr. Paul
Johnstone, Mr. H. D. Smith, H. F., Copy to H. T. S.', 26 March 1952, BBC Written
Archives, Caversham

R51/684, '"The Heritage of Britain": A Series of Programmes for 1951', BBC Written
Archives, Caversham

R51/684, Memo on 'Heritage of Britain', 'dictated by Mr. Boyd and despatched in
his absence by Beryl Kerf [sp.?] (Secretary)', BBC Written Archives, Caversham

Labour Party Archives, Manchester
'Comments on Churchill's Election Broadcast', 10 October 1951, Labour Party Re-
search Department (eds), *Campaign Notes* (London: Labour Party, 1951), Labour
Party Pamphlets and Leaflets, 1951

GS/DORK/21; GS/DORK/40

Labour Party, *Report on the 50th Annual Conference, held in Spa Garden Hall, Scarbo-
rough, October 1 to October 3, 1951*

Labour Party Pamphlets and Leaflets, 1951, *Campaign Notes*, Labour Party Research
Department (eds) (London: Labour Party, 1951)

Morrison, Box 17, General Secretary's Papers

NEC Minutes, 24 January 1951–7 November 1951 (NEC Minutes, 25 April–30
May,1951, includes 'Declaration of Principles of Democratic Socialism', pp. 1–11)

'Policy Sub-Committee, National Film Association, 25th June, 1951, Appendix A',
Labour Party NEC Minutes 27 June–25 July 1951

'Scientific Research Sub-Committee' folder, containing minutes dated 25 August 1942;
16 October 1942; 3 June 1943; 29 June 1943

Science Museum Archives, Exhibition Road, London
Box 8390 pt 1, Box 8390 pts 2 and 3

Thomas Cook Travel Archive, London
Coach Tours in Britain 1951, arranged by Cook's World Travel Service, in conjunction
with Westcliffe-on-Sea Motor Services Ltd

Daily Programme Itinerary and List of Members 1951, Co-operative Federation of
Western Australia, SS *Orchades*, disembarking Tilbury, 16 March 1951

Edinburgh Festival, 19 August to 8 September 1951, inclusive

Four and Seven Days' Holidays in London to See the Festival of Britain 1951, arranged
by Cook's World Travel Service in association with Yorkshire Service

The Holiday Maker (spring and summer 1951), published by Thomas Cook World
Travel Service, 1951

Holidays in Britain and Ireland, Festival of Britain Year 1951, Dean & Dawson Ltd

Holidays in London, During the Festival of Britain, 1951, Travelling by Express
Day Coach Service, arranged by Cook's World Travel Service, in association with
Crosville Motor Services Ltd Chester

Holidays in London, During the Festival of Britain, 1951, Travelling by Express Day
Coach Service, arranged by Cook's World Travel Service, in association with Lincoln-
shire Road Car Company Ltd

Holidays in London, During the Festival of Britain, 1951, Travelling by Night Saloon

Coach Service, arranged by Cook's World Travel Service, in association with Crosville Motor Services Ltd Chester

Holidays in Scotland 1951, Cook's World Travel Service

How to See London 1951, Cook's World Travel Service

Inclusive Tours in Great Britain and Ireland, 1951

Scottish Miners Holiday Scheme, Festival Holidays 1951 to London and Sunny South Coast, arranged by British Railways in conjunction with Thos. Cook & Son Ltd

Summer Holidays in the British Isles, 1951, Cook's World Travel Service

Greater London Record Office

LCC/EO/GEN/1/146–57; LCC/EO/GEN/1/132–4; EO/GEN/5/38; LCC/EO/PS/2/1–56; EO/PS/7; EO/PS/11/1; EO/PS/11/65; EO/PS/11/68/2/6 and 8; EO/PS/aa/86; EO/WAR/3/41–2; LCC/MIN/374/Primary ed.; LCC/FB/GEN/1/25; FGL/402–14 (plans); LCC/CL/PK/2/6–13, 116; LCC/CL/GP/2/58–61; LCC/CL/GP/2/62–81; LCC/AR/TH/1/42; LCC/CL/GP/2/152–170

Contemporary newspapers and journals

Architects' Journal
Architectural Review
Belfast Telegraph
Birmingham Mail
Coventry Standard
Daily Mail
Glasgow Herald
Illustrated London News
The Listener
The Liverpolitan
Liverpool Echo
News Chronicle
New Statesman and Nation
Picture Post
The Spectator
The Times
The Times Educational Supplement
The Tribune

Selected printed primary documents

'1851 Centenary Pavilion', *Architectural Review*, 109 (1951), p. 266.

'Architectural Preview: Festival Pleasure Gardens Battersea Park', *Architectural Review* (April 1951), 230–5.

Association of Scientific Workers, *Science and the Nation* (Harmondsworth: Pelican Books, 1947).

Barnes, L., 'A Policy for Colonial Peoples', in Lord Latham, J. S. Clarke, J. Griffiths MP, K. Martin, L. Barnes and R. H. Tawney, *What Labour Could Do: Six Essays based on Lectures prepared for the Fabian Society* (London: George Routledge and Sons, 1945), 64–81.

Barry, G., 'The Festival of Britain 1951', *Journal of the Royal Society of Arts*, 100:4880 (22 August 1952).

Bertram, A., *Design* (Harmondsworth: Penguin Books, 1938).

British Film Institute, *Films in 1951: A Special Publication on British Films and Film-*

Makers for the Festival of Britain (London: published by *Sight and Sound* for the British Film Institute, 1951).

Cambell, A., 'The Festival and Sir Thomas' (letter to the Editor), *Tribune* (17 November 1950), p. 23.

Cole, G. D. H., A. Bevan, J. Griffiths, L. E. Easterbrook, Sir W. Beveridge and H. Laski, *Plan for Britain: A Collection of Essays Prepared for the Fabian Society* (London: George Routledge and Sons, 1943).

Cole, M., *Education for Democracy: A Report Presented to the Fabian Society* (London: George Allen & Unwin and the Fabian Society, 1942).

Conservative Manifesto, 1945, Mr. Churchill's Declaration of Policy to the Electors, as printed in P. Adelman, *British Politics in the 1930s and 1940s* (Cambridge: Cambridge University Press, 1987), 64–6.

Cooke, C., Letter from Cecil Cooke, Director of Exhibitions, Festival of Britain, 1951, to E. Fletcher, Secretary of the Research and Economic Department, Trades Union Congress, dated 20 April 1951, located in TUC file MSS. 292/509.3/6, Modern Records Centre, University of Warwick, Coventry.

Council of Industrial Design (COID), *Design in the Festival: Illustrated Review of British Goods* (London: HMSO, 1951).

Council of Industrial Design (COID), *Furnishing to Fit the Family* (with drawings by Nicholas Bentley, Hugh Casson and Hilton Wright) (London: HMSO, 1948).

'Critic', 'Festival Diary', *New Statesman and Nation* (5 May 1951), 497–8.

'Critic', 'Shall Socialism Fail? II. Lost Chances and Future Needs', *New Statesman and Nation* (12 May 1951), pp. 524–6.

Edwards, R. J., 'The London of the Future', *Tribune*, 6 April 1951, pp. 6–7.

'Festival Exhibitions Review', *Architectural Review*, 110 (August 1951), 194–5.

Festival of Britain Catalogue of Events Throughout the Country. Issued by the Festival of Britain 1951, Liaison Branch 2, Savoy Court, London WC2, 1951.

Festival of Britain: The Closing Ceremony, South Bank Exhibition, Sunday 30th September, 1951 6–10:30 pm, Souvenir Programme (London: The Fanfare Press).

'The Festival of Britain in Northern Ireland', *Architects' Journal*, 114 (26 July 1951), p. 110.

Gardner, B., Letter from B. Gardner, General Secretary, Amalgamated Engineering Union to H. V. Tweson, General Secretary, Trades Union Congress, dated 16 January 1950, located in TUC file MSS. 292/509.3/6, Modern Records Centre, University of Warwick, Coventry.

Glasgow: A Centre for Tourists (Glasgow: 1951).

'Glasgow's Hall of Power', *Glasgow Herald*, Tuesday, 1 May 1951, p. 3, column b.

Grigson, G. (gen. ed.), *About Britain Guides*, 13 volumes (London: Published for the Festival of Britain Office by Collins, 1951).

Hawkes, J. *A Land* (Harmondsworth: Penguin Books, 1959).

'Herbert Steps Out' (editorial), *Tribune* (16 June 1950), pp. 5–6.

The Illustrated London News, 219:5873 (10 November 1951).

Joad, C. E. M., 'Culture and the Community', in H. Morrison, T. W. Agar, B. Wootton, C. E. M. Joad, J. Robinson and G. D. H. Cole, *Can Planning Be Democratic? A Collection of Essays Prepared for the Fabian Society* (London: George Routledge and Sons, 1944), 55–74.

Lancaster, M.-J., 'The Festival is the Present', *Ideal Home Journal*, 63–4 (May 1951), pp. 43–6.

Latham, Lord, J. S. Clarke, J. Griffiths, K. Martin, L. Barnes, R. H. Tawney, *What Labour*

Could Do: Six Essays Based on Lectures Prepared for the Fabian Society (London: George Routledge and Sons, 1945).

Mackinder, Sir H., *Democratic Ideals and Reality: A Study in the Politics of Reconstruction* (Harmondsworth: Penguin Books, 1944).

Morrison, H., *The Peaceful Revolution: Speeches by Herbert Morrison* (London: George Allen & Unwin, 1949).

Morrison, H., 'The Labour Party and the Next Ten Years', in *Forward From Victory! Labour's Plan. Six Essays based on Lectures prepared for the Fabian Society, by Herbert Morrison, G. A. Isaacs, Hugh Dalton, H. A. Marquand, Lewis Silkin, Hector McNeil* (London: Victor Gollancz, 1946).

Morrison, H., T. W. Agar, B. Wootton, C. E. M. Joad, J. Robinson and G. D. H. Cole, *Can Planning Be Democratic? A Collection of Essays Prepared for the Fabian Society* (London: George Routledge and Sons, 1944).

Nicolson, B., 'Henry Moore in Retrospect', *New Statesman and Nation*, 12 May 1951, p. 532.

Nicolson, H., 'Marginal Comment', *The Spectator*, 186–7 (11 May 1951), p. 616.

The Official Book of the Festival of Britain, 1951 (HMSO: London, 1951; Work 25/230, PRO, Kew).

Prestatyn Holiday Camp, Important Announcement Amendment to Brochure, Dancing Festival of Britain, Specially Organised for the Festival of Britain, 1951 (London: Corinthian Press; Thomas Cook Travel Archive, London).

Priestley, J. B. *Festival at Farbridge* (London: Heinemann, 1951).

Priestley, J. B. *Postscripts* (London: Heinemann, 1940).

Punch Festival (30 April 1951).

Report of the Working Party on Coloured People Seeking Employment in the United Kingdom, 17 December 1952, CO 1032/119, PRO, Kew.

'Sagittarius', 'Festival Sisters' (poem), *New Statesman and Nation* (5 May 1951), p. 498.

Stewart, J. D., 'Ulster Farm and Factory: A Guide to the Story it Tells, by John D. Stewart, with decorations by Colin Middleton', in *1951 Exhibition Ulster Farm and Factory* (London: HMSO, 1951; Work 25/230/E1/A1/8, PRO, Kew), pp. 8–29.

Stonier, G. W., 'Battersea Revels', *New Statesman and Nation* (16 June 1951), p. 678.

Summerson, J., 'The Arts and Entertainment: Lansbury', *New Statesman and Nation* (16 June 1951), p. 679.

Summerson, J., 'South Bank Architecture', *New Statesman and Nation* (12 May 1951), pp. 529–30.

'Voucher Scheme for Festival: A National Affair', *Liverpool Daily Post* (1 September 1950), p. 8; 'Festival of Britain in Liverpool' vol. 1 (22 July–12 August), H F394 5 FES, Cuttings book, Pressmark 352 CLE/CUT 3/8, p. 8, Local History Department, City Library, Liverpool.

'Warwickshire Agricultural Society Festival of Britain Show, The Racecourse, Warwick, Wednesday and Thursday, June 6th and 7th', advertisement in *Coventry Standard*, County Edition (1 June 1951), p. 1.

Young, D., 'Scotland: Time for Decision', *Tribune* (5 May 1950), p. 11.

Secondary sources

'1951', *Architects' Journal*, 179 (27 June 1984), 92–9.

Addison, P., *Now the War is Over: A Social History of Britain 1945–51* (London: Cape, in association with the BBC, 1985).

Adelman, P., *British Politics in the 1930s and 1940s* (Cambridge: Cambridge University Press, 1987).

Agnew, J. A. and J. S. Duncan (eds), *The Power of Place: Bringing Together Geographical and Sociological Imaginations* (Boston: Unwin Hyman, 1989).

Alexander, K., 'Lessons from Scotland', in J. Fyrth (ed.), *Labour's High Noon: The Government and the Economy 1945–1951* (London: Lawrence & Wishart, 1993), 195–213.

Ali, Y., 'Echoes of Empire: Towards a Politics of Representation', in J. Corner and S. Harvey (eds), *Enterprise and Heritage: Crosscurrents of National Culture* (London and New York: Routledge, 1991), 194–211.

Appleby, J., L. Hunt and M. Jacob, *Telling the Truth About History* (New York and London: W. W. Norton, 1994).

Applegate, C., 'A Europe of Regions: Reflections on the Historiography of Sub-National Places in Modern Times', *American Historical Review*, 104:4 (October 1999), 1157–82.

Arnold, M., *Culture and Anarchy*, ed. J. Dover Wilson (Cambridge: Cambridge University Press, 1932 [1869]).

Barker, Sir E., *The Character of England* (1947), as reprinted in J. Giles and T. Middleton (eds), *Writing Englishness 1900–1950: An Introductory Sourcebook on National Identity* (London and New York: Routledge, 1995), 55–62.

Barrett, M., *The Politics of Truth: From Marx to Foucault* (Cambridge: Polity Press, 1991).

Beach, A., 'Forging a "Nation of Participants": Political and Economic Planning in Labour's Britain', in R. Weight and A. Beach (eds), *The Right to Belong: Citizenship and National Identity in Britain, 1930–1960* (London and New York: I. B. Tauris, 1998), 59–88.

Benton, T. and C. Benton (eds) (at the Open University with Dennis Sharp), *Form and Function: A Source Book for the History of Architecture and Design 1890–1939* (London: Crosby Lockwood Staples in association with the Open University Press, 1975).

Berman, M., *All that is Solid Melts into Air: The Experience of Modernity* (London: Verso, 1983).

Bhabha, H., *The Location of Culture* (London: Routledge, 1994).

Bhabha, H. (ed.), *Nation and Narration* (London: Routledge, 1990).

Birmingham Feminist History Group, 'Feminism as Femininity in the Nineteen-Fifties', *Feminist Review*, 3 (1979), 48–65.

Bourdieu, P., *Distinction: A Social Critique of the Judgment of Taste*, trans. Richard Nice (Cambridge MA: Harvard University Press, 1984).

Bourdieu, P., 'Identity and Representation: Critical Reflections on the Idea of Region', in *Language and Symbolic Power*, ed. J. B. Thompson, trans. G. Raymond and M. Adamson (Cambridge: Polity Press, 1991), 220–8.

Bourdieu, P., 'Rethinking the State: Genesis and Structure of the Bureaucratic Field', *Sociological Theory: A Journal of the American Sociological Association*, 12:1 (March 1994), 1–18.

Bourn, D., 'Equality of Opportunity? The Labour Government and the Schools', in J. Fyrth (ed.), *Labour's Promised Land? Culture and Society in Labour Britain 1945–51* (London: Lawrence & Wishart, 1995), 163–80.

Boyce, D. G., ' "The Marginal Britons": The Irish', in R. Colls and P. Dodd (eds), *Englishness: Politics and Culture 1880–1920* (London: Croom Helm, 1986): 230–53.

Boyle, K., 'Northern Ireland: Allegiance and Identities', in B. Crick (ed.), *National Identities: The Constitution of the United Kingdom* (Oxford: Blackwell in association with *The Political Quarterly*, 1991): 68–78.

Briggs, A., 'Exhibiting the Nation', *History Today*, 50:1 (2000), 16–25.

Bristow, J., 'Life Stories', *New Formations*, 13 (spring 1991), 113–31.

Bud, R., 'Penicillin and the new Elizabethans', *BJHS*, 31 (1998), 305–33.

Buxton, N. K. and D. H. Aldcroft (eds), *British Industry Between the Wars: Instability and Industrial Development, 1919–1939* (London: Scolar Press, 1979).

Cairncross, A., *Years of Recovery: British Economic Policy, 1945–51* (London: Methuen, 1985).

Calder, A., *The Myth of the Blitz* (London: Pimlico, 1991).

Campbell, J., *Nye Bevan: A Biography* (London: Hodder and Stoughton, 1994).

Cannadine, D., 'The Context, Performance and Meaning of Ritual: The British Monarchy and the "Invention of Tradition", c. 1820–1977', in E. Hobsbawm and T. Ranger (eds), *The Invention of Tradition* (Cambridge: Cambridge University Press, 1992), 101–64.

Carruthers, B. G., 'When is the State Autonomous? Culture, Organization Theory and the Political Sociology of the State', *Sociological Theory: A Journal of the American Sociological Association*, 12:1 (March 1994), 19–44.

Centre for Contemporary Cultural Studies, *The Empire Strikes Back: Race and Racism in 70s Britain* (London and New York: Routledge in association with the Centre for Contemporary Cultural Studies, University of Birmingham, 1982).

Chase, B., 'History and Post-structuralism: Hayden White and Frederic Jameson', in B. Schwarz (ed.), *The Expansion of England: Race, Ethnicity and Cultural History* (London and New York: Routledge, 1996), 61–91.

Chase, B., 'Walter Scott: A New Historical Paradigm', in B. Schwarz (ed.), *The Expansion of England: Race, Ethnicity and Cultural History* (London and New York: Routledge, 1996), 92–129.

Chatterjee, P., *The Nation and Its Fragments: Colonial and Postcolonial Histories* (Princeton: Princeton University Press, 1993).

Churchill, W. S., *A History of the English-Speaking Peoples. Volume I. The Birth of Britain* (London: Cassell, 1956).

Clifford, J., 'On Collecting Art and Culture', in *The Predicament of Culture: Twentieth-Century Ethnography, Literature and Art* (Cambridge MA: Harvard University Press, 1988).

Cole, G. D. H., *The Post-War Condition of Britain* (London: Routledge & Kegan Paul, 1956).

Colley, L., 'Britishness and Otherness: An Argument', *Journal of British Studies*, 31 (1992), 309–29.

Cooke, P., 'Decentralism and the Politics of Place: An Interview with Raymond Williams', *Environment and Planning D, Society and Space*, 2 (1984), 369–74.

Cooper, S., 'Snoek Piquante', in M. Sissons and P. French (eds), *Age of Austerity, 1945–1951* (Harmondsworth: Penguin Books, 1963): 35–57.

Corner, J. and S. Harvey (eds), *Enterprise and Heritage: Crosscurrents of National Culture* (London and New York: Routledge, 1991).

Crick, B. (ed.), *National Identities: The Constitution of the United Kingdom* (Oxford: Blackwell in association with *The Political Quarterly*, 1991).

Cronin, J. E. *The Politics of State Expansion: War, State and Society in Twentieth-Century Britain* (London and New York: Routledge, 1991).

Daniels, S., 'Mapping National Identities: The Culture of Cartography, with particular reference to the Ordnance Survey', in G. Cubitt (ed.), *Imagining Nations* (Manchester and New York: Manchester University Press, 1998), 132–52.

Davey, K., *English Imaginaries: Six Studies in Anglo-British Modernity* (London: Lawrence & Wishart, 1999).

Deutsch, K., *Nationalism and Social Communication: An Inquiry into the Foundations of Nationality* (Cambridge MA: MIT Press, 1966).

Donoughue, B. and G. W. Jones, *Herbert Morrison: Portrait of a Politician* (London: Weidenfeld & Nicolson, 1973).

Doyle, B., 'The Invention of English', in R. Colls and P. Dodd (eds), *Englishness: Politics and Culture 1880–1920* (London: Croom Helm, 1986): 89–115.

Dresser, M., 'Britannia', in R. Samuel (ed.), *Patriotism: The Making and Unmaking of British National Identity. Volume 3: National Fictions* (London and New York: Routledge, 1989), 26–49.

Duncan, C., *Civilizing Rituals: Inside Public Art Museums* (London: Routledge, 1995).

Dyer, R., *White* (London and New York: Routledge, 1997).

Eldersveld, S. J., 'British Polls and the 1950 General Election', *Public Opinion Quarterly*, 95 (1951), 115–32.

Eley, G., 'Finding the People's War: Film, British Collective Memory, and World War II', *The American Historical Review*, 106:3 (June 2001), 818–38.

Eley, G., '*Distant Voices, Still Lives* The Family is a Dangerous Place: Memory, Gender, and the Image of the Working Class', in R. A. Rosenstone (ed.), *Revisioning History: Film and the Construction of a New Past* (Princeton: Princeton University Press, 1995), 17–43.

Eley, G., 'What is Cultural History?', *New German Critique*, 65 (spring–summer 1995), 19–36.

Eley, G., 'Nations, Publics, and Political Cultures: Placing Habermas in the Nineteenth Century', in C. Calhoun (ed.), *Habermas and the Public Sphere* (Cambridge MA: MIT Press, 1992), 289–339.

Eley, G., 'Nationalism and Social History', *Social History*, 6 (1981), 83–107.

Elwall, R., *Building a Better Tomorrow: Architecture in Britain in the1950s* (Chichester: Wiley-Academy, 2000).

Entrikin, J. N., *The Betweenness of Place: Towards a Geography of Modernity* (London: Macmillan, 1991).

Finer, H., *English Local Government* (London: Methuen, 1945 [1933]).

Ford, B. (ed.), *The Cambridge Guide to the Arts in Britain, Vol. 9, Since the Second World War* (Cambridge: Cambridge University Press, 1988).

Foster, K., *Fighting Fictions: War, Narrative and National Identity* (London and Sterling VA: Pluto Press, 1999).

Foucault, M., 'Of Other Spaces', *Diacritics* (spring 1986).

Foucault, M., *Discipline and Punish: The Birth of the Prison* (London: Allen Lane, 1977).

Francis, M., 'The Labour Party: Modernisation and the Politics of Restraint', in B. Conekin, F. Mort and C. Waters (eds), *Moments of Modernity: Reconstructing Britain 1945–1964* (London: Rivers Oram Press, 1999), 152–70.

Frascina, F. and J. Harris (eds), *Art in Modern Culture: An Anthology of Critical Texts* (London: Phaidon Press in association with the Open University, 1992).

Fryer, P., *Staying Power: The History of Black People in Britain* (London: Pluto Press, 1992).

Fuller, P., 'The Visual Arts', in B. Ford (ed.), *The Cambridge Guide to the Arts in Britain, Vol. 9, Since the Second World War* (Cambridge: Cambridge University Press, 1988), 98–145.

Gallagher, J., *The Decline, Revival and Fall of the British Empire* (Cambridge: Cambridge University Press, 1982).

Games, A., 'The Festival of Britain Symbol', *RSA Journal*, 143:5459 (May 1995), 55–6.

Gaskell, S. M., *Model Housing: From the Great Exhibition to the Festival of Britain* (London and New York: Mansell, 1987).

Gellner, E., *Nations and Nationalism* (Oxford: Oxford University Press, 1992).

Giles, J. and T. Middleton (eds), *Writing Englishness 1900–1950: An Introductory Sourcebook on National Identity* (London and New York: Routledge, 1995).

Gilroy, P., *Small Acts: Thoughts on the Politics of Black Cultures* (London: Serpent's Tail, 1993).

Girouard, M., 'It's Another World', *Architectural Review* (August 1974), reprinted in *Architects' Journal*, 179 (27 June 1984), p. 108.

Gold, J. R. and S. B. Ward (eds), *Place Promotion: The Use of Publicity and Marketing to Sell Towns and Regions* (Chichester: John Wiley & Sons, 1994).

Goodman, N., 'How Buildings Mean,' *Critical Inquiry*, 11 (June 1985), 642–53.

Gorer, G., *Exploring the English Character* (London: The Cresset Press, 1955).

Greenhalgh, P., *Ephemeral Vistas: The Expositions Universelles, Great Exhibitions and World's Fairs, 1851–1939* (Manchester: Manchester University Press, 1988).

Hall, S., 'Culture, Community, Nation', *Cultural Studies*, 7:3 (October 1993), 349–63.

Hall, S., 'Cultural Identity and Diaspora', in J. Rutherford (ed.), *Identity: Community, Culture, Difference* (London: Lawrence & Wishart, 1990), 222–37.

Hall, S., 'Ethnicity: Identity and Difference', *Radical America*, 23:4 (October–December 1989), 9–20.

Hall, S., 'New Ethnicities', in *ICA Documents, 7: Black Film, British Cinema* (London: ICA, A BFI Production Special, 1988), 27–31.

Hall, S., 'Notes on Deconstructing the "Popular"', in R. Samuel (ed.), *People's History and Socialist Theory* (London: Routledge & Kegan Paul, 1981), 227–41.

Hall, S., *et al.* (eds), *Culture, Media, Language* (London: Hutchinson, 1980).

Harkness, D., 'Britain and the independence of the dominions: the 1921 crossroads', in T. W. Moody (ed.), *Nationality and the Pursuit of National Independence* (Belfast: The Appletree Press for the Irish Committee of Historical Sciences, 1978).

Harwood, E. and A. Powers (eds), 'Festival of Britain', in *Twentieth Century Architecture 5* (The Journal of the Twentieth Century Society, 2001).

Hasler, C., 'Preface', *A Specimen of Display Letters Designed for the Festival of Britain 1951*, as reprinted in 'The Festival Lettering', in M. Banham and B. Hillier (eds), *A Tonic to the Nation: The Festival of Britain, 1951* (London: Thames & Hudson with the co-operation of the Victoria and Albert Museum, 1976), p. 114.

Heron, L. (ed.), *Truth, Dare or Promise: Girls Growing Up in the Fifties* (London: Virago, 1985).

Hewison, R., *Ruskin and Oxford: The Art of Education* (Oxford: Clarendon Press, 1996).

Hewison, R., *In Anger: British Culture in the Cold War 1945–1960* (New York: Oxford University Press, 1981).

Hewison, R. (ed.), *New Approaches to Ruskin: Thirteen Essays* (London: Routledge & Kegan Paul, 1981).

Hilton, M., 'The Politics of Consumer Society' (review essay), *History Workshop Journal*, 45 (spring 1998), 290-6.

Hiro, D., *Black British, White British: A History of Race Relations* (London: Grafton Books, 1991 [1971]).

Hjort, M. and S. MacKenzie (eds), *Cinema and Nation* (London and New York: Routledge, 2000).

Hobsbawm, E., *Nations and Nationalism Since 1780: Programme, Myth, Reality* (Cambridge: Cambridge University Press, 1990).

Hoggart, R., *The Uses of Literacy* (Harmondsworth: Pelican, 1966).

Holt, R. (ed.), *Sport and the Working-Class in Modern Britain* (Manchester: Manchester University Press, 1990).

Howkins, A., 'The Discovery of Rural England', in R. Colls and P. Dodd (eds), *Englishness: Politics and Culture 1880-1920* (London: Croom Helm, 1986: 62-88).

Hubback, E. M., *The Population of Britain* (Harmondsworth: Penguin, 1947).

Hudson, D. and W. Luckhurst, *The Royal Society of Arts, 1754-1954* (London: John Murray, 1954).

Iliffe, S., 'An Historic Compromise: Labour and the Foundation of the National Health Service', in J. Fyrth (ed.), *Labour's Promised Land? Culture and Society in Labour Britain 1945-51* (London: Lawrence & Wishart, 1995), 132-45.

Jackson, A., 'The Politics of Architecture: English Architecture 1929-1951', *Journal of the Society of Architectural Historians*, 24:1 (1965), 97-107.

Jackson, P. and J. Penrose, *Constructions of Race, Place and Nation* (London: University College London Press, 1993).

Jameson, F., *The Political Unconscious: Narrative as a Socially Symbolic Act* (London: Routledge, 1986).

Jeremiah, D., *Architecture and Design for the Family in Britain, 1900-70* (Manchester and New York: Manchester University Press, 2000).

Jordanova, L., 'Science and Nationhood: Cultures of Imagined Communities', in G. Cubitt (ed.), *Imagining Nations* (Manchester and New York: Manchester University Press, 1998), 192-211.

Joyce, P., 'The Constitution and the Narrative Structure of Victorian Politics', in J. Vernon (ed.), *Re-reading the Constitution: New Narratives in the Political History of England's Long Nineteenth Century* (Cambridge: Cambridge University Press, 1996), 179-203.

Joyce, P., *Democratic Subjects: The Self and the Social in Nineteenth-Century England* (Cambridge: Cambridge University Press, 1994).

Keith, M. and S. Pile (eds), *Place and the Politics of Identity* (London: Routledge Press, 1993).

Laclau, E. and C. Mouffe, *Hegemony & Socialist Strategy: Towards a Radical Democratic Politics* (London and New York: Verso, 1985).

Landy, M., *British Genres: Cinema and Society, 1930-1960* (Princeton: Princeton University Press, 1991).

Layton-Henry, Z., *The Politics of Immigration: Immigration, 'Race' and 'Race' Relations in Post-war Britain* (Oxford: Blackwell, 1992).

Leavis, F. R. and D. Thompson, *Culture and Environment: The Training of Critical Awareness* (London: Chatto and Windus, 1933).

Le Corbusier, 'Le Corbusier Parle ... 1951', trans. Emmanuelle Morgan, in E. Harwood and A. Powers (eds), 'Festival of Britain', *Twentieth Century Architecture 5* (The Journal of the Twentieth Century Society, 2001), 7-10.

Leventhal, F. M., 'A Tonic to the Nation: The Festival of Britain, 1951', *Albion*, 27:3 (1995), 445–53.

Lowenthal, D., 'European and English Landscapes as National Symbols', in D. Hooson (ed.), *Geography and National Identity* (Oxford: Blackwell Publishers, 1994), 15–38.

Lumley, R. (ed.), *The Museum Time-Machine: Putting Cultures on Display* (London: Routledge, 1988).

Mackay, J. and P. Thane, 'The Englishwoman', in R. Colls and P. Dodd (eds), *Englishness: Politics and Culture 1880–1920* (London: Croom Helm, 1986), 191–229.

MacKenzie, J. M. (ed.), *Imperialism and Popular Culture* (Manchester: Manchester University Press, 1986).

MacKenzie, J. M., *Propaganda and Empire: The Manipulation of British Public Opinion, 1880–1960* (Manchester: Manchester University Press, 1984).

Mackenzie, N. (ed.), *Conviction* (London: MacGibbon & Kee, 1958).

Madgwick, P. J., D. Steeds and L. J. Williams, *Britain Since 1945* (London: Hutchinson, 1982).

Mandler, P., 'The Consciousness of Modernity? Liberalism and the English National Character, 1870–1940', in M. Daunton and B. Rieger (eds), *Meanings of Modernity: Britain From the Late-Victorian Era to World War II* (Oxford and New York: Berg, 2001).

Mandler, P., '"New Towns for Old": The Fate of the Town Centre', in B. Conekin, F. Mort and C. Waters (eds), *Moments of Modernity: Reconstructing Britain 1945–1964* (London: Rivers Oram Press, 1999), 208–27.

Mandler, P., 'Against "Englishness": English Culture and the Limits to Rural Nostalgia, 1850–1940,' *Transactions of the Royal Historical Society*, 6th series, 7 (1997), 155–75.

Mandler, P., 'John Summerson (1904–1992): The Architectural Critic and the Quest for the Modern', in S. Pedersen and P. Mandler (eds), *After the Victorians: Private Conscience and Public Duty in Modern Britain, Essays in Memory of John Clive* (London and New York: Routledge, 1994), 229–46.

Manser, J., *Hugh Casson: A Biography* (London and New York: Viking, 2000).

Marwick, A., *British Society Since 1945* (London: Penguin, 1996).

Mason, T. (ed.), *Sport in Britain: A Social History* (Cambridge: Cambridge University Press, 1989).

McDonald, R., *The Language of Empire: Myths and Metaphors of Popular Imperialism, 1880–1918* (Manchester and New York: Manchester University Press, 1994).

McKibbin, R., *Ideologies of Class: Social Relations in Britain 1880–1950* (Oxford: Oxford University Press, 1990).

McWilliam, R., 'Moments of Modernity' (conference review, *History Workshop Journal*, 43 (spring 1997), 284–6.

Mellor, D., 'The Pleasures and Sorrows of Modernity: Vision, Space and the Social Body in Richard Hamilton', in Tate Gallery, *Richard Hamilton* (London/Millbank: Tate Gallery Publications, 1992), pp. 27–39.

Mercer, K., 'Recoding Narratives of Race and Nation', *ICA Documents, 7: Black Film, British Cinema* (London: ICA, A BFI Production Special, 1988), pp. 4–14.

Middlemas, K., *Power, Competition and the State, Vol. 1: Britain in Search of Balance 1940–1961* (London: Macmillan, 1986).

Mitchell, J., *Crisis in Britain 1951* (London: Secker & Warburg in association with the University of Nottingham, 1963).

Mitchell, T., 'The Limits of the State: Beyond Statist Approaches and Their Critics', *American Political Science Review*, 85:1 (March 1991), 77–96.

Mitchell, T., *Colonising Egypt* (Cambridge: Cambridge University Press, 1988).

Morgan, K. O., *The People's Peace: British History 1945–1989* (Oxford: Oxford University Press, 1990).

Morgan, K. O., *Labour People: Leaders and Lieutenants, Hardie to Kinnock* (Oxford: Oxford University Press, 1987).

Morgan, K. O., *Rebirth of a Nation: Wales 1880–1980* (Oxford: Oxford University Press in association with University of Wales Press, 1982).

Morgan, P., 'From a Death to a View: The Hunt for the Welsh Past in the Romantic Period', in E. Hobsbawm and T. Ranger (eds), *The Invention of Tradition* (Cambridge: Cambridge University Press, 1992), 43–100.

Morley, D. and K. Robins, 'No Place Like *Heimat*: Images of Home(land) in European Culture', *New Formations*, 12 (Winter 1990), 1–23.

Mort, F., *Cultures of Consumption: Masculinities and Social Space in Late Twentieth-Century Britain* (London and New York: Routledge, 1996).

Mulhearn, F., 'English Reading', in H. Bhabha (ed.), *Nation and Narration* (London: Routledge, 1990), 250–64.

Nairn, T., 'Scotland and Europe', in G. Eley and R. Suny (eds), *Becoming National: A Reader* (New York and Oxford: Oxford University Press, 1996), 79–105.

Nairn, T., *The Enchanted Glass: Britain and its Monarchy* (London: Picador, 1980).

Nairn, T., *The Break-up of Britain* (London: New Left Books, 1977).

National Film Theatre, *Forty Years, 1952–92* (London: National Film Theatre, 1992).

Nava, M. and A. O'Shea (eds), *Modern Times: Reflections on a Century of English Modernity* (London and New York: Routledge, 1996).

Newton, C. C. S., 'The Sterling Crisis of 1947 and the British Response to the Marshall Plan', *Economic History Review*, 37 (1984), 395–7, 404.

Partington, A., 'The Days of the New Look: Working-Class Affluence and the Consumer Culture', in J. Fyrth (ed.), *Labour's Promised Land? Culture and Society in Labour Britain 1945–51* (London: Lawrence & Wishart, 1995), 247–63.

Partington, A., 'Popular Fashion and Working-Class Affluence', in J. Ash and E. Wilson (eds), *Chic Thrills* (London: Pandora Press, 1992), 145–61.

Pearson, N. M., *The State and the Visual Arts: A Discussion of State Intervention in the Visual Arts in Britain 1760–1981* (Milton Keynes: Open University Press, 1982).

Perkin, H., *The Rise of Professional Society in England Since 1880* (London and New York: Routledge, 1989).

Pevsner, N., *The Englishness of English Art* (Harmondsworth: Penguin, 1964).

Pickering, M., *History, Experience and Cultural Studies* (Houndmills: Macmillan, 1997).

Pilkington, E., *Beyond the Mother Country: West Indians and the Notting Hill White Riots* (London: I. B. Tauris, 1988).

Plouviez, C., 'The Best of the Festival' (review of E. Harwood and A. Powers (eds), *Festival of Britain: Twentieth Century Architecture 5* (The Journal of The Twentieth Century Society, 2001)), *Festival Times*, newsletter of the Festival of Britain Society, 44 (March 2002).

Porter, R., *London: A Social History* (London: Hamish Hamilton, 1994).

Porter, R. (ed.), *Myths of the English* (Cambridge and Oxford: Polity Press, 1992).

Potts, A., 'The Museum as Social Space', *History Workshop Journal*, 43 (spring 1997), 215–17.

Powell, Sir P., '"No Visible Means of Support": Skylon and the South Bank', in E. Harwood and A. Powers (eds), 'Festival of Britain', *Twentieth Century Architecture 5* (The Journal of the Twentieth Century Society, 2001), 81–6.

Powers, A., 'The Expression of Levity', in E. Harwood and A. Powers (eds), 'Festival of Britain', *Twentieth Century Architecture 5* (The Journal of the Twentieth Century Society, 2001), 47–56.

Pred, A., 'Structuration of Place: On the Becoming of Sense of Place and Structure of Feeling', *Journal for the Theory of Social Behaviour*, 13:1 (March 1983), 45–68.

Priestley, J. B., 'Blackpool', from *English Journey* (1934), reprinted in J. Giles and T. Middleton (eds), *Writing Englishness 1900–1950: An Introductory Sourcebook on National Identity* (London and New York: Routledge, 1995): 174–7.

Robinson, D., 'Films in 1951', in E. Harwood and A. Powers (eds), 'Festival of Britain', *Twentieth Century Architecture 5* (The Journal of the Twentieth Century Society, 2001), 87–94.

Rogaly, J., 'Millennium Squanderama: Has Anyone Given a Thought to What it Really Means?', *Financial Times* (28/29 December 1996).

Rose, N., *Governing the Soul: The Shaping of the Private Self* (London and New York: Routledge, 1989).

Rose, N., *The Psychological Complex: Psychology, Politics and Society in England 1869–1939* (London: Routledge & Kegan Paul, 1985).

Rose, S., 'Sex, Nation and Citizenship in World War II Britain', *The American Historical Review*, 103:4 (October 1998), 1147–76.

Rydall, R. W., *All the World's a Fair* (Chicago: University of Chicago Press, 1984).

Rykwert, J., 'Architecture', in B. Ford (ed.), *The Cambridge Guide to the Arts in Britain, Vol. 9, Since the Second World War* (Cambridge: Cambridge University Press, 1988), 252–77.

Sahlins, P., *Boundaries: The Making of France and Spain in the Pyrenees* (Berkeley and Los Angeles: University of California Press, 1989).

Said, E., *Culture and Imperialism* (London: Vintage, 1994).

Saint, A., 'Spread the People: The LCC's Dispersal Policy, 1889–1965', in A. Saint (ed.), *Politics and the People of London: The London County Council 1889–1965* (London and Ronceverte: The Hambledon Press, 1989).

Samuel, R., 'Introduction: The figures of national myth', in R. Samuel (ed.), *Patriotism: The Making and Unmaking of British National Identity. Volume 3: National Fictions* (London and New York: Routledge, 1989).

Samuel, R., *Island Stories: Unravelling Britain. Theatres of Memory, Vol. 2*, ed. A. Light, with S. Alexander and G. Stedman Jones (London and New York: Verso, 1998).

Schoeser, M., 'The Appliance of Science', in E. Harwood and A. Powers (eds), 'Festival of Britain', *Twentieth Century Architecture 5* (The Journal of the Twentieth Century Society, 2001), 117–26.

Schwarz, B., 'Introduction: The Expansion and Contraction of England', in B. Schwarz (ed.), *The Expansion of England: Race, Ethnicity and Cultural History* (London and New York: Routledge, 1996), 1–8.

Shaw, C. and M. Chase, *The Imagined Past: History and Nostalgia* (New York and Manchester: Manchester University Press, 1989).

Sinclair, I., 'Dome Truths', *The Guardian*, Saturday Review (30 October 1999), p. 102.

Sinfield, A., 'The Government, the People and the Festival', in J. Fyrth (ed.), *Labour's Promised Land? Culture and Society in Labour Britain 1945–51* (London: Lawrence & Wishart, 1995), 181–96.

Sinyard, N., 'Film', in B. Ford (ed.), *The Cambridge Guide to the Arts in Britain, Vol. 9, Since the Second World War* (Cambridge: Cambridge University Press, 1988), 238–51.

Sked, A. and C. Cook, *Post-war Britain: A Political History* (London: Penguin Books, 1990).

Smith, A. D. *Theories of Nationalism (London: Duckworth, 1983).*

Snoddy, R., '100m showpiece for 2000', *Financial Times* (11 May 1995).

Sparke, P., *As Long as it's Pink: The Sexual Politics of Taste* (London: Pandora, 1995).

Stamp, G., 'The South Bank Site', in E. Harwood and A. Powers (eds), 'Festival of Britain', *Twentieth Century Architecture 5* (The Journal of the Twentieth Century Society, 2001), 11–24.

Stedman Jones, G., 'Class Expression versus Social Control? A Critique of Recent Trends in the Social History of "Leisure"', in *Languages of Class* (Cambridge and New York: Cambridge University Press, 1983), 76–89.

Steedman, C., 'State Sponsored Autobiography', in B. Conekin, F. Mort and C. Waters (eds), *Moments of Modernity: Reconstructing Britain 1945–1964* (London: Rivers Oram Press, 1999), 41–54.

Steedman, C., *Past Tenses: Essays on Writing, Autobiography and History* (London: Rivers Oram Press, 1992).

Steedman, C., *Childhood, Culture and Class in Britain: Margaret McMillan 1860–1931* (New Brunswick: Rutgers University Press, 1990).

Steedman, C., *Landscape for a Good Woman: A Story of Two Lives* (New Brunswick: Rutgers University Press, 1987).

Strong, R., 'Prologue: Utopia Limited', in M. Banham and B. Hillier (eds), *A Tonic to the Nation: The Festival of Britain, 1951* (London: Thames & Hudson with the co-operation of the Victoria and Albert Museum, 1976), 6–9.

Thane, P., 'Government and Society in England and Wales, 1750–1914', in F. M. L. Thompson (ed.), *The Cambridge Social History of Britain, 1750–1950. Volume 3: Social Agencies and Institutions* (Cambridge: Cambridge University Press, 1990), 1–62.

Thompson, E. P. *The Making of the English Working Class* (New York: Vintage Books, 1966).

Tippett, M., *Art at the Service of War: Canada, Art and the Great War* (Toronto: University of Toronto Press, 1984).

Tiratsoo, N. (ed.), *The Attlee Years* (London and New York: Pinter Publishers, 1991).

Tiratsoo, N., 'Popular Politics, Affluence and the Labour Party in the 1950s', in A. Gorst, L. Johnman and W. S. Lucas (eds), *Contemporary British History 1931–1961: Politics and the Limits of Policy* (London: Pinter Press, 1991), 44–51.

Tiratsoo, N., *Reconstruction, Affluence and Labour Politics: Coventry 1945–60* (London: Routledge, 1990).

Titmuss, R. M., *Essays on the 'Welfare State'* (London: Allen & Unwin, 1958).

Trevelyan, G. M., *British History in the Nineteenth Century and After (1782–1919)* (Harmondsworth: Penguin Books, 1979 [1922]).

Trevor-Roper, H., 'The Invention of Tradition: The Highland Tradition of Scotland', in E. Hobsbawm and T. Ranger (eds), *The Invention of Tradition* (Cambridge: Cambridge University Press, 1992), 15–42.

Tulloch, C., 'Strawberries and Cream: Dress, Migration and the Quintessence of Englishness', in C. Breward, B. Conekin and C. Cox (eds), *The Englishness of English Dress* (Oxford and New York: Berg, 2002).

van der Rohe, M., 'On the subject of exhibitions', *Die Form* 3 (1928), p. 121, as reprinted in T. Benton and C. Benton (at the Open University with Dennis Sharp) (eds), *Form and Function: A Source Book for the History of Architecture and Design*

1890–1939 (London: Crosby Lockwood Staples in association with the Open University Press, 1975), 165.

Vansittart, P., *In the Fifties* (London: John Murray, 1995).

Vernon, J., 'Border Crossings: Cornwall and the English (imagi)nation', in G. Cubitt (ed.), *Imagining Nations* (Manchester and New York: Manchester University Press, 1998), 153–72.

Vernon, J., 'The Mirage of Modernity', *Social History*, 22:2 (May 1997): 208–15.

Vernon, J., 'Narrating the Constitution: the Discourse of 'the real' and the Fantasies of Nineteenth-century Constitutional History', in J. Vernon (ed.), *Re-reading the Constitution: New Narratives in the Political History of England's Long Nineteenth Century* (Cambridge: Cambridge University Press, 1996), 204–38.

Vernon, J., 'Notes Towards an Introduction', in J. Vernon (ed.), *Re-reading the Constitution: New Narratives in the Political History of England's Long Nineteenth Century* (Cambridge: Cambridge University Press, 1996), 1–22.

Vernon, J., 'Who's Afraid of the "Linguistic Turn?"', *Social History*, 19:1 (January 1994), 81–97.

Wagnleitner, R., *Coca-Colonization and the Cold War: The Cultural Mission of the United States in Austria after the Second World War*, trans. D. M. Wolf (Chapel Hill and London: University of North Carolina Press, 1994).

Walkerdine, V., *Schoolgirl Fictions* (London: Verso, 1990).

Walkowitz, J., *City of Dreadful Delight: Narratives of Sexual Danger in Late-Victorian London* (London: Virago Press, 1994).

Walvin, J., *Leisure and Society 1830–1950* (London: Longman, 1978).

Waters, C., 'Representations of Everyday Life: L. S. Lowry and the Landscape of Memory in Postwar Britain', *Representations*, 65 (winter 1999), 121–50.

Waters, C., 'J. B. Priestley (1894–1984): Englishness and the Politics of Nostalgia, 1929–1951', in S. Pedersen and P. Mandler (eds), *After the Victorians: Private Conscience and Public Duty in Modern Britain, Essays in Memory of John Clive* (London and New York: Routledge, 1994), 209–28.

Webb, D., assisted by R. Wilkin, 'An Advertisement on Wheels', in M. Banham and B. Hillier (eds), *A Tonic to the Nation: The Festival of Britain, 1951* (London: Thames & Hudson with the co-operation of the Victoria and Albert Museum, 1976), 170–1.

Weedon, C., *Feminist Practice and Poststructuralist Theory* (Oxford: Blackwell, 1997).

Weight, R., '"Building a new British culture": The Arts Centre Movement, 1943–53', in R. Weight and A. Beach (eds), *The Right to Belong: Citizenship and National Identity in Britain, 1930–1960* (London and New York: I. B. Tauris, 1998), 157–80.

Weight, R. and A. Beach (eds), *The Right to Belong: Citizenship and National Identity in Britain, 1930–1960* (London and New York: I. B. Tauris, 1998).

Werskey, G., *The Visible College: A Collective Biography of British Scientists and Socialists of the 1930s* (London: Free Association Books, 1988).

West, W. J. (ed.), *Orwell: The War Commentaries* (New York: Schocken Books, 1985).

Whiteley, N., 'Utility, Design Principles and the Ethical Tradition', in J. Attfield (ed.), *Utility Reassessed: The Role of Ethics in the Practice of Design* (Manchester and New York: Manchester University Press, 1999), 190–202.

Williams, R., *Writing in Society* (London: Verso, 1983).

Williams, R., *Keywords: A Vocabulary of Culture and Society* (New York: Oxford University Press, 1985).

Williams, R., 'State Culture and Beyond', in *Culture and the State, I. C. A. Documents* (London: ICA, 1984), 3–5.

Williams, R., *Culture and Society 1780–1950* (Harmondsworth: Penguin, 1961).

Williams, R., 'Culture is Ordinary', in N. Mackenzie (ed.), *Conviction* (London: MacGibbon & Kee, 1958).

Wilson, E., *Only Halfway to Paradise: Women in Postwar Britain: 1945–1968* (London and New York: Tavistock Publications, 1980).

Wood, J., 'A "Third Way"? The Labour Left, Democratic Socialism and the Cold War', in J. Fyrth (ed.), *Labour's Promised Land? Culture and Society in Labour Britain 1945–51* (London: Lawrence & Wishart, 1995), 73–87.

Worswick, G. D. N. and P. H. Ady (eds), *The British Economy 1945–1950* (Oxford, Clarendon Press, 1952).

Wright, P., *On Living in an Old Country* (London: Verso, 1985).

Wright, Sir P., Director of Public Relations, Festival of Britain, 'The Festival of Britain: Some Memories', *RSA Journal*, 143:5459 (May 1995), 52–5.

Unpublished dissertations, theses and papers

Daunton, M., 'Ancient and Modern: Culture and Capitalism in Victorian Britain', unpublished paper presented to King's College (Cambridge) Themes in Modern History Seminar, March 2000.

Ebong, I. I. I., 'The Origins and Significance of The Festival of Britain, 1951', unpublished PhD thesis, University of Edinburgh, Department of History, 1986.

Eley, G., 'How is "History" Represented?', unpublished essay, 1996.

Forgan, S., 'Festivals of Science and the Two Cultures: Aspects of Science, Architecture and Display in the Festival of Britain', unpublished paper, presented at 'The Visual Culture of Art and Science from the Renaissance to the Present' Conference, the Royal Society, London, 14 July 1995.

LaCoss, D., '*La Leçon de L'Ile des Cygnes*: Ordonnance and Social Modernity at the 1937 Paris Exposition', unpublished paper, University of Michigan, Ann Arbor, May 1993.

Mandler, P., 'The Nationalization of Culture', unpublished paper presented at the North American Conference of British Studies, Chicago, October 1996.

Pussard, H., '"A Mini-Blackpool": Belle Vue and the Cultural Politics of Pleasure and Leisure in Interwar Manchester', MA Thesis in Cultural History, University of Manchester, 1997.

Vernon, J., 'Telling the Subaltern to Speak: Social Investigation and Formation of Social History in Twentieth Century Britain', Presented to the International Congress, 'History Under Debate', Santiago de Compostela, Spain, July 1999, www.h-debate.com/papers/sesionte/1/Vernon.html

Weight, R. A. J., 'Pale Stood Albion: The Promotion of National Culture in Britain 1939–56', unpublished PhD thesis, University of London, 1995.

Willis, K., 'The Promotion of Nuclear Power in Britain, 1945–1960', unpublished paper presented at the North American Conference on British Studies, Vancouver, October 1994.

Index

Note: 'n.' after a page reference indicates the number of a note on that page, literary works can be found under authors' names and page numbers in *italic* refer to illustrations.